TRUE AMERICANISM:
GREEN BERETS AND WAR RESISTERS

A Study of Commitment

DAVID MARK MANTELL

Teachers College Press
Teachers College, Columbia University
New York and London

© 1974 by Teachers College, Columbia University
Library of Congress Card Number: 74-2230

Library of Congress Cataloging in Publication Data

Mantell, David Mark.
    True Americanism: Green Berets and war resisters;
a study of commitment.

    (Foresight books in psychology)
    Bibliography: p.
    1. Aggressiveness (Psychology) 2. Commitment.
3. Parent and child. 4. United States Army. Special
Forces. 5. Pacifism. I. Title.
BF575.A3M35 1974   155.2   74-2230
ISBN 0-8077-2429-7

Manufactured in the United States of America

SERIES EDITOR'S FOREWORD

Now that the Vietnam war is no longer an active service area for young Americans, many of the divisions it caused are beginning to heal. But amnesty remains a fighting word for many Americans. Congress, the press, and many others are still debating whether amnesty is to be denied, to be conditional, or to be blanket and unconditional.

The debate so far has proceeded without much specific information, and it has therefore been more polarized and enflamed than it ought to be. Who are these 25,000 or more war resisters? What experiences and motives lay behind their resistance? What would it mean for them, and for us, to have them come home? In this study, the second of the Foresight Books, David Mantell lets them tell us, in their own words, who they are and why they chose Canada or Sweden rather than Vietnam. His careful unfolding of their histories, their families, and their routes into exile can provide the understanding we all need as we decide the terms under which they come back or stay away. Those Americans who are in favor of amnesty may know some young men such as these. What they read here may not be entirely new to them, though the eloquence of some of these young men may surprise anyone. Those who are opposed to amnesty have a particular obligation to get to know some of these men, and Mantell gives them that opportunity.

He also takes us into the lives of a sample of Green Berets, men who chose active combat in an unpopular war and returned to the least enthusiastic reception accorded the veterans of any American war. When we know the routes, so typically American, that led these men into their actions, we may be more understanding.

The contrasts between the two groups are striking, whether one looks at families, at school histories, at relationships with women, or at attitudes toward themselves. Mantell's point is that both represent deep streams in the American cultural experience, and both are in that sense true Americans. Whether we like them or not, we cannot disown either the war resisters or the Green Berets. Both represent us. Both are us.

The Foresight Books series is dedicated to publishing exciting research on important questions. Mantell's method—life history interviews—requires patience, tact, and sustained interest in human lives. The researcher, and now the reader, must listen carefully to people, and he must suspend judgment until he has heard and pondered both those things that are easily said and those that emerge only with difficulty. Mantell lets each man be his own spokesman. When we finish this book we have gotten to know, at surprising depth, two groups of important and representative young Americans. Both groups chose less travelled roads, and both have paid a heavy price.

Many of the basic political and social decisions that will affect these men have yet to be made. We hope that this book will be useful in making those decisions wisely.

D. F. Ricks
Series Editor
Foresight Books

ACKNOWLEDGMENTS

Many of the intellectual and emotional issues addressed in this study have recognizable roots in my childhood and adolescence. In this respect as well as in others, I feel fundamentally indebted to my family, friends, and teachers, who knowingly and unknowingly shaped my relationship to them.

The study would not have achieved its present form without the help of many people. The research was carried out while I was on the staff of the Max-Planck Institute Research Center for Psychopathology and Psychotherapy in Munich. I am grateful to its Director, Professor Paul Matussek, for his support. Ilse Ankenbranck, Reinhard Scholl, Miriam Freifeld, Werner Schuboe, and Tamar Berman helped with the data analysis. Edwina Picone transcribed the taped interviews into readable manuscript. Ilona Weinreich typed several revisions.

I am indebted to Hans Jürgen Koch, Gabriella Baldner, Dr. Leroy Milman, Professors Jerome Cohen and David Ricks, and to Robert Panzarella. Their thoughtful comments helped me sharpen conceptualizations and improve formulations. Willa Rosenblatt gave the manuscript a sensitive and careful editorial reading. Among her many credits, my wife Fredda holds that of having prepared the largest portion of the final revision.

Without the support of Colonel Ludwig Faistenhammer, Commander, Special Forces Detachment, and Mr. Ralph Di Gia of the War Resisters League, these interviews could not have taken place. Finally, I owe my greatest debt to the Green Berets and war resisters themselves, who consented to open their lives to scientific exploration and to publication. I hope they will feel I've kept my promise to be fair and just.

David Mark Mantell
New Britain, Connecticut
July 1974

CONTENTS

INTRODUCTION

Shortly after the first reports of the My Lai massacre reverberated through the American press, the mother of one of the involved soldiers told a journalist, "I sent the Army a good boy and they made a murderer out of him." At about the same time another young man stood before a judge in the Federal Court Building in New York City. I sat with his parents, friends, and supporters and listened as the judge said, "I have deep respect for your moral convictions. One day they may become the law of the land. However, I am bound by oath to uphold the law until such time as it is changed. You have repeatedly and flagrantly violated this law." This young man, one of the war resisters I interviewed, was then sentenced to five years in a federal penitentiary.

This is a study of personal violence and nonviolence, their origins and course of development, their later involvement in political events, and their relevance to war and peace. In the following pages the lives of fifty young male citizens of the United States, twenty-five Special Forces soldiers (Green Berets) and twenty-five war resisters, are summarized. The two groups were chosen because they each seemed, through their antithetical actions, to be at the forefront of pro- and antiwar segments of the American population.[1] The fact that the people in one group freely volunteered to personally execute politically commanded violence while the other group refused to support such activities in any way seemed to indicate direct involvement in and commitment to distinct courses of action. My primary interest, however, was not in the actions of these fifty young men, nor in the consequences of their acts. Rather, my interest was focused on their roots. The behavior of these two groups is one reflection of the diversity of American society, and of how American traditions have led to opposing interpretations of Americanism.

The key to these attitudes and behaviors can be sought in nonpolitical events and processes which occurred early in the lives of these men. For this

1

reason their political and social ideas and convictions as young adults were of only secondary interest in this study. Of primary concern, and discussed in successive chapters, are what these men told me of their family background, in particular their relationship with their parents, their social, religious, and sexual development, their academic performance and social relations in school, their extracurricular interests and activities, and their relation to authority figures as well as to those significant persons and situations they encountered while growing up—in short, those factors which helped shape their later attitudes and perceptions.

At one time or another most nations have been forced by futile wars, economic disasters, and social upheavals to revise some of their attitudes and institutions. With the exception of a civil war 100 years ago, the United States has managed to escape this fate. It remains to be seen whether the long-term effects of our involvement in Vietnam will run deeper than those of the Korean War, a war which became equally unpopular and was accompained by approximately the same degree of dissent.[2]

The character of a nation, its policies and institutions, reflect its family life. One cannot be separated from the other, but most parents do not fully understand the implications of their own behavior for the immediate or future behavior of their children. Few children have seen their parents kill another human being or return a draft card to its source. Parents rarely explicitly teach their children to do this kind of thing. It is my view, however, that the reactions of individual Americans to the war in Vietnam were wittingly and unwittingly created within the American family.

Selection of the Samples

The War Resisters

In the summer of 1968, I went to New York City and established contact with antiwar groups. The War Resisters League (WRL) and its affiliated organizations appeared to be the best and most central organizational framework through which contacts could be established with persons committed to an antiwar position. The League's offices were centrally located in Manhattan; it posessed a relatively large staff of paid and volunteer workers; it was a meeting place for persons of antiwar sentiments from all parts of the country; and through its counseling services to young men who were considering or had already decided to oppose the draft, it offered me access to a still larger antiwar population.

In order to balance the sample, approximately equal numbers of subjects were chosen from four different parts of this population: younger staff members of the War Resisters League who were working in the central office; field workers who could be reached through the central office; persons who had sought counseling at the central office during the previous six months and whose names and addresses were on file; persons awaiting sentencing to federal jail terms for draft evasion, whose names were on a register hung on the wall of the central office. Members of each of these groups were randomly selected and asked to participate in the study. One in ten declined to cooperate. Most of the interviews were conducted in private apartments, restaurants, or at the Manhattan WRL office; the rest took place within an eighty-mile radius of New York City.

Nineteen independent criteria (see Appendix) dealing with motives, actual behavior, and legal status were used to categorize the nature of the war resisters' commitment to an antiwar position. This analysis showed that substantial differences existed in the war resisters' personal interpretation of commitment, and that not all of them had taken an antiwar stand because of a deep, personal belief in nonviolence per se. Four subgroups of varying sizes could be delineated.

THE FIFTEEN MOVEMENT SUBJECTS

With two exceptions, I became acquainted with these people at the War Resisters League and its affiliated organizations in their combined offices, where the men worked. The movement members interpreted their opposition to war in the form of a total personal and sociopolitical commitment. Essentially, no aspect of their lives was untouched by this dedication.

Because most of them had informed their draft boards in writing that they did not intend to cooperate with the Selective Service System in any of its administrative functions, had refused induction on one or more occasion, and had burned or returned their draft card, thh faced jail sentences. The majority were waiting for a date to be set for their Federal Court trials. A few had been tried and were involved in appeals or awaiting sentencing. One movement member had already served his prison term for refusing to perform military duties after his in-service application for conscientious objector (C.O.) status had been rejected.* Another, who completed his questionnaire in jail, had just been sentenced to five years in a federal penitentiary under a special Federal Juvenile Rehabilitation Law which foresees release at such time as the juvenile is considered rehabilitated.** In this case, rehabilitation apparently meant willingness to enter the Army.

Because of their participation in marches, demonstrations, and sit-ins, eleven of the fifteen movement members had been in local and federal jails on at least one occasion. For at least several months preceeding our inter-

* My wife met him by chance in the New York City subway and gained his cooperation for this study.

** This resister was originally suggested to me by my parents who had read several articles about him in local newspapers. He was also known at the War Resisters League for his independence and zeal.

view, they had spent a part or all of their time in work and activities organized and directed by the War Resisters League or by other related peace groups, and expressed the intention of continuing movement work in the future. Most, if not all, of their close friends were also movement people.

THE THREE SOCIALLY ACTIVE WAR RESISTERS

These resisters can be distinguished from the movement ubjects in two ways. They had no affiliations with antiwar organizations and, instead, had devoted most or all of their t me to such educational and rehabilitative activities as the Peace Corps, Urban League, Volunteers in Asia, and ghetto workOne had conscientious objector status, another was applying for it, and the third was no longer eligible for the draft. This last subjnt was in fact a borderline case in some ways. Although he was not organized within the peace movement and did not intend either to formally affiliate himself with it or devote his energies privately to it, he had returned his draft card with a note in which he refused to cooperate in any way with the board. This act of protest, together with his willingness to go to jail, is striking. He had spent five years in the Peace Corps in South America and chose to return his draft card despite the fact that he was by then exempt from military service.

THE FOUR PRIVATE CONSCIENTIOUS OBJECTORS

These subjects had a completely private commitment to nonviolence. Although one happened to be a paid staff member of a peace group, none felt their private commitment to nonviolence neccessarily required them to participate in broader activities of a propagandistic, organizational, or demonstrative nature. One had received a medical deferment, the second conscientious objector status, and the other two were waiting for decisions from their draft boards on their applications for such status.

THE THREE CONVENIENCE DRAFT RESISTERS

The remaining subjects were applying for C. O., student deferment, or medical reject status when interviewed. Although all of them voiced opposition to the war in Vietnam, their private motivation was to avoid the draft in any way possible. They had no further interest in antiwar, civil rights, educational, or rehabilitative organizations and movements although they were generally sympathetic. While it would be accurate to claim that these people did have an aversion to violence, their primary motivation was personal expedience. They regarded serving in the Army as an unnecessary, disruptive, and dangerous intrusion into their lives and were trying to find a conventional solution to this dilemma which would not bring them into conflict with the courts or take them away from their work and private lives.

Their position was probably similar in some respects to that of many young men. They were not antimilitarists, and believed that the United States should maintain a military potential and that young men should serve in the armed forces, however uncomfortable and disruptive that might be. But, believing that the United States had a bad foreign policy in Vietnam and that the armed forces were being misused, they felt no moral obligation to perform military service at that time. Their behavior represented an attempt to avoid the obvious penalties and threats involved in draft resistance as well as the hardships entailed in serving in an army with which they disagreed. Their possibilities for resolving this dilemma were restricted, since they did not qualify for some kinds of deferments and had not opted for those open to them. The result was confusion, trepidation, and half-hearted attempts to work this problem out within the structure and definitions of the Selective Service System.

The four-part division into "Movement," "Social Activist," "Private," and "Convenience" subgroups highlights the manner in which the war resisters had incorporated their antiwar stand into their general life style. The presence of fifteen movement subjects within a total sample of twenty-five persons is a reflection of the selection procedure used. Hundreds of thousands of Americans protested the war in Vietnam on some occasion, and the number of Americans in agreement with this position went into the millions. In order to guarantee fulfillment of the commitment criteria, however, it was necessary that a person had done more than hold antiwar sentiments and had participated in an antiwar march or demonstration. The fact that each of the movement subjects was engaged full-time in antiwar and peace activity at the time of the interviews as well as before suggested the kind of full commitment which I had wanted to investigate.

Selection criteria always have an artificial and unrealistic component in that they presuppose clear-cut categories which may not exist or may not properly handle the phenomenon to be explored. The movement subjects were not the only young Americans who, in the summer of 1968, were demonstrating personal dedication to an antiwar position, and it would have been inappropriate and unrealistic to limit the use of the word "commitment" only to those persons who were actively engaged in the organizational structures of antiwar groups. It was for this reason that I attempted to include in the sample other people who, through circumstance and inclination, had tried to continue with their private lives while taking at least an administratively explicit antiwar stand. This relatively small group fell into the previously described three subdivisions, which undoubtedly correspond to the larger population of antiwar people in the United States. Although it made my sample unrepresentative of a general cross-section of antiwar persons, this selection was consistent with my intent to study the most publicly dedicated antiwar activists.

The Green Berets

After completing interviews with the war resisters I returned to the Max Planck Institute in Munich. A short time later I heard that a relatively large Special Forces detachment was stationed nearby. The prerequisites for membership in this group are high. In order to qualify for the Special Forces a soldier must volunteer for the unit, pass a series of psychological tests, and successfully complete a difficult obstacle course. Green Berets are specifically trained for combat duty. Self-selection and Army selection procedures appeared to guarantee a highly dedicated, prowar population.

In the late spring of 1969, the commander of a Green Beret unit gave me permission to interview his men. With the help of the company physician, a sample of twenty-five was selected at random from approximately 400 soldiers stationed at the base. There were only two criteria for selection. The soldiers had to be between twenty and thirty years of age, and be regular members of the Special Forces. The twenty-five soldiers were asked to participate in this study on a volunteer basis and none refused.

Throughout this book, the Green Berets are referred to as war volunteers, although at the time of my interviews with these men, only twenty had previously served in Vietnam. This label is derived from the fact that Special Forces members are more likely to see combat than are members of any other American military unit. A soldier who volunteers for the Special Forces is in effect volunteering to go to war.

Before I began my study of the Green Berets, I had conducted two pilot studies of Americans who volunteered for the war in Vietnam. The first pilot study was of five psychiatric referrals to the neuropsychiatric clinic of the American Military Hospital in Munich. The applications of these men for combat duty had been rejected on psychiatric grounds. The second pilot study involved fifteen combat volunteers from infantry units in southern Germany. I decided against continuing this study because the soldiers' motives for going to Vietnam did not satisfy my commitment criteria. They were primarily interested in escaping marital difficulties and the boredom of a peacetime Army. Some had been disciplinary problems in their units; others were interested in maximizing their promotion possibilities through duty in a combat area. All were motivated by the extra pay and the excitement and adventure they anticipated finding in Vietnam. When I began my interviews with the Green Berets, I had no idea that they too would express motives similar to these.

The Control Group

During the winter of 1969 and the spring of 1970, I asked all the students in my college-level psychology courses at a number of American military installations in southern Germany to complete the same questionnaire series which had been given to the war volunteers and war resisters. Only males between twenty and thirty-five years of age who had been drafted, had not served in Vietnam, and stated that they did not intend to volunteer for duty in Vietnam entered the final control group. These criteria reduced the sample from sixty to thirty-five. Time pressure and other considerations prevented me from interviewing these men. Since the bulk of the life history material was gathered in interviews, my information on this control group falls largely in the areas of attitude and personality.

Method

Before each interview, both Green Berets and war resisters were asked to complete an extensive series of attitude, personality, and biographical questionnaires. Some were my own experimental questionnaires and others were well-known, widely used inventories. The bulk of the questionnaire data is presented in Chapter 7, along with the selection rationale and evaluation procedure. Three questionnaires are used elsewhere to support and supplement the interview findings: they are the rating scales for high school social behavior and attitudes used by Bandura and Walters and reported in their book *Adolescent Aggression,* adapted into questionnaire form; the Military Life Questionnaire, based on the inventory used by Stouffer in his studies of *The American Soldier;* and the Thorne Sex Inventory.

In nearly all cases the interviews, held in one or two sessions, followed completion of the questionnaire series and lasted between five and fifteen hours. All interviews but one were recorded on tape and then transcribed. The transcriptions range in length from sixty to over 300 typewritten pages. The interviews were open ended; they were conducted this way in order to motivate the interviewee to expound at length with a minimum of direction and intervention. In this way I hoped to obtain spontaneous documents from which direct quotes could be taken. Generally, I opened the interview by requesting the subject to tell the story of his life, beginning with his earliest memories. Themes which particularly interested me, such as disciplinary practices in the home, sexual experience, and relations with parents, were specified for purposes of orientation. In this way I ensured that the major research topics would be covered, but also gave the subject the opportunity to tell his story as he saw it. This freedom enabled subjects to relate crucial experiences which could not have been anticipated even after review of the questionnaire material. Specific questioning fell into two categories. A series of questions on social, political, racial, religious, and sexual topics had been prepared in advance. Also, two independent series of questions were designed for the war volunteers and the war resisters. In each case, the questions dealt with the circumstances surrounding their decision to become war volunteers and war resisters and the experiences they had had since in these roles.

Evaluation of the interview material followed a fixed category system. All categories, whether descriptive, as the majority were, or interpretive, were rated by two independent raters.* When rater reliability was not perfect, the category was either dropped (twenty percent) or lineal scaling was reduced from five to three alternatives. Missing data averages five percent for all category results presented.

Data Presentation

In order to ensure maximal continuity each chapter is divided into two parts. The first is devoted to the Vietnam volunteers, the second to the war resisters. In Chapter 7 direct comparisons are made among these groups and the control sample of inductees on a number of the inventories.

The life history chapters contain lengthy quotations from the interview material. While thematically organized, the selection of quotations was not cut except to eliminate repetition, thematically irrelevant material, and my questions when the responses were self-explanatory. All such cutting is indicated by ellipses. By including a considerable amount of original transcription I hoped to achieve several ends. I felt it was necessary to provide the reader with the original words of these young men so that no doubt could arise as to the validity of the sources. Also, since the original material is far richer in content and meaning than analytical interpretation could be, I felt it would be injurious to this report not to disclose information, even where it is idiosyncratic, which would broaden the reader's perspective on these subjects. Finally, the original material will enable every reader to examine critically the balance and judiciousness, as well as the accuracy, of the conclusions I draw.

Notes

1. R. B. Smith, "Disaffection, Delegitimation and Consequences: Aggregate Trends for World War II, Korea and Vietnam," paper read at the conference on "The End of the Mass Army," Amsterdam, March 29-31, 1973.

2. *Ibid.*

---

*One rater was a sociologist; the other was a college student.

CHAPTER 1

WHERE THEY CAME FROM

THE GREEN BERETS

It is widely believed that professional soldiers are recruited largely from the lower social classes but this factor, as well as parental educational and occupational status, was highly variable among the Green Berets interviewed. While nearly half the parents did not complete high school, of those who did about one-quarter went on to college. The occupational distribution of the parents corresponds closely to their formal educational background. One-third of the fathers were unskilled and another third were skilled laborers. The rest included a doctor, a self-employed businessman, a white-collar worker, and three executives. When the mothers worked, they were clerical and sales employees, unskilled laborers, or nurses. The majority, however, were housewives.

The sample of Green Berets was fairly evenly divided between those born and raised in urban centers and in small, rural communities. Three spent their childhood years in the country and their adolescence in the city, or vice versa. They came from all parts of the United States and one was from the Caribbean.

A broader view of the variability of the social setting in which these soldiers grew up can be gained through the career patterns and social mobility analysis of their fathers. Through education, business ventures, and investments, many families experienced considerable upward social mobility; the grandfathers of the Green Berets were largely unskilled manual laborers, but the fathers of many of the volunteers attained greater material security and affluence. A smaller number of families suffered economic setbacks and hardships. In these cases, the fathers were unemployed and their wives and children went to work, often receiving financial help from relatives. Both upwardly and downwardly mobile families passed through critical periods. By contrast, the socially and economically nonmobile families enjoyed continuous material security. Only a minority of these families were ever poor and this was due to the downward mobility of the fathers. Eleven fathers were chronic alcoholics. In this group, however, chronic alcoholism is primarily connected with middle-class (nine cases) as opposed to lower-class status (two cases) and with upward mobility (five cases) and nonmobility (four cases) rather than downward mobility (two cases). Occupational instability, when measured by number of jobs lost, was strongest among the upwardly mobile fathers. Among the downwardly mobile, occupational instability was fatal. When a downwardly mobile father lost a job, his career was over. The nonmobile fathers rarely or never changed jobs or occupation.

Upward Mobility

The eight upwardly mobile families often moved into new neighborhoods where they felt they had to conform to the life style of their neighbors. The accompanying strains were particularly great for those families who experienced considerable upward mobility after years of hard living. Three of these fathers had been unemployed for long periods of time and another had once gone bankrupt.

One father who had had only eight years of elementary school and started work as a farmhand had been frequently unemployed and shifted jobs constantly. Later he went into partnership with another man but went bankrupt. A few years later he acquired a small greenhouse business and expanded it into a large enterprise from which he earned more than $40,000 a year (Case 207). The father who was a doctor had put himself through college as an unskilled laborer; he opened his own clinic and earned an excellent living (Case 206). Another father started as a gas station attendant, then worked as a travelling salesman, went to college, and became a district sales manager with earnings over $40,000 a year. He had had, his son noted, a "very tough childhood," being orphaned at an early age and brought up by an alcoholic uncle who beat him frequently. While working as a travelling salesman he too became an alcoholic (Case 208). Another father achieved social mobility as a military officer and, after retirement, as a salesman. He had run away from home at the age of fifteen and worked as an unskilled laborer before joining the Army. While in the military he completed one and a half years of college and became a heavy drinker (Case 212). The other fathers began as a dishwasher (Case 210), farm laborer (Case 215), and unskilled laborers (Cases 214 and 217), and moved over the years to much better jobs as a dietician, railroad inspector, investment speculator, and construction superintendent respectively. These four fathers made successful investments of different kinds.

Case 214's description of his father is representative for the career pattern and personality of the upwardly mobile fathers:

His family didn't have much. He played football in high school and worked pulling cotton and in a cotton gin. He had a kind of a bullheaded sort of determination. When he started working on something, he got it done. He wouldn't let anything stand in his way. He allowed himself few excuses for failing. That's probably his problem, I'm not sure. Expected more of himself quicker than he should have. He went to college and he worked nights and studied and played football. He was a good football player. He used to have a book of clippings on him, you know, and all that business. He stressed all the masculine virtues. He wasn't very imaginative. In fact, he was very unimaginative. I'm sure he had certain feelings of social inadequacy, not being able to get along with people, snobbish people or something. But for the most part he kept that kind of thing inside. He kept things inside. He would never talk about things that bothered him. The same way he kept pain inside, you know. Pain didn't matter. It was like he couldn't afford to lose a day's wage.

No or Minimal Mobility

Eleven families experienced no socioeconomic mobility during their children's childhood and adolescent years. The fathers were mainly skilled and unskilled workers who remained steadily employed and provided adequately for the material needs of their families. A few had farms on the side, worked by the children. In seven cases, the mothers occasionally took part-time jobs to help out financially. This enabled the families to buy luxury goods; it was never undertaken to provide for necessities.

Downward Mobility

In six cases the financial situation of the father deteriorated so badly that the family income sank below the subsistence level. Downward mobility coincided with the fathers' unemployment. In two cases (213 and 221) unemployment was caused by on-the-job accidents which prevented the fathers from resuming work, and in one case (227) chronic illness had the same result. None of these fathers received compensation. Another father's business (Case 219) went bankrupt and he never recovered from the loss. Still another, formerly a truckdriver (Case 225), lost his job because of laziness and unreliability. The last father in this group (Case 228), a former Army officer, became an alcoholic. In all these families, the mothers went to work and were the only sources of income for periods ranging from five to eighteen years. The children also had to work for such necessities as food and clothing.

THE WAR RESISTERS

More than half the resisters were born and raised in the greater New York metropolitan area; a substantial number spent their childhood and adolescent years in Brooklyn, and others grew up in outlying communities. The other resisters came from various regions of the United States: from such large cities as Boston and San Francisco, and from small communities in Wisconsin, Pennsylvania, Ohio, and North Carolina. One resister was born in Latvia and spent several childhood years in Germany before his family finally settled in a suburban New York community.

The resisters come from working-, lower-middle-, middle- and upper-middle-class families.* In all these families there was a close correspondence between education and occupation. With the exception of one self-employed businessman, the fathers with a college or graduate school education worked in professional or management positions. The skilled and unskilled workers had the lowest average educational level; only one had completed high school. The clerical workers, salesmen, and the other two self-employed businessmen were an educational middle group. Most had completed high school and a few had begun college but only one had finished.

Nearly all the fathers had always worked in the same occupation and at the same job. When job changes did occur they were usually connected with career advancement within the same occupation. Only one father changed his job more than once. The three fathers who changed occupations were special cases. One had been a teacher in Europe and while learning English began a gardening business. The second had been unemployed for several years and finally opened a small business. The third had a Ph.D. in economics, and was an inventor and peace advocate who only worked intermittently, usually as a teacher. The family existed on his salary and royalties, and his wife's salary. He gave most of his time to various antipoverty and peace organizations.

Upward Mobility

The fathers of all ten upwardly mobile families had completed college. Three had M.A.s and two had Ph.D.s. Although the mothers had all completed high school and three had received M.A. degrees, they usually had less formal education than their husbands.

There was no direct connection between upward mobility and income.

---

*Many studies have reported that student activists come primarily from professional homes and that the frequency of professionalism in family background is most conspicuous among Jewish activists. Neither trend could be confirmed in this study. Only one-third of the war resisters came from professional homes and in these cases the religious confession was usually Protestant. No fathers were medical doctors, psychologists, or lawyers. Half the Jewish fathers were unskilled or skilled manual laborers and one worked in a clerical position. The others were in professional and management occupations except for one self-employed businessman. Three of the Catholic fathers were salesmen, one worked as a clerical employee, and another as a public relations executive. There were many working mothers in all these families. In the Jewish and Catholic families, the mothers generally worked out of financial necessity and in clerical positions. The Protestant mothers were teachers and social workers and took up their occupations because of boredom with household chores or as careers.

Some of the families had incomes of more than $20,000 a year while others did not exceed $12,000. In these families the wives worked only if they were so inclined. The wife of a $50,000-a-year business executive worked as a part-time secretary, the wife of a $20,000-a-year public relations executive as a sales clerk. One social worker was married to a self-employed landscape gardener, the other to the vice-president of a large company. One mother had worked her entire adult life as a telephone operator in order to help maintain the family's lower-middle-class living standard.

Despite varied income levels, these parents possessed three major similarities. They had greatly improved their economic position over that of their parents. Most had lived in the same community since marriage. A few had moved once in connection with new jobs but remained within comfortable visiting distance of old friends. They all seem to have been satisfied with their respective living standards and were not status conscious.

No or Minimal Social Mobility

These thirteen families were heterogeneous in educational level, occupation of the father, and socio-economic status. In several cases the mothers had much more formal education than had the fathers.

More than half the fathers had a high school education or less. Most were skilled and unskilled manual laborers and the others were in sales or clerical positions. Their occupational titles included truck driver, school custodian, dispatcher in a trucking firm, shipping clerk, cutter in the garment industry, auto salesman and machine maintainance supervisor. Their incomes ranged from $6,000 to $11,000 a year. Four of their wives were housewives. Four families were dependent on the income of mothers who worked full-time as bookkeepers, an accountant, and a postal clerk. In one family the mother had always been the only source of income. Her husband had divorced her after a few years of marriage and never contributed support. Chronic illness had prevented two fathers from working full-time and left one an invalid. One father had built up a flourishing oil-delivery business, but because of his generosity in giving oil without charge to poor families, his income never exceeded $6,000 a year.

The remaining four fathers had college educations and one had received a Ph.D. in economics (this case was discussed earlier). One maintained a flourishing import-export business dating from before his marriage, and had an annual income of $25,000. His wife was a trained nurse but did not work. Another father was a high school science teacher with an annual income of $14,000. Because of his popularity and performance record he had been repeatedly offered highly paid administrative positions which he rejected in order to continue teaching. His first wife was a housewife, the second a social worker. The other father was a salesman for a large pharmaceutical company and had a constant annual income of $20,000. His wife, a former secretary, did not work.

Downward Mobility

The fathers in these two families were skilled workers. One was an electrician and the other a wood-carver. They and their wives were high school graduates and one wife had attended college. The downward social mobility of these families was caused by illness and decreased work opportunity. The electrician had been bedridden for three years before he died of a heart ailment. His wife worked as an accountant and had been the sole source of family income for many years. The father's illness and medical costs forced the family to move to a smaller, less expensive apartment. The other father carved wooden forms for hat makers; this specialty became outdated and his income shrank over the years. If the family had not lived in a cooperative apartment complex with low rentals and many benefits their whole way of life would have been endangered.

Summary

One is immediately struck by several features of the socioeconomic background of the war resisters' families: the broad spectrum of their origins; the fact that education rather than business ventures usually provided the springboard to upward mobility; and the fact that many wives, especially among the lower-status families, were better educated than their husbands. Among families of middle- and upper-middle-class status, it is noteworthy that none appeared to be conspicuous consumers. Even the upwardly mobile families whose incomes enlarged considerably did not get caught up in status pressures, and therefore did not experience radical change in their life styles, either materially or socially. The absence of fluctuations in life style, combined with their economic self-sufficiency, undoubtedly added to their basic stability. These features may also be viewed as among the more important social-psychological preconditions for the emergence of the value structures and behavioral patterns which were to play an increasing role in the lives of their sons.

There was only one family in which status pressures contributed to family disharmony. In this case the husband was better educated than his wife but had not been able to provide her with many of the middle-class luxuries to which she aspired. This situation was complicated in part by an interconfessional marriage—he was German-Catholic and she Polish-Jewish—and the fact that the husband had been an ambulatory, passive alcoholic for many years.

Seven mothers had considerably more schooling than their husbands—in one case the mother had completed college and her husband only the eighth grade; six fathers had a considerably higher educational level than their wives. The fact that these discrepancies in formal education did not lead to friction can be attributed to several factors. The families placed strong emphasis on informal education: reading, music, visiting museums, and going to the theater. It was not uncommon for the formally less well-educated parent to be better read and more interested in the arts and literature than his or her spouse. The fathers, irrespective of their relative educational levels, were unaggressive and self-assured. Several wives continued their education at night and increased their sophistication through political activity and community work. Many parents shared each other's political views and were engaged in common political activities. The virtue of hard work was a central value to all the families. Therefore, the fathers' labor was respected regardless of occupation, and the wives enjoyed equal respect whether they remained housewives or became employees. Several families were further solidified by ethnic bonds, political beliefs, communal living, and religious beliefs.

CHAPTER 2

FAMILY LIFE DURING CHILDHOOD

THE GREEN BERETS

CASE 204

Well, if my mother and father hadn't trained me, I wouldn't be what I am today. . . . You know, they took the time with me and my brothers and sisters. . . . As far as I'm concerned, they gave me a good home life and everything. They were real good to me. . . .

CASE 205

My parents were hard-working people. . . . Our family, we—we never had anything to say to each other. You didn't sit down and have any drawn-out conversations. My mother and father were working all the time. They were tired, that jazz. My mother was there all the time but she didn't have much to say.

CASE 206

My memory of my parents was that they seemed quite happy. There didn't seem to be any problems at all. . . . Yes, they were very concerned about us and gave us everything we needed.

CASE 207

I would say that I had a real good home life except, you know, for the money. It was not that much.

CASE 209

Well, we weren't ever close, but we always got along. Uh, we never disagreed. I always did what they wanted. . . . Well, it seems like we never talked that much and when we did, we just never discussed anything really . . . but I'd say I had a happy childhood. . . . They gave me enough attention. Maybe they could have given me a little more. But I don't feel that was important. . . . Well, I didn't like staying around the house. 'Cause unless you just like to sit around and watch television, there was nothing to do. There was nothing at home. It seemed like everything that was happening was somewhere else. I never hated anything at home. It was just boring.

CASE 214

Had the feeling that they [his parents] weren't going to hold me back, that I didn't need them because when I felt like I needed 'em they weren't there. . . . It was a matter of I wasn't getting what I needed where I was so I went looking for it. . . . I cut out the first time after I beat my Dad. That's the first time I left. I could always leave from then on. That summer I was gone, was at friends' houses. It was always, if you don't like it you can get out. That was one of my Dad's main lines. Sometimes I'd leave and sneak back up in the garage, where they couldn't find me. Sleep up there. Then out again as soon as they'd gone to work. I'd always sleep in somebody's car or something, you know. . . . When you're hungry you always find somebody to feed you.

CASE 215

In my estimation, I have undoubtedly the finest pair of parents any individual could have. . . . I couldn't describe a better pair of people to anybody, as far as I'm concerned, I think.

CASE 221

We knew right from wrong. Both me and my brother was raised up, I should say real decent. I mean, even when we was younger, we had to go to church every Sunday, you know, and this and that. And we never did go out and get in trouble, but we had just as much fun as any of the other kids. . . . I'd say I really had probably the best mother and father anybody had.

CASE 228

Well, we weren't ever close, but we always got along. Uh, we never disagreed. with my mother, my wife is more affectionate.

Parental Relationship

CASE 209

They got along fine. Nothing really out in the open. Like once in a while my father would go out and come back drunk. But my mother never, you know, never got angry or nothing. Just never said nothing much.

CASE 213

Did your parents get along well?
Oh yes, they, uh, they've been married more than twenty-two some years now and, apart from quarrels and arguments, I only remember one time that—that my Dad, slapped my mother. Just one time, I guess if I were to, well, I was a young kid then. I didn't really know the circumstances but if I could see

that again—maybe—maybe she asked for it, I don't know. Maybe. You know how women get now and then. They start rattling off at the mouth and you're just at the point where you can't take any more and then quiet them down. I mean, naturally it's not proper but, uh, and who's to know what a—what a—a person who has a lot on his mind, well, what the reflex will be when something like that blows—makes them blow their top, you know.

Were you there at the time that he slapped her?
Oh yeah. . . .

And what did your mother do, do you remember?
She cried a little bit and that was all.

CASE 221

Well, he was furious. He would have just—she was trying to cook and I don't remember, this was just told to me, I mean I was real too small. Anyway, yeah, he was just—it was at my grandparents' house there in Arizona. And she was fixing something to eat and he come up and goosed her or messing around with her or something. And it must have just caught her 'cause she had a knife in her hand and he turned around and she took it and threw it. I know one good fight they had because she was at fault. It was in—we was living in Portland, Oregon and I don't know what started it, 'cause I guess he was drinking and she kept hitting on him and slapping him and he threw her under ice cold water in the shower. That's all he did was keep her under the shower till she cooled down.

That time that she threw the knife at him, you say that he smashed her. Where?
He slapped her.

Did she kind of cool off after that?
Yes.

Did your parents ever have any arguments besides those two times?
Oh yeah. Constantly. She almost run him down once with a car. She caught him out with a barmaid one time on New Year's Eve. I was in the eighth grade too, that's right. It happened in Phoenix. And my brother—my brother—well, my father's—well, I guess you could—my uncle, him and my father are just like—they're both big men, 250 pounds. And they're always kicking around, you know. Running around together. And my mother and my aunt caught them in a bar making some advance to some barmaids and they really had a fight that night. But Dad didn't do anything to her. She did it all. She was pulling his hair, pinching him and all this bit.

You said she tried to run him down with a car?
Yeah, she stopped right before, 'cause he said, you know. She cursed him out to start with and we was going home and he took out walking and she went to chase him, you know, with the car.

CASE 223

They got along real good except my mother didn't like him going hunting or fishing all the time.

CASE 226

Well, in the early days they got along real good and, uh, it seemed like, uh, the last ten years, uh, ten years before he died, it seemed like he started drinking quite a bit and going out with women and they quarreled quite a bit. And, had a few fights. Other than that, they got along okay. . . . Oh, he'd come in drunk and, uh, and use cuss words, uh, say he was with some gal or woman and then. . . . I hadn't been out with a woman and, you know, it wasn't very good to hear. But I could understand my mother's feelings and I didn't blame her for them.

CASE 228

Now when you were young, do you remember the fights and arguments that your parents had with each other? And when I say remember, I don't necessarily mean in detail, but do you remember arguments in the home?
I don't remember arguments, I remember that they had some pretty knock-down drag-out fights occasionally.

What's a knock-down drag-out fight?
Blows are struck and recriminations. . . .

Do you remember who hit whom at the time?
Well, I remember Mother had a black eye once. I assume that he hit her. They didn't, uh, they didn't really fight in front of us. I mean, well, maybe they were in the next room or something like this. After we went to bed or along these lines.

Discipline

CASE 204

When either mother or father would tell us to do something we went ahead and did it. Like with mother, you know, I mean, if we were bad, she'd spank us with a hairbrush. She usually took care of most of the whippin'. And we'd go ahead and behave. Her beatin's weren't as bad as our father's, 'cause he'd usually get out the belt, you know. He'd wear us out.

CASE 207

My Dad was never, I don't think he was very strict. He was a real serious man. If he said something, he wanted it done, you know. He said we'd be in by ten, and we had better be in at ten or otherwise there was a punishment.

CASE 209

Well, they'd just bring out the strap and whip us a few times. That would usually straighten us up. That was the usual way or send us to bed early sometimes, when we were younger. . . . Well, for fighting, calling somebody names, destroying something around the house. Just did something you weren't supposed to do, you know. . . . My mother usually dished it out 'cause she was around more when things happened and took care of it on the spot. My father used a board a couple of times. That's, uh, maybe why I feared my father more [chuckles]. . . . My mother whipped me, you know, it's hard to recall, but I'd say, about twenty or thirty times. Something like that. Maybe a couple of times a week. . . . My father would hit me maybe five or six times [with the board], that'd be enough. Most of the time you knew you deserved it. . . . No, they weren't too hard in that respect. . . . Yeah, it was hard to know 'cause it was up to them, you know, how they felt at the time. They were nervous people and you'd get on their nerves after a while. . . . There were certain things you did every day. You didn't think about 'em. You just did 'em. And you never talked back.

CASE 212

My mother never administered punishment just due to the fact that, uh, she's only five foot two and I've almost always been bigger than she is and she just never figured she could ever hurt me, I guess.

Your father?
My father is six foot eight. . . . There's an automatic built-in terror there [laughs].

What do you mean, a built-in terror?
Well . . . when Dad finally stands up, you know [chuckles] he means business and so it's best that you correct yourself immediately, so every time he said something I had a tendency to listen. He also told me when I was younger that the day I decided I'd go against his wishes, we'd go out in the back yard and square it away. When I was about sixteen, I thought I was big enough to try it. And we went out and . . . he let me hit him three times and then I took off running and he caught me. And so after that I decided to listen. . . .

Would you say your father was a strict man?
Yes, I'd say he was strict.

In what ways?
Well, basically anything concerning mother that was out of the way, or anything that, uh, concerning—well, anything concerning the house, I would say he was strict on—like no swearing in the house, you know, and he better never hear about your doing it any place else, uh, respect for your mother, I never could get a reading on that except the fact that she was my mother. That's why I should respect her. So, I mean [chuckles] I just took it for granted that I should respect her. Then, lying, I'd better not lie to anyone. Be home on time. When— when I was told to be someplace—be there at the proper time and the proper clothing. Your hands washed and face washed to go to dinner or something like this.

CASE 215

I can never remember my mother whippin' me. I don't know if she ever did or not but I can't remember her ever doing it. Now I can remember her always threatening to whip me and I also remember her threatening to tell my father what I had done and that he'll whip me, which he did a few times. He wasn't very hesitant about puttin' the belt to my backside. I'm not talking about a severe beating. I'm just talking about a couple of quick swats on the butt that hurt for about maybe an hour 'til I understood the meaning he was trying to put across. I can't say that they were ever cruel or unusually hard punishing me.

Do you remember any incident in which—you told me that if you really pushed your father hard that he'd really have a bad temper. Do you ever remember pushing him?

Yes I do. I remember coming home drunk one night when I was about seventeen years old and I was supposed to go fishing with him at three o'clock in the morning. I remember coming through the front door of the house and he was sitting on the couch reading the paper. He had gotten up ready to go fishing and I hadn't come home yet. And I don't know what I said to him because this is what I remember: I came in the door, he got off of the couch and then he asked me something and I remember saying something smart and laughing to myself and I woke up the next day and I had a black eye. He hit me. I thought of what I said and he'd never tell me what I said and he stayed away from the house for two days, he didn't come home. Don't know where the hell he went. My mother was worried out of her mind.

What time did you come in into the house?

It was about four o'clock in the morning. . . . He just got all upset. I guess, I can't blame him too much.

Was your father a strict man?

Not really. He was level-headed. I mean, if I did something he thought was wrong and he said you aren't gonna do that again, I usually didn't. He was the authority but I wouldn't call him strict at all, not really. . . .

Do you remember ever holding a grudge against your father for anything at all?

No, nothing.

Would you say your father was the central authority in the family?

Oh, yeah, definitely. My mother did what she was ordered. If he said something, that was it. She went along with it. I tried to get her to argue for a while but she wouldn't do it [laughs].

CASE 217

My father never spanked me. He was too big, strong as a bull. He was afraid he'd hurt us. He's about six foot four, 240 pounds. I always did what he said. When he said something, we did it . . . 'cause he looked mean [laughs]. You was looking up at a giant. . . . My mother stopped hittin' me when I was about five. I was too big and just laughed.

CASE 218

I reckon they just had normal rules, you know. You must say yes sir and no sir, ma'm, yes ma'm and no ma'm. It's normal being from the South. You say it anyway. It's a habit. I don't remember anything particular rules that were set up there about anything. Just normal stuff. Like you should be there maybe when they had dinner or something. You should be there to eat it there. And you get some—tell them where you're going or something like this, see. Uh, it's not anything—normal stuff.

Well, give me an idea what you consider normal. What were they?
Well, uh, you know, you had to, uh, eat your supper at a certain time. You had certain things to do that you—I was supposed to do. And maybe I was supposed to sweep the floor and maybe I had to wash the dishes. These weren't rules, just things to do. And you didn't—you don't talk back to grown people. And just, uh, just normal stuff.

Now, give me an idea of what kinds of things you used to get punished for when you were a kid and who punished you?
Well, I got punished for anything that I would do. Maybe I would, uh, I'm supposed to be somewhere at a certain time, I wouldn't be there. I probably got in trouble in school, maybe the teacher would write home a note or something or other. And my mother always gave me a whipping. I'd get whipped for—I'd go to somebody's house to play and I'm supposed to be back at twelve and I come back at, say, three in the afternoon or something like that. Uh, go to the show on Saturday and they normally had a western, you know, and the continued picture and so forth. And instead of seeing it one time you sat there and seen it twice and this was something you might get punished for, if they specifically said to be out of the show at such and such a time.

CASE 219

My father seldom spanked me, very seldom. My mother did quite often because she didn't believe in waiting for my father to come home from work. . . . He laid down strict laws. If he set down a rule, then he kept it for sure. And there were no ifs, ands or buts about it. . . . On a few occasions he did bat me on the head. Probably, I think, it was back talk to my mother. You should never talk back to my mother. . . . He very seldom spanked me and very seldom smacked me in the head . . . I guess, he thought if I thought I was a man I should stand there and take what was coming to me, which I'm sure I justly deserved. But he does lose his temper kind of easy. When I was older I definitely kept to any rules, to any policies he put down for me. Actually, when I was older, I wasn't much of a problem for him. Was busy studying.

CASE 221

Do you ever remember your father giving you a whipping?
No, he hit me one time though. . . . I was in high school at the time. . . . Well, one thing my father is really choosy about is his cars. He's—about every two or three years he buys a brand new car. And he really takes care of them. In fact, he has one right now, won't give up—he bought a '57 Buick brand new, Roadmaster, and it's just like brand new now. And he had a pick-up and I took it out and I messed up the side—these truck mirrors on the side, I messed it up. And he started chewing me out about it and I wised off and that's when he hit me. But that's about the only time I can remember he ever hit me.

With his fists, with his hands or what?
Uh, he hit me with his fists . . . in the jaw.

CASE 226

Who would you say made the decisions in the family?
My father.

Was there ever any doubt about that?
No.

What kinds of rules and regulations were there about family life and family discipline in your house?
Well, anytime I do anything, well, until I got older, he always'd whip us with a belt, big black belt. Like I said, we were real close and, uh, I think there's a lot of love in our family. We couldn't go swimming by ourselves or couldn't go fishing by ourselves, couldn't go hunting. A couple of times, that's when I was younger, I slipped off into a pit and got hung. I knew what I was in for. I knew that I was going to get punished. Couldn't smoke, couldn't cuss. If I went to a movie, I had to go during the day, no nights. Couldn't go at night, you know. Couldn't talk back. We couldn't talk back. They were my parents. I wouldn't talk back to them. I knew we were well disciplined. I think if we had more—more discipline like I had when I grew up today, rather than sitting trying to talk some, I think it would be better.

When the kids broke the rules and regulations in your house who punished them?
My father.

Always?
I can remember my mother spanking me about twice.

And what did she spank you with?
I remember once I stole two packs of my father's cigarettes. Went out into the bushes and smoked them. I come back and I was drunk. And all right, she went into the bathroom and got this syringe, a syringe hose, and boy, she beat me blue.

A syringe?
A syringe. Well, hot water bottle, you know, which always has a rubber hose into it. I don't know what you call it.

CASE 228

Well, my father was a heavy—heavy-set, stocky individual. Uh, pretty stern and disciplinarian, I would say. When he told me to do something, it wasn't my normal course of action to ask him why. 'Cause often as not he would say, because I told you to. But on the other hand, uh, a lot of times he'd explain his reason behind something. He seemed to know what he was doing and how he wanted it done, uh, which was, I guess, for an Army officer it's a pretty good way to go. And it was a pretty good approach to a problem and apparently it led to some successes in the Army because he made major in five years which back then, in some cases, you make it either very quickly or very slowly, I don't think you make it you know, one of these twenty-three-year-old Air Force colonels or anything like this.

Do you remember what kinds of rules there were at home, in the family?

Not really anything I can remember clearly. I was taught at a very early age to say, yes, sir, no, sir, sir, ma'm, yes ma'm and that. . . . Yeah, I got whipped pretty often . . . My mother did it pretty often too. But I think my father had a little more impression on us . . . About three times a week . . . We usually got whipped with a rope. I suspect that it was the first thing that came into hand. I recall once or twice with a riding crop or the reins of the bridle . . . Yeah, it was somewhat unpredictable . . . The last time was at about fourteen. That was my mother. . . . Yeah, we stood still because I don't think we would have gotten away with running away from it.

A basic contradiction lies at the center of the relationship between the war volunteers and their parents. The latter conscientiously inculcated their children with a long and exacting list of moral imperatives, but exhibited to their children what would have been considered faulty behavior in others. They used physical measures to punish their children and simultaneously declared violence to be bad. They scolded, nagged, and screamed at the children, but prohibited their emotional release. While unleashing the full fury of their anger they ignored and trampled their children's feelings and demanded courtesy and consideration in return. The parents regarded their own behavior and its acceptance by their children as self-evidently correct. What the children therefore learned was that anger, punitiveness, harshness, and violence were the self-evident rights of the strong and that the same behavior on the part of the weak was morally wrong.

Although more than half the volunteers experienced general indifference from one or both parents, I do not consider these findings to represent a basically indifferent parental attitude or a fundamental disinterest in their children's welfare. They reflect different components of a family pattern and style of child-rearing in which concern for the child is strong but expressed in demands. The child is not cared for but supervised, not comforted in difficult moments but expected to be strong, not seen as a being with emotional needs but as one whose dependency requirements must be squelched rather than outgrown. This pattern of childrearing insists that children should be seen and not heard, that childhood should end quickly. It does not imply, as the previous quotations illustrate, that children reared in this manner feel rejected.

It is important to recognize that none of the volunteers came from morally, educationally, religiously, or materially impoverished family backgrounds or from an impoverished social milieu. Their parents were intent on raising law-abiding, hard-working citizens and executed their responsibility as they understood it. Despite an occasional passing setback, they were successful in this endeavor.

The Home Atmosphere

Most of the Green Berets came from families which were both physically and psychologically intact during their most important developmental years. Only four families were so seriously affected by divorce or the death of a parent that long-term outside support was required or the child was given in care to relatives or an orphanage. For the most part the families were self-sufficient units and appear to have enjoyed respect and social acceptance in their communities.

Two of my colleagues independently rated eighteen characteristics of the Green Berets' home environments. Their judgments, shown in Table 1, provide a view of the inner fabric of these families which, to some, may appear inconsistent with the initial description of them as outwardly stable, self-sufficient, and psychologically cohesive. My colleagues felt that the inner character of nearly all of these families was strongly conformistic, hard, autocratic, intolerant, and nonintellectual, and that the great majority could be described as aggressive, overbearing, irritable, emotionally isolated, rigid, tense, violent, and cold.

This portrayal seems to me to correspond closely to one kind of rugged family life offered for mass consumption in Western movies and television productions. Strict rules are imposed by parents on their children. Each person in the family has prescribed tasks. Parents are stern, cold, and objective with each other and with their children. Punitiveness in the form of threats, deprivation, blows, and other forms of intimidation are generally used to secure the children's obedience. There is little or no room for private feelings and opinions. Usually, only one opinion exists, and it is voiced by the dominant parent. Moreover, it is not expressed as an opinion but as an absolute law. At the same time parents take many extra privileges for themselves which are inconsistent with their otherwise strict code of personal discipline. They may lose their temper, strike out in anger, make arbitrary decisions and are not expected or obligated to explain or justify their behavior. The major differences among such families are found in such secondary characteristics as their wealth, their glamour, their social prestige, the degree of refinement they employ in disguising their methods, how many people work for them, how talented their children are and how pretty and devoted their women.

In fact, there is no inconsistency between the description of the Green Beret families as externally intact, cohesive, and socially accepted on the one hand and the partial portrayal of them given in the interviews. This family pattern has proven its functional vitality over many generations. The more interesting question concerns the explanation for this vitality. Why are they able to function so well despite the tension, latent and expressed aggressiveness, and suppressive and inhibitory forces within them? A satisfactory answer to this question must include a discussion of dependency and power relationships, values, habituation, and the social context in which such families thrive.

The family life of these volunteers was governed by an overpowering network of conformistic demands. Deviation from the rules laid down by the superior family member(s) brought swift and often severe disciplinary action. The rules were established independently of the needs and feelings of the

TABLE 1

Home life atmosphere ratings for war volunteers (in the raters' judgment)*

	Number	Percent		Number	Percent
Warm	4	16	Rational	6	24
Neutral	6	24	Neutral	5	20
Cold	15	60	Irrational	14	56
Friendly	7	28	Relaxed	4	16
Neutral	6	24	Neutral	3	12
Hostile	12	48	Tense	18	72
Peaceful	3	12	Sharing	7	28
Neutral	4	16	Neutral	6	24
Aggressive	18	72	Unsharing	12	48
Secure	10	40	Flexible	2	8
Neutral	5	20	Neutral	6	24
Insecure	10	40	Rigid	17	68
Stable	13	52	Togetherness	5	20
Neutral	3	12	Neutral	1	4
Unstable	9	36	Isolation	19	76
Nonviolent	3	12	Calm	5	20**
Neutral	5	20	Neutral	1	4
Violent	17	68	Irritable	18	72
Democratic	1	4	Easy-going	2	8
Neutral	1	4	Neutral	5	20
Authoritarian	23	92	Overbearing	18	72
Gentle	0	0	Tolerant	2	8
Neutral	3	12	Neutral	3	12
Hard	22	88	Intolerant	20	80
Individualistic	0	0	Intellectual	3	12
Neutral	3	12	Neutral	1	4
Conformistic	22	88	Non-Intellectual	21	84

*The alternative "neutral" was used when the rater could not decide which of the adjective pairs best portrayed the family atmosphere. The rating scale had five alternatives in all all, for example, "Very Warm," "Somewhat Warm," "Neutral," "Somewhat Cold," "Very Cold." Although a number of families were described as "Somewhat Warm," "Friendly," "Secure," etc., almost none received the rating "Very." Since these families, nevertheless, represented exceptions from the overall trend among the volunteers and because exceptions were found on each of the eighteen descriptions, a separate analysis was made to see whether there were exceptional families responsible for the exceptional ratings. This analysis showed that exceptional status on one variable was unrelated to exceptional status on another. There were no exceptional families but rather families who deviated from the general pattern in one detail or another.

**In one case, the information was not sufficient to evaluate this aspect of the home life.

weaker family members, in accordance with custom and personal inclination, and were not disputed. Any needs or desires on the part of the weaker family members which were not heeded by the stronger members were voluntarily subordinated to the prevailing system and usually remained unexpressed. Dissatisfaction was handled similarly. Emotional sensitivity and the expression of affection were regarded as signs of weakness, especially for males, and as such were discouraged. Therefore, the Green Berets learned at an early age that affection, as well as consideration for individual emotional needs, would occupy a very circumscribed role in their families and that their occurrence, as with punishments, would depend primarily on the mood of their parents.

Underlying, cementing, and legitimizing this family pattern were moral values and behavioral standards. These declared family life to be good. They also demanded unswerving loyalty to the family unit. Habituation, in this context, refers to the tendency for people to come to regard anything as good which is intact and functioning. Such a tendency is highly compelling when that which one has cannot be exchanged for a new and better one, as is the case with a family. Although during moments of unhappiness children may fantasize about how different their lives would be if people other than their parents were their parents, they gradually learn to accept their family life with its imperfections, and defend it against attack. If, irrespective of the inner workings and the actual benefits accrued from an institution, its members accept it and continue to function within it, they adjust to it, regard it as a normal condition, and harmonize with it. They identify with it, regardless of what nonmembers think and despite the objective conditions of their lives. It is difficult to live in a permanent state of rebellion, and rebellions rarely occur when people do not have standards of comparison or do not see the chance of changing their circumstances. This fate is especially obvious in the case of children.

The Parental Marriage

Approximately equal numbers of parental marriages were appraised by the Green Berets as tending more towards harmony or more towards disharmony. Of the six rated as very disharmonious, four ended in divorce. By and large, the parents adjusted well enough to one another so that their marriages were not threatened. In fact, a collapse of the marriage only became a possibility when the father proved an unreliable provider. This was usually but not always connected with his alcoholism, occupational instability, and a nearly complete loss of prestige. By and large, the stability of the marriage was unrelated to the frequency of disputes, expressed affection, or aggressiveness between the parents.

Nearly half the volunteers could not recall ever having seen their parents express affection verbally or physically to each other. The others recalled the occurrence of an occasional kiss or embrace, but suggested that these expressions were mechanical and reserved. Only one-quarter of the parents shared common interests and only one-sixth engaged in common spare-time activities.

There are virtually no families in this sample in which serious arguments did not take place. According to the soldiers arguments were initiated by mothers more often than fathers, but were caused most often by the faults of their fathers, and sometimes by the faults of both parents; in only one case was the mother alone considered at fault. In the majority of families the arguments were carried out in the children's presence. Differences were rarely removed through discussion and mutual agreement. In most families, the mothers would eventually submit to the fathers but in one case it was the reverse. In three other families, the docile husbands seldom replied.

How the parents of the war volunteers behaved toward one another during disagreements helps us understand why they were unsuccessful in resolving their differences and why temporary solutions were not more enduring. When the fathers were angry and wanted their standpoint to prevail, their most frequent behavior was to yell, to bang doors, to smash objects, or to nag. The mothers were most likely to nag, to yell, bang doors, and smash objects. One-third of the fathers physically attacked their wives and one-sixth of the mothers physically attacked their husbands. Often, fathers walked out of the house or remained silent. No mothers walked out during arguments but a few did remain silent. Only a few parents used rational discussion with each other at any time during arguments.

One childhood and adolescent memory of the Green Berets was of one parent overpowering the other and arguments remaining unsolved. Very few of these soldiers experienced rational discussion in their homes. This, as are many aspects of family life, is undoubtedly related to the general dominance-submission relationships which prevailed between the parents (see Appendix). Only one volunteer came from a family in which the father and mother were equal in the overall supervision and direction of family life. In most, the father was clearly the dominant figure, but five Green Berets felt that their mothers had unquestionably dominated their fathers. In three families, the parents rarely interfered with and generally ignored each other.

It is often the manner in which families approach their problems and their skill in solving them which determine their emotional welfare as well as the number, severity, and consequences of the problems they experience. If family members are not attuned to each other's needs, if they treat each other harshly, and if the dominant family member(s) fulfill themselves at the expense of the others, their problem-solving ability is more fictional than real. Discontent arises and is intensified and aggravated by new abuse and by the fact that mounting resentment can be suppressed only through intimidation. Such a situation may seem to stabilize, but the underlying anger and lack of understanding and perspective lead to further problems. Such families are likely to move into frequent crisis periods in which large reservoirs of anger are released. The weaker family members are prone to release their anger upon persons outside the family. Still, the family retains the aura of being intact and viable and therefore the children are likely to regard this kind of family life as "normal."

Among these families, a total of sixty-six crises were reported. (Family crises do not include the considerably larger number of enduring conflicts and recurring arguments which, in the majority of these families, were a part of everyday existence. Family crises also do not include the sudden and arbitrary release of anger or general hostility, both of which were accepted aspects in the lives of many families.) A crisis is here considered a situation in which the relationship among family members was so badly strained that family life became chaotic and ceased to function. In some of the cases previously illustrated, it took the form of passing revolts. The weaker family members, usually the passive recipients of abuse, reacted. The wives and children of domineering fathers, the husbands and children of domineering mothers, rebelled. They threatened to leave home and did; they yelled and hit back in allowing themselves emotional release. As a result, the families entered a state of disequilibrium. Confusion arose because the customary pattern of dominance and submission was interrupted. Equilibrium returned after a few days or weeks without an explicit reconciliation. It would seem that everyone found the new situation too uncomfortable, uncertain, and explosive, and therefore welcomed a return to the former condition. Things then went along as before until a new crisis erupted, and evaporated in its turn. Sometimes the children went off to live with relatives and stayed away for periods ranging from one week to six months.

The primary cause of these crises in the families was not likely to be severe illness, in-law problems, death, or other unforeseen or unavoidable problems. The family crises were usually prompted by the manner in which the family members treated one another, by the overflowing of mutual anger and hostility precipitated by a relatively minor event. Other more concrete occurrences, such as financial problems, unemployment, alcoholism, and extramarital affairs, also prompted crises. However, they too provided the opportunity for the family members, particularly the parents, to express their general hostility within the context of a tangible problem.

It is my feeling that this pattern explains the capacity of these families to remain intact despite the intensity of strife and dissatisfaction within them. The children learned that it was their moral obligation to obey their parents and to suppress their feelings. Therefore, even during family crises, even when family members left home, they returned physically and psychologically to the old system because they saw return as their moral obligation. Perhaps the one prohibition which best exemplifies this system is the father's prohibition of personal inconvenience. Since he could arbitrarily decide at any time what a personal inconvenience was, the rest of the family was subject to his whims. The family existed to satisfy him.

Fathers and Sons

CASE 201

He was pretty easy going and we got along real good. He used to back me up against my mother, you know, say I had a point. . . . He lets everything mount up and then he tells you what is happening. Like if you do something wrong, he probably wouldn't tell you. He would wait until you do five or six things and then the next little thing you do, whether it is stupid or not, the slightest stupid thing you do, then he puts everything on you, socks you one. So other than that we had a good relationship. . . . Yeah, he smacked me in the head, knocked my head because I had some wet clothes and he said he'd have to pay the doctor bills.

CASE 205

My father was very quiet. He never said anything. . . . He never punished me.

CASE 206

My father is the kind of person who lavishes a lot of affection on a child. I mean, he provides for them well, makes sure they're well fed and well clothed and in his own way he loves them very much. But he's not an outwardly emotional person. And this bothered me at times because there were a lot of times I wanted to go out and do things with him but he was too involved with his practice and never had time. . . . When something comes along and makes him mad or disturbs him, he clams up. He doesn't say anything. . . . He's very devoted to his practice, his clinic. He spends about nineteen hours a day at his practice. . . . Actually, he's not really cold as such. I get the impression more that he wants to be very close but doesn't know how to really get emotionally involved with my brother and I. Like I said, he's not a cold person, but it's hard for him to exhibit or show emotion

CASE 209

They were always talking about not smoking and not drinking, especially, you know, my father. And he was the one who smoked and drank. . . . He took up flying for a while but he never pursued it. He never took, you know, no special interest in anything.

CASE 213

Well, I always felt guilty about not doing more things with my father. Say my school days, for example, uh, I remember I didn't force him, but I didn't, uh, get with him more on say attending my school functions more. He didn't attend like my mother, you know, concerts and, uh, football games. He did go to a few football games. . . . He—he did enjoy . . . the ones he did go to. And, uh, more companionship. Uh, say around my friends, having him meet my friends more. . . . I wish I could have had him closer to me in other words.

CASE 214

How has your father been vengeful?
Well, by vengeful I mean . . . if you don't go out and mow the lawn I'm going to kick your ass! Why don't you pick up your ass, you know. Well, lots of it is vengeful in the sense that he was taking out his dissatisfaction, uh, with himself for both being drunk and for feeling like—for the same feelings that were probably making him drunk. He was taking those out on us.

Did he actually ever kick your ass?
Well, he tried to one time but I kicked his instead. . . . That was when I was a freshman in high school. It was the first time I ever left home.

CASE 215

My father's very well tempered. He has the ability to get quite angry. No doubt about it. I had to push myself a couple of times to avoid his temper. . . . But he is a very fine teacher for anything he tried to teach me. He was very patient with me and extremely helpful.

CASE 219

He likes to be at home. Like as my parents go, basically as far as character goes, I think both of them have a lot of principles and character. Like my father, he doesn't go to church because he doesn't believe. He thinks a lot of people are hypocrites. They go to church and it's just for show. It's better for their business or their occupation if they're seen in church every Sunday. And they go out and party hard the rest of the week. Well, my father doesn't believe in this. He's a family man. He likes to have—he's not against drinking or smoking. He likes to drink and smoke. He basically likes things to go smoothly and he likes to be at home and enjoys television and listening to music. . . . My father was pretty stubborn and hard headed really. He was a perfectionist, a real perfectionist. He used to make my mother so damn mad. He always expected everything in the house to be, and he's still that way, pretty much, he expects everything in the house to be exactly in its certain place. And, uh, I don't know if this is just a personal characteristic or if he became this way while he was in the army, uh, demanding exact precision as far as the cleaning of the house, the placement of things and the alignment of things. But he was real exact with us and he had a very good eye. He has very good vision and I remember one example my mother told me about. This one particular vase on the table, a vase. Uh, every day when he came home he'd always—he just made a routine inspection, like it was a barracks. When he came home, you know, he'd walk around and he'd move this ashtray or that ashtray or check this or that. Every day he always moved this one vase just a fraction of an inch, you know, to put it right in the middle. And so my mother, this made her so mad. So one day she took a ruler and she measured it right down to the exact center of the table and placed the vase right exactly in the center. And my father came home and he looked at the vase and he started to move it and he looked at it again and he said it was exactly right [laughs]. That made it worse because my mother expected him to move it a little fraction and then she was going to say, ha, I caught you this time, you know. But no, it's exactly right.

And, uh, I remember on two occasions I didn't make my own bed. As long as I can remember this was one of my tasks that he made me learn how to do as soon as I was able to and that was to maintain my own room and to make my own bed. This one time I overslept and I didn't get up. In fact, if I'm not mistaken, I was an altar boy then and I was late getting up and going to church and so I didn't make my bed. And so for the next two weeks to make sure I had plenty of time to get my bed made I had to get up an hour early [laughs]. And so it was pretty decent punishment. It made me think about getting up and doing what I was required to do and then the second time that I did it, I was a little older but he made sure that I didn't go anywhere for a week or two. I forget, a week or two, something like that. After school I had to come immediately home and, uh, work around the house. And he believed in, uh, if I wanted something I should work for it and get it myself, to have ambition, you know. For some reason, he always stressed the military. He always wanted me to go into the Army. And, uh, I remember this, very many times he talked about the army and that it's a good life and that it's good for a man to be in the Army. . . . But I think more or less in his mind he pictured a fairly secure way of making a living and something that would be more or less interesting for a young man. You know, one that is possibly aggressive or interested in a little bit of adventure. I think maybe he pictured himself actually. I think he always mentioned that he regretted that he got out of the Army. He always wanted to stay in the Army. And I think since he wanted this so much for himself, he wanted me to do it.

Did you ever get the feeling when you were growing up, while on the one hand your father was encouraging you to join the service that he was also pretty much of an army man in the way he lived?
He was very much because, like I mentioned, the way he'd more or less conduct inspections. Every day he'd come home and he'd insist on preciseness. And not only that. He was real systematic about other things that he did, such as, oh, just little minor examples, such as the way he would, uh, he was real fanatic about the way he would, like before he'd go to work he'd pack his lunch. Everything had to be just so so and always he was prepared hours before it was time to go to work. He always insisted on everything being—he had a certain place and he'd put his cigarettes and his thermos jug and his lunch and his jacket and a certain pair of shoes and socks. And he wore a uniform. In his later years, on his present job, he wears a uniform and he always keeps a spotless uniform.

Tell me something. Is it possible that your father emphasized military virtue, you know, in terms of responsibility, discipline, neatness, orderliness, stuff like that, but never in connection with any particular set of values? You have to be disciplined and orderly and neat because you have

to protect this, that, and the other thing. For example, a person would say, uh, you might have had the training that you have to be patriotic and fight for your country, you know.

He never indicated patriotism.

Right. I get the feeling your father was more interested in just the general military value.

I believe so.

As opposed to the general military value in defense of a particular set of values, as for example the U. S. and what it stands for. Is that true would you say?

That's true. I never thought about it before but this is basically true because every time he mentioned military, the way he mentioned it it had to do with certain, uh, things, self-discipline or neatness and precision or being a man as far as building, he never actually mentioned character so much, anything that would lead toward, for instance, punctuality and neatness had something to do with a person's character. He never indicated this but I think he pictured the military life as being a well-disciplined man that was neat and orderly. But he never mentioned patriotism or defending any such thing as the U. S. anything like this, never. No.

Do you think it would be fair to say in the case of your father that he was more interested in the form of the military life and what the military life represented than in any particular virtue like, I mean, these were the virtues, but he wasn't interested in the concepts of good and bad. You know, this is evil, this is good?

That's true. I would say he was more interested in the military life. . . . He never really expressed too many feelings or thoughts about, I think, he more or less thought that it was understood that you should do good. If it's in your mind to do good and not to do bad. Uh, I mean, he was a good man in that way but he never really did much to try and form my character. He never really did much, only to the extent that he wanted me to be punctual and well disciplined and neat and this form of the military life.

Something I'd like to know a little bit more about is the kind of relationship you did have with your father while you were growing up. So far you've given me the impression that, uh, there wasn't a heck of a lot of communication. You apparently do respect him, sufficiently to not oppose him on all the regulations he set, you know, around the house and behavior around the house. And perhaps you did have a fear of him because you said that your mother had to protect you on a couple of occasions. So, in fact you said he did have a bad temper, but you seem to have really, for a while looked outside the family for other people because of a lack of contact, you know, emotional contact that you had with your father. Are these impressions correct?

True, that's true. Uh, throughout my entire life I have never really—when I was younger my parents went on a few picnics and I went with 'em a few times. But as we were growing up I never went for walks with my father. I never—on a few occasions I helped him wash the car but he never took me camping. He never took me fishing or hunting. He never really took the time to . . . sit down and talk about anything as far as, uh, we never talked about literature, never talked about life, never talked about good or bad or character or anything. Uh, very little. My parents never really—I never really talked with my parents a great deal. Now when I was at home maybe they would watch television. They were television fiends. They think that everything revolves a-round the television set and so when I was at home, mostly I would watch television with them. . . .

I was always at fault. There was no doubt about that in my father's mind and we had a lot of open conflicts there and there was times when I tried to control my—uh, I became pretty angry a couple of times and I'd clench my fist. I never attempted to hit my father. That's for damn sure. I would be so mad I'd want to say something. But I tried to control my feelings and I wouldn't argue against him because I knew it was useless. I knew I could never win against my father. He was very stubborn in his beliefs. . . . During that time period we did have quite a few arguments.

CASE 221

Well, I mean, she [his mother] didn't want me to, you know, go out and don't want me to fight, don't want me to, you know, anything that was dangerous. She didn't want me to do this and that, you know. And thank God! My old man. He—he cut her off short, you know, 'cause my old—well, anyway, my old man also was very interested and used to take me and show me how to knife fight. . . .

Do you remember why your father wanted to show you how to knife fight?
Yeah, because I asked him to. I mean, he used to do all kinds of things when I was small. Teach me how to march and stuff like this. You know, all basic movements that you do in the Army. I got interested in knives because he gave me an old Navy Burnett, a Burnett he had. And I asked him to show me how to, you know, to use it. How to work with it. 'Cause he used to box when he was in the Army. And he used to show me how to box and wrestle.

CASE 228

My old man built a rabbit trap. I guess we had a lot of rabbits around there or some damn thing. It was a kind of unusual rabbit trap. It was constructed out of half-and three-quarter-inch pine or a similar type wood and, uh, a pretty unusual method of getting a rabbit. The idea was the rabbit would come in—the box was baited, well, it was just constructed in the shape of a box. The box was baited. You take the bait and set the trap off and there's a quarter stick of dynamite in it. I don't think we ever caught any rabbits with it or the rabbits took the bait.

It would have blown the hell out of the rabbit, wouldn't it?
Yeah, it killed the shit out of the rabbit.

Would there have been anything left to eat?
No, I don't think so. . . .

I remember one time in Michigan, we were living on a lake. And, uh, one of the neighbors threatened to turn him in to the Child Welfare People for beating us. We must have been hollering pretty good although noise carries across the lakes quite a, ways, but the next neighbor was, well, half a mile away maybe.

It would appear that the fathers of the Green Berets took their duties and responsibilities as parents and providers seriously. In many, if not most cases, they must be described as family men. Some had outside interests and some spent many hours at bars, with friends, or with other women. Yet the fathers who came home after work, played with their children, worked at a hobby, or puttered in their garden were as familiar figures in these interviews as the ones who were rarely seen by their families or who retired into voluntary isolation within the confines of their homes and property. The homogeneous qualities among the fathers have less to do with how much time they spent at home than in what they did when they were there.

Parents influence the attitudes and behavior of their children in three major ways. They serve as models for imitation, so that their children acquire their loyalties, values, attitudes and many of their gestural and behavioral idiosyncracies. They transmit a social, ethnic, and national background to their children which lasts throughout their maturational years. Finally, the personal relationship between the parents themselves and between the parents and the children play decisive roles in shaping children's personalities.[1]

The value system of the Green Berets' fathers was very clear-cut. The boys were expected to develop their talents and strive for success through hard work and diligence without asking for help. Their fathers expected them to be neat and clean, well-mannered, and outwardly respectable at all times. In their social relations with other people the boys were to show respect for adults, obedience to their superiors, and conformity to the standards prevailing in the community. Respect for property was of cardinal importance. The fathers expected their boys to be physically strong and emotionally tough. They were taught that relaxation and self-indulgence were luxuries which had to be earned. In some cases the fathers tried to teach their sons to help other members of the family in times of need. A few fathers valued intellectual achievement, rationality, individual privacy, kindliness, respect for life, community responsibility, and philanthropy. One spoke of social justice and another was interested in the arts and literature.

The fathers underscored their expectations for their sons with very specific prohibitions. Prohibitions were issued in connection with behavioral infractions on the part of the sons and also whenever the fathers felt the need to impart their views on "right" and "wrong." Many of the prohibitions represented specific illustrations of the values just described. Lying, cheating, stealing, disobedience, bad language, sloppiness, bad manners, and the destruction of material things were prohibited. Most fathers also forbade fighting, drinking, smoking, and sex. The majority prohibited their sons from showing affection and emotionality; this corresponds to the value of emotional toughness. Very important in this context is that many fathers considered their own personal convenience to be inviolable and therefore categorically prohibited their sons from disturbing them.

The most frequent disciplinary practices were physical punishments, threats and sternness, negative criticism, restrictions, and deprivations. The disciplinary practices employed by the fewest fathers, and then only rarely, were tangible rewards, physical isolation, reasoning, and withdrawal of love.

It should be pointed out that four of the war volunteers were never punished physically by their fathers. Three of these reported that their fear of their fathers had been so deeply ingrained in them in early childhood that it never would have occurred to them to "cross him"; an "evil look" sufficed. The remaining volunteer was orphaned at an early age and could not remember having been punished by his father.

I asked the Green Berets to describe the circumstances in which they received physical punishments, the instruments of physical punishment, and the regions of their body which were struck. They said that their fathers struck them when they broke house rules, destroyed property, the father was annoyed, and when they harmed others. Further circumstances which provoked their fathers to strike them were when they broke an "agreement" with him, showed lack of courage, harmed themselves, got into trouble in school, showed physical weakness, when there was no apparent reason, and when they were in trouble with the police.

There is considerable variation in the reports of the Green Berets on the frequency with which they were physically punished by their fathers. Only one reported that his father beat him daily. Many said that they were beaten between once a week and twice a month. The majority stated that their fathers beat them either two or three times a year or two or three times altogether.

Nearly half the fathers confined beatings mainly to the sons' covered buttocks. Several beat mainly on the head, a few mainly on bared buttocks, and a few indiscriminately on all parts of their sons' bodies. The most frequently used instrument of punishment was the father's hand. However, most of the fathers also used belts, sticks, and/or whips. Four Green Berets reported that their fathers grabbed "any convenient object" and two stated that their fathers also used boards, iron rods, or chains on occasion.

When a parent punishes a child and particularly when this punishment is severe and physical, it is important to know how the child's reactions to pain affect the parent. Only three of the fathers stopped a beating when their sons started crying, nearly half continued the beatings, and three intensified them. Four Green Berets no longer remembered how their fathers reacted when they cried, or said they never cried.

Broad similarities emerged among the volunteers' fathers in the manner in which they related to their sons. For the most part, they had relatively little contact with them. What contact there was, shown in Table 2, was experienced by the entire sample of Green Berets as somewhat more pleasant than unpleasant.

TABLE 2

Raters' judgment of relative frequency of pleasant and unpleasant contacts between the war volunteers and their fathers*

	Positive		Negative	
	Number	*Percent*	*Number*	*Percent*
Frequent	3	12	2	8
Occasional	10	40	6	24
Rare	8	32	15	60
None	4	16	2	8

*These judgments are based on quality of father-son contacts related by the Green Berets. When frequent father-son contact was reported (five cases), the raters' judgments concerned the relative proportion of positive and negative content. When the soldier mentioned several positive and negative contacts, the alternative "occasional" was checked. When only one to three kinds of contact were described, the alternative "rare" was checked. When neither positive nor negative contacts were described, the alternative "none" was used.

The explanation for this evaluation has a perceptual and a content component. Since the fathers generally paid little attention to their sons, the latter were grateful for any attention they received. Although many of the fathers were temperamental, nervous, and easily annoyed, their sons took pains not to upset them. Therefore, irrespective of the actual amount of time they spent together, it was often possible for them to share pleasant experiences.

For the most part, the fathers determined when they had contact with their sons as well as what they did together. They set the tone, content, and boundaries of the relationship. Their sons subordinated their wishes and needs to the temperament, values, and accessability of their fathers and therefore rarely made demands upon their fathers. Except for the fact that they gained privileges with advancing age, for example, the right to use and own a gun and could then join their fathers and relatives on hunting trips, the essential pattern of the father-son relationship did not change from childhood to adolescence.

In short, the overall relationship between these soldiers and their fathers tended to be formal, ceremonial, and cold. Few fathers took more than a distant, supervisory interest in their sons' development and then mainly in regard to the fulfillment of the external behavioral guidelines they had set for them. The temperamental differences between the fathers account for the fact that approximately half were remembered as generally impatient and the other half as generally patient. The fact that only nine were described as having been helpful, three understanding, three affectionate and emotionally responsive, and two respectful of their sons' individual rights illustrates the narrowness and superficiality of nearly all these relationships. Eleven soldiers could not recall ever having shared an interest with their fathers.

The Military Experience of the Fathers and its Influence on the War Volunteers

During childhood the Green Berets were exposed to a value and disciplinary system which harmonized well with military life. Beyond this, many soldiers also had specific military training in their homes in the form of drills, marching, saluting, and room inspections, as well as specific modes of greeting and behaving toward superiors. These practices were more likely to occur in the homes of the thirteen Green Berets whose fathers had served in the military during World War II. Of these, ten had related adventuresome and glamorous war stories to their sons, six had brought them war trophies, and five had taught them how to fight with a knife.

This training seems to have had an impact on the later behavior of the Green Berets. Those who had "personal kills" while in Vietnam (nine out of fourteen cases with kills while in Vietnam) usually had been exposed to one or more of these specific military practices. On the other hand, two of the fathers with military experience in World War II did not put their sons through military drills and did not tell them adventuresome war stories; instead, they told their boys about the horrors of war. These two men and one other had also been exceptional in their opposition to their sons' decisions to join the Army. Their three sons were the only Green Berets who hoped to avoid combat duty and who were considering leaving the Army.

Mothers and Sons

CASE 201

Well, my mother, she has kind of a—not a bad temper, but she don't let you get away with anything. When you're wrong she tells you that you're wrong and when you're right she tells you that you're right. Since I was the youngest, she used to protect me against my brothers and sisters but then she quit protecting me and every time I did something, whether I was wrong or not, she licked it to me, you know. So I used to figure she was whipping the others all the time when she knew I was wrong. . . . Everything I did, whether it was right or wrong, was incorrect to her. . . . I always let her know I knew the difference between the birds and the bees and she didn't dig that too much, you know. . . . But eventually we all made up and, you know, had a pretty good relationship. I write pretty often and send money for stuff and so on. . . . She used to get a broom or something and suddenly she comes on me and socks it to me. And sometimes she never cools off and I keep on gettin' it. If she tells me she's going to give me five and I only get one, she's goin' to give me the other four if it takes her five or ten days to give it to me, you know. It's not a regular sweeping broom, you know. It's the bare half of a coconut tree with kind of prongs, you know.

CASE 205

She's a little hot tempered, you know. There was always the thing that, you know, you don't want to say the wrong thing and get her started. . . . She did most of the punishing. For about just about anything. She had heart trouble and didn't like any noise so I didn't play much. So I didn't run around the house and this jazz. She was, uh, the type of person who said something once and she was stern. When she said, move, you moved then and there or you got killed. She'd take us and beat us half to death . . . with anything . . . yeah, with a chair too [laughs]. If she was standing there. You're going to do what she says or she'd beat you to death. . . . Hell, no. You din't run. You stood there and took it until she decided to quit. You'd get it for anything. . . . She used to get on my ass. . . . I realized, shit, she was just the type of woman, you know, just got furious all of a sudden and that was it. . . . No, my mother wasn't affectionate with anybody except my younger brother.

Did your mother ever hit you with a belt?
Hell, yes.

On your bare bottom?
Shit, yes.

Did you ever have welts?
Bled.

You actually bled?
Hell, yes. My mother didn't play.

Did she hit you on the head too?
Shit, yes. Anywhere, wherever she connected, that's where you got it. . . . Hell, it would hurt like hell, you know. You'd cry and then she would continue beating you until you stopped crying and shit, you know. And she had a thing, that you didn't look at her while she was beating you, you know. You wouldn't dare look up at her. I never understood it. She called it, rollin' your eyes. I mean, if you looked up at her she would beat the hell out of you. The last time I told her I wasn't goin' to cry, I told her, shit, I wasn't going to cry anymore, you know, and if she beat me to death I wasn't going to cry. She continued beating me and, hell, I wouldn't cry.

What was she beating you with?
A stick.

And you just stood there and took it?
Yes, till I got so weak. She was beating me till I just couldn't hold up anymore, you know. So when I slumped down to my knees, you know, and then she had one of these heart flutters or something and her heart wouldn't hold it out any more. So when I went down, hell, she almost went down too. But I didn't cry for her anymore. I figured, well, the hell, I wasn't going to do that shit anymore.

Was your Dad around when she beat you?
He'd always go out of the house. He never dug shit like that.

But wouldn't he say anything about it?
No, 'cause he didn't want to get into an argument.

So, in other words, your mother pretty much ran the house?
She did run the house. She ran the whole business. . . . No, my father didn't say anything. He wouldn't say anything.

Did you ever get into arguments with him about that?
My father?

Yeah.
We never talked.

Pardon me?
We never talked.

I mean, did you ever have the feeling that you wanted him to stand up to her?
Yes.

Did you ever tell him that?
No. We never talked before so I never said anything.

CASE 206

I remember, once in high school I wanted to go somewhere and my mother said, no. And I said, I may have to obey you but I don't have to like it. And she was really hurt. So I apologized for it. . . . She was a warm, outgoing person. Maybe a little overprotective. She was afraid I would hurt myself. . . . No, I couldn't ever talk to her. Don't know why. Maybe it was her overprotectiveness. . . . She was the one who really impressed on us, my brother and I, our sets of values as far as moral restrictions and codes are concerned. And my father backed her up. . . . She wouldn't let me do a lot of things, like go to beach parties because she said it would be a beer bust. . . . And I started dating a girl while I was a sophomore in high school and she was afraid I'd get her in trouble and have to get married. She [the girl] was older than me. That was another problem. Also my parents didn't know her parents socially and were unsure of her background and all this sort of thing. . . . She's [his mother] a very intelligent woman. Very gifted artistically. Same as my father. They're both gifted with their hands. She's a very attractive woman and was very involved with church work. She's a very patient woman. Had to be with two boys and being the only woman in the family. She has a gift for understanding people. Very warm, outgoing person for any, well for most people. Very easy to talk to. My brother and I, neither of us could talk to my mother or father. I don't know why. We just couldn't. . . . She was pretty dominant about making decisions. She pretty much gave the yes or no answer and he'd back her up. . . . I think, he was afraid.

In many ways it is easier to generalize about the Green Berets' mothers than about their fathers. In their sons' portrayals they appear as tough, determined, and, for the most part, hard-working women who not only had to carry the burden of the household and the upbringing of the children, but in many cases also worked to help support their families. The majority were easily irritated and volatile and did not hesitate to strike out at their children as long as they were still physically able to do so without fear of reprisal. Their displays of affection were rare, and as unpredictable as their loss of temper. Although they were all stern, demanding, and strict disciplinarians, several tended to become soft, affectionate, and overprotective at times, only to lapse quickly back to their usual irritable manner. Most of them had unusually problematical relations with their sons, and this strain was most evident during the late childhood years (eight to twelve). The ebb and flow of the mother-son conflicts are intimately bound to the entire structure of these families and, in particular, to the especially difficult position of nearly all the mothers, being subservient to their husbands while trying to maintain authority and control over their father-oriented sons. In the mother-dominated families, in contrast, there was far less open conflict between mothers and sons, since the mothers reigned as undisputed authority figures.

The general unanimity between mothers and fathers on major values and behavioral standards guaranteed a certain and consistent framework for bringing up children. The functional vitality of the family life, especially during the volunteers' childhood years, was decisively determined by their mothers' efforts. In fact, the very reason the family structures remained intact and bringing up the children proceeded along the lines previously described can be attributed to these women. They exercised daily authority and demanded compliance with family standards more thoroughly than their husbands could.

Although the differences are not appreciable, more mothers than fathers required personal discipline, obedience, orderliness, thrift, good manners, conformity with social norms, and respectful-subservient behavior towards adults from their children. These represent the core values and behavioral standards which guided parent-child relations in the Green Beret families. Fewer mothers than fathers were concerned with individual achievement, independence, and love of animals and nature, and therefore voiced such values less often, if at all. Whereas the fathers were unusually concerned that their sons be physically strong and emotionally tough, the mothers seem to have paid little explicit attention to these "masculine virtues." On the other hand, the culturally determined feminine orientation of some of these women was expressed in their attempts to teach the virtues of kindliness, love of life, philanthropy, and intellectual achievement. Very few of them, as was the case with their husbands, voiced such values as sociopolitical engagement in the community and nation, rationality, social justice, respect for the privacy of their children, or cultural appreciation.

The attempts of some of the mothers to implant the spirit of humanitarianism and aesthetic appreciation in their sons reflect, at best, a secondary concern on their parts. Moreover, within the context of the overall family life, these values were hardly perceptible and of minimal impact. The minority of volunteers who did experience warmth, understanding, attention, respect for their person, and other gentle qualities from their mothers, rejected them at the time as signs of overprotectiveness or because they did not appear credible in view of the mothers' general behavior. Yet as adults, they tended to remember such moments with gratitude.

While the mothers voiced prohibitions more frequently than the fathers, as would be expected because of their dominant role in the child-rearing process, both parents generally declared the same behaviors taboo. If possible, the mothers were more concerned with their sons' external propriety, were far more conservative, restricting, and disapproving on sexual matters, and were especially sensitive about inconsiderateness.

Despite the tension in the mother-son relationships and the isolated criticisms of them in several interviews, these women essentially represented goodness to their sons. This, combined with the unusually strong roles they played in their sons' character development, enabled them to give the family system its moral fiber.

As mentioned earlier, the Green Berets' mothers used physical punishment in the rearing of their sons more often than their husbands; only two did not. More than two-thirds beat their sons once a month or more well into the boys' early adolescent years. As with the fathers, most mothers used their hands, but those who also used belts, sticks, whips, and straps ran a close second. None used boards, chains, or iron rods but nearly a third used "any object at hand" when they got angry.

The mothers' reasons for punishing their sons differed somewhat from those of the fathers. They punished most frequently when the son harmed others, harmed himself, destroyed property, and broke house rules. Other frequent occasions were when the son got into trouble in school, when the mother did not want to be bothered, or for no apparent reason at all. Five mothers punished their sons for not showing enough courage and one for physical weakness.

I found that four of the fathers beat their sons exclusively on the head. No mothers showed a similar partiality for the head region. However, one-third indiscriminately beat their sons anywhere and everywhere (head, arms, legs, backside, neck, and so on). The majority beat them on their covered buttocks and one on the bare buttocks.

The relationship between the individual volunteers and their mothers was influenced in part by a number of factors: the boy's sibling position, the mother's work schedule, her physical stature and psychological stability, the relative harmony and balance of authority between the parents. For instance, one volunteer had never felt physically intimidated by his mother because he had outgrown her in height and weight in middle childhood. Another, under the same circumstances, had been unmercifully beaten by his mother throughout childhood and early adolescence. Some of the mothers were perenially cold and distant, others wavered between coldness and bursts of warmth, while still others generally expressed a hostile and rejecting attitude toward their sons. Despite these and many other idiosyncratic differences, several pervasive characteristics emerged in nearly all the mother-son relationships. None of them demonstrated empathic sensitivity, they demanded fulfilment of their behavioral propriety standards above all else, they exacted compliance with their expectations as they saw fit, and regarded obedience to parental demands as the best evidence that their children were on their way to becoming good citizens. The mothers spent surprisingly little time with their sons beyond that necessary to discipline them and care for their physical needs. While many volunteers recalled having received lectures, virtually none recalled talks. Yet the relatively greater contact between mothers and sons, particularly during the childhood years, and the mothers' stronger propensity for emotional expression, undoubtedly accounts for the fact that they had more frequent disagreements with their sons and were more often the object of their sons' anger than were their husbands. The interesting feature of these families is that even under these circumstances the volunteers felt that their fathers had exercised a far greater influence upon them; it was only in the five matriarchal families that the maternal influence was perceived as greater.

The behavior of the mothers was not always consistent and did not always conform with their proclaimed standards. This is also partly responsible for the strain in many mother-son relationships. Eleven mothers tended toward protectiveness in expressing maternal concern, for example, that their sons "dress warmly," or "not hurt themselves." Their sons experienced this as overprotectiveness and rebelled against it. Of these eleven mothers, four were gradually overpowered by their steadily growing sons. In all four cases these women were portrayed as affectionate, nonirritable, patient, helpful, understanding, permissive and respecting their sons' rights.

The Family in the Community

Only a few of the volunteers' families visited their neighbors with any degree of frequency. The majority of families had either very little contact or none at all with their neighbors. When neighborly socializing took place, it was usually characterized by each family member seeking out his own contacts or by the parents and children going their separate ways. Only in three cases did families exchange visits as a complete unit. Relatively few of the volunteers' families had any close friends, and those who did seldom had more than one or two.

The families had a different relationship with their relatives. The majority visited with their relatives, tended to have a close and spontaneous relationship with them, and were most likely to visit as a complete unit. However, fully one-quarter of them rarely or never saw their relatives, the relationship they had with them tended to be formalistic, ceremonial, and emotionally distant, and the family members did their socializing independently of each other.

An important aspect of community life is the mutual help relationship among its members. Families are in need of emotional and material support at different times, and the cohesiveness of a community rests in part on the willingness of community members to help each other at such times. Since only a few of the volunteers' families enjoyed close relationships with their neighbors, it is not surprising to find that only several gave help to neighbors, still fewer to friends, and only one to strangers. The help that was given was usually short-term, consisting of cooking and caring for sick people, helping with household work, and driving children to school. The fathers were rarely involved in these helpful acts. Only two families received help from neighbors, friends, and strangers.

The mutual help relationships were strongest within the extended family. Help was given when relatives were ill and needed assistance on the farm. In a few cases the children of relatives and grandparents were taken into the home. Most of this help was also of brief duration, but the fathers were more actively involved, particularly when outdoor manual labor was required. The help received from relatives tended to persist over longer periods of time. Relatives cared for the children during holidays and summer vacations, during family crises, or took over the care of the children permanently. Relatives also helped out when the father or mother was ill, when heavy work had to be done, and when financial aid was needed.

It is important to point out that the person-to-person help relations between the families of the volunteers and others did not cross racial, religious, or class lines, either in the giving or the receiving. The mutual help activities of these families did not extend into the broader community except where impersonal organized charities were involved. Although short-term help was given by some families to non-relatives, they did not accept help from non-relatives. The people outside the extended family whom they did help belonged to the overall in-group.

I was puzzled at first that the volunteers reported their families were more helpful to friends and neighbors (even though this involved only a minority of the families) than their friends and neighbors were to them. The pattern is exactly reversed with relatives. They reported that their families received help from relatives more often than they helped relatives. Perhaps the explanation for the differing reports lies in part within the traditions and values surrounding the giving and receiving of help. American tradition says that it is good to be charitable, but to receive charity, particularly from strangers, is demeaning. It therefore becomes a matter of pride and respectability not to be on the receiving end, unless this occurs among relatives. This leads people to deny help when it is offered or to call help by a different name if it is accepted—a loan, good neighborly relations, or God's work.

Very few fathers participated constructively in the affairs of their communities. Thirty-six percent had no organizational ties whatsoever and seventy percent of the organizational ties of the rest were purely social. The social clubs in question were usually restricted to men; members passed through initiation ceremonies which in most cases were handled as secrets. Five fathers belonged to political groups whose meetings were also open to women. These groups served as lobbying platforms for local businessmen's associations or to keep minorities out of the community. Three fathers engaged periodically in routine charity work through their churches and fraternal organizations. They helped collect and distribute money for veterans, the blind, the aged, and youth groups. One father attended PTA meetings as a passive observer.

Several fathers did hold relatively prestigious positions in their communities. One was a church elder and a member of the Board of Church Directors. Another was a deacon, a Cub Scout pack leader, and coached the local Little League basketball team. Two were Boy Scout scoutmasters. Another coached both the Little League baseball and football teams in his community. Still another managed a mayoral campaign in his community.

Very few of the volunteers' mothers actively participated in organized communal life. There are several possible explanations for this. For one, the double burden of full-time work and running a household undoubtedly left some with little time and energy for outside interests. Beyond this, few of the Green Berets portrayed their mothers as civic-minded women. For the most part, they were work- and family-oriented people whose horizons did not extend beyond their own personal and family needs. On the other hand, there were several who did hold responsible positions in their communities. One was a Youth Director and organized United Nations Children's Tours through the United States. Another was very active in veterans' organizations and the Women's Auxiliary of the American Legion. She collected funds for the groups and visited Veterans' Administration hospitals. Three mothers taught in Sunday and Bible schools and four participated occasionally in their local PTA chapters. In all, fifteen mothers had no organizational affiliations; of the nineteen associations the remaining ten women belonged to, almost half were women's social clubs.

THE WAR RESISTERS

CASE 100

My parents did a fantastic job of working together on things. . . . Most of my growing up was sort of positive and solidifying things and with my brother in the acceptance of each other. I never felt that I could do anything that would shock my parents. I mean, if I like joined the Nazi party it might shock them [laughs] but beyond that I didn't feel there was anything that would shock them.

CASE 104

Most of the discussions that went on were in terms of theoretical large groups and there was a lot of talk about justice. And Dad would comment on things that he'd read in the paper. We'd talk about discussions I'd had in school or Tom [his brother] had had in school. You know, or Mom might bring something up that's come out of the work she was doing [as a social worker] . . . . It was not a person-oriented thing. We were not really connected with other people. We didn't have visitors, go visiting, that sort of stuff.

CASE 105

My family is very, very honest and open. . . . You know, like people walk into the house and they'll bring a friend in, and if Granny is having a fight with my brother, nothing changes. They just keep fighting. Not any kind of airs or anything. It's like a very homey kind of thing. And that's nice. I have no idea how it came out like that but, uh, that's the way it is. . . . Like we set up almost a therapy kind of thing where we all sit down and everybody expresses what's making him mad lately.

CASE 109

When I started accumulating my own record collection my parents requested every so often that we have an afternoon or evening concert in which I played my newer records. We just all sat around and listened. . . . I've always felt that whatever I would create would be viewed at least benevolently. And it's not that I was never criticized because I have definitely produced things that my parents don't like and that my mother doesn't like. She says that it doesn't say very much and that I could be better in such a way or this or that. . . . In other words, I feel that my mother and also my father are people I can really talk to. . . . As I told my closest friend Ronnie, I told him, I think, the fundamental part of my relationship with my parents is that I can regard them as people, people who happen to be my parents. . . . I don't know how anybody can say this but I esteem my parents as people as well as parents. And that perhaps esteeming them as people is more important because it's enabled the relationship to continue to grow after the parental functions have just been entirely outgrown as far as I'm concerned.

CASE 110

It's a very independent family. . . . In the respect that it thinks it does what's right, no matter what, you know. . . . No, it doesn't think it's unconventional. But I think it is. But the family's ego concept is very hung-up in the feeling that it would do what was right, no matter what. Somehow that's inherent in the family ego-concept although I don't know where it came from 'cause in practice they never do anything the least bit, uh, outside the mainstream. I got

really so little that it was easy for me to break away in a. very complete way.
. . . I never had the feeling I was losing anything if I disassociated myself from
my parents' feeling or beliefs or home or anything.

CASE 111

The atmosphere in which I grew up wasn't too authoritarian so it let me change.
And when I did change my parents didn't get all tight about. . . . I was pretty
much able to do what I wanted to do. . . . As I said, when I did things that
didn't live up to their expectations, uh, they were disappointed, you know, without punishments. . . . They were really great parents. Always together. We did
lots of things together. They've always been very, very concerned about us.
And they're good people like that . . . and that's why—that's one thing I feel,
it's the duty of every child, if nothing else, it's a duty that he owes his parents,
is to at least inform them of why he has to do something.

CASE 117

Well, we might have had humanitarian more than really political kind of morality
going on in the house. There was always talk about politics and morality and
truth and justice. . . . We used to get into arguments all the time. . . . They
instilled a very strong sense, uh, of morality in me. . . . Well, my mother was
a poet and my father was an engineer, so usually they differed. My father looked
at things from a practical standpoint and my mother, well, we always watched
educational television. . . . Music was always important in our house. My father
used to play the 'cello and my mother played the piano and my brother played
the violin. Father and I used to play the recorder and the 'cello and then I
took up the flute. . . . My parents always took the sides of minorities and Negroes.
. . . Like when the Sunday *Times* came my father took the magazine section
and I took the sports section and I'd try to help him with the crossword puzzles.
. . . My mother used to be anti-television and my father was pro-television. There
used to be television fights and my mother would get upset when my brother
and I would watch and said, ''Television makes small minds'' and that we should
read books. I never read.

CASE 118

I mean, my mother and father worked a lot. Especially my father worked day
and night. . . . And most of the job of taking care of us was in the hands of
my grandmother and grandfather. But there weren't any particular problems I
don't think. . . . And it really didn't make that much difference to me in a certain
sense whether my parents were home or not. . . . But there really wasn't a hell
of a lot of family life as such, I guess. We just all sort of lived there.

CASE 119

We were never a really close family in terms of intense personal relations but
then on the other hand we all recognized the fact that we were a family, that
we had obligations, responsibilities to one another, uh, a certain amount of

love involved, but not the ideal open relationship that you often see in families.
. . . My parents lived on this one block within three buildings of where my
mother had lived from the time she was a child, so as a result everybody in
the whole area knew her family and knew me as her son and knew all the
brothers and sisters and cousins and uncles and aunts. . . . I would say it was
generally a happy family, a happy environment. My parents didn't have all kinds
of fancy things but we had all that we needed. I mean, we had food, there
were beds for everyone. We even had a television set relatively early in the
game. A very quiet family. My father'd work long hours. Uh, he would leave
at about five-thirty or six every morning and didn't get back until seven or eight
and by that time he was so exhausted that, you know, he just had strength
to eat. . . . But then I can recall weekends, you know. Saturdays and Sundays.
Picnics and things like that. Playing ball with him.

My mother was more important in terms of day-to-day relations. I think
we always had a close relationship. . . . I think that both my mother and father
led us, we were taught to believe things. We certainly heard all things about
equality and being concerned with other people, the starving children in Europe
to make you finish the last bit of food on the plate. You've heard that line?.
. . . The big emphasis was, you know, this is a good life, this is a good country.
You have the ability to get ahead . . . you can do it. It's a matter of picking
what you want to do. We didn't have all the opportunities to do all these things
and we'll make sure that you get the educational background at least so you
can do the things that we weren't able to do. . . . And I can remember lots
of happy scenes. We went away every summer. I can remember having a good
time, and huckleberry picking and things like that.

CASE 121

It was a quite warm, very affectionate family. Very free. Very giving. . . .

Our family was a small family and, uh, very close. Also, you know, as
I say, I was brought up in policitally aware areas, made politically aware ever
since I could think, you know. Ever since I was born I was made to know
about cruelties, of other people's cruelties. . . . And I was aware of just the
things that go on. . . .

He's very warm, you know [father]. Yes, quite affectionate. Like every toy
I ever had was made by him. . . . Well, we did everything together. You know,
anything I wanted to build he was always there to help with. Always tried
to understand and he, unlike my mother, wasn't one of these judging types,
so I didn't feel this indirect pressure that my mother would put on me, I suppose.
Yeah, so he and I got along quite well.

Perhaps the most striking feature of the war resisters' accounts of their
families is the sensitivity they indicated toward family members and the
relationships between them. It is within the context of their heightened
awareness of interpersonal events that we can begin to analyze and understand both the deep affection most of them continued to feel for their parents
and the ongoing and consciously experienced anguish and disaffection
some of them felt because of family conflict. None of the resisters seemed

inclined to overlook or to make light of the faults they saw in their parents and their family life. In this respect many demonstrated what some might regard as an oversensitivity to the problems and conflicts which arise in most homes. That this sensitivity existed and was often combined with a strong moral overtone is largely attributable to the standards their parents passed on to them.

Conflict between values and behavior became a problem which increasingly plagued the resisters in their later lives, and led to guilt and self-recrimination. The origins of this conflict are to be found within the contradictions between value and behavior in their own families. To some degree all the resisters experienced such inconsistencies and responded to them. Those few, however, who came from seriously disrupted family backgrounds were also those who had the most problematical and disrupted interpersonal relations in later life, who were personally most troubled, and whose path to war resistance was marked by the greatest indecisiveness, anxiety, guilt, and excessively demonstrative behavior. Just as these war resisters could not excuse their parents for their shortcomings, they were unable to excuse themselves for their own.

For the most part it seems that the resisters' concern for standards—justice, proper treatment, consideration—was an outgrowth and reflection of their parents' concerns. Their parents did not merely demand compliance from their sons; they attempted to justify their actions and views. These attempts often failed, and these attempts at justification, as well as their inevitable and apparent failure in many instances, opened the parents to attack and criticism, removed the aura of infallibility with which many parents surround their behavior, and thereby introduced the central notion into the experiential and cognitive world of their children that power and authority require justification but often cannot be justified. There was no absolutistic authority in the war resisters' families.

The Home Atmosphere

The rating analysis of the family atmosphere in which the resisters grew up revealed many elements of diversity. Of central importance for this study are the qualities of friendliness, nonviolence, calmness, tolerance, and intellectuality, which were noted in eighty percent or more of the cases (see Table 3). Physical violence or the threat of it, while occurring in about half the resisters' accounts of their childhood memories, played a subordinate, peripheral, and fortuitous role in the arsenal of methods their parents employed to control them. The parents did not employ violence against each other or threaten violence. On the other hand, in more than twenty-five percent of the cases the family atmosphere was characterized as generally tense, and in forty percent of the cases family members appeared more isolated

TABLE 3
Raters' judgment of the war resisters' home life atmosphere

	Number	Percent		Number	Percent
Warm	18	72	Rational	19	76
Neutral	4	16	Neutral	3	12
Cold	3	12	Irrational	3	12
Friendly	21	84	Relaxed	16	64
Neutral	2	8	Neutral	2	8
Hostile	2	8	Tense	7	28
Peaceful	18	72	Sharing	17	68
Neutral	7	28	Neutral	6	24
Aggressive	0	0	Unsharing	2	8
Secure	18	72	Flexible	19	76
Neutral	3	12	Neutral	2	8
Insecure	4	16	Rigid	4	16
Stable	18	72	Togetherness	11	44
Neutral	4	16	Neutral	4	16
Unstable	3	12	Isolation	10	40
Nonviolent	21	84	Calm	20	80
Neutral	4	16	Neutral	2	8
Violent	0	0	Irritable	3	12
Democratic	18	72	Easygoing	17	68
Neutral	4	16	Neutral	3	12
Authoritarian	3	12	Overbearing	5	20
Gentle	19	76	Tolerant	20	80
Neutral	3	12	Neutral	3	12
Hard	3	12	Intolerant	2	8
Individualistic	16	64	Intellectual	20	80
Neutral	2	8	Neutral	2	8
Conformistic	7	28	Nonintellectual	3	12

from than united with one another. These findings point to the chronic problems which disturbed a minority of the families as well as to the personality qualities, economic conditions, and interests which separated family members and which reflect more formal and perfunctory relationships among them.

The Home Life Atmosphere ratings introduce most of the specific findings discussed throughout this chapter.

The Parental Marriage

Most of the war resisters felt that their parents were satisfied with each other and that they got along well. These marriages were characterized primarily by mutual respect and companionship. In the majority of cases the parents had common interests. The husbands and wives granted each other considerable independence. Tension arose periodically in the majority of marriages but resulted in continuous open hostility in only two cases. With these exceptions, all the parents tried to find ways to deal with each other based on consultation and rationality. The reports of the war resisters offered numerous examples of how the parental relationship, especially their manner of communicating with each other, solidified the marriage, generated the feeling of parental unity, and helped keep problems from straining family life unduly.

Mutual consent was one of the major themes in the resisters' accounts of the relationship between their parents. In most cases mutual consent meant that the parents actively consulted one another on most matters and did not preempt each others' opinion by independent and one-sided decisions. In a few cases, however, mutual consent should be understood as having more a nominal than an active character. These parents rarely consulted each other directly. Each had his or her area of competence and functioned independently without interference from the other.

Half the resisters felt that neither parent dominated the other, but that both worked together. There were several cases in which resisters felt that either their mother or their father had been a more dominant figure in the marriage. One described a situation in which his father dominated his mother through dictatorial behavior. Except in this case, dominance should be viewed as a form of leadership. In these cases, the dominant parent was the more extroverted, contributed overtly with greater frequency to the regulation of family life, and therefore made his or her personality more visible. Although several war resisters had mixed feelings about the passivity of a parent, particularly if it had been the father, none of them felt that the dominance of one parent was carried out expressly at the other's expense. The more retiring parent retained his or her right to initiate, criticize, and make an opinion prevail.

By discussing problems, the resisters' parents were usually able to resolve their differences. Arguments generally centered around issues specific to a particular family. Two couples had trouble with in-laws who were living with them. In three marriages there had been strong disagreements about parochial school education and discipline of the children. Other couples argued about finances, purchases, and occupations. These arguments, however, had a passing character. Temporary strain followed by reconciliation was characteristic. The only general theme which repeatedly arose and therefore presented a more continuous source of strain between the parents was the wife's feeling of neglect. This problem arose in seven families. The sons sensed strain between their parents and tended to curtail contact with them until the problem was resolved.

All but five resisters felt that the positive bonds between their parents outweighed the negative ones. They also reported that positive communication between their parents was more frequent than negative communication. In most cases the war resisters were reluctant to place the blame for arguments on one parent. They felt that both of them had strengths and weaknesses as well as irritating quirks. While emphasizing that they were confident of their parents' mutual regard and that the parents' relationship provided them with a feeling of security, the sons reacted with discomfort and sometimes with deep pain and confusion when arguments between their parents persisted. At the same time they felt that their parents were fundamentally in agreement with each other on most issues.

The resisters reported twenty-four family crises during their childhood and adolescent years. The majority of these occurred in six families. Ten families experienced no crises at all and four families only one. The causes of the crises, their duration, and their consequences varied considerably from family to family. In some cases there was a temporary emotional release after a long period of tension. Other families were exposed to particular strains which led to a series of secondary disturbances. Still other families were hit by a number of serious problems simultaneously. There did not appear to be any connection between the number or duration of family crises and the manner in which they ended.

Most of the crises were precipitated by concrete disturbances, usually involving financial hardship, such occupational drawbacks as long hours, and serious illness. All of these problems had had a persistent and disruptive influence. Three families had provided many years of constant care for physically and/or psychologically ill grandmothers. This imposed many restrictions on family activities: the mothers were preoccupied with their care, other family members felt neglected, and the entire family experienced an intensifying conflict between their feelings of obligation and the burden of the grandmothers' chronic illness. Two couples also experienced long-term strain under similar circumstances. Both husbands had worked at low-paying jobs for many years. They had become increasingly frustrated and withdrawn from everyday family life over the years. Their wives were energetic, extroverted, critical women who were particularly annoyed by their husbands' passivity in family affairs.

Four resisters came from homes broken by divorce. Two sets of parents were divorced when their sons were less than two years old. One man said he missed not having a father and the other seemed unaffected. His father came for occasional visits when he needed a place to stay, and was accepted as a house guest. The other divorces occurred after many years of seemingly satisfactory marriage. One wife felt neglected, began an affair, and divorced her husband to marry the other man. Her second husband, formerly a prominent attorney, lost his practice and position due to alcoholism. The mother also became an alcoholic, and it was in this climate that several of her children, including my subject, spent seven of their late childhood and early adolescent years. A somewhat similar situation arose in a second family. Within a six-month period the father began an affair with his secretary, accused his wife of frigidity, began sleeping in the living room, moved out of the house, obtained a divorce, and remarried. Except in the case where the father came for visits after his divorce, the divorce proceedings, the preceding, attendant, and later difficulties severely shook all involved and created lasting bitterness.

Two of every three resisters felt that their mothers played a dominant role in their upbringing compared to their fathers. In all but one of the remaining families both parents were felt by their children to have played equally influential roles. The relative dominance of the mothers and fathers in the parent-child relationships correlates strongly with the frequency and kind of contact between parents and son. The mothers spent more time with their children, exercised a greater portion of everyday discipline, performed an equal share of severe discipline, were less likely to employ corporal punishment, and were more likely to express warmth. The resisters who felt that both parents played equally influential roles in their upbringing had fathers who compensated for their absence during the day by actively participating in family life in the evenings and especially on weekends. With a few exceptions, none were exposed to strong corporal punishment, and most of them were rarely or never spanked. Nearly all parents agreed on child-rearing practices and most displayed comparable leniency and strictness.

The fact that the war resisters did not have an ingrained fear of their parents is a significant finding of this study. Four resisters did, however, report strong anxiety in connection with their parents, only partly related to parental disciplinary practices. The one subject who came from a traditional patriarchal home and whose father had been a strict and sometimes harsh disciplinarian had feared his father. The other three—one in particular—had been fearful that their mothers might restrict them or withdraw affection. The one who had been most fearful of a loss of maternal love described his mother as an unusually cold person. He said, "I was always afraid [of losing] the little bit of love she gave."

Fathers and Sons

CASE 100 (brother is CASE 104)

He [father] was an employee of the Selective Service before he entered the Army and that only lasted for about two weeks because he told everybody who registered their rights as a conscientious objector . . . and too many people in the office where he was working applied for a C.O. and they fired him. . . . He was a pacifist before the war but like many pacifists he questioned his ideas before it came about and finally decided to join and he participated in the bombing of Hamburg which was more destructive than the bombing of Hiroshima was. Mass bombing. Fires all over the city, people melting in there . . . really melting and suffocating. . . . And after the war he was really horrified by it all and spent twenty years trying to prove that disarmament wouldn't lead to an economic disaster. No, he isn't a pacifist anymore. He believes that violence is appropriate in certain circumstances. . . .

A goodly portion of my sense of ethical values comes from my father . . . who took most of his time for his peace work and his economic studies and didn't have that much time to spend with the rest of the family.

CASE 101

My father has worked as a person within a company, you know, he hasn't belonged to a union and has never been a policy maker, you know, or anything of that nature and has generally taken instruction and orders and did the things that had to be done. He just sort of had to fit in and, you know, be able to take it or else he could lose the job any time, pretty much. And I think that has produced in him a certain amount of unwillingness, although it's more subconscious. . . . I don't think he would recognise it as such . . . not to be involved or not to be concerned about things that don't immediately affect [cough] immediately affect him and no particular, you know, desire to try and go out and experience anything, you know, outside the context of my mother, and a few close friends, you know, in the neighborhood and his job.

CASE 103

Well, he's almost totally, uh, objective and unemotional. He never struck me, for instance, uh, hardly ever shouted. The only time he'd get emotional was when, you know, you'd be arguing with him and he'd either accuse you of being a smart aleck or he'd say something like "So now it's my fault" and kind of walk out, but that was about the height of his emotion. . . .

My father, as I say, didn't seem to have any emotional stake in the household itself at all and lived in his own, you know, trivial little world of taxes literature. He needs a lot of sleep, he also gets up very early in the morning, he reads his tax books and it just doesn't seem anything for him to do, I mean, he comes home, has a drink, sits around for a while, goes down in the basement maybe, putters, comes up, eats dinner at seven, and then they watch television around eight or so and sometimes at eight or nine, with nothing else for him to do, he'll go to bed. And the next day he'll wake up early in the morning at four or something and read his tax cases or something. And that's really his life, day after day.

CASE 104

I tended to be constantly fighting with my father over his intense rationality. He has a very rational mind—rational in the sense that excluding, taking into account irrational factors in other people. I mean, he will be able to react, based on a catalogue of his total estimate of a situation. . . . But . . . he could react to any situation in a very cool, logical fashion until he ran up against irrationalities, and he couldn't understand them. . . .

My mother's a good example. But my brother and I, well he just, I mean, she would go up to a certain point and it would become illogical and she'd be stubborn about something and wouldn't want to do it, you know, or he would be doing something which was logical in the course of where our lives were going and she wouldn't want to do it because, you know, she just didn't want to do it. She had no reason for it but she just didn't want to. And Tom and I, you know, we were kids, we were irrational, and I still think, you know, we reacted appropriately irrational to some things. And he couldn't understand it.

CASE 105

He's a good man. He's a good person . . . if you meet him. But he has just no sense of responsibility at all. And, uh, he has no confidence in himself at all. No self-respect. He just can't do anything, you know.

CASE 109

I can't stand my father when he's angry. He can just say all sorts of things he doesn't mean. And he's capable of making statements like, you know, he wants nothing more to do with this or that person or this or that person is the greatest idiot that ever lived and things like that. And . . . of course, you can say that a person is the greatest idiot that ever lived in a jocular fashion but my father is very angry when he says things like that. . . . When my father is angry, he can dominate the whole household because he won't talk.

He was a sergeant, I hope that's right, in the Army. No, he didn't see combat. He was involved in something that was educational . . . an office job. My father doesn't discuss that very much. . . . If I ask him he'll tell me. But I've never known him to talk about it.

CASE 110

My father lost his parents very early, the last one when he was three, to violent circumstances 'cause they were Jewish. . . . Yeah, in Russia. The Cossacks. . . . He has told me about the Russian Revolution and how he thought the ideals were a good thing but that he wouldn't pick up a gun. . . . Basically that's what it came down to. Killing people and violence was just distasteful to him. Very emotional about that. . . . Yeah, my father is very proud of the fact that he didn't support the Russian Revolution. He wouldn't take up a gun in the Russian Revolution. He didn't take up a gun in World War I. World War II he wanted to go fight but he was too old. . . . It may very well be an awareness on his part that his parents died violently. . . .

CASE 111

Um, he's, uh, he's hard-headed, opinionated, conservative, um, a [New York] *Daily News* reader, and I'm somewhat like that myself. I got a lot from him, kind of hard-headedness, and this always causes my—some of my problems 'cause we always argue. I take one side and he takes the other side and he never gives down. Um, he's able to make quick decisions, and, he likes people, doesn't like to sit around very much. He's kind of a—somewhat of a nonconformist in, uh, in the fact that he's pretty honest with people. He doesn't make fakes of them. Does a good job, works hard, uh, doesn't know the facts on a lot of the things he tries to talk about politically, takes more of an emotional stand than an objective stand.

CASE 112

He was a staff sergeant . . . and in the United States the entire time [World War II]. He didn't talk very much about it. He believed in the war effort but didn't try to romanticize the Army life.

CASE 113

And my dad—my dad is an alcoholic. And he's a functioning alcoholic. I mean, he goes to work and never misses a day. He functions, he makes money, does his job, but he's an alcoholic. . . . He's a very lonely man. . . . His bark was worse than his bite. He would holler every once in a while and he had sort of a stern demeanor. . . . But I knew his bark was worse than his bite and I knew that he wasn't mean or nasty or anything. He was just—would sort of growl a little now and then.

CASE 117

I think my father's hypocritical. Now I do. Before I never used to.

CASE 118

They left Latvia because the Russians were coming. It was a capitalistic family. And it was the assumption at the time that we would all be coming back in a couple of years when all the troubles would be over with. . . . Well, my parents are just kind of anti-Communist and that's it. And the Hungarian uprising took place and they were very pissed-off at the United States for not helping out. . . . My mother has mellowed over the years. Social work has done a lot to change her. And I did too. . . . She's a sane sort of person now. My father sticks to the *Daily News* to this day. . . . [He thinks] Communists are the same. They're everywhere and subverting everything and they definitely have to be done away with. . . .

Well, the key to my father . . . is that he's basically a Latvian peasant. And his father was a peasant. And so on. And he—I never did quite figure out how it was that he came to go to the university in a big city. But, statistically it should never have happened. He should have stayed back there on the farm in Latvia. And so on. And he's just somehow never made the adjustment probably . . . from the peasant to being a sophisticated New Yorker. . . . He's the kind who is not involved with the family very much. He's involved with his business. Very gregarious with his friends, but they're the same old friends. . . .

I couldn't get along with my father at all. I never really talked to him or confided in him or anything like that. . . . For me, at least, he was very hard to talk to. And really the only thing we talked about was how is business going. We had a brief spell at least in junior high school where, uh, we would watch the fights together on television. . . . He is usually quiet and has a bad temper. When he loses his temper, he shouts. And he is very irritable. He's very compulsive. He's always involved with little things. He's putting little things together all the time. He is extraordinarily touchy about cleanliness. He reads primarily mechanics magazines. He's very mechanically inclined and works well with his hands. He is conservative politically. He considers himself open-minded. He's a hard person to approach emotionally. He doesn't express emotions at all. And he withdraws pretty much from everyday events of the family life. He lives in his little world of what he does with his hands and with his business.

CASE 121

My father came to the States [from Russia] when he was twenty-two. He left before he would have been drafted into the service. . . . He left during the Revolution. . . . Well, I suppose he was pretty much pro-Revolution. . . . Well, he left because they tried to kill him. The White Russians came to his family. They pulled a machine gun on top of his parents. They lived in a town which was based around a hill. They just put a machine gun on top of the hill and started to shoot clear out, you know. . . . Why? Well, the White Russians were against the Revolution. And not only that, it was a Jewish town so they just tried to kill all the Jews. . . . I remember during World War II my father although he made nothing always sent money and sent food to Europe since his brothers were in camps and I was always formally aware the stuff was going. . . . I was taught . . . and shown that this thing can still happen, to be very well aware of the fact that this could, you know, cruelty is happening around the world like in Germany still today.

CASE 128

He was a gunner on a bomber. From what he says he came close to being killed several times but was never wounded. Yes, he participated in the bombings of Germany, in fact, we've talked about it. And he says if he were placed in a similar situation now there would be no way he could be able to do it. He just—he found that the whole thing just sickened him . . . And he was involved in one very bad area over a series of oil fields in which most of the American bombers were knocked down. [Pause]. And, uh, it left a pretty big scar on him which he doesn't show very often unless he's talking to someone whom he knows well. . . . The fact that so many of his own friends were killed, the fact that he was involved in the death of so many people he didn't know. . . . The bomber was dropping the bombs and the people were dying.

Did this trouble him a lot too?
He says it did and I have no reason to disbelieve him. He's very sensitive and I suspect that towards the end, the only thing that carried him through was just [pause] sheer guts. He just pushed himself to finish.

Have you talked to him about the war?
Well, he was—it took some time for me to draw him out on it. I would say we only really started to talk about it after the time I had left school and was

living at home. And we had had a number of occasions just to sit and talk in the evening. . . . He seemed to maintain that a certain distance from that part of him because, I think, the disturbance he felt over what he had done. . . . I do remember during high school one thing that stayed very clearly in my mind. That was a television show one night about the bombing of those oil fields, the one that he had been involved in. Apparently they had taken comprehensive films of the whole thing. And he was crying. Apparently there was nothing he could do to help himself, because the whole thing came back to him so vividly. Apparently several men on his own shift were either wounded or killed. But he never made a big thing out of it. He never tried to impress me with his stories. . . . I can't ever remember him glorifying the war or himself. Our later discussions that were more serious showed me that he saw no glory in what was going on. It was just a mean, dirty thing for him. And he felt at the time it had to be done. He has very little time for that sort of militaristic thinking. To him, to use his own words, it's bullshit. . . . It seems as if he couldn't help making those sorts of statements. It was sort of burned into his mind. There was never any glory after they had taken off from the field and had gone across the Channel to Germany. . . . He said he almost turned off his mind. . . . And even when you managed to get back to the base, even then, there was nothing glorious about it except that you were just, just there.

Disciplinary Practices

CASE 103

Well, sometimes they threatened to spank me but I didn't antagonize them too much, you know, I rarely did things wrong. . . . My father, once, I kind of surprised him in the dark and he kind of, you know, "What did you do that for?" and gave me a shot in the back of my head. Uh, and I remember that 'cause that's the only time he ever did that. . . .

Well, the basic idea was that any order given I should be able to ask a reason for it and get a rational response. And I could argue and if on those few occasions when I could make my logic prevail, you know, I could have the right to do what I wanted.

CASE 104

Punishment. Well, it was just, you know, whatever happened to come along. Like, we'd do some kind of damage and refuse to apologize for it and he said, "All you have to do is apologize for it." And he'd get very angry if we really got stubborn about it and we'd be sent to bed without dinner or something like this or get paddled occasionally. . . . Yeah, well one time I had cut my finger at breakfast on a shredded wheat biscut. That sounds impossible, but I did. And, well, my father said, "Well, what'd you cut it on?" I said, "I cut it on a shredded wheat biscuit," and he hauled off and slugged me with an open hand. My nose was bleeding down my shirt, blood all over the kitchen, you know. He must have just hit something in the right way. It really blew my mind, you know, he said, "That's for being a wise-guy." Well, you know, nobody in their right mind would believe someone could cut their finger on a shredded wheat biscut. . . . It took me two days before I could explain to him that I really had. I mean, I just shut him out of my world entirely. But this sort of thing didn't happen very often. In fact, that's one notable exception.

CASE 107

If I did something wrong, let's say it involved the neighbor down the block, they would make me go to the neighbor and apologize. . . . That would be almost the type of punishment, something that had a benefit to it as a punishment.

CASE 111

Well, when I was younger, fighting with my brother, when I got older, not listening to my parents and not giving them the respect that they thought they should get. And for that I'd get hit, usually by my father, a slap in the face, mainly when I was younger, uh, a spank. Sometimes he'd just hit me on the arm a few times.

CASE 112

I remember as a child feeling tremendously frustrated. . . . I simply couldn't do the things I wanted to do. I—I don't know quite what I wanted to do but my parents were standing in my way.

CASE 125

Oh, it was fairly permissive with definite guidelines. . . . I can remember fairly easy, uh, when I was below thirteen, because at thirteen we moved. Before I was thirteen I was going to start writing. I was going to start a diary and start writing how my folks were taking care of it 'cause they were doing such a great job. And I knew that I was going to be a parent some day and I figured that I would want to use their tactics. . . . Even while being under their rearing I thought they were pretty sharp at their job. . . . There weren't too many hard and fast rules. . . .

They've never been authoritarian . . . like in terms of them saying, you can't do this or you can't do that. There's never been very much that I've wanted to do that they objected to, you know. . . . It was very open.

CASE 128

They encouraged both my brother and myself to think for ourselves whenever it was feasible. . . . Well, first of all we had certain responsibilities at home. They were, you know, that either my brother or I had to take care of like the garbage or cleaning our rooms. Helping to keep the house straight or helping to keep the yard clean and things like that. And they very, very rarely interfered with my reading. Quite often if there was something that puzzled me in a book or something, I would come and ask for an explanation. And they usually solved it. . . . Once I had gotten into high school there was never any big trouble about hours. Like if I was going to stay at a friend's house late Friday evening or Saturday evening, I would call up and say, you know, this is where I am and I'll be here until such and such a time and then I'll be home. And unless there was a particular reason to be home he [father] would say, fine, see you later, see you in the morning. . . . They never put any limitations on where I was going. Where I went, what I did, the friends I had, there never seemed to be any interference with it. The only things that they would say to me in some situations, when they felt that I wasn't considering all the factors that were involved and they would say, "Look, we think there are other things involved in this that you don't realize. We think it would be wiser if you did this." And, you know, of course there wasn't total freedom. . . . Yeah, they felt that the most sane approach was to introduce me to thinking for myself as early as they could and to teach me to be responsible.

Although the mothers usually played a more important role in the war resisters' early socialization, the fathers exercised a strong and sometimes more decisive influence on the moral, social, and political development of their sons.

Values and moral standards seem to have played a strong role in the fathers' lives. The interlocking character of their values and behavioral standards precludes neat, mutually exclusive categorization. Social ethics, such as respect for people and life, kindliness, and humanitarianism had direct implications for the resisters' personal conduct. Conversely, such personal conduct standards as rationality and hard work belonged to the fathers' definition of sound personal and social character traits. Despite this overlapping I have maintained the distinction between "social ethics" and "personal conduct standards" for the sake of presentation.

Both areas appear to have been equally important to the fathers. Their cardinal social ethics were respect and love for people and life, kindliness, humanitarianism, social justice, sociopolitical engagement and love of the arts. Many fathers also stressed respect for property and philanthropy. The fathers' cardinal "personal conduct standards" were hard work, diligence, individual intellectual achievement, independence, rationality, and good manners. Several fathers also emphasized respectability, thrift, orderliness, and cleanliness. The resisters' fathers were not always rational and they certainly did not always act in accordance with their principles.

Although the sons often deferred to their fathers' judgment, and were punished by them, they did not feel that this had intruded upon their basic feelings of worth, negated their fathers' respect for them, nor meant an attempt to submerge them under arbitrary dictates. The resisters did not describe themselves as ideal, perfectly well-behaved children, but they seldom provoked their fathers to definitive proclamations. At the same time there was a clear understanding that lying, cheating, stealing, destructiveness, and fighting would not be condoned. Several fathers also prohibited bad manners, disobedience, back-talk, excessive emotionality, sloppiness, and bad language. These prohibitions seem to reflect idiosyncratic differences among the fathers as well as the particular habits of some of their sons.

Sexuality was neither tabooed nor glorified and sexual activity was generally left to the sons' judgment. Likewise, the fathers explained the dangers and disadvantages of smoking and allowed their sons to decide the issue. The consumption of alcoholic beverages seems to have been alien to these families. Only one father and one stepfather drank heavily. The consumption of alcoholic beverages was rarely a problem because they were either not present in the home or were used only on special occasions.

Most of the fathers maintained personal interests and areas of privacy without excluding themselves from family life or indulging themselves materially or psychologically at the expense of other family members. Although substantial differences could be found in the frequency and intensity of father-son contacts from family to family, and a few resisters felt that they had been badly neglected during their childhood years, the fathers did not appear to have overindulged or neglected their sons.

The Disciplinary Practices of the Fathers

Consciously or reflexively the fathers encouraged their sons to follow desired patterns rather than punishing them for transgressions. This is reflected in the fathers' use of praise, reasoning, and reward as their major disciplinary measures. When their sons did not respond to reason, when they were particularly stubborn, or deviated from established family standards, punishments ensued. The most common punishment in such situations was negative criticism (scolding, nagging, yelling). Most of the resisters vaguely recalled having been spanked by their fathers while they were small children. Several fathers occasionally punished with threats, sternness, restrictions, deprivation, and physical isolation.

Several were described by their sons as having had bad tempers. When very angry or irritable, they were as likely to yell as to remain silent, but they seldom employed violence. Yet many resisters recalled one and sometimes two or three occasions on which their fathers had struck them in anger. This took the form of spankings during childhood and slaps during adolescence. The five who had been slapped by their fathers displayed a vivid recollection of this unusual event.

None of the physical punishments reported can be viewed as beatings and even the five adolescents who had been slapped by their fathers pointed out that physical punishments were almost always precipitated by apparent deviations from well-defined and highly valued standards. Corporal punishment was not administered arbitrarily or lightly and the concrete reasons for it varied from father to father. Some fathers spanked their sons for breaking house rules, others for hitting a smaller brother or sister, and still others for breaking things. Two boys had been spanked for misbehavior in school and three for breaking an agreement. Another experienced his only spanking after sticking a pin into his father's "enormous buttocks" in the presence of houseguests.

Only two boys recalled more than four spankings from their fathers and the remainder remembered only one or two. The boys were spanked with an open hand on their covered buttocks. Two fathers had used a leather strap on the sons' covered buttocks but apparently did not strike their sons hard. The spankings did not involve many blows and were generally discontinued when the boys cried. The sons' behavior during spankings did not result in their intensification.

Despite considerable variety in the kind and intensity of contact, the analysis of the overall father-son relationship revealed the following predominant qualities: helpfulness, mutual respect for each other's rights and individuality, patience, affectionate expression, understanding, acceptance, and freedom of movement and expression. Many fathers took an intense interest in the sons' hobbies, thoughts, and school work while others were more reserved, peripheral figures in day-to-day life. None of the resisters felt that they had been materially or psychologically spoiled or overindulged. Several did regret that their fathers had not spent more time with them or demonstrated a more continuous interest in their development. These sons felt that their fathers had always been available when they were needed although the infrequency of contact led to inhibitions and communication difficulties.

In only seven cases did the general openness and cooperation between father and son coincide with a relationship which the sons felt had been consistently warm and emotionally close. Six fathers were described by their sons as especially quiet, reserved, or withdrawn, and three others as generally irritable. These sons experienced the strongest communication difficulties with their fathers. Most of the subjects described their fathers as highly rational men who habitually intellectualized most matters. They felt that their fathers had generally been at a loss when they could not grasp something through reason alone and that this had hampered and often precluded emotional communication. However, few sons described their fathers as "overly emotional" and explained that their inability to employ reason at particular times had introduced difficulties into their relationship.

One of the more striking aspects of some of the war resisters' accounts is the high esteem in which they held their fathers. Praise, pride, and gratitude were not expressed as hollow statements or as lip-service to an abstract ideal of parental respect, but straight forwardly. Even the minority of sons who had had communication difficulties with their fathers or severely criticized them for particular shortcomings felt that they had had many redeeming and positive qualities. None of the father-son relationships disintegrated into continuous, open hostility. Lines of communication remained open and attempts were made to reduce strain.

Military Experience of the Fathers

More than half the fathers had been on active duty in the American Army, Navy, or Air Force during World War II; one had served in the Latvian Army. A few had seen combat either in the Pacific or in Europe and two fathers had participated in bombing missions. None told adventuresome war stories, brought trophies home, gave their children military drill, or tried in any way to glorify military virtues or life. Rather, they expressed sentiments which ranged from belief in the senselessness of war and military routine to deep pain and horror over the loss of life they had witnessed or helped to bring about. At the same time they felt that their participation in World War II had been necessary; none had adopted an antiwar position at that time.

Mothers and Sons

CASE 101

Her main thing was to provide a home and provide for whatever children she had. . . . She had always done the pray-to-God bit and she feels, you know, grateful in a sense that she's been able to live and, you know, attributes a lot of this good fortune to God in heaven and the Bell Telephone Company. . . . I don't think my mother was equipped to, uh, you know, to be able to relate to me, except in terms of her pulling the shots, you know, which is unfortunate. But, you know, this is the type of powerful almost domineering woman that my mother could be. . . . My mother, to this day, still sees my not graduating from Columbia, my refusing to cooperate with what's left of the service, in a sense, as a personal thing against her. . . . It's almost impossible for my mother and I to communicate. Because as soon as I say how I feel which she doesn't want to hear, then she immediately goes into this quasi-screaming thing and then, "Joseph, Joseph," you know, "Pray to God" type of thing, you know, and, you know, it's . . . almost impossible to be able to communicate with my mother.

CASE 103

Well, she was—she was subjective entirely for dealing with me, but emotionally she—like she never used to scream and she, uh, you know, wouldn't cry more than twice a year or something. Uh, most of the time she's annoyed, she just looked annoyed and that was about it. . . . I used to have to kiss her when we came to the dinner table, it was a very perfunctory sort of thing. And that was about the only contact we had. . . . My mother's a sweet woman who doesn't do a lot of thinking. And her opinions haven't changed, because I don't really think she has any well-formulated opinions. . . . It's hard to describe her. My mother seems to lack a very sharp definition. She never went to college and she's basically, uh, well not . . . very intelligent. . . .

My contact with her consisted in one of her usually bugging me about either working harder in school or, uh, when I went and asked her for something and discussing whether I needed it or my brother got it or something like that. And she—another thing about her is she's, I don't know, I guess she is sick but, you know, she's constantly ill in some way or other and one gets the feeling one is constantly burdening her with, you know, by asking her to do something for you and not doing what she asks immediately. And then she'll do it if you don't do it immediately, and that always bothered me.

CASE 105

We have a tremendous love for my mother. And we knew it all the time. And it was the thing that held the family together. . . . She, just sitting down and telling us she loved us and that's why she was working and that she was sorry she couldn't be with us more. Stuff like that. It wasn't like an all-the-time thing. But, you know, sometimes-little-things-mean-a-lot kind of thing. When you didn't expect it she'd be saying something to let you know. And when our birthdays came around you knew that whatever we got, you know, she tried really hard to get it for us . . . it was like a beautiful thing. . . . We knew that this love was there. . . .

My mother's like, uh, a very understanding woman . . . sort of grown with us. . . . Right from the beginning she has always been working hard for my brother and me. She worked as a barmaid and then she worked as a babysitter on the weekends . . . and now she works in the Post Office. . . . And very few people would do things like she does. You know, like to bring up a kid when your husband left and went to go with another woman. . . . I think that's an amazing thing to have that much feeling for a kid. You know, to know that he needed a place to stay. . . . Last year I brought home a kid who, uh, I bring black people home all the time. That's no problem. This kid wasn't only black. He was an ex-convict and a drug addict. She put him upstairs in my room and cooked for him and made him soup and stuck with him. . . . I told her how much it meant to this kid and even though she was scared and even though she was on vacation, and she needs, you know, vacations for her are really important . . . she did it.

CASE 107

My mother was an R.N. and she has compassion. . . . When the situation calls, somebody needs help . . . she'll give it to them when the time comes . . . and like when my sister's boyfriend will come in, you know, she'll have lots of food and she'll be hugging and kissing him and talking. . . . She—she's like a—she's a Jewish-type mother. . . . Almost, you know, as I see it, a fairly intelligent, naive blond. You know, that kind of atmosphere and feeling at times, you know, which is a beautiful thing. . . . She was sensitive like at times somebody would be sick in the family she'd act as a nurse and like I could see her being a wonderful nurse. Very tender in all different ways. I could see that . . . and then there were other moments when she showed just as much aggression, not physical aggression, but aggression of tightness and nervousness, you know. Noise. . . . She can function in either extreme.

Well, she just won't cook, man. I'd come home and I'd throw a steak in the oven, you know, like she usually didn't bother. I mean, like we usually don't have big dinners in the dining room, with the whole family around with the table cloth and stuff, you know.

CASE 109

I think, my mother is basically an extremely creative person who unfortunately has never found an area where she can express this creativity very directly. I know she wrote a lot of poetry when she was younger and she was very interested in reading and writing poetry. . . . What she did was she encouraged me a great deal whenever she found it. She would encourage all my creative efforts and I would generally go to her first with something new that I had written. . . . One thing that has always impressed me is the way she reacts to my friends. And I think she goes out of her way in a very, very demonstrative, uh, kind of way to make my friends welcome and to express interest in them. . . . I feel she is basically a very creative and sensitive person. She—she's extremely rational. I mean, she doesn't get broken down or upset or high-strung about things very often. But she feels very deeply. And she'll generally express them in terms of a very animated kind of concern which I saw this morning when she was telling me how she felt that it was necessary to go out and politically do something in a very active way about what is happening in this country and urging me to do so.

CASE 110

Oh, I was a very good kid. I mean, uh, there was just so little warmth coming from my mother that I didn't dare risk losing what there was. . . . I know that my mother is talking about her own feelings and isn't even aware of them, you know, that she's just so out of touch with herself that she isn't even aware of what she's talking about. . . . She just had a whole set of criteria that fit no conventional pattern but her own and she was sure that they were right. It was very important for her to be a "good mother," but she's very definitive and very opinionated in a stupid way. She's like really an ass. . . . She has definite feelings about what she thinks is right, and she always expresses things in terms of what's right. And you know, consideration for others is her theme somehow. . . . Somebody who's not giving her what she wants has no consideration for others, quote unquote. . . . My mother had a really strong but thoroughly illogical, I mean inconsistent, feeling of justice. . . . Mother's not the model of woman, she's the model of this other thing, sort of asexual, bitchy, old, you know. Really old and decrepit and bitchy and I really hate them, all of them, all the old women in the subways and all the women who walk, you know, with shopping bags and you can't get around them on the sidewalk, and kvetch at you and call you up and give you a hard time, I really hate all of them.

CASE 112

My mother is the type of person who, I suppose, because of my father has reached a liberal position. She's well-meaning, extremely naive and innocent as far as political events occur. She can't—when we say that someone has done something that is illegal or someone has taken a bribe or someone has passed a bill that shouldn't have been passed, it's about beyond her understanding how this can take place. And she'll ask extremely naive questions, "How do they do this?" Uh, so her political interests derive from my father's more radical position. I imagine that she has been pretty much shaped by him. . . . She took great concern as to what we were doing, where we were going, and to the extent that it became quite annoying in later life as I grew older to have to practically report to my mother and the tie was finally broken with some angry words, some understanding on the part of each of us.

CASE 117

My mother's very, uh, permissive and liberal, and my brother and I, when we were still living at home, we could smoke at home, I mean, like there was less reason for me to want to move out of the house, because, you know, I could have a pot party over at my house and my mother wouldn't mind. Matter of fact, we turned my mother on once. She hasn't smoked since then. . . . My relationship with my mother has deteriorated rapidly since, uh, since the thought of moving out, well, since—right after my father moved out, my mother just kind of went freaky.

CASE 122

One thing about Mom that I think is significant: she's a wonderful person to go for a walk in the woods with. She knows the different birds, many of the different quacks and certainly enjoys life and certainly enjoys nature. . . . You can feel her excitement about life when you walk in the woods with her. This is an important, significant thing. . . . She started to drink a lot [since her divorce] and she started to smoke a lot. And she went along with my stepfather most of the time. She used us in her bitter campaign against my dad in many ways. . . . What's it been now, fifteen, sixteen years, and my mother is still so bitter that—that every fifth word out of her mouth, even though she's been remarried now for fifteen years, is bitter denunciation of my dad, and it makes it very uncomfortable to be with her. So I try not to be. . . . My mom, and my stepfather, they are not fit parents [slight laugh]. Quite frankly, they, they shouldn't—they're a couple of people who are not responsible and should not have [slight laugh] growing young minds under their control. . . . As human beings she's never respected us, any of us children, as human beings. And, she's not an easy person to live with.

CASE 123

One time I remember a cousin came to visit us and, uh, he was a mechanic and the oil had settled in his hands and he couldn't get it out. You know, it was just his hands. That was his hands from that time on. He would be grease-stained for the rest of his life. And I remember that he came to shake my hand and I went to shake his hand and I saw his hand was all black and covered with grease and I wouldn't shake hands with him. I remember my mother hit me very hard and said that, uh, told me that, you know, a man makes his living with his hands and that sometimes that hand might not be clean but it's clean because he makes a living by it. That was the only time that any strong thing ever happened, any physical action had ever taken place in morals.

CASE 125

She's a real arbitrator of family disputes and misunderstandings. And always reminding other people when other people's birthdays are. Letting other people know that this or that comment would hurt this or that person. She's a real—she should be a labor negotiator in New York. She's very good at it . . . very sportive. . . . Tremendous amount of independence. . . . My mother's very, very neat, noticeably so, you know. It's sort of, uh, not pretentious, but it's just obviously so. . . . She used to clean houses to put herself through high school. Comes from a very poor farm family of about twelve kids. And so she went to high school, in order to buy her clothes and pay for her books and stuff like that, she worked as a maid in different houses . . . and so keeping houses clean is a part of her personal history. So our house is immaculate. You could eat off the floor. When I walked in I used to grab a pillow off the davenport and throw it on the floor just so it's not exactly perfect, you know. . . .

Well, she too will help out people who are sick. You know, clean their house for them, sort of her forte kind of thing, you know. Had a relative who was, you know, alcoholic and she would help take care of that family for some time until he got back on his feet. And, uh, I don't know. It's just by the way the things they say. If not so much their actions as the things they say. And their actions don't deny the things they say or, you know, the way they talk. The actions that I know tend to support the idea of a very sensitive person.

CASE 126

Because of acute conflict with my mother, I left home. . . . My mother I disliked and in part, I'd say, blamed her for the divorce, uh, well, for losing him. And I didn't like her, I didn't get along with her on a day-to-day basis. In fact, I really despised her.

CASE 128

I think, another example was the business with the church. . . . On several occasions after I stopped going to church the pastor would show up at the house and want to talk with us and find out why I wasn't going and why I wasn't going to Catholic school. And on a couple of occasions my parents or my mother—this was during the day when my father was away at work—would say, you know, why don't you ask him, don't ask me. She would encourage me to tell him myself why I wasn't interested in going.

Disciplinary Practices (Violent)*

CASE 101

We were playing cowboys and Indians, so I'm running up the back with my pistols and all that shit, running up the back calling "You fucking bastard, you fucking bastard." All the neighbors had their heads out the window and I'm

---

*Instances of violence by mothers against sons were rarely reported. The two recounted here were unusual.

sure that's what my mother reacted to more, you know, than calling that. Although she reacted to that because that's probably a sin, if not a mortal sin, certainly some type of grave offence. I didn't know what was going on. I felt guilty, you know, just from the tone of her voice as I knew from prior experience that I'd done something wrong. So I came running up the stairs and, you know, it's a three-story house, you know, and went up the stairs and down to the second floor. Well, then my mother's now waiting to take off my trousers and she starts running upstairs, takes the tomahawk, throws it at me—whack!—just out cold!

CASE 129

They would yell at me in one instance and slap me in another. . . . He [father], hit harder, he also seemed to be just, well, like when he'd lose his temper he was scarier. My mother would sort of be, when she'd lose her temper, she was, well, it's just that she was very worked up and I didn't feel as threatened. . . .

And I lighted the cherry bomb and I tossed it out onto the street. The problem was that when I tossed it out of the window it exploded in the air right next to the guy painting on the ladder. Fortunately he was a young cat, you know, and he went like he fell off the ladder but he didn't hurt himself. You know, my mother comes in and blah-blah, and she just knew I did it. She just figured it out. And my mother had a hang-up about lying. She couldn't stand lies. And she said, "You used the money that you were supposed to put in the church collection." And I said, "No," you know, but she was really furious. She was really furious. She really thought that I was lying to her and had taken that money and had said that I was giving it to that church thing, you know. And that I had just, you know, turned around and had gone and spent it. And on firecrackers no less! [slight laugh]. And she really—she started to hit me, you know, and I had to put my hands up. She was—she was—I was amazed, she was really furious. She gave me a black eye [slight laugh]. Yeah. And of course afterwards, you know, I was still really pissed at her because she found out afterwards, you know, my father came home and like I didn't want to just blow it and say that my father gave me the money. He came home and, you know, "What happened? The kid's mad. You can tell that something is wrong." My mother must have explained it to him and he said, "Aw, I gave him an extra quarter. What did you do? I gave him the money, you know." And then my mother like apologized, but then I was still really pissed. Like I was mad because she didn't really give me any chance, you know. And she really flew off the handle.

The war resisters felt that their mothers in comparison to their fathers had played as important and sometimes more decisive roles in their development. Many more negative statements were made about mothers than fathers. Particularly in the childhood years, the mothers were usually more deeply involved in their sons' day-to-day problems and gave them more individual attention. Some mothers were social and political activists who contributed their time and professional training to community organizations. Several were described by their sons as having been more rational and socially conscious than their husbands. The mothers tended to balance the marital unit by being the emotional and subjective wives of overly rational husbands or the rational wives of emotional and subjective husbands.

In view of the basic similarity between the war resisters' parents, most of the descriptive material on the values, moral standards, disciplinary practices, and sociopolitical sentiments of the resisters' fathers are equally valid for their mothers. However, important differences between the parents are found in some areas. Most of these differences appear to reflect the mothers' more active position in the home and in their sons' upbringing. A few seem to stem from the mothers' special interests and inclinations.

The value system of most of the mothers was broader than their husbands' and placed a stronger emphasis on external respectability and compliance. More mothers than fathers were concerned about good manners, obedience, respectability, and behavioral conformity in the community. This in part explains the tension that existed between many resisters and their mothers during childhood, and the resentment some of them continued to feel. As a group, the mothers also appear to have been less theoretical about societal processes and the responsibility of the individual to his fellow man. This is reflected in their greater stress on the importance of individual acts of helpfulness within the family as well as to outsiders. They seem to have taken a more active interest in the arts than most of their husbands and therefore were more likely to bring cultural appreciation into the home.

The mothers' more active role in the home and in the resisters' early socialization was seldom accompanied by compulsiveness, harassment, punitiveness or overprotectiveness. Most resisters felt that their mothers had not shown an exaggerated concern for the formal aspects of their conduct and appearance. It seems as though the mothers were compensating for their husbands' noninvolvement and lower standards in these areas but also felt that overexacting demands for neatness and social formalities were less important than such character traits as honesty, industriousness, and a strong social conscience. With a few notable exceptions, perhaps the most striking feature of nearly all the mothers' values was the absence of puritanical attitudes. They did not place taboos on sexuality, smoking, and drinking, and many gave their sons their first sexual instructions.

The more frequent day-to-day contact between mother and son meant that the mothers had a larger share of discipline. Most of them also tried to encourage their sons to reap rewards through good behavior rather than to punish them for noncompliance with established standards. Fewer resisters recalled having been spanked by their mothers than by their fathers and the majority spoke of their mothers' use of the incentive of tangible rewards as a standard disciplinary procedure. They also felt that they had been both praised and criticized more often by their mothers.

The relative warmth and understanding in most of the mother-son relationships underscores the problematical character of the others. The causes of the mother-son conflicts varied from case to case. One war resister described his mother as a cold though well-controlled and fair woman who strove to be a perfect housewife and mother. He had always found it difficult to talk to her and as a child had not dared to misbehave for fear of losing the little affection she gave him. Another had been deeply distressed since middle-childhood by his mother's behavior. She had divorced his father and gained custody of their children. Her second marriage was to a punitive, irritable and autocratic man whose standards she adopted; she expressed unceasing bitterness toward the boy's father, and prevented them from seeing each other for more than one day a month over a six-year period. During the second marriage the woman began to smoke and drink heavily and only after the boy rejoined his father did the mother-son relationship improve. The remaining mother-son conflicts were not as serious as the ones just described. These men said that they had always felt closer to their fathers and that the communication problems stemmed from their mothers' "overconventionality," "constant bickering," "hard veneer," or "use of material coerciveness."

The serious conflict in two mother-son relationships and the communication problems of varying severity in several others do not seem to have had a direct bearing on the moral-political stand taken by these men as war resisters. Particularly in the first two cases the tense mother-son relationships appear to parallel idiosyncracies in the boys' developmental patterns and to be connected to particularities in their personalities, both of which will be discussed in later chapters. The common roots of nearly all the resisters which led in a more or less continuous line to their antiwar position lay in the interlocking influences of the child-rearing practices and moral-social-political climate in their homes. It should also be pointed out that most of the boys who felt inhibited with their mothers because of their coldness, irritability or overrationality felt that they had been able to relate better to their fathers.

Violence in the Family History

Victimization played a major role in five family histories. The grand-parents, parents, and relatives of four Jewish families had been caught in upheaval and violence in Russia in 1905 or 1917. They left Russia in order to escape the wanton massacres of civilian populations and also to avoid forced Army conscription. The war resisters said that although their grand-parents and parents had sympathized with the ideals of the revolution of 1917, they had refused to carry arms and participate in the "blood bath." Some relatives had lost parents, brothers, sisters, and cousins in massacres. The aversion to violence, militarism, and political-economic oppression which they brought with them to the United States became incorporated into the family tradition and was expressed in strong social-political idealism and engagement. The other (non-Jewish) family fled Latvia as the Russian Army began occupation of that country after World War II. They spent several postwar years in displaced person camps in Germany waiting for the Russian Army to leave. Finally they emigrated to the United States.

The Family in the Community

The families of the war resisters differed widely in their propensity for contact with neighbors, but showed similarity in respect to friends and relatives. A minority of the families had frequent and close relations with their neighbors while the majority of them seem to have restricted socialization to friends and relatives. Most of the families had several or many close friends, and the majority of them had close, unceremonial, and frequent contacts with their relatives. The most characteristic aspect of socializing was that it included the entire family.

The person-to-person help extended and received by the war resister families has several distinctive characteristics. It usually extended to friends, neighbors, and strangers as well as to relatives. In many cases the help given imposed long-term burdens on the entire family. The families that gave help were also more gregarious than the minority of families that did not. Helpful acts extended across ethnic, religious, and racial lines in most cases. There were a few families who apparently helped only relatives and friends, or only strangers. These families gave much more help than they received.

The extension of person-to-person help was as typical of fathers as of mothers, and in many cases involved the entire family. In addition to grandparents, other people were taken into the home for short periods of time; these included high school students who were estranged from their families, a drug addict, and neighborhood children whose families were undergoing hardship. One father with poor eyesight spent a substantial portion of his spare time reading and talking to blind people. Two mothers who were trained nurses gave their services to people through clinics and hospitals. Helpful spare-time activities of fathers included community work in slums, directing a teen-age lounge, helping in the organization and administration of a home for old people, and giving financial help to friends. Mothers' activities included helping blind people, going on door-to-door fund-raising drives, organizing recreation for handicapped children, tutoring a Chinese woman in English, and offering social worker services to different community organizations.

Many of the fathers' organizational affiliations and private actions involved criticism of social and political institutions and policy. Although none of the fathers was a member of a left-wing party, several had histories of left-wing dissent and sympathies; these men were equally divided between first-, second-, and third-generation Americans. A few had been social revolutionaries during the 1930's, had flirted with and then rejected the American Communist Party, had protested against Mussolini in 1929, Senator Joseph McCarthy in the 1950's, and the war in Vietnam and the Selective Service System in the 1960's. However, only a minority of the fathers had clearly defined left-wing political sentiments and even they remained skeptical of left-wing political groups. Their political dissent had an individualistic character and was not carried out in conjunction with party platforms and politics. These men remained politically nonaligned and unaffiliated critics, more concerned with particular social and political inequalities and errors than with radical politics or revolution in the United States. The only father with a longstanding sociopolitical affiliation belonged to the American Civil Liberties Union. He campaigned actively for Senator Eugene McCarthy in the 1968 Presidential primaries and, as did several other fathers, joined the War Resisters League after his son decided to become a conscientious objector.

The sociopolitical engagement of the politically moderate and conservative fathers had the same sporadic quality as that of their left-wing counterparts. They campaigned, collected signatures, and attended political meetings for Democratic and Republican Party candidates.

Only one father belonged to a purely fraternal organization. Others belonged to Jewish and Protestant groups whose activities extended into the broader community. None belonged to hunting, sports, or rifle clubs. The fathers' disinterest in and, in some cases, antipathy toward organized religion was reflected in their minimal participation in formal religious practice. They were not affiliated with confessionally bound fraternal organizations unless these groups were dedicated to social action programs. Two fathers held prestigious positions as lay members of their congregations, one as a Presbyterian deacon and the other as initiator of a Sunday morning discussion group in lieu of prayer at a Unitarian Church.

While not all fathers had organizational ties and not all fathers engaged in "individual acts of conscience," there were only two fathers who did neither one nor the other. In a majority of cases the fathers did both. Another striking aspect of the fathers' sociopolitical activities is that they were not combined with political dogmatization of family life. Several of the politically active fathers did not demand that their wives and children adopt their views, and rarely discussed their views at home, although some wives, and later their sons, showed a similar engagement. A number of fathers were politically outspoken at home but not in public.

The organizational affiliations and sociopolitical activities of the resisters' mothers have a distinctive pattern. In many cases this pattern is related to religious denomination and practice and to the social and political interests of their husbands. The most conspicuous aspects of this patterning are: near-ly seventy-five percent of the mothers' organizational ties were with secular organizations dedicated to philanthropic, educational, community health, and political goals; less than one-third of the mothers were associated with social groups and these women also participated in philanthropic and/or educa-tional groups; the mothers who attended church regularly had the fewest number of secular organizational ties, and several were affiliated with neither church nor nonchurch groups; the six mothers with ties to political groups were intense political activists both at home and in the community; only a small minority of mothers had apparently never affiliated themselves with secular or church groups.

Most of the war resisters' mothers extended help directly to family members, friends, neighbors, and strangers, and in some cases this had been done through association with hospitals, clinics, community welfare institu-tions, or through agencies for the blind and physically handicapped. Many mothers did not possess the skills, were not inclined, or were prevented by work and family obligations from extending regular direct help to persons outside the family. Some of these women expressed their concern for physi-cal and mental health problems through participation in national and local fund-raising organizations. Nearly half the mothers were active in local PTA chapters, and one had served as president of her chapter. Most of the mothers' church and synagogue associations involved groups which served both philanthropic and social functions.

Both the number and quality of values and behavioral standards empha-sized by the war resisters' families clearly illustrate the overall moral climate surrounding their sons' upbringing. I feel that this and the many rights the resisters enjoyed in their homes contributed substantially to formation of the position which they took as war resisters. As children they were confident of their right to an opinion, even though it was sometimes ignored, their right to privacy, their right to make mistakes and, in most cases, their right to receive an apology when unfairly criticized or punished. At the same time these boys knew that incorrect behavior, particularly infringement on others' rights, would result in discussion, reprimand, or punishment.

Notes

1. R. E. Lane, "Fathers And Sons: Foundations of Political Belief," *American Sociological Review*, 1963, 502-511.

CHAPTER 3

ADOLESCENCE

THE GREEN BERETS

CASE 207

I've always wanted to do something adventurous like jumping out of planes which I do. I'm going to start skydiving tonight. I'm in a skydiving class that starts tonight. And, uh, I raced stock cars for a year. Nothing big-time like, you know, like you read in the papers. Just a little dirt track. But I think a lot of that had to do with the kid that lived downstairs. He was, like I say, he was two years older than I was and we always grew up together. And ever since I can remember, we've always done something exciting, you know. We've always done dangerous things for some reason. We jumped off bridges and in the water, you know. I guess all kids do it. Today I look at the bridge where I used to jump off and it scares the hell out of me, 'cause it seems so, it was about a hundred foot drop into the water and, you know, you wonder why you did something like that. At the time I never gave it a thought of getting hurt. And if my folks knew about it, I would have got whipped. And, uh, I think, he, he and I together more or less built adventures, you know, an adventuresome attitude in us because he's, he's now a professional stock car racer. You know, I think if I had gotten out of the Army last year, instead of reenlisting, I probably would be, you know, racing this year. . . . The best thing that ever happened to me was, well, I won a race one day and I thought that was about the greatest thing.

CASE 208

I went out for track, made the varsity, got to go to the state meet, on a relay team. I thought that was really great, 'cause, uh, we spent a whole weekend in a hotel or motel. I think we stayed up all night, phoning people on the phones and drinking cokes and stuff. We didn't do too good at the meet the next day. It was a pretty good weekend. And then that summer, that summer was the fateful summer. I got caught stealing cars right before my junior year was to begin. Not really stealing them. We'd get up in the middle of the night and somebody'd leave the keys in the car and we'd drive it around for about two hours and then park it about two blocks from their house and then, you know, go home. But what happened was, we had this one car out one night, it was about three o'clock in the morning, I guess. The cop wanted to stop us to see what two sixteen-year-old kids were doing out at three o'clock in the morning. He said that the taillight was off, but I don't think the tail was off. I think it was 'cause he was interested in, you know, what are these two kids doing out this late. So we got out and ran and he fired one shot and I kept running. The guy I was with stopped and hid. And in about five minutes they had about five squad cars all over the area. I had already gotten out of the perimeter where they were, and I was on my way home, and I remember, I always feel it in my stomach, never had in my life, was when I walked up my street and came around the corner and there's my house—every light in the house is on. Go around and dug in a window and sure enough my door is open. Knocked on the back door. The first thing my father said when I walked in was "Thief." That's the worst feeling I ever had in my whole life. I thought I was going, I had that feeling where I just didn't care anymore 'cause it was out of my hands. I—there wasn't really anything I could do anymore about it. And it was those poor feelings where there's nothing you can do. I thought for sure I was going to jail for the rest of my life. . . . They—they questioned us, him in one room, me in the other room. And finally, they finally got all five cars out of us. They brought me in and my parents' hearts were broken. They took it pretty good. I—I've put them through a whole lot of stuff that I regret now. . . .

Did your parents ask you why you did it?
Yeah.

And what did you tell them?
I don't know. At the time—the first time—the first couple of times it seemed like fun. Then it wasn't even any fun anymore. Actually, what it was, it was just more daring than anything. Just for the thrill. Just to say you did it.

Was it your idea or your friend's idea or both of yours?
Uh, it was just—just by mutual agreement. Like that. He'd come over and tap on my window about 11:30, 12 o'clock at night. I get bored laying in bed anyway.

Pardon me?
I said, I get bored laying here in bed anyway. I'm—what I'm surprised is, uh, we never got caught before that. We're lucky we got caught out in the suburbs, because we'd take cars down into the city and stuff like that. And the Chicago police are like flies down there. They're all over the place. And I know if we were to run in Chicago, we'd have had a slug in the back instead of shooting into the ground, which is lucky. . . .

If we had any family problems? I never had any problems with my family at all, except I used to get in trouble. I think it was mostly because I didn't hang around with the wrong crowd, I mean, they'll all be successes in life, but they're a rowdy crowd. You know what I mean. What you'd term as trouble makers. And not really—really trouble makers like vandalism and stuff like that. I think, when we took those cars, we would have gone out just to wreck them, strip them down and sell them. But what we did was purely out of boredom, actually nothing else to do. The only reason we did it in the middle of the night was because probably, because we didn't have enough guts to do it in the middle of the day and stuff like that. . . .

Then there was something else I'll never forget. Uh, I saw a train hit a car, with six people in it. Dragged it about half a mile. These people were—you couldn't even recognize them. They were arms, legs, heads, feet, fingers, toes and everything all along the tracks, intestines all inside the car. . . . I saw it happen. I saw the car being dragged down the tracks and just pushed out, rolled under an embankment. It's kind of like slow motion. It just sort of tumbled right on down.

And how old were you then?
Sixteen.

Do you remember how you felt?
Well, actually, it was—more in a state of shock than anything. I couldn't believe it was happening 'til I actually got right up there. We drove on and then came back. After they had dragged the car back across the street to this, uh, junk yard that happened to be across the street. It was sitting there, this big crowd of people, and looked at the car and there were—the trunks of the bodies were— three of the bodies were still inside. Completely severed in different directions and smashed and pieces of intestines all over the—not just blood but I mean chunks of human bodies laying all over the hood and the trunk and the roof and hanging out the sides of the doors and stuff. It looked like they took a plate of spaghetti and meatballs and threw it at the car. Really sickening. I don't think—I don't think it did too much to me then.

Did you get sick at the time?
No, that's what's funny. I wasn't nauseous at all. The girl I was with got sick. She didn't throw up or anything, but she started feeling to her stomach. But that sort of stuff never bothered me that much. I'm more interested, you know, in what happened than really stopping and thinking about what really happened.

CASE 202

Yeah, my school was pretty bad. Cops in there all the time. Three people got killed. You know, Bedford-Stuyvesant. . . . One day, I was supposed to be the baddest thing there, and these guys were ribbing me, you know, saying I was a quitter and then followed me into a candy store and just kept ribbing me, ribbing me. So I ordered another Coke and told him not to open it, and so while they was ribbing me I was shaking the Coke up and pretty soon I just turned around and hit him with it. . . . He was playing with his knife. . . . Shaked it up to get pressure inside. When it bursts, then it blows glass all over. . . . Hit him on the head. . . . He got cuts, on the top of his head, and a pretty good one right here. . . . I think he was unconscious. Maybe he wasn't. I don't know. I just hit him and left. . . . No, I wasn't nervous. I was elated.

CASE 209

Well, uh, they [his parents] never wanted you to get into juvenile trouble, you know, not get into trouble with the police. . . .

Did you ever had any trouble with the police?
No, I didn't.

Nothing at all?
Well, I never got picked up. Well, one time.

Did you ever do anything you could have been picked up for?
Yes, I have. I smashed a couple of windows. I used to take car parts. Uh, this is later on. When you're younger, I used to in the wintertime, always bomb cars with snowballs and then one time they were having—I guess, we were in eighth grade, and they were bombing the school with snowballs and I guess somebody broke a few windows and the same night they took a priest's car and pushed it down the street. I wasn't in on it. I saw them pushing the car, but I was there. We got our names taken down by the police that night, but that was the only time. I guess I was in trouble with the police, but I never got in trouble for it.

That was pretty minor. Did you ever do anything else that you could have gotten into trouble for, if you had been caught?
Oh, later on, when you get into high—like, uh, we got into high school, you'd be drinking, you know, underage. I guess most people do that now. I guess later on when I got just out of high school I was smoking some grass a little bit, a couple of times. Some guys would be getting it. And, you know, and then go across the bridge into Canada. Like we'd go up there and sell the Canadians a lot of booze. They have their Yorkville, up in Toronto, and we'd go up there on weekends sometimes, like our senior year in high school and go and sell the Canadians a lot of booze, 'cause they couldn't buy it up there. Go across the border. But that's nothing great. No great crime or nothing.

CASE 210

You say that your hobby was boxing.
Right. PAL, Police Athletic League. My uncle got me interested in that. He was a detective. . . . Well, like we went up to Golden Gloves. Pennsylvania doesn't have any Golden Gloves. I had to go to another state for Golden Gloves, but the Police Athletic League is equal to the Golden Gloves and I did pretty good.

Did you get to hold any titles when you were in PAL?
Oh yeah, oh yeah. I won the PAL Junior Championship, which was for one season, one year, and that was the last year I was there.

What were you? Lightweight?
What? [laughs] Lightweight! I was 100 pounds when I came in the Army.

Start wherever you want and tell me about school.
. . . I graduated out of there. I had one problem in that school. I got in a fight [laughs]. It was a good one too.

What happened?
Well, some kid threw a stone and hit me in the head and cut my eye. The next day, I came back, well, I came from home and went to school and seen him at recess and I asked him why he threw the stone at me. He cut me and, uh, he was sorry . . . and he said, he was sorry and so I swung to hit him.

So his friend picked up for him. He was a little bigger that I was. So I said, well, after I'm finished with you, I'll go back to you. I remember that now. I beat the heck out of that guy. We just rolled on and cut up our knuckles. That was the only time I was ever suspended, uh, taken to the principal's office and sent home and letters for both of us, for our mothers to come in [laughs]. My mother was mad. But my father was real proud, you know, to see that I was defending myself, because all the time before that I used to get beat up and so finally my uncle started teaching me to box. I couldn't figure out why everybody could whip me and I can't whip anybody. I have two hands just like they do. So I started to learn how to fight. That was the first fight I had in school. That was in the fifth grade. . . .

Then there was this teacher, for automobile mechanics, but we played a prank on him once, all the guys got together. This is—not thinking now—now I wouldn't do anything like this, but being younger at the time and not realizing the symptoms it could cause a person. He had to drink mineral water. That's all he could drink. Well, they emptied his thermos bottle and put tap water in. So he was out of school for about 4 days [laughs]. At the time it was comical, but in a way it's—you think about it and you could have killed the man maybe if it was very serious. He had to have this kind of water. . . .

How did it come about, I mean your taking boxing lessons?
Hmm? 'Cause my uncle didn't want me to get in any mischief, uh, this police uncle of mine, 'cause he came around to my house, well, he used to come over every Sunday, you know. More or less the family has a big dinner on Sunday. All the kids would sit in here. All the big people were at the table. This was something that always happened every Sunday. It was a get together of the family, once a week. And, we were all at the table, and after everybody ate, my uncle—we sit down here and we used to just spar around. And he used to talk boxing, and I could fight all these—swing like that, and, uh, well, we were playing around and he threw a punch and I ducked and he knocked me out [laugh]. That's how heavy-handed he was. And so, you know, it didn't knock me out, it just blacked me for a second. So, I woke up and my uncle said, you ought to give this kid boxing lessons. . . . You know, my uncle reminded me more of a gangster than a cop. Then this other uncle of mine was a paratrooper. Not everybody can be a paratrooper. All my uncles were outstanding in some way. Now this one uncle, he was more or less my ideal. And, uh, everything he ever done, I tried to copy . . . and my other uncle, it seems like whenever this man fights, every bit of hate, he has nothing but hate, and when he fights, he fights to win. . . . All right, it's just like, well, say, James Bond movies, okay. Everyone walks around now playing this James Bond bit. Everybody thinks he's the greatest thing since bubble gum, or these Italian Western movies, this Clint Eastwood series now. People are trying to imitate this. It's more or less what I was always trying to imitate my uncles. Which I know I can't do because I'm me and they're them. . . .

And then this one time I'd seen my father fight, and I never seen my father get really mad in my life. . . . [Someone] said something about my mother and then had a butcher knife and my father—my father took the butcher knife and beat the heck out of this guy. I walked around, you know, the kid walks around being proud of his father and he told me not to tell my mother. . . .

CASE 212

Well, I did deer hunting, pheasant, dove. That's about it. I used a twelve-gauge shotgun and a 30-30 rifle. I wasn't a very good shot. I only hit a deer but usually got the pheasant or the dove. . . . Well, once when I was younger, as a matter of fact, that's the only time I remember getting into trouble. I found some matches and, uh, I built a fire in the garage and then I found some shotgun shells and I threw them in the fire and one of the rounds went off and blew a hole in the roof. My father came out and spanked me and told me I shouldn't be playing with matches and stuff like this. This upset me. Now that I look back on it, you know, I could have killed myself.

Did you have any fights at school?
No, not really. It's surprising. All my life I've been bigger than everyone and so this is one reason I've never had to fight. People just leave me alone. They're always looking for somebody, it seems, that's smaller than they are. And basically, I don't want to hurt somebody that's smaller than I am. Now in a combat situation, it's different.

CASE 214

Did you ever get into trouble with the police during junior high and high school?
Yeah, I had about a dozen arrests for disorderly conduct and that business. One for petty larceny. One for burglary. . . . We were all drunk one night. Out of money. No booze. Decided a good way to get some liquor would be for two of us to . . . walk into a liquor store, grab a fist of whisky and run. Figured they'd never be able to catch us. I'm sure we worked well. Except, when we came running out of the store there was a cop car at the intersection. Well, they located us real fast, chased us down, took us to jail. And that was it. . . . The burglary? My little brother and I broke into a school on the corner and stole some gas for a go-cart. A big haul [laughs]. I was about twelve, I guess. What happened was, some kid saw us breaking in the school, went home, told his parents. And his parents looked it up in the school directory where we lived and the police came to our house, told my parents, told us we should appear in court on such and such a date. And we appeared and the guy [judge] said, "Well, since your parents are such upstanding people, if you ever get into any more trouble, we're going to have to bring this up again." . . . Yeah, my parents were heartbroken. I remember that. . . . Oh, for the liquor store thing, paid a twenty dollar fine. Went to jail, spent the night in jail and, uh, I don't remember who bought me out on that. Somebody bought me out on it.
    Jail made me hate everybody and everything. That's the most base thing I can ever imagine. It made me hate authority. It made me hate the police. It made me hate authority, really actively hate authority. I probably revolted against authority, actually viewing an authority structure and disliking it and hating it. Can't remember ever having as much contempt as I did for it. That's

changed quite a lot now. I've reassessed that quite a bit since I've been in the Army.

CASE 215

Between my freshman and sophomore year in college I worked for the sheriff's department. I took the job. See, the rifle team I used to shoot for was under the sheriff's department, the sheriff's department rifle team for the parish. I knew all the people there very well 'cause I shot with them 'til I was eighteen years old. One of the people I got to know very well became sheriff of the parish. Once in a while, when they were short, I used to ride in the car, like go out for a traffic accident or something like that. And that was my first introduction to brave things. I worked there about a week and there was a car from Dow Chemical Company that hit a truck from Dow Chemical Company at about sixty miles per hour and the damn thing blew up and burned up eight people. And I helped clean up the mess. You asked me earlier, did I ever throw up. Yes, I threw up that day. That day I got sick. . . . It was still burning when I got there and it was a good hour until the flames were under control. And then we had to wait until things cooled off a little bit and we had to take the bodies out of the car. And it was somewhat of a mess. . . . The bodies were charcoal. There wasn't much of anything left. The thing that made me sick, it wasn't seeing all the bodies in the car, it was after we had taken all the crusted bodies out of the car that I looked in the back seat and saw something that was crusted and I picked it up. And it was a hand, the back of it. It was just red. It was all burned and it was crusted on one side and I picked it up and it fell apart between my hands. That did it.

How old were you when your father first introduced you to guns?
Six or seven. . . . I've been shooting ever since.

Have you ever been in trouble with the police?
Well, I had quite an advantage because when I did get into any kind of trouble I had them [sheriff] to help me out. I did get into trouble a little bit one time. Got a young lady drunk one night and her father called the police. Thank God they called the sheriff's office where I happened to be working. They got me out of the whole thing. She was only sixteen or seventeen and the legal age for drinking was eighteen. I bought a bottle and I got plastered.

CASE 217

I remember all the way through clear up to when I got into high school, I had to get into a fight with every kid in the class, 'cause I could beat everybody. The first thing was to beat everybody at school. Didn't fight so much in high school. Started growing up, started getting a bit older. No use for fighting.

Did you have fights in high school?
Yeah. The biggest fight I got into was with a guy, he was the middle age between my brother and myself. My brother was a senior and I was a sophomore and this guy was a junior and on the football team. He got into a fight with my brother. It was my brother's fault. He's a loud-mouth and wise guy. He was about 240 pounds and my brother was only 150. And the next day I got a

hold of him and did him in a number. Broke his nose, couple of ribs. Put him in the hospital. Actually didn't even know him. We got to be good friends. ... No, I didn't even get scratched. At that time I had been studying karate for a couple of years. Also had been weight lifting since I was thirteen. ... No, I didn't get into trouble. Where I come from out in California is quite a rough place. Gang fights, hoodlums and everything else. Bloody motorcycle gangs and car clubs. A lot of gang fights going on all the time. A few broken ribs and stuff is nothing. Nobody even looks at it. It's a waste of time for the cops.

Were you ever involved in any gang fights?
No.

Why?
More or less, the—the people that I ran around with, the gang that I ran with weren't thugs or anything but the football team. And I weighed 230 pounds and I was the smallest one, and we always went around together. We had two guys that weighed 310, and we always stayed together, and nobody'd mess with us. We always had eight or nine of us together. And nobody wanted to fight us. Never had to get into any fights, gang wars. Didn't cause anybody any trouble.

CASE 218

What kind of hunting did you do?
Oh, uh, quail hunting, dove hunting, squirrels, deer, turkey. Shot some pigs. I've done just about every kind of hunting that can be done. I've hunted for bears and things. But we don't have too many bears in [subject's home state]. ... Started hunting at about eight or nine ... had various different guns. Then I had a 410 and then I got a rifle and later on I got a twelve-gauge pump and an automatic. I had altogether what you need to shoot with. Most of them were given to me.

While you were growing up, did you ever have any problems of any kind with the police?
No, no, I never did. None whatsoever. People that have problems with the police are normally people from big towns and everything, or that, uh, the police picking up maybe from a small town there. You don't have maybe one or two police anyway and they hardly ever picked up the kids. They usually listen to their Daddy or something like that there.

Did you ever do anything when you were a kid that you could have gotten picked up for?
Sure, sure.

Like what?
Oh, I stole a watermelon, shot out street lights, pushed cars down the road. Several things.

Anything else?
That was enough then, I think. Throw firecrackers at people, you know. Stuff like that.

Have you had many fights?
Sir, I've had 99,000 fights.

Can you tell me about some of them?
Well, down at Fort Bragg, that was a long time ago. I went down to the beach, me and two friends of mine. There was a big dance hall and we bought six gallons of moonshine for about eighteen dollars a gallon. Everybody got drunk and we started to fight and fought for about an hour. . . . Yeah, with everybody in the place. The cops arrested everybody. Put everybody in jail. And everybody was bloody. Some people didn't have no teeth . . . it was a good one. The first one, the town at the time was a little bit—it's changed a lot now—was a little bit rougher. I mean the people would—it looks like they would go to town just to Saturday night fights, is about what it was. They'd fight on the street, in the bars, and somebody was always insulting somebody else. And, uh, being from the South, and almost all the people—a lot of the people being from the South, and, see, uh, pride was the thing. It was, you know, you cannot be insulted. It hurts your pride and all. So you have to fight.

And who would you usually fight against? The guys that weren't from the South?
No, we'd fight Southerners just as well. Fight anything. In fact, I'd probably fight him quicker because he ought to have better sense [chuckles], the Southerner.

Were you ever in any grudge fights?
Grudge fights, I don't know whether you classify—how you classify grudge fight there. Uh, I really didn't hold any grudges against anybody for any period of time that I know of. We used to go to the county line and we'd get ten of us people and we'd go out and we'd try to whip up ten of the people from the other county. At the county line you'd do that. But I wouldn't call it a grudge. It was more or less just fun.

You used to do that when you were a kid, I guess?
Yes sir.

And how often would you say you did something like that?
Oh, maybe say, once a month or something like that. And everybody, say, we'd go and whip them and go to the county line down there and they'd send ten and you'd wrestle them, hit each other.

Did you get bruised up in those things?
[laughs] You're doggone right. You didn't have nobody kicking nobody or nothing like that. Just more or less hitting and shoving and wrestling.

CASE 227

Yeah, we broke into a leather factory and in the leather factory they take the leather, buck this leather down smooth. Well, they got a machine that scrapes it down real smooth and this all goes through a duct down into a big pit as big as this room. We used that one day. We used to take and play in it, you know, get on the rafters and jump into the stuff and have a ball. Well, she didn't like the idea, 'cause the day I came home, actually looked like a colored guy. It was black leather that they used and I had black leather all over me. It took about two days to wash all that stuff off. I got home and that was the last time I went down there. I got a real whipping from her [his mother], you know. But, I mean, that was the last time.

My overall impression as the volunteers talked about their adolescent years was of an outwardly happy and successful period of their lives. With few exceptions, it was also a hectic time for them. They were busy with work and play, had many friends and girlfriends, were popular in their social circles, and had little or no open conflict with their families. Particularly striking is their high activity level, the intensity with which they pursued their interests and, in many cases, their ability to pursue several activities simultaneously and to achieve a notable measure of success in each. Most of them were average to good students academically and many held prestigious positions in their schools, in athletic organizations, in the scouting movement, and in their churches. In these respects, they conformed closely to the popular and socially sanctioned image of the clean-cut, well-mannered, hard-working, athletically talented, popular All-American Boy.

The Green Berets' public image, however, was usually in sharp contrast to their private lives. Most of them were involved in petty acts of juvenile delinquency, led a sexual life which would not have met with public approval, engaged in daring and adventuresome acts for thrills, were exposed to violent death as the passive witnesses of suicides, drownings, traffic accidents, and as active hunters, and were also involved in numerous fights. In a sense, the Green Berets led double lives. They were outward conformers who were able to break easily with the standards prevailing in their communities. At the same time, they remained sensitive to social and legal sanctions, and altered undesirable behavior once they were detected and punishment became a real threat.

During the Green Berets' adolescent years, more than half their families spent little or no time together in common pursuits, and in the remaining cases few activities involved the entire family at once. Family activities were not only limited in time. In most cases, the fathers went off with their male children and the mothers with the female children. Outdoor activities, such as picnics, hiking, boating, hunting, and fishing were favorite pastimes. Some fathers and sons worked together on cars, building a garage, or house repairs. Three mothers tried to interest their sons in music, art, or literature. Nearly half the families went to church together and nearly one-quarter to the movies. However, only four families took vacations together. None of the Green Berets reported that politics, current events, social issues, international affairs or any other social, political, artistic, literary, scientific, or creative issues or subjects were discussed in their homes.

With the exceptions of three fathers and four mothers, the parents of the Green Berets gave their sons little or no personal attention. By personal attention I mean the expression of interest and concern in the form of a chat, a discussion, or a constructive argument. This form of personal contact between parents and sons is absent in nearly all the childhood and adolescent histories of the soldiers. The problematical nature of this observation lies in the fact that most of the Green Berets did not regard the absence of a close parent-child relationship as evidence of parental neglect, nor did they feel that their family relations and their personality development had necessarily suffered because of this lack.

Family Life

The absence of a profound, friendly, and casually emotional relationship between parents and children is well illustrated by two further findings. Neither positive nor negative contacts were characteristic of the Green Beret parent-child relationship during the adolescent years. This is a further indication of the routine coldness of the family life, but also seems to be somewhat paradoxical in view of the tension within the families and the fact that some parents did spend time with their sons. There appear to be two explanations for the paucity of emotional contact between the parents and sons during these years: the parent-son relationship was still characterized by formality and control, and the sons appear to have stayed away from home as much as possible.

It is interesting to note that while the father-son relationship did not change substantially between childhood and adolescence, the mother-son relationship did. The mothers began to have less and less contact with their sons and in many cases what contact they had was more likely to be unpleasant than pleasant. Many volunteers perceived their mothers' attention to be increasingly overprotective, nagging, and a threat to their masculinity, and they rebelled. The growing assertiveness which they showed toward their mothers occurred much less frequently in their relationships with their fathers. However, in the few cases and on the few occasions where the volunteers did rise against their fathers, the interaction was highly emotional, verbally aggressive, and physically violent. It should not be forgotten that most of the Green Berets deeply feared their fathers. When they did assert themselves, their assertion met with condemnation from both parents. However, whereas the mothers could no longer physically intimidate their sons as easily as before, this was less true in the case of the fathers. The fathers did not—as did the mothers—try to reestablish their subjective feeling of moral righteousness and superiority by condemning the assertive actions of their sons. Instead, the fathers were now faced with the same kind of physical assertiveness which they themselves had once practiced. Their position of authority was challenged. The outcome of such a challenge is necessarily violent.

Encounters of the kind just described occurred in only in two cases. The adolescent years of the majority of the Green Berets did not include the kind of parent-child conflicts and differences normally expected among teenagers. The overwhelming majority of the volunteers rarely allowed any feelings of anger to be released toward their parents. In fact, only four of them ever openly disagreed with their parents. If disagreement was voiced at all, it occurred almost exclusively within the context of parental discipline. Yet, when physical punishment was inflicted, the volunteers rarely offered any form of opposition. Only three of the Green Berets countered with verbal opposition and only two subjects ever hit one of their parents.* On occasion, several tried to escape a beating by running away. This natural fear reaction on the part of the sons usually spurred the parents on to more severe punishment.

The passivity of the Green Berets in their relationship with their parents is remarkable. Given the stringency, arbitrariness, and punitiveness of their parents, more filial opposition might well have been expected. Realizing that minimal opposition occurred within the context of physical discipline, it would be interesting to know whether the sons who did show opposition were still being beaten by their parents at a later age than those who showed no opposition. It would also be interesting to find out if verbal punishment met with more opposition than physical punishment.

In order to answer these questions we need to know how old the volunteers were when they were last beaten by their parents. Only three of the parents stopped beating their sons before the child's tenth birthday.** The majority was still beating them well into the early teen-age years and one-third of the parents continued beating their sons through the middle teen-age years. A few of the fathers continued the beatings longer than did the mothers but there were also four Green Berets who were never beaten by their fathers and whose mothers were still beating them during their early and middle teen-age years.

A clear statistical relationship between the age at which the Green Beret was last beaten and whether he opposed beatings is precluded by the above data. The majority of parents beat their sons into the early and middle teen-age years and only a few sons protested. More specifically, the three who verbally opposed beatings and the eight who sometimes tried to run away were still being beaten in their teen-age years. However, there are just as many who did not offer verbal opposition or try to run away who were also being beaten during that age period. The adolescents did react to verbal punishments more defiantly than to physical ones. During the middle teen-age years, several occasionally argued in defense of their positions. The majority

---

*The father of one was a chronic alcoholic who badly mistreated both the mother and the children. The other subject engaged in a test of strength with his father at age seventeen and lost.
**In one of these cases, the parents had died during their son's early childhood.

remained passive when verbally rebuked and did not voice differences of opinion either.

It is to be expected that with advancing age adolescents become increasingly sensitive to physical punishment, restrictions, and other forms of parental discipline, and may protest against this kind of parental intervention. Therefore, defiance and sensitivity can express the attempts of a youth to protect and maintain his self-esteem. However, the adolescent histories of the Green Berets contain very little opposition of any kind. Disagreements on values, ideas, standards, interests, inclinations, or passions are rarely reported. The Green Berets seem to have absorbed and accepted the entire system of parental values and standards without questioning it. This would explain their almost total lack of criticism of their parents and, as will be shown in later sections, toward other authority figures as well.

Parental Attitudes Toward Education

The parents of the volunteers held achievement standards for their sons which corresponded to the ones they had set for themselves. These parents, as most upward striving parents, wanted their children to have a better life than they themselves had. Only three Green Berets felt that their fathers set no achievement standards for them at all and only five felt that their mothers were unconcerned with their occupational and material futures. Not one parent expressed an achievement standard for a son which was lower than his or her personal standards. Not one of the parents thwarted the ambitions of their sons by belittling or ridiculing them. In fact, some of the fathers and mothers adopted a "pushy" attitude in that they nagged their sons to set high goals. Many of the mothers and fathers gave their sons encouragement and support in the pursuit of their ambitions. On the other hand, several Green Berets felt that their parents had no particular ambitions for them beyond wishing them well.

The parents' attitude toward their sons' school performance emphasized formalistic values: being a good student and not getting into trouble. Some parents admonished their children to do their homework but only one father and five mothers ever directly helped them with it. Only one father and six mothers ever went to school to talk to their sons' teachers. It is important to note that only one father and two mothers tried through discussion to stimulate their sons' interest in their school studies or, more generally, in education and knowledge.

The overwhelming majority of the Green Berets felt that their parents did a "good job" in raising them. They stated that their mothers and fathers punished them "just enough," although a few felt that they were either punished too much, especially by their mothers, or too little by their fathers. Further, the overwhelming majority reported that both of their parents were "sometimes unfair" and two that they were "usually unfair," but only three felt that a parent was "always unfair." In these cases, only mothers were regarded as having been always unfair.

In assessing the current attitudes of the volunteers toward their parents and how they were raised, I also considered such important areas as: Does the Special Forces soldier respect his parents? Is he proud of them? Does he have a friendly relationship with them? Does he feel he has learned something of value from them? Does he feel that his parents set a good example for him? The overwhelming majority of volunteers answered these questions positively. Among some soldiers there was a noticeable tendency for the fathers to be rated higher than the mothers. Only one mother was rated higher than a father. Despite generally positive attitudes toward their parents and their parents' efforts on their behalf, not a single Green Beret had a very close relationship to either one of his parents. On an emotional level their feelings toward their parents ranged from a vague feeling of closeness to complete distance.

Religious Development and Practices

The Green Berets come from families of widely varied religious practices and convictions. Many mothers emphasized and practiced their religion more vigorously than their husbands. Almost half the families attended church together with considerable regularity. In fact, church attendance and picnics were the activities which these families most often engaged in as a unit.

The Green Berets' religious practices seem to have been those of young people who have adopted the beliefs and practices of their parents without giving them much thought. Their adolescent religiosity is another aspect of the respectability and community conformity which they demonstrated in accordance with their parents' demands. This interpretation is based on several lines of evidence. Not one subject placed a deep, personal, or philosophical importance on his religious practices during those years. They did not reflect upon the meaning of religious values and practices, or report that religion had had more than a superficial influence on their standards or behavior. (The exceptions here are the few subjects who attended Catholic parochial schools; their behavior was stringently controlled by nuns and priests.) Once they left their home communities and entered the Army, most discontinued church attendance or attended church services only on rare occasions. The overwhelming majority of the Green Berets no longer considered themselves religious at the time of this study although they still believed in or at least accepted uncritically the religious dogmas of their youth. Since they left home, they had not again found themselves in situations which would precipitate a resumption of religious practice, although one soldier did find himself praying in Vietnam after a battle in which several of his companions were killed. In short, religion was no longer significant in the lives of these soldiers.

Two soldiers converted to Catholicism during their late adolescence. Here too, their motivations seem to have been superficial and formalistic. They found the ritual of the Catholic church more colorful, the music more powerful, the communion wafers more genuine, the organization of the church more exact. The differences in religious beliefs between the Protestant and Catholic churches did not particularly interest them and had little to do with their decisions to convert. The two Green Berets described their reasons for converting in these words:

CASE 212

I just didn't seem to get anything out of it . . . so I started going to the Baptist church which was closer to home. I didn't quite go along with their communion ideas of giving you a soda cracker and some Welch's grape juice. . . . So by sixteen or eighteen I started taking up Catholicism, started taking catechism classes and I became a Catholic. . . . No, I wasn't very religious at the time. . . . Well, the children in our town are basically Catholic. Now I'm not saying I became a Catholic because all the rest of the kids are Catholic. Like I said before, when I went to communion it seemed to be presented in a manner that was completely unbelievable. . . . Presenting Christ to you in this manner of a Saltine cracker with it written on the side as Saltine and Welch's grape juice or something like this.

CASE 219

When I was little my parents were Methodists. But they never went to church. My brother and I went to church every Sunday. When I was ten or twelve I got a little tired of going to that church mainly because my very best friend that I went to school with, he was an Episcopalian, and so I started going to church with him and became an altar boy. It's the most similar religion to Catholicism. I got real close with the minister and took an active part in it. Then I had a real close girlfriend in my eleventh year of high school and she was Catholic and so I started going to church with her. . . . My father was threatening me to move out of the house if I changed over and that made things worse. . . . And I was trying to go along with the beliefs of the Catholic church. . . . I took private instruction two or three nights a week for about a year. And then I convinced them [his parents] that I wanted to change before I got out of school because I was planning to go into the Army and wouldn't have time. . . . Well, when I went there I knew very little about the religion. It seemed to me the people were more dedicated to their religion. The priests impressed me because they dedicated their entire lives to being priests. The actual ceremony itself, the Mass, impressed me with its tradition.

Do you think it was the particular theological principles that attracted you to Catholicism?
No, I don't think I had this too much in mind.

Was it the fact that it was much more disciplined and much more dedicated?
Yeah.
There was more ceremony?
This is what drew me.
The ceremony was colorful, well prepared, and well executed.
This is what drew me more than the actual meaning behind the theo—how do you pronounce that word?

In High School

At several points during the interviews, the Green Berets were asked to talk about their high school experiences. Very few made more than brief and superficial statements about their teachers, classmates, schoolwork, or grades. When made, such remarks were usually in response to direct questions. Their reluctance or inability to discuss this period at first appeared paradoxical since I knew from the biographical data form that the majority of them had been quite successful in a number of extracurricular activities, and therefore presumably had also been well-known and prominent personalities within their high school communities. A possible explanation for this inconsistency emerged later and is discussed at length in Chapter 5 in connection with their motives for joining the Army. The explanation suggests that the Green Berets recall their high school years with self-recrimination because they failed to take advantage of their educational possibilities and instead rode high on the waves of social and athletic adventure and popularity.

Despite the dearth of interview information on the soldiers' social and authority relations and their ways of handling hostility and anger in high school, it was possible to gain important insights into these areas through questionnaire results. All subjects were asked to complete a questionnaire based on the work of Bandura and Walters.[1] The Green Berets' answers show a far greater similarity to Bandura and Walters' control group of nonaggressive and nondelinquent students than to their aggressive, delinquent sample. This fact deserves special attention and illustration. To compare the results from the Green Berets with those from the inductees and the war resisters, see the High School Questionnaire in the Appendix.

With only two exceptions, the Green Berets indicated good to excellent social relations with their teachers and classmates. They reported that they liked and respected "most" or "all" of their teachers and felt that "most" or "all" of their teachers were "very much interested in them and always ready to help." Further, they stated that their teachers were "rarely" or "never" unfair and that they "rarely" or "never" received unfair grades. Most of them remember that they were angry with a teacher "occasionally" and that teachers were "occasionally" angry with them. As students they did not express their anger directly; they did not swear at the teachers or strike them. Instead, they would either "bury their anger so that no one would know it "or they would try to avoid contact with the teacher." Some of the Green Berets reported that they occasionally argued with their teachers and always regretted it afterwards. During and after such an argument they felt very uncomfortable. Their discomfort was not caused by remorse but by fear. Their usual response to anger at a teacher was "to do nothing" or "swear under my breath."

Nearly all the volunteers reported that they were "very well known," "very much liked," "very popular," and had "very good relations with their classmates" in high school. There were few students whom they did not like and no students at all whom they hated. They reported that very few students disliked them and that nobody hated them. They argued "occasionally" or "frequently" with other students but tried to avoid students whom they disliked. Very few of the Green Berets reported arrogance or rudeness to other students, or challenging other students to fight. Instead they reported that they "usually tried to avoid fights but were always ready to fight." Perhaps this attitude toward fighting was responsible for the fact that many had fights in high school for which they retrospectively held themselves as much to blame as the students with whom they fought.

Not one of the Green Berets was an academically outstanding student and not one was a failing student. Their grade point averages ranged from average to good. All of them indicated when questioned that they could have earned better grades if they had tried harder. Most felt that they could have done "much better" academically and some that they would have been "excellent" students if they had taken their studies more seriously. Nearly all of them strongly regretted not having spent more time and energy on their school work during high school.

The general picture emerging from these results is of affable, sociable, and cooperative students who paid only the necessary attention to their studies while spending most of their time and energy in the pursuit of other goals. Despite the fact that they often experienced hostility and anger, both at fellow students as well as at teachers, they tried to avoid direct confrontations. They were well aware of the social boundaries for aggressive expression and, with a notable exception, were not found in the principal's or guidance counselor's office for violation of school regulations. The Green Berets did not violate social sanctions in structured situations where such behavior was prohibited or where they were under the direct supervision of authority figures. They were and are highly responsive to various expressions of social control and behave in accordance with the required standards. If these standards do not allow for the expression of anger, hostility, and violence, the Green Berets are uncomfortable and perhaps even seem docile and repressed.

The emergence of this behavioral pattern is most visible in the experiences of six Green Berets, of whom five attended Catholic parochial elementary schools. Their experiences placed them in a minority position in comparison to the other soldiers. Judging from their statements, they misbehaved more often than Green Berets who attended public schools. They also reported having been physically beaten by the nuns and priests who were their teachers. Judging from the frequency of these disciplinary acts, the teachers were not able to maintain the level of control over their students that they wished. This may reflect unreasonable standards, generally disorderly students, or simply the response style in such schools for the kind of infractions which occur in most classroom settings. For our purposes, however, it is important to emphasize several points. None of these students ever dared talk back to one of his teachers, let alone curse at or strike one—as the following quotes indicate, they were simply afraid. The took physical punishments as an expected and "normal" feature of teacher-student relations. In the one case in which a Green Beret talked of getting back at a teacher, his behavior was sneaky as well as calculated to do physical harm. He pushed a ladder out from under a nun while she was changing a light bulb. She fell and broke her leg. This pleased the soldier unendingly.

CASE 201
Yeah, the teachers slapped us around quite a bit. You didn't fool around.

CASE 208
One time I threw a ball of yarn to a kid and missed him and hit the teacher in the back of the head. So she sent us both down there. We had to paddle each other first. And then the principal gave us a swat. And the next time was for throwing snowballs—paddled that day. . . . I was late coming home for lunch, the principal told me to tell my mother why I was late. I told her I was having a snowball fight. . . . My father had given the principal instructions if I ever messed up, just bring out that paddle, 'cause he was on the teacher's side all the time. I can see he was right, because I was always wrong.

CASE 225
Was there any corporal punishment in the parochial school? I mean, if you misbehaved—the kid misbehaved, would he ever get slapped or spanked?
Definitely, there were no qualms about hitting children in the Catholic school.
Did you ever get hit?
Quite often.
By whom? Anyone in particular?
No, I think they each took a turn.
Did they hit hard or did they just hit to alert you?
Well, they hit—they hit very hard.
And where would they hit you?
Across the face, usually.

With what?
The hand. The back of the hand or the palm.

Did you ever see any of the kids get hit harder, hard enough so that they got a cut lip or something like that?
Yeah, I saw one boy—they broke, uh, someone broke all the knuckles on his hand but that—she used a ruler, put his hand on a glass paper weight and swat him. . . .

And why'd she do that?
He was cutting up in class and, uh, she was very quick tempered. She couldn't control herself very good and she'd just go sort of wild, you know.

Anything happen about that?
Yeah, she was reprimanded . . . we had a few that were pretty bad. There was one—she was the science teacher and she ran the lab and a couple of the guys were fooling around and she grabbed [one of] them and she put his head in a bucket of ammonia, but of course it didn't touch his face itself but she held him there for about, I'd say a good minute. And, well, she was so mad—the reason she was mad, they were—they were using sulfuric acid for an experiment and one of the kids threw some at another kid and just hit him on the outside of his eyeball—on the eyelid, you know, and she just went into a fury over that. And she was another one who couldn't control herself very well.

CASE 227

Could you tell me what parochial school was like?
Yeah. Strict [laughs]. And if you did something wrong there it wasn't the nun that took care, it was the priest.

And how would he take care of you?
He had my rear end—not my rear but my hands switched a couple of times for things I did wrong in school.

Do you know what he switched you with?
Well, he had like a—I wouldn't say a ruler but a big long stick, about that big, two feet in diameter, for doing this wrong, for doing that wrong.

And where would he hit you?
On the hands.

Bottom or the top?
Well, it all depended how bad you were. Put them this way, fine. Put them that way. Whatever way he wanted it. And then when I was in the seventh grade I broke this nun's leg, actually.

You broke her leg? How?
Yeah, she was standing on the ladder and I pulled the ladder out from underneath her.

On purpose?
Yeah.

Why?
Well I—well, it's just one of those things. Like I—she didn't like me and I didn't like her, and she kept me after school before that quite a few times.

Most of the Green Berets completed high school in the expected period of four years. Five voluntarily dropped out of high school before they received their diplomas, but later earned diplomas in the Army. Seven Green Berets went to college directly after their graduation from high school and stayed for periods ranging from six months to two years before dropping out. Right after terminating their formal education voluntarily, most of them joined the Army.

Extracurricular Activities and Hobbies

During their high school years, the volunteers were very active in sports, clubs, church organizations, and scouting; they also pursued such hobbies as hunting, fishing, mechanics, and building. Several of them were elected to student council and class leadership positions. Three of them worked for their school newspaper and the school yearbook. Many also had chores to do around the house, ranging from small jobs like cutting the grass to hard manual labor on the family farm. The majority had part-time jobs with which they earned pocket money. There were only three who did not actively participate in several activities during their high school years.

The capacity of the volunteers to engage in many activities and to attain a moderate to high degree of success in them appears to reflect several pronounced personality traits. They appear to have had the ability to recognize their strengths and act accordingly. They emphasized achievement and social recognition and therefore chose activities which were socially valued and hence offered prestige. They enjoyed being well-known. They placed emphasis on activities which required physical stamina and agility, and the ability to use these qualities efficiently. They selected activities which required a high degree of self-discipline. Success and prestige in these activities also provided them with a special status among their peers: they were envied and honored and had special privileges as well.

Of the twenty-five volunteers, nineteen played on one or more high school varsity teams and earned letters in the following sports: track (twelve), football (ten), basketball (nine), swimming (four), cross-country (two), baseball (two), wrestling (two), cricket (one). Participation in high school sports secured for these soldiers considerable prestige and social recognition in their peer groups as well as in their communities. It also provided them with the opportunity to exercise and challenge their bodies and to experience adventure, as well as to ventilate their aggressiveness without fear of sanction, as the following quotations indicate.

CASE 217
What was your favorite sport in high school?
Football.

Why?

Body contact. Plow over everybody else. That you would beat the other person. And when they'd come into tackle, you'd be able to hit them back harder and move them out of the way. I couldn't do any of this zig-zag fancy stuff. Just a straight line. . . . As long as you're going after the ball it's legal. Stepping on legs and breaking ribs and stuff, going for the ball. It's all legal.

CASE 218

Which sport did you like the best?
Football.

Why?

Well, it was just, uh, more I guess, more—well physical, I suppose. More hard and you'd hit people and everything. Show your cruelty in there.

The success the Green Berets had enjoyed in high school athletics ended with graduation. Only one was an outstanding athlete who could have participated in college-level athletic competition. The excitement of high school sports, the roar of the crowds, the limelight, the resulting success with girls, the uniforms, the honors, the adventure, the challenge of physical competition were all over for the others once high school was past.

The other extracurricular activity which appears nearly as often as athletics in the volunteers' responses is scouting. Many pursued their scouting activities with an intensity and success equal to their sport activities. Most moved up to high honorary positions within the Scouting Movement. Several became Life Scouts, one was a Three-Palm Eagle, and another received the coveted God and Country Award. A number went on to become Explorer and Sea Scouts. One even advanced to the position of assistant scoutmaster at the age of eighteen. There was only one soldier who neither engaged in competitive sports nor belonged to a Boy Scout troop during his adolescence. Instead, he joined the Civil Air Patrol and the National Guard prior to joining the Army. One was a member of the county rifle team and engaged in shooting competitions. Some soldiers also belonged to church-sponsored youth organizations. Two were members of 4-H Clubs.

Another noteworthy aspect of the volunteers' adolescent activities is their apparent lack of interest in solitary, artistic, intellectual, or scientifically oriented hobbies, although a few did collect stamps or butterflies for a short time. These hobbies did not seem to absorb much time and did not become a passion. One subject read many books during high school. Hunting is the only solitary hobby which appeared with considerable frequency in their histories. Several also enjoyed fishing and one went trapping. None engaged in community or civic activities or political youth groups and only one joined the Civics Club at his high school. Other hobbies mentioned by the Green Berets were weight lifting, stock car racing, chess, and debating.

The Other Side of the Green Berets: Adventure, Violence, and Juvenile Delinquency

One of the most notable findings about the volunteers generally is their consistent preference for aggressive and violent situations, some sanctioned (athletics, hunting, warfare), some bordering on the illegal (fighting, drunkenness, brawls, the seduction of minors, or indiscriminate fornication), and others clearly illegal (drunken driving, smuggling of alcoholic beverages across state lines, peddling of hashish, forceful entry, theft, vandalism). The clearly illegal examples were least frequent and disappeared after a single detection. The others persisted and were augmented by new variations after entry into the armed forces. Many of their personal historical heroes were military men, and their favorite movies tended to be spectaculars, such as *Ben Hur, Spartacus, The Silver Chalice, The Life of Christ, The Ten Commandments*, and the James Bond series. Their favorite actors included John Wayne, James Cagney, and Gary Cooper.

During middle adolescence most of the boys began to consume large quantities of alcoholic beverages. This was usually done during house and beach parties or after football games. Often, these parties ended in the intoxication of all participants and in brawls, coarseness, automobile accidents (one was a hit-and-run incident), and attempts to overpower girls. Eleven teenagers were involved in acts of juvenile delinquency and fourteen had at least several serious fights. Most were also eager to prove their daring by jumping from high places, racing cars at high speeds, challenging "tough guys" to fights, and so on.

Despite the detection and prosecution of most of their acts of juvenile delinquency none of the Green Berets was sent to a reformatory or spent more than twenty-four hours in jail. This seems to be because they were apprehended only once, and came from solid, respectable families. To me, one of the most striking aspects of these experiences is that the adolescents did not repeat these offenses. A single confrontation with the police and the courts taught them not to engage in punishable illegal acts. They did not curtail their aggressiveness or the quest for adventure and violence, but they did learn to keep their activities largely within the bounds of legality.

In most cases, the delinquency took relatively common forms. Many students play hooky from school at least once. Most children and adolescents have participated in adventuresome acts which meet with social and perhaps with legal sanctions when discovered. No crime committed by a Green Beret during his adolescent years was terribly alarming to me; there were no incidents of armed robbery, of unprovoked or premeditated assault with a deadly weapon. The delinquent and semi-delinquent acts of these adolescents have a strong flavor of the ordinary. Even the boy who smuggled liquor across the Canadian border and the one who stole a bottle of liquor did not commit rare crimes, statistically speaking. The first had the good fortune not to get caught. The second was treated more harshly than would have been the case had the bottle of liquor been a candy bar.

In my opinion, the significance of the prosecuted criminal acts does not lie in their legal status per se, but in the fact that these and similar acts permeated the adolescent years of these soldiers until they were caught. At the time, they were all aware that they were doing things which were either socially undesirable or clearly illegal. This added to the adventure inherent in the acts, but did not prevent their execution. The boys did not feel guilty either before, during, or after these acts and the subsequent prosecution. They were not remorseful in the sense of having broken with their own personal ethical standards. They did not suffer privately because of self-recriminations for immoral behavior. Their reactions were those of persons caught red-handed, of persons respectful and fearful of authority. Instead of feeling pangs of conscience, they criticized themselves for their stupidity and poor judgment. In short, they learned a legal lesson, not a moral one. Several did use the word "guilt" in connection with these acts of juvenile delinquency. But in their vocabulary, "guilt" meant fear and shame.

The physical violence of the adolescent years must be viewed differently from the juvenile delinquency. A great deal of the violence occurred in socially sanctioned situations, for example, on the football field, in the boxing ring, and while hunting. These forms of violence were encouraged and rewarded. The most frequent form of socially marginal, largely undetected, and rarely punished adolescent violence is fighting. The adolescent fights of the majority of the Green Berets exceeded in frequency and particularly in ferocity the more common pushing and wrestling matches of most young boys. The fights were conducted with vehemence and often with the goal and result of bodily harm to at least one participant. In some cases fighting became a kind of extracurricular sport activity. In other cases fighting appeared to be one expression of a massive inferiority complex. Sometimes the youths of a neighboring county were physically humbled. Sometimes all new male classmates were humbled ritualistically. For the majority of the Green Berets fighting was an easily precipitated aggressive reflex with which they attempted to secure and defend their social positions. It could be triggered by the most minimal external stimulation. Very few of the boys ever engaged in grudge fights. Their opponents were usually unknown to them previously. In this sense, most of their fights were impersonal. Of the three who participated in grudge fights, one fought to uphold his brother's honor even though he felt his brother had provoked the fight and was at fault. Some felt that the fights were forced upon them. These adolescents varied in weight from 100 pounds to well over 200 pounds. Some won most or all of the fights. Only one reported having lost most or all of his fights.

On the other hand, a few of the Green Berets reported that they had not had any serious fights during their adolescent years. They described themselves as having been unusually big and strong for their age. They felt that their size, strength, and athletic reputation guarded them from provocation and attack, and seemed to have been satisfied with their ability to intimidate others; all three said that they did not look for fights. Their physical prowess and social stature provided them with considerable self-confidence. As one of them pointed out, "Nobody bothered members of the football team." One Green Beret explained that he did not fight for fear of getting into trouble.

All the incidents of adolescent violence were saturated by a deep respect for and fear of authority and power. After every act of violence which led to a confrontation with a superior, the adolescent had regretted his behavior, and usually discontinued it. During this period, their punished violent behaviors ceased. New outlets for expressing anger were found outside the bounds of legal and social detection. This reveals the need and the willingness of the Green Berets to break with the prevailing moral standards of their homes and communities as well as to curtail such behaviors when the threat of detection and punishment arose. This behavioral pattern also reveals an acute sensitivity to and testing of the perceived boundaries of social and legal prerogatives. When official danger was imminent they reacted rapidly and with self-control.

One further aspect of adolescent exposure to violence is worthy of special attention: most of the Green Berets witnessed violent death during their childhood and adolescent years. One boy witnessed a friend being stabbed to death. Another boy watched a person burn to death in a traffic accident. Still another youth saw the corpse of a man who had committed suicide by shooting himself in the mouth, and the body of a victim of a traffic accident. Two youths watched people drown. One was following his girlfriend to a party in another car when she had an automobile accident and was killed. He also viewed the body of another girlfriend in a funeral parlor. She had committed suicide by shooting herself in the head. Others witnessed people die of heart attacks, gunshot wounds, electrocution, and in massive train and truck accidents. One saw the body of a child hit by a car. Another watched a young man fall to his death while mountain climbing. Still another came upon the body of a girl who had just been shot in the head. One adolescent assisted in a funeral parlor.

I do not know of any statistics that deal with the probability of witnessing violent death or seeing a dead body before one's twentieth birthday, but I am amazed by the frequency with which this occurred during the late childhood and adolescence of the Green Berets. I do not think that all of these exposures were purely accidental. It seems more logical to assume that the Green Berets felt drawn to this kind of violence and that death held a fascination for them.

The reactions of the boys to these incidents is very important. Two examples were quoted earlier in this chapter. In each situation, many people were crushed, dismembered, and burned to death. Despite the number of people involved and the manner in which they died, both soldiers pointed out that at the time they were not physically or emotionally upset by these tragedies. They were fascinated by the accidents and the events surrounding them. One reported experiencing some sense of aesthetic beauty in the mangled remains of a car rolling off the train tracks and landing under a bridge. The young man who had to clean up the dismembered and charred remains in another incident was not at all affected by the "mess." His only "soft" reaction came when he picked the crusted remains of something up from the back seat of the wrecked car. As it suddenly broke apart in his hands he realized that it was a human hand.

In both these cases, and in others not quoted here, the adolescents were initially onlookers. They came upon the scene after the accident, suicide, or murder had taken place, or they saw the body in the funeral parlor for the first time. As neutral onlookers, they were in no way responsible for the deaths of these people. That a person died was relatively unimportant to them. What counted was how the person died. In some professions, the capacity for clinical detachment and intellectual fascination with injury and death is a precondition for success. A surgeon, a mortician, or a soldier cannot afford to become upset by broken bones or blood. These seemingly accidental experiences show that the capacity to tolerate another person's anguish and death had been tested and proven at an early age among the majority of the Green Berets.

There may be a connection between the capacity of these young men to react with nearly complete personal detachment to the death of human beings and, among other things, their previous training in hunting. The overwhelming majority of Green Berets hunted or trapped during their childhood and adolescent years. Almost all of them owned weapons. Most of them killed mammals as well as other kinds of animals. The high frequency of hunting and killing in their backgrounds cannot be overlooked. Not everybody goes hunting and not everybody volunteers to go to war. I do not wish to claim that all hunters are destined to become future soldiers or, conversely, that nonhunters never volunteer for combat duty. However, the hunter owns and carries a weapon, stalks his prey and shoots live ammunition into a living creature with the purpose of killing it. The parallels between deer hunting and hunting Viet Cong were explicitly voiced by several of the soldiers and are quoted in Chapter 5.

From earliest childhood, the Green Berets interviewed were accustomed to being both recipients and initiators of violence. To them, violence has been and still is a clearly sanctioned and authorized part of life.

Persons of Personal Reference During Adolescence

Thus far my treatment of the Green Berets' social models had been from the perspective of a critical outsider. It is equally if not more important to examine this aspect of social learning experience through the eyes of the subjects themselves. Toward the end of the interviews I asked each subject, "Which people do you feel had an influence on you when you were growing up? Looking back over your entire life, which people do you think have influenced you in becoming what you are today?" This question was then broken down into different life periods. I also asked the interviewee to describe the person who influenced him and to explain in what way he felt he had been influenced. I call persons so named Persons of Personal Reference.

A few theoretical remarks are necessary before presenting the Green Berets' answers. Obviously, my attempt to isolate the social models of the Green Berets' development years lacks the methodological rigor of laboratory experiments. Data gathered in interviews and questionnaires were retrospective, therefore it is not possible to make specific statements as to the exact determinants of imitative learning. At best we can only gain a broader understanding of the kinds of social models whose presence was consciously recorded by the Green Berets. This undoubtedly includes only a small segment of the total population of social models to which they were exposed, but it is a highly salient segment. Their characteristics, however partially and imperfectly recalled, reveal key insights into the volunteers' dominant perceptual and cognitive sets, may allow for generalizations as to how these sets emerged, and may also allow for generalizations as to the probable composition of that unrecalled and far larger group of social models. It is also important to point out that under particular circumstances people deny the influence of social models on their own behavior.[2] Since we do not yet have a set of principles to explain when the influence of which models will be both registered and voiced, one recourse is for the researcher to attempt to extrapolate modeling effects from his own observations combined with those of the people he is studying. It is to distinguish clearly between these perspectives that the social models described here are called Persons of Personal Reference.

The answers of the volunteers are among the most interesting aspects of their statements. The most concise formulation of their feelings on this matter might be that people played an unimportant and peripheral role in their lives. Although they led active social lives and knew many people, they did not mention having had intellectual or emotional ties to anyone. They seemed to perceive themselves as always having been alone in the world. A few Green Berets answered the question, "Which people do you feel had an influence on you while you were growing up?" with the word "Nobody." Most of them were surprised at the question and unsure of how to answer it. Some named friends, teachers, ministers, and other people they knew while they were growing up but were unable to say how these people influenced them or to describe what these people were like. When they were asked what characteristics of the persons of reference they found attractive and what drew them to these persons, the most frequent answers are, "We hung around together" or "We got along." They seem to be men who simply did not have strong ties to anyone during their developmental years.

Again a strongly pronounced paradox is evident in the backgrounds of the volunteers. In reviewing their childhood and adolescent years, there is very little material to suggest that the Green Berets were in any way isolated in their social relations. They belonged to different kinds of clubs and organizations, they reported having been well known, having had many friends, and having spent a good deal or most of their free time with other people. With the exception of hunting, they did not pursue solitary hobbies, and they were usually accompanied by their fathers, relatives, or friends when hunting. Most of them went to church regularly and knew their priests and pastors. They had coaches, scoutmasters, teachers, buddies, and girlfriends. Why then did most of the Green Berets indicate that they essentially knew nobody who influenced them while they were growing up? And when they did mention persons of reference, why did they have such difficulty in articulating how they were influenced?

I think these questions have several answers. Most of the soldiers told me that I was the first person who had taken such a deep interest in them. All of them told me that I asked them questions about things they had never thought about before. For these reasons it is understandable that they were psychologically unprepared for the interviews and often did not know what to say. I am not suggesting that they were afraid to say things which might discredit them in my eyes. Indeed, in this respect, I think they were unusually honest in their reports and did their best to answer my questions. However, very often they did not understand the questions. This was not because of limited intelligence; when I asked them questions about their feelings, emotions, and the nature of their relationships to other people, they all showed varying degrees of helplessness. The reason for this seemed to be that the Green Berets were largely unfamiliar with these regions of experience. Their vocabulary for these themes was limited. They had not had practice in this kind of communication. From the time of their earliest childhood memories, there is a record of near total abandonment of their inner lives. It seems as though no one has ever been interested in their feelings. Similarly, they have rarely been interested in the feelings of others. Their relations with most people have been emotionally superficial and utilitarian. This becomes most apparent in their sexual lives.

The few positive remarks made by the Green Berets about persons of reference are most revealing. Parents were named most often by nearly all the Green Berets as the key people in their lives. Grandparents, especially paternal grandmothers, were also named very often. The fascinating aspect of the paternal grandmothers is that they were nearly the only people mentioned by the Green Berets who ever showed them kindness and understanding.

CASE 202

Grandma has a kind word for everybody.

CASE 213

My grandmother on my father's side who I adore so much because she's always been so kind and generous. She's always had all good intentions.

CASE 224

She was a real nice woman. I would have liked to stay with her all the time.

CASE 225

I talked to my grandmother.

A few Green Berets made fleeting references to other people who gave them personal attention or possessed soothing and mellowing qualities. There was a "quiet, nice, old maid lady who gave advice," a "quiet grandfather," an "eighth-grade teacher who played chess with the students during lunch hour," a "man in town who was everybody's friend," a "minister and his wife. . . . They were good companions on picnics. . . . We went ice-skating together. His wife was very pretty and broad-minded. They did everything together as a family," and "a friend of mine's father. He was always a gentleman. Quiet and reserved. Knew what he was talking about. He did things with his son which my father didn't."

These quotations show that some of the volunteers are aware of what they missed while growing up, that they did have fleeting exposures to gentleness and warmth which remained in their memories. The Special Forces soldiers also recalled rare moments of warmth and understanding with their parents. They remembered when someone took the time to talk to them. The memories are described in very few words. I think this is partly because there is not much one can say about experiences of such brevity, and partly because the Green Berets do not talk about pain.

There are several other statements about persons of reference which are different from and originally longer than the preceding ones. There is a "college friend who was a black belt in karate," a "track coach who squeezed everything out of me when I thought I couldn't do any more," an "uncle who taught me to fight," a "college friend who wanted to be a jungle killer and convinced me to join the Special Forces," a "friend who taught me responsibility . . . and is now in jail on forgery," and a "scout master who helped guide me to do the right things when I had fallen away from Boy Scout ways. He helped me stick with the Boy Scouts and go camping and stuff. You know, things that are healthy and good for boys."

I was very much puzzled for some time by what seemed to be an unusually blatant contradiction in the statements of the war volunteers. They said that they had ideal parents and teachers and were very successful in their home communities. Yet they were leading the rootless life of professional soldiers and did not feel homesick. How were they able to sever most of their ties with their families and home communities without any signs of emotional conflict? I believe that part of the answer to this is that they really did not feel that their parents or teachers were ideal. Beneath the facade of their praise was deep resentment, bitterness, and unhappiness. The outward success of their high school years was a result of a game they felt compelled to play. Underneath they were filled with anger and contempt which they did not express directly. "It is not smart to express anger. . . . I buried my anger so no one would know. . . . I clenched my fist in anger. . . . My mother beat me to the ground but I wouldn't cry. . . . My father was big, hairy and mean. You didn't mess around." And so on. The people who were nice to them were peripheral figures in their lives. They did not establish close and enduring relationships with anyone.

THE WAR RESISTERS

During adolescence, the war resisters entered a period of intense and often painful self-discovery. Feelings of obligation both to themselves and to the world around them developed, along with the crystallization of a firm sense of independence, individuality, and self-importance. Throughout this period, but particularly during the period preceding their antiwar activity, an intensifying personal struggle ensued in which they attempted to harmonize their beliefs with their actions. This process is marked by repeated acts of conscience, self-criticism, and self-doubt, and intense intellectual and emotional turmoil which in several cases was accompanied by neurotic anxiety and conflict. This then culminated in the decision to refuse military service.

The intellectual and emotional growth of the resisters during their adolescent years was spurred in part by particular experiences which placed them in exceptional positions with regard to their peers. By chance, interest, or achievement each war resister became a member of an academic, cultural, athletic, political, religious, or racial minority, and in most cases two or more minorities simultaneously. These events paralleled an intensifying estrangement from traditional sources of religious, moral, social, and political authority and the institutional structures which represented them. The only formal institutions with which most of the teenagers maintained a relatively although not always unproblematic and harmonious relationship were their own families. Their questioning, criticism, and protest, particularly in the later teenage years, and the resulting estrangement from many American institutional structures, ended neither in personal alienation nor in radical political affiliations. A few resisters found a reconciliation with reformed concepts of their churches and became strongly religious. Others affiliated themselves with government- and community-sponsored social welfare institutions. Many devoted their energies to peace groups, while a few continued their education in preparation for an academic career. Despite the heterogeneity of their activities and their sometimes antithetical views on particular institutions and issues, all of the war resisters gradually gleaned a similar set of fundamental ethical concepts from their homes, schools, churches, and the American political heritage and fused these into a relatively simple and obvious code of personal conduct from which they have refused to deviate. Nonviolence, the equal worth of each human being, and the responsibility of each citizen to speak up for his beliefs were the cornerstones of this code.

Had the United States not been involved in Vietnam and had the political climate in the United States been different, it is doubtful that more than a handful of the war resisters would have taken such an explicit antiwar stand. In all but one case it is also questionable whether these men would have opposed military service had they themselves not been faced with conscription. Their adolescent and young adult years were passed in a particular moral-political climate which made protest both possible and relevant. The heated sociopolitical debate and upheaval began and actualized at a time when most of them were still preoccupied with hobbies, schoolwork, and girls. I do not feel that they would have become war resisters had circumstances not forced a decision upon them.

It must be emphasized that the decision they made was not a necessary outgrowth of the sociopolitical conditions of their time. Millions of young Americans reacted differently—they volunteered for the armed forces, allowed themselves to be drafted, left the country, or avoided and evaded the draft in a number of other ways. Furthermore, the American armed forces contained a substantial percentage of soldiers who were not in agreement with the American involvement in Vietnam and who had a distaste for violence. These observations suggest that the rejection of violence and coercion in one's personal relations and in a given international conflict does not preclude cooperation, support, condonement, or submission to their institutionalized employment in general or in that very same international conflict. Obviously, other elements and conditions must be operative to enable a person to give consistent public expression to private sentiment.

Many resisters explained that their decision to refuse induction was attributable to the temperamental qualities of nonviolence and independence which they had possessed since childhood. In other cases I offered this interpretation. Yet in order for these qualities to continue to develop into an attitude and behavioral set capable of actually generating and perpetuating these actions considerable further supportive experience was required. It is in this perspective that the adolescent years gain their special importance.

Family Relations During Adolescence

CASE 103

And I told my mother, "All these years you've been coming on as though you love me . . . you're sacrificing yourself for me but actually . . . you want to sacrifice for me. I mean, that's the kind of person you are that gets pleasure from doing." . . . But, you know, I wasn't going to change my living patterns for her and any time she really became excited I said, "What you really love is, uh, the person you want me to be . . . but I'm not prepared to do it. What you should love is the real me, the real me being long-haired and radical." That would always get her because there was no argument to that.

CASE 115

Again in school I wasn't doing poorly but I wanted to do better. The bickering in my house sort of built up tremendous pressure. And then one night there was just some silly old argument over something and all along, ever since I was small, I never said anything but just kept quiet and then this time I just ran out of the room and started screaming and jumping up and down, "Shut up, shut up!" and started crying and laughing intermittently. . . . They got very quiet. They didn't know how to deal with me. My mother suggested that I go outside for a while and my father was completely upset and in a dither. He didn't know what the heck is this. So then my mother suggested that I go outside and I did. And I ran for about three or four miles and then I came home and, uh, [chuckles] I sat down and I felt very awkward and very uncomfortable . . . and I got something to eat and then my father sat down. "We want to understand what you did that for. What's the problem?" And they sort of like kicked it off again. . . . Then my mother suggested that maybe, uh, I [should] go away from the house for a while. She wanted to come with me. But I decided I would go away on my own but I went with my cousin. We went down to Florida by bus and he stayed for a week and I stayed for about a month or so, a month and a half, and I got a job at the race track pretty quickly.

CASE 116

Toward the very end I became much, much more interested in my father's earlier history and his political stuff and I think we became—we got closer, you know. And had he lived, you know, he would have had very different opinions than me, but I would have been much more interested in his early experiences and stuff. That was just beginning to develop. . . . And I remember after he was around more [father was ill and at home] he was very warm and affectionate . . . and we were just beginning a rapprochement. . . . And then he died that summer while I was in the South.

CASE 117

After my father moved out my mother just kind of went freaky . . . and my mother kind of resented the fact that we wanted to move out and she would scream and yell at home, "Go live with your father and Mrs. ——!" . . . The woman used to call up all the time and I'd listen in on the conversation and she'd call my mother a "worthless wench" and [say] "how could Hitler have missed you" . . . I mean, he [the father] carried out this affair in a way that it was very sloppy and messy when, you know, it could have been done better. . . . There used to be big fights between my mother and father . . . and I called up my father and said, "What the fuck is going on?" He tried to explain to me that, you know, sometimes people get upset and that they say things they don't mean. I kind of agreed with him but it still hurt me and it still bothers me. . . . Well, for about the next three months that's about all we heard in my house was the Nazi bedding down with my father. . . . My mother was very upset. . . . We used to get phone calls at three o'clock in the morning. But she's calming down . . .

CASE 128

I remember talking more with my father, really getting some idea of what he thought and felt. And this is when we talked about the war. We talked about politics. We're able to talk to each other quite frankly now. You know, it doesn't really matter what the subject is because he knows where I stand politically. In fact he's in agreement with me in a lot of things. . . . Whenever I would voice an opinion that my father would disagree with, he would say, "Well, I don't agree with that," and he would say, "Now this is why I don't agree with it." But he never, you know, he wouldn't force it upon me and say, well look, you know, this is the thing you ought to believe.

The resisters' parents had initiated most family life during childhood, but the opposite pattern emerged during adolescence. Most of the parents maintained an interested and benevolent attitude towards their sons' development. Most rarely interfered with their sons' activities. It was the sons who brought their experiences home, asked for help and counsel, raised new questions, and in so doing demanded that their parents find adequate responses. Some parents responded with patience, knowledge, understanding, and flexibility, thereby contributing crucially to the continuing harmony and closeness of their relationship with their sons. This observation is confirmed by the conflict that occurred in other cases when parents responded with intolerance, anger, material coercion, or hysteria to their sons' nonconformity. And as the previous quotations show, a few families were seriously disrupted by marital problems.

Several war resisters who had not had a close relationship with their fathers during childhood began to seek their counsel more during adolescence. The quiet, rational fathers gained new value in their sons' eyes because of their knowledge and analytical minds. The sons found them interesting, astute people with whom they could engage in fruitful discussion. Several outgrew their mothers intellectually and came to perceive them as naive and ill informed, particularly on academic and political issues. Despite the reconciliation between several fathers and sons and the growing intellectual distance between a few mothers and sons, most of the teenagers continued to consult their mothers more often on intimate, emotional matters. This can be attributed to the mothers' success in establishing a close emotional relationship with their sons during childhood.

The resisters' fathers tended to be more worldly people with broader interests than the mothers, and this too added to their ability to enjoy a stronger intellectual kinship with their sons during adolescence. Also, their more circumscribed position in the home during the resisters' childhoods often enabled them to make a relatively unproblematical transition from a father-child to a more equal father-son relationship. In a few cases the war resisters explained that their fathers' earlier remoteness had made them very curious and had initially prompted them to investigate their thoughts and feelings. The mothers generally found it more difficult to go beyond the mother-child pattern that had existed for so many years. Nevertheless, there were few cases in which resisters became estranged from either of their parents during adolescence.

Five families experienced prolonged conflict during this time. In two cases this stemmed from disharmony between the parents, and in three cases it seems to have been localized in value and personality conflicts between the parents and their nonconforming sons. These disputes severely strained family relations and resulted in considerable bitterness. Three war resisters succeeded in reestablishing lines of communication with their parents and felt that most of the strain and tension had been eliminated. At the time of our talks, the others were still estranged from their parents and had only minimal contact with them.

Religious Development

CASE 101

My main objection to the concept of organized religion, uh, is this whole thing of—you sign up, you join, you take your thing and then you sort of—I wouldn't say you sold out, but you relinquish, uh, to your bishops, to your Mother Superior, to your abbess, to your Pope or whatever, and you accept the framework they give you. Obedience and that sort of thing to their dogma, their particular whim. Well, I object to that.

CASE 123

I thought the church should stop looking so much to the structure and to the money that it gets and look more to the individual and his relationship to God. How can they practice or preach on one hand that to kill is wrong and on the other send a priest or a cardinal out and bless a bunch of troops before they go kill? . . . I thought this was terrible. You just don't do this. And, uh, I guess this is the point where I started to realize that not only the church is wrong but that the government was wrong. It was wrong for the government to be tied up in a situation where they're killing and wrong for the church not to say anything against it . . . and that it might be time to start doing something about both of them. . . . And my wife said that if there's something that you're opposed to you don't just sit back but you stand up and actively . . . protest it.

CASE 128

And I went into kindergarten. And I can remember being very scared the first day, because I was going into something I knew nothing about. It was sort of a dark gloomy building with these dark gloomy nuns in their black habits. The whole setting seemed to be black. I think the biggest memory for those years in school was the schoolroom, because it was such a very, very strange contrast to my life at home. The nuns had pretty much free reign as far as corporal punishment was concerned. I can remember them laying into people quite often with pointers or rulers. And there were kids in school who seemed to be encouraged by this. People who were bullies anyway. Maybe they were just excited by the whole thing. . . . Yeah, there were a couple of pretty vicious people there. And the nuns never seemed to take too much interest in what was being done. I can remember there was one kid in particular who was a constant scapegoat. And, uh, I remember one day they took him off into the bushes and beat the hell out of him. . . . The best description that I can think of is medieval. Uh, the nuns never seemed to be—with a couple of exceptions— never seemed to be very concerned about what you learned, as long as you learned your catechism and followed the straight and narrow path. And I think the only reason I avoided serious trouble was because sometimes I was taunted for being a bookworm. . . . I remember a particular nun one day taking a child and beating her head against the blackboard. And the people, the bulk of the people who sent their children to these schools had seemed to accept this very matter-of-factly. You know, this was all part of a good, average Catholic upbringing. And it always disturbed me. What the hell is the point of all this? We're not learning anything. The day I graduated from elementary school I was really happy because I knew that I was going to public school. . . . You know, I'm willing to admit that there's certain things that I am intolerant about. I'm intolerant as far as the Catholic Church is concerned, because I think with their [condemnation of.e birth control they're probably one of the most destructive forces in existence.

CASE 103

I dislike making categorical statements, so I usually put myself down as agnostic. . . . An atheist denies the slightest, you know, even theoretical possibility of

God existing and I wouldn't want to go that far. . . . Agnostic is probably pretty good because it does suggest a measure of indifference in this sort of question which I really feel. I used to be more concerned with it but there are more important problems to worry about than that.

CASE 107

Well, I don't believe in organized religion but I feel I'm very religious as far—I feel I've developed my own sense of values and I'm religious in the way that I live by them like I try to live by them. Well, I believe all religions teach the same thing, no matter what they are. . . . You know, it's the same old story. When you're young they teach you these things, values whatever, and as you get older they tell you don't live by them or you're going to get hurt. And I'm just trying to live by them.

All the war resisters experienced long periods of deep religious preoccupation, were strongly influenced by religious thought, and reached the conclusion that the religious institutions in which they were reared were badly in need of a humanizing reformation. The course of their religious questioning during adolescence was strongly influenced by the religious context in which they had been raised. This in turn was often connected with their denominational background and the conformistic religious pressures which had been exercised upon them.

As a group, the six resisters brought up within the Catholic tradition experienced broader and more consistent formal religious training than those of Protestant or Jewish background. They also reacted more sharply and critically to their church; only two maintained a Catholic identification. Whereas all of the resisters expressed differing degrees of skepticism toward organized religious institutions, intense hostility, bitterness, disillusionment, and condemnations were only expressed by those of Catholic background.

The roots of this estrangement had both common and individual aspects. Three boys attended Catholic parochial schools where they were appalled by the disciplinary practices employed by the nuns and priests, the doctrinaire treatment of church tenets, and the neglect of academic subjects. The others experienced similar reactions to their Sunday school training and priests. Three boys came from interconfessional marriages and had been exposed to the religious practices of Protestant and Jewish relatives. This broadened their religious perspectives and engendered interest and tolerance for other religious traditions.* In high school and particularly in college, all of these boys established close friendships with classmates of other faiths in which discussions of religious subjects often played a central role. The only two Catholic war resisters who did not reject Catholic theology found that this

*The three boys who were sent to Catholic elementary schools came from interconfessional homes. The mother of one was Episcopalian, the other Jewish. Neither woman was religious. In the third family the father was a nonpracticing Baptist.

contact had led to a deepening of their devotion to fundamental Christian and Catholic beliefs. However, they also rejected the institutionalized form of the Catholic Church.

Many Protestant—but even more Jewish—war resisters reported fewer disputes with the organizational structure and theological foundations of their faiths. But at the same time, only three of the Protestant war resisters still took an active interest in their churches. One had entered the Lutheran ministry, a second experienced a revelatory conversion and decided to become a minister after his release from jail. The third's interest in the Unitarian Fellowship paralleled the growth of his father's involvement with this movement. Another resister, also of Lutheran background, majored in religion in college but did not identify himself with any particular Christian denomination. Two other resisters came from an interconfessional family, with a Protestant father and a Jewish mother; they identified themselves as Protestants but their major interests were in Oriental religions and yoga.

Nearly all of the war resisters with Protestant and Jewish backgrounds had received nominal religious instruction during childhood at afternoon or Sunday schools. Their attitude toward this religious training was expressed by one who said, "My mother thought that it was good that I was understanding the Jewish heritage when in fact I was learning to duck spitballs at times." Two had attended yeshivas for several years in which their academic studies had been divided between Jewish cultural heritage (Hebrew language and literature, Jewish history) and regular academic subjects. One maintained a strong Jewish ethnic identification while continuing with his engineering studies. The other chose not to attend college and instead devoted his energies to the peace movement. He no longer found any significance in his cultural training and said that he regretted not having learned Spanish since there were more Spanish-speaking than Hebrew- or Yiddish-speaking people with whom he would like to be able to converse.

Few resisters with Protestant and Jewish backgrounds came from strongly religious homes, but most of their parents had definite religious-cultural identification and maintained a few traditions in their homes, attending religious services only on special holidays. The sons stopped attending church and synagogue services after confirmation and Bar Mitzvah, and gave relatively little thought to religious questions, especially religious doctrines, until later adolescence. None felt that they had become atheists but all reported having outgrown the debate over the existence of God, turning instead to the moral principles by which they wished to conduct themselves.

One major difference emerged between the overall religious outlooks of the Protestant and Jewish war resisters. While both groups expressed a fundamental concern with the unifying ethical precepts of all faiths, the Protestants more frequently maintained a religious Christian identification. The resisters of Jewish background did not appear to be concerned with denomina-

tional questions. They expressed affinities of varying strengths for ethnic and
cultural aspects of Judaism while identifying themselves with general humanistic values.

High School Experiences

CASE 104

My brother and I started a discussion club . . . [in] which we showed things
like human reproduction, planned parenthood, and some medical films and stuff.
And this was beginning to come slightly under fire from the school administration. . . . We also objected to things like the Army assembly, showing armed
forces films, the Lord's Prayer, Pledge of Allegiance, this sort of stuff. But nothing
really happened until this very maladjusted friend of mine . . . was suspended
unendingly for refusing to wear a belt on pants that didn't require a belt. He
couldn't see it. And I, I couldn't understand it. I was still very straight-laced,
you know. "Why the heck shouldn't he wear a belt for Pete's sake?" You know,
why cause trouble over that. But he wrote a letter attacking this English professor's old lady who sucked her teeth all the time. She had false teeth, sort of
the laughing stock of the whole school, but was head of the senior class. And
he ran it off on the business school's machines with the help of all the student
secretaries in there and passed it out. And among other things it addressed the
teacher by her first name, attacked her in a logical fashion rather than a deferen-
tial one and, you know, the most horrible thing he could have done was to
address her by her first name, you know. This brought the roof down. They
kept careful watch on the mimeograph machines after that, so we, you know,
in order to try and tone him down and get it to where we might get some
sort of discussion going. He was a radical and I was a liberal and I wanted
to see something happen, but he was turning off a whole pile of people who
wouldn't have been if he had done it in their style. So I took his stuff home
and we went over it . . . and I exerted some sort of editorial policy on what
he was writing but left it with its original flavor and ran it off on a ditto machine
that Dad had and passed them out at school again. We passed out about three
of these things . . . and the whole school went up in arms. Camps divided immediately, student council collapsed, there were all sorts of discussion about what
sort of student council there ought to be. And we got the reputations for being
villians, trying to destroy the school, putting a black mark on the record of
the senior class. And all the kids from across the track came over to our side.
The maladjusted people and all my academic friends went over to the other
side and this was an abrupt change from everything that happened. Nothing
ever really developed in terms of long-lasting alliances 'cause it was almost
the end of that school year. But it was the beginning of things, this was '64,
summer of '64 which was the beginning of things happening in this country.
The real change, the beginning, you could see it, see it turning up.

CASE 112

My years of growing, I guess, in high school there was that feeling of desperation,
of being muffled, being squelched, uh, the feeling was such that the high school

had a minimal amount of knowledge to offer me, that I wasn't getting anything out of the high school. I thought that in many subjects I was discovering more on my own through self-education, through reading, than I was in high school. Besides, I clashed several times with authorities. I found myself having to either do what I thought was ridiculous or pay the consequences. . . . I was finding myself, compromising myself perhaps in everyday life and walking through the halls of that institution . . . as far as disciplining myself to obey the authorities that existed . . . having demands being put upon me which I thought were foolish, everything from saluting the flag to not perhaps expressing my true thoughts at times, to being marched down to a military assembly, to pledge allegiance to the flag . . . I saw no purpose for it. I thought it was ridiculous. Besides not believing in what I was saying I saw no practical purpose for it. It didn't even help to make people patriotic and that was its purpose. I clashed on that and I didn't stand up and I didn't salute. And I had a session with the principal and the dean. And they entirely agreed with me, "When we went to high school we had none of this and we didn't miss anything." . . . They said that the law had been passed in a time of hysteria during the McCarthy era and they agreed with me. It served no purpose but they were enforcing it because that was the law and they weren't going to lose their jobs. We worked up the compromise that I would have to stand up but I wouldn't have to salute or pledge and that's what I took for the next two and a half years. . . . So actually I was developing more than a political outlook. I was developing an attitude towards most of the people that I came into contact with in everyday life. I was beginning to demand that there be some other reason for their ruling over me than simply that they have the might to do it. And I eventually found by my eleventh year, I guess, that there are many other people who felt precisely as I did. And so to that extent it was a comfortable position to know that I wasn't alone. But to know that there wasn't anything that I could do was frustrating.

CASE 128

There were a couple of kids there in tenth grade who became involved in the Student Peace Union. It was in 1961-62. They explained to me the aims of the group: nuclear disarmament and so forth. And I became really interested. So we formed sort of an informal chapter . . . in the high school. And there were about seven or eight members, and we would talk with other people who were curious about it, and . . . wore the nuclear disarmament peace button. We decided to pass out the literature . . . and about the middle of my sophomore year all hell broke loose because some of the local—I should call them townies or the bullies or the whatever. I think the expression at the time was "rocks." I seem to recall that they were very unhappy with this whole thing. In 1949, there had been a very serious riot at a [nearby] concert [by] Paul Robeson. And the American Legion had come up and had literally started a riot. They had started to stone people who were attending the concert. . . . People started leaving in a mad rush . . . and all their supporters just lined up down the road for several miles. And they stoned cars and buses. A number of people were very seriously injured. I don't think any criminal charges ever were pressed against any of the people who started the thing. But since that time, . . . [the town] had been pretty badly divided. And the American Legion had been pretty popular among the Italians and the Irish Catholics. Anyway, as these kids decided, well, we don't really like what you are doing, you're a bunch of Communists. So they started to push us around. I remember they grabbed the literature sometimes and ripped it up. And I remember they tore off my button and they tore off buttons of several other peoples' jackets. And it started to get pretty serious. We were getting pushed around and the school administration was taking no interest in it. Really. So three of us went down to the principal and we said, look, you know, we're being pushed around. We're not doing anything. We're wearing a button and we're passing out literature people ask us for. And you're just sitting by and doing nothing. And he was a very wish-washy character . . . and we were forbidden to wear the buttons or distribute any of the literature on school grounds. And nothing was ever done to the people who had started the trouble, who had pushed us around. I don't know, maybe that was my first radicalizing experience. Very likely. But I was really disgusted with the principal. I remember this one American Legion member who wrote a letter to the local newspaper during the whole hassle. And he was not a very bright man . . . but he wrote this letter which, in essence, accused us all of being Communists. And I remember particularly one phrase he used: "Red Fascists." It was the first thing that stopped me when I read his letter. So I wrote a letter in reply and pointed out what we were doing and what we believed in. And, I guess, from then on I gained the dislike of the American Legion and this one individual in particular. But a good number of the townspeople supported us . . . a number of people in general who just felt that we had done nothing wrong or had done nothing offensive.

Fights

CASE 100

I don't remember ever being beaten up except one time in high school in gym when I was helping a guy do some exercise and some other guys were bothering him so he couldn't do his exercises. And I told them, "Why don't you leave him alone?" And they were in this other guy's class and not mine. And when I got into the shower they grabbed me and punched me in the stomach and told me not to interfere in the affairs of their class. . . . And I got harassed for a lot of my political beliefs and people, the arch-conservative Goldwaterites pushed me in the hall. . . . I took Ghandi's stand here that nonviolence isn't for chickens.

CASE 107

When I first went out for football, I was very young. There was a lot of adventure and glory in it. Well, I sort of came into more maturity as I got older. And you're not vicious when you play football. I'm not. I played offense. . . . Yeah, I always played quarterback and it wasn't a vicious type of thing at all, especially from my standpoint. . . . Oh, I got hit and I hit people plenty, but contact is a different thing. You're not trying to kill anybody. I mean, you're not trying to destroy. . . . I'm afraid to punch somebody in the face 'cause I'm afraid I'm going to hurt them, break a bone or whatever. I can take care of myself . . . I guess, I'm nonviolent. I've never hit anybody in the face. Like with my parents. I argue with them strongly but when I get to the point where I might get fresh I'll walk away.

CASE 109

There may have been a couple of isolated times when I'd say I was picked on. I can't remember ever aggressively pouncing upon somebody but once. That was when I was fourteen. And there was just this one fellow whom I, you know, just really couldn't stand. And he made one point about how he wanted to fight with me and that's the one point I can remember in my life when I had absolutely blindly lost my temper. . . . We were separated. I mean, there was no physical violence. . . . Well, we grabbed at each other. I don't think we really hit each other. It was in a kind of struggling and wrestling kind of way. . . . I regretted it. Although I don't think I thought too much about it directly afterwards. When I think back a little bit now, whenever it's recalled, I regret it because I don't think there was any purpose to it.

CASE 111

Yeah, I remember a couple. A big boy was hitting this kid who had [had] polio who was okay now and could walk but he was about eighty-five pounds and he was very short. And this guy was a pretty big guy, so I picked up a medicine ball and threw it and hit him right in the stomach. And he came after me and swung at me and I ducked and I came up with an undercut, whatever you call it, and hit the guy right in the jaw and floored him.

Balance in intellectual and social growth is clearly apparent in the breadth of the war resisters' extracurricular activities during their high school years. Through athletic and academic achievement, scientific, musical, artistic, and literary creativity, and unusual interests and talents, nearly every war resister secured a position of distinction among his peers. Several came into conflict with teachers, administration officials, community organizations, and other students because of their social, moral, and political views. Most had regular duties to perform at home and the majority also held part-time jobs with which they earned their pocket money and began to save for their college education.

Nineteen of the twenty-five resisters played one or more varsity sports in high school and two were voted "outstanding athlete" in their high schools. Fifteen held such honorary positions as president or vice-president of the student council or junior or senior class, captain of athletic teams, editor of school newspaper, literary magazine, or yearbook, member of academic honor societies, and leadership status in innumerable clubs and organizations. One was elected to the student court. Eleven wrote for school publications, five organized discussion forums, and four debated.

In addition to their official high school activities every resister pursued an intellectual, manual, athletic, or creative solitary hobby, such as reading, creative writing, poetry, musical composition, folk singing, painting, bridge, carpentry, mechanics, electronics, ham radio, photography, astronomy, tropical fish, zoology, biology, veterinary medicine, nature hunting, chess, stamp and coin collection, old books, acting, crabbing, fishing, hiking, and walking. All but one of the resisters who did not participate in high school athletics played tennis and baseball, swam, sailed, or skied for relaxation.

None of the war resisters had ever hunted or owned a gun. Several had kept a menagerie of small animals. Of the six who participated in scouting, two became Eagle Scouts, one a Star Scout, and two were elected to the "Order of the Arrow." Twelve also participated in civic organizations sponsored by their communities. The two resisters who were least active in high school had had special interests. One had spent all his spare time as a riding instructor, caring for horses and working in stables or at race tracks. The other had danced for church groups and sung in a church choir during his childhood. He later performed on Broadway for several seasons in "The Sound of Music."

I do not feel that the significance of the resisters' adolescent activities lies in their achievement per se, nor did I have the feeling while talking to them that they were anxious to boast about those years or were still sentimentally attached to them. They stood apart because of their seriousness and, in most cases, their innocence. The cynicism of high school politicians and the status orientation of "college prep" students seem to have been equally foreign to them. Underlying their actions was an implicit understanding that each individual was responsible for developing his talents and interests. They regarded awards, honors, and other acknowledgments as confirmations of achievements, not as goals. I see the basic significance of the resisters' high school accomplishments in the way they themselves perceived them. They took advantage of the opportunity their high schools offered them to realize their potentials. Individualism took precedence over conformism. Yet their individualism was neither rugged nor antisocial. By exploring and developing their own personalities many of them seem to have come to a clearer understanding of themselves as well as of their obligation to others and society at large.

Their individualism found a less pleasant expression n conflicts over principles, politics, and policies with students, teachers, and community groups. Five helped organize discussion forums in their high schools. This activity resulted in heated and socially fragmentizing debate within the entire school and often overflowed into the community.* Several other resisters came into similar though more circumscribed conflicts while opposing con-

*The antiwar stand of these teenagers emerged at the relatively earliest age. Four of these five also came from the politically most active family backgrounds. The influence of the fathers' political sentiments on the sons' behavior was most apparent in these cases. One evaluated this influence most concisely when he said, "My father was out protesting against the war while I was still too lazy to get out of bed."

formistic pressures. By marking them as dissenters and subjecting them to threats, assault, and ostracism, these events left a deep impression on the teenagers.

Many of the war resisters took points of view equally unpopular with their friends. One teenager quit a social fraternity because his proposal to "adopt a poor family for Christmas" with extra raffle funds was met with ridicule and laughter. The other boys wanted to use the money to throw a party and get drunk. Another broke off friendships with several members of his high school football team because they made a practice of yelling "Nigger" out of the window of their car while speeding through black neighborhoods. Many voiced critical opinions during social studies and history classes and were harassed by students for their views. One teenager elected to attend a military prep school because of its academic reputation. He said, "I realized after about two days of being there and wearing the uniform that I had made a bad mistake because it was very militaristic and very authoritarian. . . . I had the most demerits of anybody in the class. . . . I detested and despised drill. They had a forty-minute drill every day. Imagine this, having kids march forty minutes a day, carrying guns, out often in the cold. It's a horrible thing. . . . Of course, they had excellent programs of all kinds, you know, excellent teachers, excellent science equipment which sort of kept me interested in part. By and large I was a kind of black sheep in the whole thing. But I knew I had to get out of this militaristic situation because at that point I saw militarism, you know, for what it is."

I think that the protest and individualism of the resisters' high school years can easily be given a disproportional importance. None of them had as yet evolved a broad political philosophy. Insofar as they had had contact with politically radical student groups or were aware of them, they demonstrated the same reserve and skepticism that many of their fathers had displayed earlier. At that time, as well as later, their dissent was not indiscriminate, but a personal reaction to very specific issues and particular persons. Their position hardened in proportion to the coercive and sometimes hysterical pressures placed upon them. Had teachers and principals shown flexibility and reason, excesses might not have occurred. The major significance of these events for the resisters lies in the fact that they dissented initially, that they did not submit to coercion, and that they did not respond with coercion. Similar examples of dissent multiplied during their college years.

Another misunderstanding could arise if these actions were to be viewed as those of perpetual rebels. While it is clear that many resisters questioned where others accepted, dissented where others conformed, protested where others remained inactive, and stubbornly defended their positions when others submitted, I do not feel that the resisters' adolescent years allow for glib generalizations about a fundamental hostility toward authority figures. Their dissent began as an expression of opinion and was only transformed into a conflict when it met with intolerance.

Social Behavior

Nearly all the war resisters spent their childhood years in socially segregated, ethnically homogenous communities. This resulted in an unavoidable exclusivity of social contacts, emphasized when they attended parochial schools. Automatic social segregation began to disintegrate during high school. Four of the six Catholic boys attended ethnically and religiously mixed high schools where their closest friends were Jewish. A few of the Jewish boys attended predominantly black and Puerto Rican high schools and became integrated in those communities. Most of the Protestant boys experienced a similar social integration in their high schools with Jewish, Catholic, and black students. The few boys who continued to attend schools which were religiously and ethnically homogeneous experienced social integration in college.

I think this process of social integration was made possible by several factors. Although most of the resisters had spent their childhood years in ethnically homogeneous environments, their parents had not indoctrinated them with ethnic, racial, or religious chauvinism or prejudices. Quite to the contrary, at least on a theoretical level, nearly all the families displayed interest, tolerance, and sometimes deep concern for the welfare of other ethnic groups. Many of the families had also had social contact with people of different backgrounds through their professions, community welfare activities, helpful acts, and friendships. Academic achievement and extracurricular activities brought the resisters into close contact with students of different ethnic and political backgrounds. These new contacts were not restricted to school hours, because the boys did not see any reason to assert ethnic parochialism in their friendship relations. There was only one case in which vestiges of religious parochialism temporarily and consciously inhibited social integration—one student elected to attend a Catholic college because secular universities had been stereotyped as Godless by the students and faculty of his Jesuit high school. A further significance of this process of social integration was that it again placed several boys into ethnic minority positions within their friendship groups. Equally important is that the combination of their athletic, academic, and creative abilities enabled most of the war resisters to belong to several different kinds of social groups at once.

Aggressivity

While the war resisters were prepared to engage in heated verbal disputes few had resorted to intimidation or physical violence. They also did not commit acts of juvenile delinquency. Although most of them had been involved in the typical wrestling and shoving matches experienced by most young children, very few of them were involved in fights during adolescence. In nearly all cases these fights arose when they were assaulted by others or when they intervened on behalf of students who were being intimidated or beaten. None of them fought for fun or to assert themselves. Their aversion to violence encompassed more than their personal relations: it led them to oppose it even when they were not personally involved. It seems that almost every time the war resisters were exposed to violence during their adolescent years, they were its target or they intervened on behalf of its victims.

There are several further features of the war resisters' adolescent fights which illuminate other aspects of their personalities. Several of the resisters were unusually large, strong, and well coordinated. When asked why they did not have many fights and particularly why they had not hurt anybody during fights, they explained that they did not like to fight and tried to resolve problems without resorting to violence. When they saw no other alternative they had been strong enough to restrain their opponents without hurting them. A few of the resisters had been challenged to fights by much larger and stronger boys who had reputations for being "bullies" and "tough kids." Although it would have been possible for them to try to talk themselves out of these certain defeats without loss of face, they accepted the challenge.

It is interesting that all three teenagers who played football in high school were quarterbacks. They did not view their role as violent and explained that they had not tried to hurt their opponents. At the same time they made a distinction between pacifism and destruction. None considered himself a pacifist; all were willing to play sports which entailed hard, physical contact. However, they refused to employ violence for destructive ends. Obviously, this distinction was important to them.

Persons of Reference

CASE 109

I've had a piano teacher since 1965 who has had a tremendous influence on me. This is reflected like in the outlook that she has upon the idea that the more you can learn, to use what is natural within yourself through your own efforts, the closer you come to being a really creative person. She believes that people who fundamentally cheat creativity through stilted techniques, fakery, repressing what's inside and twisting what's inside, will ultimately produce corrupt art. And our discussions have gone into much more than simply piano playing, the nature of piano playing. We've touched on politics. We've touched on the whole nature of art and what it's for.

A friend of mine went to Mississippi in 1963 and 1964 and this made me directly aware of the civil rights movement. I said to myself, "Well, why aren't you going to Mississippi?" Not in terms that I necessarily should be going to Mississippi but that I should know why I'm not going to Mississippi.

CASE 110

I talked with my cousin about the war, and being basically legalistically-minded and fairness-minded, the thing I hit upon immediately was Nurnberg. . . . Then I sought out . . . [a friend] who was doing a Nurnberg thing and helped him out a bit. . . . He was a noncooperator on the grounds that the Constitution says that treaties signed by the President and ratified by the Senate become part of the law of the land and take precedence over anything else but the Constitution, meaning all laws made by Congress. Nurnberg was such a treaty. Nurnberg specifically outlawed some of the things we were doing in Vietnam. Therefore Nurnberg made it mandatory for him to refuse to cooperate with Selective Service as an arm of an illegal policy. . . . He's in jail now. . . . I thought he was very brave and proper. He was doing the right things and I started getting involved and getting on the mailing lists.

CASE 111

There was a liberal minister down there who changed me quite a bit. . . . And then my first friend. We're still very close . . . He's an extremely honest guy. We were very honest together and never hid anything that had any importance from each other. . . . He made me think about myself and my standards and how I saw things. Criticized me up and down the line. It was an honest dialogue and I hadn't had an honest dialogue. . . . He took a pretty liberal stand for civil rights and for peace. I was the one who started the peace thing really. But he, kind of a civil rights, human concern bag. You know, care about human beings . . . yeah, [laughs] now he works across the street in an insurance company. . . . He's got a wife and kid. He'd kind of like to become a resister but doesn't have it in him. Became a little more bourgeois.

CASE 112

I made one lasting friendship in the eighth grade. His parents were refugees from Europe. He was blunt . . . very rebellious towards authority. Eventually we got quite close. Discussed things together . . . developed an outlook, each of us changing in our own ways and each, I think, influencing the other. By the ninth year I had read Thoreau and the Duty of Civil Disobedience . . . was also watching civil rights demonstrations in the south and the the Battle of Summit Bridge. Things of that sort again made me feel something was very wrong, but there's still, I think, a certain faith in the ability of the United States as a country to correct its evils. And I don't think I recognized, as I do today, how ingrained our social ills are. How difficult a task it will ever be to rid ourselves of them. So it was more or less realizing certain things were wrong, but they could be corrected fairly easily if we get right down to it. . . .

I didn't know that there were many more people in prison for having done similar acts. So when I realized that I wasn't alone, when I met a fellow in the Resistance office who hadn't registered, I felt wonderful. Here was a person, in the real live skin and blood, who had done what I wanted to do, and it was quite heartening.

CASE 128

In college I met a fellow who impressed me from the outset. He had been born with a withered arm and very seriously deformed legs. . . . I was immediately impressed by the number of things he could do despite this. You know, he drives, builds things, just all sorts of things. He's been able to overcome it without the aimless bitterness you'll find sometimes. . . . He sort of sets an example for other people by his decency and his kindness. And I suppose I've learned some of that from him.

CASE 129

Well, as a freshman I had a sponsor, an older student who lives in the freshman dormitory, who was a C.O. I really respected him an awful lot, wanted to be like him. . . . Well, he was a very quiet, very sensitive kid. He'd gone to Mississippi the year before on a registration drive and had been severely beaten along with a rabbi and another person at a railroad crossing. . . . He just seemed like a much more attractive and highly principled Christian than I ever encountered in the church and I was really impressed. . . . He was so much stronger a man of his convictions that I was. I had never been called upon to display mine or bear witness to them in any public fashion, and he did it with such grace and integrity and without even, you know, a second thought.

Perhaps the most interesting paradox surrounding the twenty-five war resisters is the relationship between the promise they showed in high school and college and the fact that the majority of them were ready to exchange their personal futures for jail cells. The decision to do so emerged slowly and painfully within the context of all the events and influences described thus far and was spurred on through contact with particular people. These people showed them what they could become and they decided to follow this example.

People played a central role in the war resisters' lives, a role of which these men were aware and to which they ascribed a fundamental importance. Any description of their movement toward resistance is incomplete without adequate attention to the impact that particular people have had upon them. It cannot be accidental that the period of the resisters' strongest concern for the welfare of others coincided both with their movement away from social, emotional, and intellectual conformity and their decision to "bear witness" to their conscience. Equally nonaccidental is that these developments followed a long series of encounters with people who embodied ways of living which deeply moved and challenged them. They felt that they had been influenced as strongly by females as by males, by much older and younger people as well as by their peers, by close friends and chance acquaintances. A number of historical figures had inspired them as well.

In trying to explain how they had been influenced by other people, the

war resisters distinguished between people who had influenced them positively and had served as prototypes for them, and others who had behaved in
ways which had shown them what they did not want to become. The most
significant persons of reference entered the resisters' lives at times when they
were prepared for a reshaping of their personalities, a redirection of their attention, the opening of new emotional and intellectual perspectives, and the
further development of others. It was primarily in these person-to-person
relationships that the resisters experienced adventure. For them adventure
meant an emotional and intellectual discovery, an awakening, or a shared
experience, a feeling of being understood and giving that feeling to others.

Conclusion

Paradox permeates the accounts of the war resisters' teenage years. Outwardly, nearly all represented the conventional image of well-adjusted, striving achievers who were regarded by both teachers and fellow students as
likely to be successful in later life. Most were academically superior social
leaders and innovators, and often locally prominent athletes. Yet in one way
or another they remained beyond the cliché value and behavioral patterns
which were integral parts of their high school and college cultures. Among
the socially better integrated, this freedom of spirit was initially less visible
and appeared only in critical situations in which highly held principles were
being compromised by the group. The socially less firmly integrated began
their dissent earlier and spoke out more often and visibly. The more deeply
the resisters were involved in their conventional high school and college society and the more closely they saw their personal destiny within this framework, the longer it took them to extricate themselves from this life style.
This process, this extrication from outside influences, went hand in hand
with the rise of their personal fortunes. It would appear that they systematically exhausted each of the institutions which were designed to frame their
lives. They then became critics of these very same institutions.

Notes

1. A. Bandura and R. Walters, *Adolescent Aggression: A Study of the Influence
of Child Rearing Practices and Family Relationships*, New York: Ronald Press,
1959. Bandura and Walters interviewed twenty-six adolescent boys with long histories of aggressive antisocial behavior and a second group of twenty-six adolescent boys
who had been identified by their high school counselors as being neither markedly
aggressive nor having delinquency or disruptive behavior in their histories. The parents of the fifty-two subjects were also interviewed. In order to analyze their interview material, Bandura and Walters used a procedure similar to the one used in this
study. They developed a series of rating scales for the parental interviews and for
the interviews with the adolescents. Some of the rating scales developed for the inter-

views with the adolescents deal with the student's behavior in high school and his feelings and attitudes toward his teachers, classmates, and schoolwork. For my own investigation, I modified these latter scales and converted them into questionnaire form. The resulting questionnaire was then given to my subjects.

2. D. Mantell and R. Panzarella, "Reconstructing a Series of Similar Tragedies: Verbal Correlates of Behavior in the Milgram Experiment." (Unpublished manuscript). In a modelling variant of Milgram's base-line condition, subjects were exposed to a defiant model. Although this experience significantly reduced the percentage of obedient subjects, both obedient and defiant subjects denied that the model's behavior had had an influence on theirs.

CHAPTER 4

Sexual Development and Experience

THE GREEN BERETS

First Intercourse

CASE 204

She was some old prostitute down in North Carolina.

CASE 207

She was about, say 18 or 19 . . . I was about 15 then. . . . She was, you know, pretty used to it and I guess she really did it more or less, you know. I mean, I was real interested. Don't get me wrong. But, you know, I really didn't know what I was doing at the time. . . . She knew what she was doing. . . . Just saw her once again. That was on a date.

Did you have any particular feelings about her?
I talked about it a few times. But if I—I don't, you know. . . . I don't know who she was. I don't know if it'd be true or not. I do remember what she was like at the time.

And how did you feel at the time you were making it with her?
Oh, I thought she was the greatest thing in the world, you know. She was good and all that. But right now I wouldn't want to have anything to do with her, you know. 'Cause I know the type of girl she is.

CASE 208

Oh yeah. It was in the front seat of a goddamned Corvair and I never saw a girl bleed so much in my life. But it—the funny thing was, I really got along with this girl. She was half crazy. . . . Yeah, I had known her for about two months. . . . Yeah, I liked her a lot. I was really sorry to see her go 'cause, I mean, she—she was real friendly. Real easy to get along with. Not extra friendly but just, you know, kind of fun to be with in a crazy sort of way.

And how old were you then?
Sixteen, I think.
And how did it happen that night? I mean, had you been talking about it or what?
No. . . . We'd been doing some pretty serious petting and stuff like that. I just decided to try something new and different. So I stuck it in.
And how did she feel about it? Do you remember?
How did she feel? I don't think she had any guilt at all. She just said it hurt and that was it.

CASE 209

I had been seeing her for about two months. . . . She had probably had it before a few times. . . . It was in her house, in her bedroom. . . . I was petting her for a while and getting my hands up there and she seemed like she was going to go all the way, so I asked her, let's go in her bedroom, since it seemed like a safer place. Then I started undressing and she undressed, 'cause I knew she was going to let me then. I didn't think it was going to be that easy but that was just the thing. . . . Well, I continued seeing her for a few months. Then I broke up with her just because I was going out with different friends and I just got kind of tired of her. Just seeing her, 'cause, I guess, I didn't like having a girlfriend right so close even though I liked her that much, you know. . . . I never went seriously with any girls.

CASE 210

I went to the, uh, Via Cuna, Mexico. . . . I went down there and went to what they call Boy's Town. This is where the prostitutes are. . . . Well, being sixteen years old and seeing something like this is real unusual and I was curious about sex at the time. So I told the prostitute I was—I was—I told her I never went to bed with a woman before and she said it cost two dollars. So I went to bed with her. She gave me back my two dollars. It was what you call a ''cherry boy,'' [laughs] which is comical. But that was my introduction to sex. . . . [I was] scared, didn't know what to do really. . . . She showed me but it was funny. . . . She looked young. . . . I can remember what she looked like. She looked pretty.

CASE 214

How old were you?
Thirteen.
How did it happen?
Oh, it's very childish. I really don't want to talk about it [laughs]. Well, the girl had a bad reputation at school [laughs]. I chided her. I began chiding her a little bit. Not derisively so but just kidding her a little bit. But she responded and I approached her sexually, you know. The first time I'd ever approached a girl sexually. I was, of course, very bashful about it, and I was successful. . . . She was the same age. We were both in the seventh grade. . . . Well, I—we

finally—we got into the habit of going to—during the lunch hour, we'd head up to the old balcony in the school auditorium and have intercourse there.
Is that where you had intercourse with her for the first time?
Yes [laughs].
Did you use a prophylactic?
No.
Did you have an orgasm?
Oh yes.
Were you aware of things about pregnancy at that time?
Yes, but for a long time I was terribly irresponsible about everything. I couldn't have cared. If she had gotten pregnant I would have said, fine, bye. That's all. I was callous about it. I didn't consider it.
Who took the initiative in that one?
Well, it's a funny thing. I did. Kind of childish and then she did just to see how far I would go, you know. . . . It wasn't a personal thing.

CASE 217

She was year behind me in school. Was her idea. [I] didn't know her too well. . . . We read books about it so we tried it . . . at a grammar school dance. She'd never done it and I'd never done it. Went out on the grass, outside the dance. . . . From then on there up 'til . . . I was twenty-one, I sort of been to bed with her once a month. Never seen in public with her once. All she liked to do was go to bed. Didn't have to spend money on her.
Did you ever start using prophylactics with her?
No.
And she never got pregnant?
I don't know.
Did you always have an orgasm?
Yeah.
Did you ever get close to her emotionally? I mean, did you ever feel strongly about her?
Never.

CASE 219

I was just about sixteen when I met her but she was one year older . . . When I first started going with her for six months we made love. It wasn't anything outstanding . . . in her house the first time. . . . I couldn't wait to tell my best friend 'cause we always compared notes.

CASE 221

I was six. That was with a girl right there when I was in the second grade. . . . We didn't know what it was but we enjoyed it. . . . It was just a quick affair, you know. It didn't last very long, naturally. We didn't take no clothes off or anything. . . . Yes, it was full intercourse. She used to have to help me, you know. But we got pretty good at it after a while 'til we got caught. We did it about three months, I guess. . . . She was just a little girl, a flirt. She used to kiss me all the time and tell the teacher I kissed her.

Early Intercourse

CASE 201

Did I fall in love with them? Uh, let's see. Kind of. Yeah. I mean, when I'm with them, yeah. . . . They know what I want and I know what they want so there's no point in feeling guilty about anything. There's no point in anything excessive behind anything. . . . Yeah, there was one . . . didn't see a great deal of her. Knew her for about two years. Yeah, I felt close to her. . . . She felt close to me until somebody told her, you know, I was messing around with another girl and she actually found some rubbers in my pocket. . . . She was about the best girl I ever met. . . . but I really didn't care then, you know, because I was having a ball with other people.

CASE 207

. . . Yeah, it was just more or less like, uh, four or five guys all with this one girl and she was just, you know, for everybody . . . if it was your night, you was lucky . . . I mean, if you picked her up. If you just happened to be down where she was at, you know, you was pretty well guaranteed. . . . She was about, I think, fifteen, real young. . . . No, I didn't really care too much for her. . . . With a girl like that you didn't worry too much.

CASE 214

Who was the second girl?
That was _____'s next door neighbor. The next one was in the eighth grade. She was kind of a bashful girl, kind of a shy girl. Had intercourse with her at a party. . . . We wouldn't get completely undressed. It'd just be drop and try. . . . Well, I could tell you some stories that'll curl your ears. . . . There were a lot of girls back at that age that I had experiences with. There was _____. We went steady for a while and almost from the outset we'd pet, you know. I don't know how many times a week I went to bed with her but I went with her for two or three months. Saw her about once or twice a week, two or three times a week probably, and went to bed with her almost always. . . . After that I don't know. Gracious. . . . Got tired of her . . . That's all. . . . Yes, I was fourteen, fifteen. . . . While I was at Saint _____ High School, there was a girl . . . who went to bed with several fellows at school. I made her downstairs standing up in the shower room. . . . During high school, I just went to bed with everybody. There was this one girl whose father owned a chain of stores. I went to bed with her a dozen times or so. We used to go to Howard Johnson motels. . . . Then there was my friend's sister that I picked up. Then there were gang-bangers, you know, and whores and stuff like that. . . . Then there was this fat girl and another one we'd ride around with . . . like with this fat girl there really wasn't much emotional involvement. We sure did have

a good time and a rag, you know. We had a good thing. . . . One time I tried to think of how many people I've been to bed with and I came up with fifty names. . . . I had a girl who was a cheerleader at _____ High School during my senior year. There was a party and I picked her up. She got drunker than a skunk and I laid her at [a friend's] house. Then there was _____ . She was a fine girl. Probably a little bit nuts. I went to bed with her. Kind of liked her too. She was very open about sex which I wasn't for a long time. Just a little moralistic, I suppose, you'd say. That summer after I graduated high school there was _____. That was on top of a downtown building in _____ City [soft laugh]. . . . No emotional involvement.

What about the girls you liked?
Well, there was _____. She was damn good-looking. She'd been married once. She didn't like responsibility at all. Anything tending to tie her down, she'd steer away from it. We spent a hell of a lot of time together. She never gave me any kind of trouble. She loved me. I liked her for that. We had a good time together. . . . There was another girl just about like that. Beautiful, just a beautiful body, not much upstairs. . . . Saw her for about three or four months. We had a damn good relationship. Hell, we had a good time which at the time was all I cared about. . . . I was running wild . . . saw her for three or four months during the latter part of the school year. . . . Don't know what happened. She didn't care. I didn't care anymore.

The week before I left for basic training, I called up every girl that I'd ever screwed just about. Everybody that was around and laid everybody I could get my hands on. Just to say I did it, you know, and that was the first time I ever really had just a complete fill with sex and I didn't even care. So I screwed. I screwed when I didn't have to, you know. It—I just—it's not such a neat thing, you know.

CASE 217

Oh, she was a special girl. . . . Later on we got engaged. . . . I have a lot of feelings toward her. Quite a respect. She's a good girl, an outstanding girl. . . . She was a brain. . . . She was real good-looking. Her measurements were about 40-25-36. She was about five foot six, very chesty. . . . She was active in everything that was possible. . . . She was very domineering. . . . She was spoiled rotten. . . . She was the sole heir to about eight to ten million dollars. . . . She was kind of conceited. She had everything going for her. . . . Maybe it was just habit. I went with her for six, seven years. . . . Oh, what did I like about her? She had a good personality when she wanted to use it. A lot of good times together. She definitely was faithful. . . . Yeah, we started having intercourse after a year and a half. . . . Only once a month while she was having her period because she didn't want to get pregnant. . . . Well, I just sort of stopped writing. That was it.

CASE 218

I'm like a bumble bee. Go from flower to flower . . . oh, it must have been five, six, eight years there because they all lived in the same community. . . . I became the regular Pan of the neighborhood.

CASE 221

Oh yeah, the next one I had, I think, was in the fourth grade. It was a cousin of mine. Me and her started messing around playing this doctor and nurse and then I had it again with her. Well, we had it a couple of times together after we got the routine set up and everything. We got caught for that and I got my butt busted for that. . . . We had this one girl who used to ditch school with us and she was sort of our plaything. The three of us would always run around together and everytime we ditched, she ditched and we'd all—we'd all have intercourse with her . . . and then during the ninth grade . . . I was going with whatever different girl I could. I was going to church then all the time.

CASE 227

I went out with this home town girl for about three and one-half years . . . The first eight months nothing but then we were doing it regularly. . . . I almost married her. . . . She lived about . . . thirty miles away and as far as driving up there every night, it was just senseless really. . . . Just made it on the weekend and in the meantime she met this other guy and we just broke it off or she did. . . . I was upset . . . and I felt badly about it. . . . I was in love with her. . . . It took me about a week or so to get over it.

Sexuality was one of the Green Berets' favorite subjects. Their statements were unusually long and repetitious. One of the things which particularly struck me was that the quality of the soldiers' descriptions of their relationships with pick-ups, dates, and "special girls" contained many similarities. The sexual behavior of the Green Berets offers important insights into their personalities, social relations, moral values and life styles. The onset of sexual activity varied considerably from soldier to soldier, yet psychological uniformity permeated each phase of their sexual development. Chronological diversity and psychological homogeneity were most apparent in conjunction with their first sexual intercourse. The varied aspects of their sexual development converged in late adolescence into a pattern typical for nearly all the soldiers.

Early Sexuality

With the exception of one boy who received what he considered to be a sound sexual education from his parents, the others received their sexual instruction from friends, "dirty books," girlfriends, and prostitutes. The most striking aspect of the Green Beret's early sexual development was their disinterest and aversion to masturbation. Many said that they discovered girls at an early age and found heterosexual play preferable. Others were caught by mothers who punished them severely, or were exposed to stringent religious condemnations. Several had never masturbated and could not explain this. Only among the Catholic soldiers did cultural influences appear to play a perceptible role in connection with masturbation. A few of the Catholic boys were the only ones who felt guilty about masturbating. They also masturbated longer and more actively than the others.

Throughout each phase of sexual development few Green Berets reached orgasm exclusively or primarily through masturbation. When such periods did occur they were brief and usually preceded first intercourse. The men who had relatively infrequent sexual contacts with prostitutes and girlfriends continued masturbating after they joined the Army and while they were in Vietnam.

In nearly all cases the first signs of sexual awakening were rapidly followed by full sexual intercourse. The diversity of circumstances surrounding the first intercourse contrasted sharply with the similarity of the boys' psychological reactions to this event. This contrast gives their first coitus its special character.

At the time of the first sexual intercourse, the boys ranged in age from six to nineteen, with an average age of 15.1. At thirteen years, one-quarter had already experienced coitus, at fifteen the figure rose to one-half, and at seventeen only three boys were still virgins. Their partners ranged in age from six (she had intercourse with the six-year-old boy) to twenty-one. Five were prostitutes, two pick-ups, eight casual dates, six acquaintances, and three close girlfriends; thus, in fifteen of twenty-five cases the girl was a stranger or near-stranger at the time of the sexual act. The six boys who experienced first intercourse with a girlfriend had had a casual and superficial relationship with them previously.

The boys' reactions to first intercourse were strikingly similar and consisted of physical pleasure or "nothing." Only five soldiers spoke of having had an emotional reaction. Two of this group found intercourse emotionally satisfying; one man spoke of disappointment; two others said they felt disgust. Intercourse rarely had an impact on the relationship between the boy and the girl. Most continued to see the girl, either "just for sex" or because they liked her and enjoyed her companionship anyway. Only four soldiers felt that intercourse caused a change in the relationship. One, who was fourteen at the time, morally rejected his sixteen-year-old partner. Another said that intercourse was followed by an emotional crisis because the girl was a devout Catholic. Two soldiers said that intercourse had deepened the relationship.

The first act of sexual intercourse was emotionally and interpersonally insignificant to nearly all the boys. Intercourse rarely coincided with or led to a deepening of the boy's feelings for the girl. She served a utilitarian function and it can be surmised from many reports that the feeling was mutual. Moreover, the strong taboos on sexuality to which most of these boys were exposed seem to have had little impact upon them, as their later sexual behavior indicates.

Only four boys experienced long periods of sexual inactivity between the time of their first coitus and Army induction. This period ranged from five months to nine and one-half years, with an average length of four and one-half years. Most of the soldiers could not recall the exact number of their coital partners. Generally the greater the time span between first intercourse and Army induction the larger the number of girls mentioned. The twenty-one Green Berets with pre-Army coital experience mentioned an average of more than five different girls. They reported a regular and uncomplicated change of sexual partners, and experienced intercourse indiscriminately with almost any available girl.

A few boys dated girls with whom they did not have intercourse, and these girls were subjected to tireless efforts to seduce them; the relationships were fraught with conflict and guilt. Only one boy did not try to have intercourse with his girlfriend—he did not want to "degrade her." With this exception, the seventeen boys who had sexual relations with their girlfriends had intercourse intermittently with other girls. The four boys who did not have sexual relations with their girlfriends had no intercourse at all.

Most of the Green Berets mentioned "special girls" whom they dated for as long as seven years. It was difficult to assess the depth of their feelings for these girls. The duration of many of these relationships suggested that strong mutual affection must have been present, and they included full sexual intimacy in most cases. Yet, the Green Berets were seldom specific and never voluntarily made reference to their feelings of affection for these girls. Intercourse did not appear to be a source of dissension in the relationships, but the soldiers did not feel that it increased their understanding, depth of feeling, or sense of obligation towards the girls. None attributed a deeper significance to these relationships and none of the girls was mentioned as a "Person of Reference."

In most cases the soldiers' perspective on these relationships seems to have been realistic and accurate. Although many relationships lasted several years, they were not stable. The boys dated other girls intermittently. Their interest in their "special girls" was based strongly on their external attributes—looks, figure, sexual compatability, wealth, and scholarly ability. Some of the Green Berets said they loved these girls, but they allowed the relationships to deteriorate by neglecting them or repeatedly dating and having intercourse with other girls in the community. Temporary comfort and a measure of mutual compatability seem to have been the central features of these relationships.

Three soldiers had unusually problematical friendships with their "special girls." Each proposed marriage several times and was turned down. In these cases the reluctance to attribute significance to the friendships seems to be based on deep pain and the unwillingness to discuss it. In two cases premarital pregnancy was involved. One girl repeatedly refused sexual intimacy for fear of becoming pregnant. One soldier, who was seventeen at the time, was refused permission to marry by his mother. Shortly after these men joined the Army the girls became pregnant by other men. Both soldiers were still ready to marry the girls. The first was refused again and the second permanently alienated the girl "by telling her off" while drunk. The third soldier's fiancée joined him in Europe and then began dating his best friend. He dismissed this betrayal with the words, "Wouldn't you know." In my opinion, these girls were important but because of pain, damaged pride, and bitterness, the men were unwilling to admit this.

Sexual Experiences in the Army

CASE 207

Well, in Vietnam and Malaysia. . . . you'd go downtown for five dollars. You bought what you wanted. . . . I had a real good time in Malaysia. I took out an Indian girl, a Chinese girl while I was there. I had a real good time there. They were nice girls. They were professional prostitutes, you know. . . . I don't consider them as prostitutes even though they were really. . . . All they [Vietnamese prostitutes] wanted was the money. They didn't have too much feeling. . . . You settled on a price and you just jumped up and went back in the back room and stripped and got it and came back out. . . . Five mintues . . . only takes a couple of times to get used to it and then it doesn't bother you after that. . . . Pleasurable? In a sense it was and in a sense it was disgusting because it was just, you know, you never thought too much of the girls themselves. You—sometimes you felt sorry for them when you see a really young one. Maybe they averaged about fifteen years old. . . . I ended up with the clap . . . 'cause I wasn't careful.

CASE 208

They're a lot grosser down here than they ever were in college, down in Group [his army unit], the sort of things they do down here. Some of these beach parties they have down here are pretty bad. This stuff's going to be pretty gross. We had one last Saturday and there are about twenty-five people out there and there are about eight or nine girls and they got drunk real fast and it was right on the Isar River and this one girl passed out. She just fell asleep. We couldn't wake her up. So we threw her in the river [it was winter] and, uh, she woke up and she was running around and stuff. So somebody took off her clothes and wrapped a blanket around her then laid her down, you know. Try to make her go to sleep. This Canadian come by and just takes her blanket and spreads her legs and starts eating her out right there. So then everybody did [laughs]. She didn't do a thing. She was so drunk she couldn't move. They did stuff like, uh, go to a place called the Wine House. Everybody gets drunk and they jump out the second story window and on to the street and land on the people walking on the sidewalks and stuff. . . . They try and act like animals which they really aren't. 'Cause they're trying to put on a show. . . .

The only time you see them when they're really animals and they're not trying to show off is when they get drunk like last Saturday.

Is that typical?
Sure, it happens every day, every night.

The married men in the corps too?
Yeah, we got a couple of married guys there. There's a lot of adultery going on in the army which I'm sure you're aware of. . . . If some of the guys do weird things like this, actually it's not really frowned on by the rest of the people because most everyone else has participated in it, let's say. I hope I don't get kicked out of the army. Most people consider this an unnatural sex act but I think we don't, most of us. Like in some of our special bars we've had pussy-eating contests, and, uh, in public or maybe a team will hire a broad to sit there on the table while we're all throwing money to, uh, and maybe the team leader or someone will, uh, eat her pussy right there and we'll time it and see how long, you know, and have pussy-eating contests.

Hold it a second. A pussy-eating contest. Well, what do you time? I mean, where is the contest?
The time is from the time you stick your tongue in and you don't come up for air. You just continuously drive on [laughs]. Not without air 'cause you can still breathe. But how long a person will stay there eating a woman's pussy. I mean, maybe, you know, after ten, fifteen minutes or so he'll just get tired of doing it or he just doesn't want to do it anymore or after she gets her feelings a couple of times it might get pretty sloppy down there, you know. But I think the record is about two hours and forty-five minutes in the Sportsman's Bar in Saigon. That is a Special Forces Bar. . . . But most of us we used to have a real good joke. We used to pretend we were homosexuals a lot. Just as a joke, you know. We'd be in a club and we'd walk up and kiss each other all the time. . . . It didn't matter where we were. We'd kiss each other on the ear . . . and we tried to pretend like we were homosexuals, just because other people, you know, in a lot of places they thought that many of us were homosexuals [laughs] but it was a hell of a lot of fun for us.

CASE 214

Then there was this girl in _____. Intelligent and pretty witty. It took me a month of running back and forth to _____ before I had that girl. Of course I told her I loved her. That's as good a way as any to express things. I was honest with her. She used to propose to me every night. It got to be a game. Ha, I didn't want to get married ever, unless I decide I really want to have a son. . . . Just can't stand the extra weight.

CASE 215

I feel that if a man is gone for two or three months from his wife and just has sexual intercourse for the sheer physical pleasure of it then there's nothing really that's wrong with it. . . . And if a woman's husband is gone and she can have an affair with a man and not get involved, I wouldn't condemn her for it. . . . We have a saying in the Special Forces. When you leave a place you throw your key on the table and say to your buddy, "There's the key to my house. There's the key to my car. You can have my wife, my clothes, and my house. But please don't wear my jump boots. I just spit-shined them." Just a standard joke . . . but everybody knows what goes on, too. When a man is gone for a year to Vietnam and his wife is at a place where thousands of men know her, it just seems logical that sooner or later somebody's gonna do it. To me it seems logical. . . . If my wife did it? What can you do? You can act hurt. If you've done it yourself, how hurt can you be?

CASE 219

One prostitute in Germany. . . . It must have been the ugliest woman in the world I made love with. . . . I really didn't have my heart in it. . . . Well, it was kind of late and I figured it might be a new experience. . . . Something I've never tried. . . . Something like her. Uh, she was from Turkey. That's the only reason I made love with her really 'cause I found out she was from Turkey and I wanted to add her to my list of countries [laughs] . . . I've been with a lot of prostitutes . . . I stayed shacked up in Mexico ten days one time and basically prostitutes are the same all over the world. They're interested in your money, they're not really interested in making love. They just get on and make you have your feeling as fast as possible so they can get the next customer in. . . . Usually when I'm around a prostitutes area I like a lot of variety but in this one case [Taipei] I stayed with this one. . . . We were very happy. . . . I stayed with her because she was really a nice person. I mean, for a prostitute . . . I mean, being a prostitute is not the worst thing in the world. In many countries it's very accepted and especially in a poor country, many times it's the difference between starvation and making a living. . . .

The first time was out in Colorado. . . . A pimp came up to me and asked me if I wanted to, uh, make love with a particular girl that was getting out of a car. She was looking real nice and for a colored woman she looked real clean. . . . Actually this didn't turn out to be too good an intercourse for me. . . . My nose kept running because it was very cold in _____ at the time and she got real mad at me because everytime I put my hands on her, my hands were extremely cold. . . . All during the intercourse my nose kept dripping on her. . . .

From there we went to Mexico. . . . Invariably every night we made love to at least five different Mexican prostitutes.

A basic tool of our trade to be friendly, to begin with, and to have a good line of what we call bullshit, you know . . . be able to just sit there and lie to the broad all night long. If you feel like lying or you feel like telling her the truth, it doesn't matter. . . . Show the woman a good time, you know. Really laugh and have good, clean fun, you know. . . . It's just like a mission, I think, with most of us. It's kinda like sport. I know that's the way it always was for me and I know for most of the other guys it's the same way. If it takes a month to get into bed with a certain woman that you've set out to get, a month, two months, it's regardless. You use the technique, you've got to analyze the woman first of all. Find out what kind of woman she is, how intelligent, what her likes and dislikes are, any bad things that might have happened to her in the past. Just friendly conversation, and she won't realize she's feeding you information all the time which for a person in the intelligence field is good ... and so after a couple of dates with a woman, she's usually given you so much information that you can use as tools against her to get her into bed. ...

As it turned out she has this little girl, two little girls in fact and, uh, so this is one technique I always tried to exploit when I was going out with a divorced women, if they have children. I always showed a real big interest in their children and offered to take them to a movie or picnics or something like this. ... I always tried to pick up a different type of woman. Try to throw 'em off guard by taking them and their children on picnics in the afternoon.

Army life had a levelling effect on the war volunteers' sexual behavior. The previously inexperienced young men lost their virginity. Most of the soldiers married and had active extramarital sexual contacts. The majority of soldiers, including those who had never or only infrequently patronized prostitutes, began to do so regularly. A more conspicuously bizarre element appeared in their sexual activity.

The sexual behavior of the Green Berets during this period cannot be viewed separately from the style of life imposed upon them by military duty. At the same time it must be remembered that these soldiers did not find this kind of life incompatible with their needs or values. A soldier is forced to satisfy his sexual drives under a variety of circumstances. He moves frequently, often finds himself in new and unfamiliar surroundings and without private quarters, may be separated from his usual sexual partner for extended periods of time, and is often the object of suspicion. All of these circumstances converge, particularly during combat duty, when the soldier may risk his life, be surrounded by death and misery, and find himself in the midst of a hostile indigenous population.

The soldiers satisfied their sexual urges in several ways. Although there was some variation from man to man, their major sexual outlets in the approximate order of their use were pick-ups, prostitutes, wives, fiancées, girlfriends, orgies, masturbation.

Prostitutes and Pick-Ups

Sexual contact with prostitutes and pick-ups occurred during combat tours in Vietnam, as well as in the United States, Europe, and elsewhere.* Because of the large number of contacts, their brevity, and the overall time

*The nations and regions in which the Special Forces soldiers reported sexual contact with prostitutes are in numerical order, Vietnam, Germany, United States, Mexico, Latin America, Japan, Nationalist China, Korea, France, Thailand, Scandinavia, Philippines, Pacific Islands, Greece, Italy, Morocco, Puerto Rico, Ireland, Lebanon, Dominican Republic, Portugal, Spain, Turkey, Canada, Malaya, Cyprus.

span involved, the soldiers were only able to estimate how many sexual partners they had had since their entry into the Army. Eighteen soldiers estimated the number of prostitutes with whom they had had intercourse: many gave up counting after about twenty-five. As a group they recalled 513, or an average of 28.5 each. The ranking soldier gave an approximate figure of eighty-five. I did not pursue the subject of pick-ups in a statistical fashion and can only report that in most cases these contacts seemed to be more frequent than those with prostitutes.

Three soldiers said that they never patronized prostitutes. One said, "It just doesn't appeal to me. I felt like if I couldn't talk a girl into bed on my own . . . I didn't deserve to be in bed anyway." Another explained, "I've thought about it. A lot of these guys do it, but I don't know. It seems like—dirty and that's the way I get the impression it is." The other soldier, Case 212, had no fundamental aversion to intercourse with prostitutes. He attributed his abstinence to bad luck:

Don't get me wrong. I had planned on it a couple of times but every time I seemed to get ready one member or more of my team would get killed and I'd wind up staying out in the field. We didn't have any women out there. We had a couple of mountain broads and they got to looking pretty good by the time I started to come back to the United States. I was more concerned about not bringing back any type of venereal disease.

The soldiers felt that the risk of venereal disease was the major drawback of sexual activity with prostitutes. At least fourteen of the men had had syphilis or gonorrhea once and several were infected more often. They were alert to this danger and had themselves treated at military dispensaries at the first signs of the disease.

The soldiers' sexual contacts with pick-ups are particularly revealing because of the seduction strategies employed and the characteristics of the females involved. These men responded most energetically to a girl or woman's efforts to maintain her "respectability" and to feel that she was held in positive regard before sleeping with a man. They demonstrated considerable patience in soothing fears, and were prepared to spend both money and time, travel long distances, lie, cheat, manipulate, betray confidences, and exploit weaknesses. After the conquest the women were discarded. Many of the Green Berets also had affairs with married women whose husbands were away at work, on trips, or on combat duty in Vietnam. Some of the affairs with married women are particularly interesting because the women provided the living quarters and gave the soldiers pocket money and other amenities. In these cases the soldiers had in effect assumed the role of male prostitutes.

Extramarital Sexual Contacts

The analysis of extramarital sexuality does not include contacts with prostitutes and is restricted to non-hardship tours of duty when the Green

Beret was cohabiting with his wife. Seventeen of the twenty married or engaged soldiers had intercourse with pick-ups as well as prostitutes during these periods, while the other three soldiers restricted extramarital sexuality to times of prolonged separation from their wives. By circumscribing the consideration of extramarital sexuality in this way I felt that situational pressures were properly weighted, an unnecessary second discussion of contact with prostitutes could be avoided, and the analysis of extramarital sexuality focused on the psychological aspects of this behavior. Many military assignments allow for the presence of the soldier's wife in comfortable family quarters. If the soldier repeatedly had intercourse with other women under these circumstances, the explanation must be sought within his personality and his marital relationship.

Soldiers are frequently separated from their wives for periods ranging from one or two days to a few weeks. Many extramarital sexual contacts with pick-ups and dates took place at such times. A substantial number also took place during stag and beach parties in the local housing area, during evening excursions into town, and with local waitresses, barmaids, and salesgirls.

The Green Berets enjoyed the novelty, excitement, and sense of conquest provided by new sexual partners, and regarded these contacts as a natural expression of their sexual needs. They were not seeking emotional involvement or stable relationships. As long as their own marriages remained intact they returned to their wives and the excursions had no immediate perceptible influence on the marriage. Some planned their adventures in advance while others were more likely to react spontaneously when an opportunity presented itself. Most were surprisingly blasé about the dangers of detection. A few had been suspected or caught by their wives. The ones who had received ultimatums said they had since become more careful. None of the soldiers felt guilty, although several granted that their activities entailed risks to their marriages. Several explained that they committed adultery only when they were far from home. As one soldier put it, "If you shit in your own front yard you're likely to step in it."

It is usually impossible to lead a carefree and active extramarital sex life without jeopardizing close relationships. Five of the seventeen married soldiers were in their second marriages. These men could not explain why they married their first wives and several were not sure of their feeling for the second one. Until the day of their marriages, two had dated other women whom they liked better. None loved their first wives, and welcomed separation when shipped overseas. All the second wives were German. From their husbands' descriptions these women appeared to be more self-sufficient, determined, and dominating than the first wives. A substantial number of the other soldiers' marriages were tension ridden and on the verge of collapse. One soldier had been divorced for six years and did not intend to remarry. Another had been engaged for six years and was unable to make the decision to marry. Several soldiers had children from previous marriages and rarely or never visited them. A few had fathered illegitimate children, but only one soldier had seen and supported these children. Many soldiers did not know or care if they had fathered illegitimate children.

Here is the exceptional statement of the one married soldier who had not committed adultery with either prostitutes or pick-ups.

CASE 213

Well, I love my wife and I adore her and I love my son and it wouldn't be fair. . . . I strongly believe in the marriage. This is why I waited this long, not that it's long enough anyway but, uh, for some people. . . . But I waited more than . . . others do. The biggest thing that I see in this is I wouldn't want my wife to go out on me, see, so I know she feels the same way about me, she wouldn't want me to go out on her and, uh, well, I'm happy with her, there's no problem.

Concluding Remarks

Where does all this information leave us? Are the Green Berets nothing more than sexually uncomplicated and forthright studs with international experience? Or are they just average young men who through the exigencies of their work find it necessary to have sex in convenient places? Are they the only men who take advantage of the young, the widowed, and the weak in the service of their own satisfaction? Are they more unscrupulous than diplomats, athletes, or construction workers? Is there a pathological feature to their sexual behavior? Are they incapable of establishing a good working relationship with a woman and caring for a family? The limited material available on the sexual habits of different occupational groups suggests that there is nothing unique about the Green Berets except their aversion to masturbation. The only obvious pathological aspects of their sexual behavior were its self-defeating character, emotionally superficial and exploitive attitudes, occasional outbursts of excessiveness, and the underlying and probably unconscious compulsive need for potency confirmation.*

Bravado and conceit in sexual matters is widespread. Most men employ one strategy or another in approaching women and vice versa. Many young men feel drawn to older women. The Green Berets did not inaugurate prostitution, but simply made unreflective and unfeeling use of existing facilities. Yet their sexual behavior is not as uncomplicated as it may seem at first glance. I think the unusual feature of their sexuality lies in its extremeness.

*Every subject completed the Sex Inventory, a questionnaire containing 147 questions designed to measure sexual drive and interest level, sexual frustration, neurotic conflict associated with sex, repression of sexual desires, loss of sexual control, homosexuality, sex-role confidence, and promiscuity. The only scale on which the Green Berets received an elevated score was promiscuity.[1]

Whereas some people are willing to compromise principles in the service of sexual pleasure, the Green Berets seem not to have had principles to sacrifice. Situations which would have deterred and inhibited others left them unaffected. Transient sexual contacts constituted not just a part, but nearly the whole, of their sexual experience. Superficiality and insincerity were the only stable emotional features of their response to women. There were almost no indications of guilt, embarrassment, reflection or self-criticism in their accounts of their activities. They told their tales with unabashed candor and conveyed the spirit of adventure. When relationships appeared to be deepening the soldiers shook themselves free from the impending "burden." Moreover, they did not tire of superficiality, fleeting relationships, or exploiting others for their own pleasure. Their behavior is a clear indication of emotional immaturity, or perhaps more accurately, emotional retardation. They did not seem to possess the capacity to show sensitivity or to appreciate the feelings of others unless this could be incorporated into a strategic calculation. Either they could not or were not willing to give a genuine response to another person's pain or love.

Wild parties, with the vulgarities, flamboyance, exhibitionism, and voyeurism which two soldiers suggested were standard features of Special Forces life, seem to me to be extensions and elaborations of the soldiers' earlier social and sexual habits. This is not to say that Army life has not had an influence on their sexual behavior, however. It has given them the freedom to fornicate around the world within sympathetic and supportive subcultures of like-minded people. It is abundantly clear that the war volunteers were notably lacking in scruples and had a remarkable degree of insensitivity. However, it cannot be claimed that they employed physical coercion in soliciting sexual partners. On occasion they got the girls drunk before the act but I strongly doubt that many of these girls could honestly have pleaded innocence. Most of the Green Berets' sexual partners seemed to have been willing participants. Aside from the girls and women whose confidence was betrayed, I do not think it possible to understand the Green Berets' ability to seduce so many women without recognizing that there were large reservoirs of like-minded females who were willing to be seduced. We should recall that a substantial number of the boys were seduced by their partners at the time of their first intercourse.

I think that one may justifiably wonder what differentiates the behavior of three thirteen-year-old boys taking turns with a female classmate from five twenty-five-year-old soldiers taking turns with one fifteen-year-old Vietnamese girl. What differentiates a high school beach party with couples having intercourse within earshot of each other from a private free-for-all party in an apartment, and the "pussy-eating contest" in the Sportsman's Club in Saigon? How is one to distinguish between the behavior of a sixteen-year-old with a prostitute and that of a twenty-five-year-old in the same position?

Are there substantial differences between transient sexual contacts with prostitutes and pick-ups? It should not be forgotten that the Green Berets had nearly as many kind words for prostitutes as for their nominally more respectable sexual partners; actually they had very few kind words for any of their sexual partners. It was not true that contacts with prostitutes were short and that those with pick-ups necessarily lasted longer. Many Green Berets lived with prostitutes for days, weeks, and in one case for nine months. Although there are circumstantial differences to which one can point, in my opinion the Green Berets did not find fundamental differences between prostitutes and pick-ups. The pick-up was perhaps more of a challenge and offered a measure of superficial external respectability, but the prostitute was more secure and could be discarded without fear of complication. The choice between a pick-up or a prostitute seemed to be largely a matter of time, place, mood, and chance.

In some instances they did seem to feel that particular practices, such as urinating on a girl's leg or opening one's fly while talking to a girl, were unusual or "unnatural." They also seemed to be somewhat unsure of the normality of their orgies and homosexual games. However, there was no way for me to determine whether the soldiers were expressing personal misgivings about their own behavior or making defensive statements to a potentially critical outsider. At no point do I recall a soldier betraying embarassment and yet I am inclined to think that they themselves may have wondered at times what drove them to sexual excesses.

The Green Berets outwardly displayed nearly complete freedom from social and sexual anxiety, showed a sometimes remarkable degree of perception, and usually demonstrated full control over their feelings and actions. They prevented sexual adventures from tarnishing their public image by restricting them to distant places or to situations which enjoyed the tacit approval of the participants, public, military superiors, and local business people. Most of their special relationships remained undisturbed. Their feelings for a particular girl did not become confused or uncertain. This was most apparent when they were having sexual relations with other women while cohabiting with their wives, fiancées, and steady girlfriends. I feel that these behaviors indicate a weak sense of masculine identity and lack of sexual confidence. The behavior is too compulsive and indiscriminate and suggests underlying uncertainty and the need for repeated confirmation at all costs. The disadvantages accrued by the Green Berets through their sexual habits were a greater likelihood of marital disharmony and venereal disease. They were not disturbed by either.

The soldiers' sexual habits might seem to imply that they did not have different moral standards for men and women. But this is not true. Both in questionnaires and during the interviews they clearly stated that sexual liberalism should be reserved for males. They disapproved or condemned premarital sexual relations for women but approved of them for men. Their descriptions of girls who went to bed with them included such words as "weird," "nymphomaniac," "sluts," "whores," "easy lay," "knuckleheads," "lacking common sense." This view was not modified through consideration of their own habits, direct confrontation with widespread promiscuity in the military community—to which they have made substantial contributions—pleasant relationships they had with women, or the fact that very few of them married virgins.

This double standard and its implicit moral condemnation of women appears to serve several purposes. By categorically putting a low moral value on any woman who sleeps with them, they found easy justification for their own behavior, avoiding the necessity of self-criticism. Since they know that their intentions do not go beyond their own sexual gratification, the double standard allows them to express scorn for any woman who falls for their line. In this way they avoid the problem of guilt. If all women automatically become whores the moment they engage in sexual relations, then one need not ever feel badly, no matter what one has done to get them into bed. The double standard also provided them with a permanent feeling of sexual superiority.

The full character of this attitude becomes more apparent when it is connected with their strong disapproval of masturbation. Their reasons for condemning masturbation had little to do with explicit moral concepts, although a residue of parental prohibitions could be seen in a few cases. They rejected masturbation because they perceived it is as a sign of weakness, a blow against their manliness, an indication of social and sexual failure. At the same time they sought compulsively to have their potency confirmed, and this often led them to unscrupulous seductions. But instead of expressing gratitude to the women for submitting to them, they rejected them and called them whores. Since in their minds a whore cannot confirm anything, the Green Berets have remained perpetually discontented.

THE RESISTERS

First Intercourse

CASE 103

I met her in college. . . . Basically we were both more or less lonely. She wasn't as articulate as I might have wanted. I had difficulty speaking to her. We only went to bed after maybe three months or so.

CASE 104

She was considerably older. I was about twenty and I was getting involved psychologically and emotionally with her. . . . I had sort of a physical relationship with her for quite a while, I guess, heavy petting for about a year or more. It just slowly progressed into something. It developed after a very close communicative, emotional relationship had developed. . . . In order to feel effectively attractive, I have to grow into knowing somebody. And this had been going on so long. . . . I had been making love to her for a long time with the exception of my final act on it. It wasn't any huge move from where we were . . . it just evoked a very, very good feeling. . . . Before that she hadn't wanted to do it and it didn't really occur to me to push it. And at that point it wasn't pushing. It was just a suggestion. We'd had so many discussions on the philosophical aspects of love, long before it came up as a primary subject. And when it grows like that you can sense where a person is at all times. In an intense situation you can fool yourself into thinking something. Over a long period you can't. You know exactly how you feel.

CASE 105

After I broke up with this one girl—I went with her up until my freshman year in college—I just had a desire to get laid. It was an ego-thing. You know, I hadn't been laid before. So this girl was around, I knew her from high school, and I got laid. No, I don't think it brought us closer, which is unfortunate.

CASE 110

It was very awkward, very beautiful in its awkwardness. I think it was a lovely thing. . . . She didn't seem to think it was as beautiful as I thought it was. She wanted a mature, adult living relationship and I liked the high school romance, so she just sort of outgrew me in that way very quickly. . . . She was very warm and very sensual and very feeling and very knowing of the fact she was touching and being touched.

CASE 120

I was seventeen. It was with a girl in the neighborhood and, uh, I don't know if she was a prostitute or not. The thing was arranged for me by the older kids in the neighborhood. It was really the most horrible experience that I know of. I was very, you know, very frightened by the whole thing at the time.

CASE 122

Twenty years old. I wanted to marry her. . . . We had been rolling around in bed for a year and a half before we finally had intercourse. . . . Well, we waited until we felt we could wake up in the morning and be happy.

CASE 123

There was a girl in one of my classes. I wasn't going out with her but she was very pretty. She didn't live too far from me and I remember going over there one day. She was at a friend's house who lived down the block from me and I went over there and . . . there was a record playing and we were dancing. Her friend was upstairs cleaning and we were downstairs and we went into the basement of the house and there had intercourse. And I remember feeling guilty about it for a long, long time because . . . at that time I remembered that all through my Catholic school days sex was taught as something bad, bad, bad. Something strictly taboo except for married people, and I felt very guilty. I knew it took me about six months before I went to confession [laughs] 'cause I was afraid to tell the priest what had happened. But I finally did and I went to confession and they bawled me out for it, of course, and I really was feeling extremely relieved when I left. About three weeks later [laughs] I went out again and I met that same girl [laughs] and it happened again. And I said, "Gee, what are you doing?" [large laugh]. So it went on that way and I remember I didn't go back to confession about it. I figured, you know, I already heard the story he's going to give me, so why bother?

Virtually all the war resisters expressed feelings of sorrow, regret, and disappointment in themselves about the "unfortunate" aspects of their early sexual experience. These misgivings were stated within the framework of a particular vision of communicative human relations characterized by emotional openness and sensitivity, self-restraint, and sharing. Most of them felt that they had been unable to demonstrate these qualities in some of their earlier relationships, and that among the numerous consequences of this failing they had lost out on opportunities for personal growth and had been able to see their own inadequacies more clearly. None of them rejected the idea of sexual pleasure as something unacceptable in its own right, but they did feel an aversion to one-sided sexual contacts because they represented a negation of the deeper purpose of human encounters.

These attitudes are among the few commonalities to be found among the resisters on the theme of sexuality. Their patterns of sexual development, their sexual experiences, and their sexual conflicts do not allow for broad generalizations. By linking various biosocial milestones in their sexual development with the stiuations in which they occurred and the resisters' responses to these events, we find several relatively consistent patterns.

Sexual Training and Experiences

More than half the war resisters received sexual instruction from their parents and from older siblings. In a few cases this was augmented by sex education programs in high school.* For many, private reading constituted an important additional source of instruction. They began with biological and anatomical discussions of the male and female reproductive organs and then

---

*Most of the boys who received sexual training at home had an unproblematical sexual development. This was also true for several others who had not received any formal sexual education. The few boys who experienced conflicts, guilt and more than one "bad" sexual experience had not received formal sexual instruction from their parents. Their early experiences with intercourse were further complicated by the residue of religious taboos, frustrating love relationships, and the conquest and consumption attitude towards sexuality prevalent in their circle of friends.

gravitated to philosophical and social-psychological essays on heterosexual and human relations. Erich Fromm's *The Art of Loving* and Martin Buber's *I and Thou* were frequently mentioned in this context as strong influences in adolescence.

Some of the resisters began to masturbate during late childhood and others during early, middle, or late adolescence.* The statement of one is representative of the naturalness with which nearly all of them viewed this aspect of their sexual development. "I just tried it one day, you know, I found it quite enjoyable. It just seemed like the time to do it. Like a woodchuck coming out of hibernation or something." Having begun, most masturbated regularly and with pleasure. Except for periods in which they were having intercourse, masturbation was their major method of attaining orgasm. While all of them considered intercourse preferable, they did not view masturbation as an unusual or uncomfortable practice. At the time of our interview, they felt that the relief of their physical needs through masturbation was more satisfactory than purely physical contacts with women. Since they viewed masturbation as a self-evident practice, most of them did not immediately understand my asking why they had not experienced guilt or conflict in this connection. Some gave me the feeling that this question could only be posed by someone who had sexual conflicts, others said they had not been indoctrinated with sexual taboos, and still others replied rhetorically with, "Feel guilty about what?"**

On the average, more than four and one-half years passed between the resisters' first masturbation and their first complete sexual intercourse.*** This statistic demonstrates awareness of sexual urges as well as a relatively unhurried movement toward full sexual activity.**** It may be that their satisfaction with masturbation partially explains why for many years most of them did not approach girls just for the relief of their physical needs. Other factors are probably of equal, perhaps greater, relevance. One correlate of early sexual activity is strong sexual taboos in the home. These were absent in nearly all resister families. Among males, early and conquest-motivated sexual activity also correlates with subcultural norms and behavioral patterns

---

*First masturbation occurred between the ages of ten and nineteen. The average age was 13.5 years.

**The impact of religious training and childhood religiosity were apparent in several boys' early sexual development. The only resister who had not masturbated was Catholic. Two of the three boys who experienced guilt in connection with masturbation were also Catholic and attributed their initial guilt feelings to the taboos on sexuality expressed by the nuns, priests, and students in their parochial schools. The other boy with guilt feelings over masturbation had been a devout Lutheran.

***This time gap ranged from one to ten years. The most typical gap was between three and seven years.

****This was the feeling expressed by the youngest (seventeen-year-old) war resister who explained that he was not particularly interested in girls and that intercourse was too important to be rushed.

in which males dominate females and condescend to them. These conditions too were absent in the resisters' families and in most of their peer groups. As we saw in the last chapter, during the war resisters' high school and college years, most of them, and their closest friends, engaged in a variety of creative, intellectual, academic, and athletic activities which they perceived as their central outlets for personal actualization and peer-group and social confirmation. Ego bolstering through sexual conquests was therefore rarely conspicuous in their subcultural norms or their personal life styles. And finally, though sexuality was not tabooed in most of their families, it may be assumed that the gravity of sexual intimacy in human terms was emphasized in their general moral and social training. It was undoubtedly presented to them as something to be taken quite seriously.

Patterns of Sexual and Emotional Expression

Both before and after first intercourse, most of the war resisters had had close heterosexual relationships both with and without sexual intimacy.* The major key to their later sexual behavior lies in the circumstances surrounding their first intercourse. Those boys who experienced it initially within the context of a love relationship had intercourse subsequently only with girls they loved or felt very close to. Varying degrees of emotional superficiality and interpersonal insignificance at first intercourse corresponded to similar circumstances during most of their subsequent sexual contacts.

There does not seem to have been a single determinant for this pattern. First intercourse was imbedded within the entire framework of the war resisters' sexual training, social and emotional maturity, peer group relations and heterosexual experience. The eight resisters who viewed their first intercourse primarily as an emotionally enriching experience for themselves and their girlfriends also possessed other distinguishing characteristics. As a group, they had received the most extensive sexual education at home. They also waited longer before first intercourse (an average of 5.1 years after first masturbation), and during this time met girls with whom they were able to establish durable and emotionally close relationships and with whom they were able to share first intercourse. The girls were also inexperienced and were portrayed as having demonstrated tenderness, excitement, and sincerity. It seems that the depth of feeling and the mutuality of their first experience left such a deep impact on these boys that they could not envision sexual intimacy under other circumstances. While some of them subsequently had intercourse with women they did not love, even this sexual intimacy was described as only a component of an otherwise strong relationship.

*The exceptions to this were two who had no further relationships after marriage. One had had intercourse for the first time after his marriage and the other married his second girl-friend.

When the second subgroup of seven war resisters experienced inter-course for the first time, they were one year younger (18.25 years) than the former group. First intercourse was with girls they had known and liked, but with whom they felt no deep emotional bonds. These men had not received a uniformly thorough sexual education at home; some of them had none at all. While they began to masturbate at the same age as the first subgroup (at an average age of 13.5 years), first intercourse took place approximately one year earlier than in the first group. Most of them enjoyed first inter-course and some felt that it had deepened the relationship with the girl. However, this event was not remembered as intensely and deeply as by by first group. In their subsequent dating, these men were seldom able to combine sexual intimacy with a love relationship, although, with one excep-tion, they slept only with girls they liked and had dated regularly. Many of these relationships were long and contained a good understanding. The ele-ments of deep fascination and emotional involvement, however, were absent. These resisters averaged 7.2 different sexual partners, or twice as many as the first group.

Five war resisters initially experienced intercourse with a casual date. Some had known the girls for several years and others had just met them. Intercourse was a chance and casual aspect of the contact, without direct inter-personal or emotional significance. These boys averaged 17.5 years of age at that time, almost two years younger than the first group and one year younger than the second. Their onset of masturbation averaged two years later than the first two subgroups and their first intercourse was from 1.2 to 2.3 years earlier. Only one of them had received sexual instruction from his parents. Most had had sexually intimate relations with girls they liked but only two were able to combine sexual intimacy with a love relationship; both relationships were short-lived. This group did not have sexual inter-course with more women than did the previous group, but their sexual expe-riences tended to be more superficial. Both those with large numbers of dif-ferent sexual partners and those with few had rarely been able to combine sexual and emotional intimacy with a girl. This subgroup contained the only war resister who had never masturbated. He had never had an emotionally close heterosexual friendship. His interest in all five of his sexual partners had been primarily physical. He was also the only resister who had partici-pated in sexual relations in a group setting and who did not see any neces-sary connection between personal and sexual intimacy.

The distinguishing feature of the last subgroup of four resisters is that they had all had intercourse with a prostitute. In three cases this had been their first intercourse. These boys had begun to masturbate earliest (at an av-erage age of 12.2), and had waited as long as the first group for first inter-course. Their second and more decisive characteristic was the diversity of their sexual behavior. They had had intercourse just for physical pleasure, with women they had liked, and at least once within a love relationship. To-gether they compiled the largest average number of sexual partners (17.2). Only one had received any sexual instruction at home or in school.

No single factor can be isolated as a general key to the war resisters' sexual development. It may well be that a good portion of luck as well as the ability to select women who would return their feelings enabled the ma-jority of them to have many and in some cases exclusively positive emotional and physically intimate relationships. When this did not occur, the signs were much clearer. In each of the four subgroups, there was at least one and sometimes two who experienced periods of confusion, frustration, and deep pain related to sexual behavior. Several had been deeply hurt by broken ro-mances, others felt they had had bad luck in general with deeper friendships, and still others had been briefly exposed to the pressures of social groups—football teammates, college fraternities, sexual liberation groups—in which matter-of-fact consumption of exploitive attitudes toward sexuality pre-vailed. A few required several years to come to grips with the religious in-doctrination they had received on sexuality.* One or more of these addition-al disturbing influences combined with serious conflicts within the resisters' families during childhood or adolescence corresponded with feelings of in-adequacy and difficulty in establishing and maintaining a stable heterosexual relationship with sexual intimacy.

Self-Perception in Sexual and Emotional Matters

All but one of the resisters felt that he had been emotionally immature for several years after his first intercourse. Those who had had intercourse only within a love relationship regarded their immaturity primarily in terms of learning how to open themselves more fully to emotional experience, and how to develop the ability to attend to women's feelings more closely. A similar perspective was also voiced by several war resisters who had not as yet experienced a durable love relationship. They felt that this had been part-ly due to an unwillingness on their part to show the necessary openness and

---

*Three of the six war resisters who were raised as Catholics consciously experienced guilt and conflict in connection with masturbation and intercourse. None experienced first intercourse within a love relationship. Three passed through extended periods of confused and superficially exploitive sexual activity and of the two who had experienced sexual intimacy within a love relationship, one had not been able to relate to this situation. From a confessional standpoint, these resisters had the greatest conflict, anxiety, and dissatisfaction in sexual matters. While all of them attributed this largely to the sexual taboos in their religious education, the differences in their personal response to that training reflect the presence of other important influences, as previously mentioned. Two distinct patterns of dealing with sexual conflicts emerged among the Catholic war resisters. Those who were more extroverted and less introspective repressed these conflicts. This was followed by "carefree" sexual activity. The more introspective ones experi-enced their conflicts acutely, and their relationships with girls to whom they were sexually at-tracted were fraught with anxiety, passivity, and, in one case, periodic impotence.

sensitivity which would have solidified some of their friendships. The few who lost a love relationship felt that this had been largely a result their own immaturity.

These self-perceptions can only be understood within the context of the war resisters' view of themselves, and their vision of the nature of a close emotional relationship. They were not hesitant to attach such labels as "childish," "insensitive," or "emotionally closed" to relationships and feelings which others might very well find acceptable and satisfying. Each of them seemed to be searching for a fuller form of communication, a more complete means of relating to another person. Some felt that they had been opened and brought closer to this by particular women who had possessed these qualities. The men grew in these relationships and found the mutuality they had sought. Some came to recognize this possibility only after losing the women they loved. Others came to this realization after one or more superficial sexual contacts.

While nearly all the war resisters had been able to enjoy intercourse as a physical experience from the time of their first intercourse, with growing experience and maturity they began to find it increasingly difficult to separate the emotional and physical components of their needs. This merging toward a more total experience seems to have had a close chronological connection to the emergence of their social conscience and the beginning of their sociopolitical engagement. When they finally discovered the basic incompatibility between their "real" needs and the social pressures which had been shaping them, they rejected more than the outward structure of their immediate social environment. They also discovered that they could not function on a personal level within a framework which systematically led to superficial, selfish, and exploitive interpersonal relations.

These insights were most clearly apparent among the few resisters who had attended fraternity parties. Initially they had forced themselves to go along with what they considered the coarseness and sexual promiscuity of the other students. Two had intercourse with girls whom they had not known before, because this was the accepted standard and they wanted to "belong to" the group. One had "liquored up a girl in the customary fashion," but said that he could not bring himself to "use her body" under such circumstances. The conflicts of these men as well as those who had had independently initiated similar experiences highlight their struggle to make claim to an individual identity and to give their sexual expression a deeper meaning. They reached a point in their lives at which they could not longer maintain sexual pretenses. They could no longer suppress their real feelings in favor of an artificially constructed alter ego. These war resisters, in comparison to the others, were exceptional in the sense that their insights were gained at the cost of greater pain and disappointment.

Love Affairs that Failed

One indication of the resisters' capacity for deep emotional relationships can be found in the intensity and duration of the pain they felt when their feelings of love were not returned. Several experienced much pain and suffered for months and years thereafter. One described an early experience: "I was in the ninth grade. It sounds crazy, but I was really in love. And this girl broke up with me and it took me five years to be able to look at her without feeling pain." Others had similar experiences which left them deeply hurt. Some tried to overcome this pain by indulging in superficial sexual conquests. Eventually they recognized that, as one put it, they "really needed a very serious, you know, deep relationship with a woman . . . not just in a physical way and not in a casual way."

Pain was felt not only when a woman was completely lost or during periods of loneliness and reminiscence; all of the men experienced moments when they came to recognize what they were missing and where they had failed. When these occurred within a durable relationship, pain led directly to new discoveries and joys, since the resisters were able to act on their insights and achieve a closer understanding with their girlfriends and wives. Others felt that their painful self-perception had led them to new readiness for a deep relationship, that the women they had loved had taught them how to relate to people, to enjoy another person's companionship, to be "decent," to "enjoy life," to "share," to be "compassionate," and to "treat each person as an individual."

In two cases, emotional pain combined with other factors led to emotional isolation from women. Both resisters had had serious conflicts with one or both parents. Both had fallen deeply in love with girls who later broke up with them. At the time of their interviews, neither man had recovered from this experience. They had both had unsatisfactory physical contacts with other women, and their renewed attempts to consolidate romances failed. They felt they had compromised themselves and the women in the purely physical contacts and had not been able to handle the complexity of their more promising relationships. Both had sought celibate ways of living. One had retired to a Catholic monastery and the other planned to devote his energies to the peace movement and possibly to remain celibate. For him, there were "too many hassles" with women.

Attitudes

CASE 101

We went sort of into this male chauvinism thing. Occasional necking, petting and that sort of knocking-up thing once in a while. But as far as a relationship was concerned, it didn't occur ... and then when I was nineteen there was this gradual opening with one other person and myself. Just an emotional opening. It really opened me up as a person. ... And we saw each other for two and a half years.

CASE 105

So, like between the age of nineteen and twenty-three, I got laid as much as I could by anybody. Almost anybody. And there was very seldom any emotional feeling. I just grew out of that. Now, instead of sex coming really quickly, I'm sort of building on a relationship. ... Most of the time I'd rather just sit and hold hands with a girl.

CASE 111

I'm just not the type of guy that goes and hustles. When I ran into the fraternity scene I just hustled chicks left and right. ... It was a bad scene ... a fraternity, you know, you had a great house, the best on the campus, and chicks wanted to get into that house. So there was no trouble at all. But I didn't like it. I found myself being phony and superficial and not how I really am which is very shy. ... Now I'm not really looking to go to bed. I mean, if we end up going to bed together, o.k., but I don't look for that. I'm after something a lot more.

Prostitutes

CASE 104

Unless I'm emotionally involved with somebody, I'd probably be quite impotent.

CASE 105

No, I wouldn't [go to a prostitute]. But if I had enough money, I would at least take a few hours and sit down and talk with them. I think I'm going to do that.

CASE 106

I can visualize it [intercourse with a prostitute] abstractly as an experience, but I don't think I would [actually have the experience]. I don't feel it's anything I would need or necessarily profit by at this time.

CASE 107

I don't have any guilt. It's kind of useless. It was something I don't think I'd want to do again, not because there's anything wrong with it but it's just something that's not too worthwhile. ... No, I wouldn't want to be in her position. If you think what her life must be like I guess you have to feel bad. ... Like the things she went through, the way she grew up. ... The reasons she's a prostitute, that's the worst part of it. You can't have sympathy for people because that's useless. You might want to change them or help them.

CASE 110

A very strange friend of mine . . . uses prostitutes in his work to make sales. That whole subculture is very strange to me. He offered that to me for a birthday present when I turned eighteen, but I didn't feel like it. Now I think I'd take him up on it out of curiosity.

Do you have any particular feelings of remorse or sadness about the fact that there are prostitutes?

Only that there are also garbage men. . . . There are people doing all sorts of distasteful things.

CASE 119

I would have sort of mixed feelings. One getting sexual pleasure, physical pleasure out of it, but at the same time feeling somewhat disgusted with myself when I wasn't able to control my emotions and ended up going to a prostitute . . . a little bit, somewhat debased. . . . No, I couldn't do it, I mean, I could do it but it wouldn't be nearly as enjoyable, it's just a fraction of the pleasure of a total relationship. It just seems artificial and false.

The resisters saw themselves and women as equal sexual partners, irrespective of the context of their sexual contact.* Sexual intercourse was experienced as a mutual undertaking, whether its immediate goal was physical pleasure alone or was coupled with emotional expression. The fact that none of them employed derisive or slanderous terms to describe these women seems to have been due to two factors: they were more concerned with the deficiencies in themselves which had led to such contacts, feeling that they would not have allowed superficial sexual contacts to arise had they been more mature; equally important, they suspected that these women had had similar problems, as well as enjoying the right to the same sexual freedom that men enjoy.

These sentiments help clarify the resisters' feelings about sexual intercourse with prostitutes. They saw such a possibility or past experience as a reflection on themselves as well as in terms of the total life situation of a woman who has to sell her body for money. The four men who had had intercourse with prostitutes spoke about these experiences in much the same way as those who had had intercourse just for physical pleasure. Those who had never slept with a prostitute could not concretely picture this act; one planned to go to one to satisfy his curiosity. Many saw no fundamental difference between patronizing a prostitute and "making a pick-up"; others emphasized the impossibility of exploiting a disadvantaged person.

---

*The only exception to this involved intercourse with prostitutes and with emotionally disturbed girls. The few resisters who had had such experiences felt that these women had been in a disadvantaged position and that their own behavior had been regrettable.

Conclusions

There was a reciprocal connection between the war resisters' emotional maturation and sexual experience. The variability in the chronology of their sexual development and in the quantity and kind of their sexual experience contrasts sharply with the gradual emergence of a largely uniform attitude toward sexual expression. With growing maturity all but one of them came to regard intercourse as undesirable outside a love relationship. The fact that this orientation toward the use of their own and others' bodies followed vast differences in previous sexual experience and attitudes indicates that within relatively few years a major transition had taken place in many resisters' outlooks. It was in these cases that this transition accompanied the beginnings and consolidation of an antiwar commitment. This finding strongly suggests that once these men accepted the idea that a part of their personal fulfillment was contingent on the establishment of a deep and durable love relationship, they could no longer remain detached from the larger political and social issues of their time. The fact that in many cases the desire for this kind of intimacy had not as yet been realized when the decision to resist had been made supposes that the vision of a particular form of human relations was sufficient to guide both their private life and public behavior.

The similarities between the resisters' attitudes toward sexual expression and their overall approach to people and politics cannot be overlooked. For some of them, this seems to have resulted in continuous frustration. A utopian view of society stands little chance of realization, and therefore confronts the dreamer with perpetual torment. He cannot reconcile his vision with imposing realities. Some of the resisters suffered so acutely from their disappointments in love or placed such high demands on themselves that they seemed to be living in painful hesitancy in their relations with women. The depth of this conflict was great enough to drive two to consider celibacy; these extreme examples illustrate the tendency of a few others to express general love of mankind but to fear the strain of the intimate personal love relationship they desired.

There does not appear to be any connection between the resisters' degree of success in establishing a love relationship and their willingness to make personal sacrifices for their antiwar stand. Among the politically most active, there were married, engaged, and lonely, single war resisters, just as there were among those who saw their antiwar stand more in terms of a private commitment.

Notes

1. F. Thorne, in *Journal of Clinical Psychology*, XII (1966): "The Sex Inventory," 367-374; "Scales for Rating Sexual Experience," 405-407; "A Factorial Study of Sexuality in Adult Males," 378-386. Also F. Thorne and T. Haupt, "The Objective Measurement of the Sex Attitudes and Behavior in Adult Males," *Journal of Clinical Psychology*, XII (1966), 395-403.

CHAPTER 5

Acts of War

Patriotism

CASE 204

Yeah, well, I'll support my country, right or wrong.

CASE 206

I realize that nobody's perfect and many people have got their thumb in the pie over there. That's definitely the case. But whatever happens, I'll stick by them.

CASE 212

Patriotism is the ability to die gracefully.

CASE 213

Well, ever since I can remember, back in grade school, when we used to say the Pledge of Allegiance in the morning, even through high school and even now, I get this tingling sensation.

CASE 218

Well, all people can't serve in high places and somebody has got to be the cog in the wheel. The cog that pays the taxes and tries to obey the laws that are set down by the federal government. And a patriotic person should vote. If he had a dissatisfaction he should let it, the dissatisfaction, be known to his Congressman and something like this here.

CASE 219

Patriotism in my opinion is a funny thing. I don't really consider myself too patriotic. I hate politicians. I hate politics. I'm not very fond of the President. In fact, the last couple of Presidents I haven't really cared for. I don't believe in waving flags. When I go to a foreign country I don't like to go around broadcasting that I'm American. I consider myself, rather than being patriotic, I consider myself a professional soldier. Regardless of why we're fighting, it doesn't matter to me why we're fighting or where we're fighting. It's my job as a soldier. I'm professional. I got there and I fight and if I think about an ideal, the ideals behind it get so involved with the god-damn corrupt people and the governments and the trade and industry that it makes me feel like getting out of the Army again and being a mercenary in some isolated area of the world where I don't have to put up with so many corrupt people and politics. I hate communism actually. But in many countries it could be a good thing.

I'm not patriotic really, but I hate to see a damn person shirk their obligation. . . . If I were given a mission to assassinate people like this, I wouldn't hesitate. . . . In fact, my team has even discussed it and a lot of other people would gladly volunteer our services but the government would never go along with it.

CASE 221

I believe in fighting for the American government, for the way our government operates and I don't know if you'd call it patriotism or not. . . . A lot of it has to do with—'cause I enjoy the business and another thing I enjoy, we get, as you know, extra pay.

CASE 226

Uhm, I don't know . . . I really don't know how to express myself. . . . [I] believe in, fight for, uh, what my country stands for, uh, our way of life, uh, I really can't express myself.

CASE 228

Well, you know, I'm guarding the country. I get a big charge out of the "Star Spangled Banner" being played.

Going to Vietnam

CASE 215

Well, in the spring semester my roommate walked in and told me about this great deal he had found on becoming a jungle killer and I laughed at him and joked with him about it for about three weeks. And he kept talking about it and talking about it and one Saturday afternoon we just went down and joined. . . . I had met some Green Berets earlier and I was quite impressed with them. They weren't the average soldier. They were part of a demonstration team and they cleaned up a bar quite well.

CASE 217

Well, their whole concept. The whole way they train and everything is based on Vietnam. The whole attitude. You're just indoctrinated for Vietnam. The whole attitude. . . . All your training goes through Vietnam. It's all jungle warfare. Uh, almost everybody you get in is coming from Vietnam. And that's all you hear about. That's daily conversation. And you just, you know, it's just a part of you. You're just about in Vietnam there [during training]. . . . I hate the Army part where you just sit around and wait and wait. You actually got to get out and do something you've been trained to do. You earn your money. I'm a firm believer in earning your money. When you just sit around garrison duty you don't earn it.

CASE 218

Well, uh, just like I say. I guess it's some kind of a basic excitement to start with and, uh, curiosity. I mean, if you train a—you take a good athlete. You train him boxing, football. If you're trained, you're curious to see how you perform.

CASE 221

Well, I had been trained for nine months on guerilla operations, combat operations, on how to kill and I just wanted to see if I could put it into use, I guess.

CASE 227

Well, more exciting for one. Everything was cloak and dagger and stuff like this. And this is what I want. . . . I ended up getting in. When I got there it wasn't as cloak and dagger as, you know, they had led it on to be. It's been a good life, I've enjoyed it.

CASE 228

That's the only war we've got, you know. It's a good training ground for our troops. It's a good try-out ground, testing ground for our equipment and doctrine, tactics. And I think a by-product is that a lot of these kids go through Vietnam and they come back, I think, they make a little bit better citizens. . . . Well, I think you get a better grasp on reality and they're more mature.

Professional Soldierism

CASE 201

You would have some excitement like a war or something. Then if it's going to be peaceful that wouldn't make sense. I mean, I—I don't mind being in peacetime, you know. But then you won't be a soldier. You would be just a civil servant in a uniform. So you're going to be assigned a desk job or something, and, that's no use to me. I mean, if I'm going to be a soldier I want to be a soldier. You know, mercenary and stuff. But not to be sitting around at being a sergeant at a desk or something. 'Cause I don't get anything out of it then.

CASE 212

I don't enjoy just going out and shooting people. I think everybody enjoys a job he can do well. That's a fact of pride. . . . You can go one step further and say you actually enjoy killing people, but we're using a harsh word here.

I don't think it's necessary. I did the job. I would do it again. I would do it to the best of my ability. ... Personally speaking, I'm very efficient at my job and this is what my country wants me to do and this is what people like yourself or the people of the United States have chosen for me to do as long as I'm willing to stay there to do it, because some people won't do it and if there isn't people like me then the job won't get done ... so I'm just doing the dirty end of the work somebody else won't do.

CASE 215

Would you say that you have found a home in the Army?
Yeah. Definitely.

And you consider yourself a professional soldier?
Yes.

What does that mean to you?
Okay, that means that I feel that my profession is the military. I am very patriotic to the United States. However, I feel that I have chosen more or less my life now to be the military whether it is being in Special Forces and that it could be a pilot. It's still the United States Army or the Army period. And I feel that if tomorrow the United States government were to be overthrown and a new government would come into power, I feel that with a little bit of readjusting I could be feel like that it's my line of work.

You said that if the government was overthrown that you think you could make the adjustment to be a good soldier in anybody's Army, fight for anybody's cause. Why?
Well, because I feel that I have been in the military long enough, I have learned enough about the military to know that when you get down on the lower level it doesn't really matter who or why makes the decision. But really all—all that really matters is how well the people in the lower echelon are disciplined to take the orders. And I feel quite capable of taking orders or giving orders to almost anybody.

Why do you think you'd be able to fight anybody's cause?
Well, I wouldn't say anybody's—I'd—I'd say if the [chuckles] the United States would be overthrown by another power, that they'd definitely have the upper hand and I just think I could readjust and become part of their military. Uh, I shouldn't say for anybody's cause 'cause there are some causes such as the black militants that I don't think I could quite fight for them. I'd be more inclined in the rule of the civil war in the United States. A really big civil war, I would be more inclined rather than go to the other side, if the government were to be overthrown, I'd be more inclined to move into deserted areas like we're trained to do and form resistance groups against the new government, but I'd prefer to either form the resistance group or become a soldier for another country, rather than take another job somewhere.

CASE 221

I know what I'm doing. I know what my job is and I know how to conduct and control indigenous people and I do what I'm supposed to do. That is, sometimes I question. Most times I don't question what I'm told to do. And well, I wouldn't do anything else but stay in Special Forces.

Who were you thinking of fighting for in South Africa at the time you were thinking of it?
Any cause. It doesn't matter. At that particular time, uh, the mercenaries had already lost in the, uh, there was this one band of mercenaries that were led by a British exile, he was an ex-officer.

In the Congo?
In the Congo, yes. I figured by the time I was ready to get out of the army, 'cause I still had a commitment and I wouldn't be free until this November, I knew this would be out, this would be over with, because, uh, things like that don't last that long. But I figured if I went to South Africa and got a job.

And that wouldn't bother you?
No, I don't like niggers but I wouldn't mind. It's being paid by blacks to kill blacks. What the hell. But the thing of it is, I mean, that's an expression I use, but, see, I would plan on working in one of these other places in between wars, in between. Mercenary groups aren't always needed. It's a seasonal job . . . in between I would keep active as a militarist by training small groups of people as local defenses for plantations .

CASE 223

Do you think it would be possible for you to fight for another country, to be a professional soldier for another country?
Well, I probably would if the money was good, but not for the same reasons that I'm in the Army of the United States.

CASE 226

Do you consider yourself a professional soldier?
Yes, I do.

And what does that mean to you?
To me it means that . . . anything that I do in the Army I do to the best of my ability. . . . And I'm ready to do anything that the Army says I must do. Everything I do is for the Army. That's about all I can say about it.

Soldiers at War

The soldier makes war. His job performance is measured by his effectiveness in combat. In organizing the statements of the Green Berets on their combat experiences I concentrated mainly on the number of combat kills, the circumstances of the kills, who was killed, the killing weapon, the immediate reactions to the kills, atrocities committed, atrocities seen, and retrospective feelings about war experiences.

With the soldiers' help a personal kill was defined as killing someone and being absolutely sure of having done it oneself. This definition was adopted as one of the central guidelines for the discussion of combat experiences because it removed the impersonal elements of modern warfare and allowed me to gain insight into the soldier's immediate responses to his own actions. I felt that this approach would be most successful in helping them to reconstruct the circumstances of their combat experiences and to recount them from a personal standpoint. A few soldiers told me that they had never discussed these matters previously. Nevertheless, they all took the opportunity to give detailed and realistic accounts. They only required prompting on the question of their feelings about what they had seen and done.

At the time of our interviews, twenty Green Berets already had had one or more combat tours in Vietnam. While all of them were confident of having participated in kills, six soldiers denied having made personal kills. They explained that they fired along with many other soldiers in the direction of the enemy or called in air strikes on enemy positions but could not be sure that they themselves had ever fired a fatal shot. The other fourteen were confident of at least one personal kill and reported an average of nine. Among the dead were women, children, and old people, both armed and unarmed. A substantial number died from bullet wounds inflicted by the soldiers. Not every soldier killed women, children, and old people but most of them killed one or the other in addition to armed adult males. Eight soldiers admitted active or passive involvement in the torture and mistreatment of prisoners. Passive involvement is defined as watching others without physical or verbal intervention.

Each of the fourteen Vietnam veterans who was sure of at least one personal kill was carefully questioned about his emotional reactions to what he saw and did in Vietnam. Since as much as five years had elapsed in some cases I was doubtful at first about their ability to recall initial emotional responses to a first kill, a mutilated American body, or a destroyed village. Although they often required prompting and I found it necessary to repeat and rephrase questions, I was surprised that recall for their feelings seemed to be as fresh and vivid as their accounts of the events themselves.

For a first analysis, the soldiers' feelings were divided into subcategories corresponding to who was killed. There were separate categories for armed and unarmed women, armed and unarmed children, and for dead Americans. In addition there was a category titled "feelings at the time of the kill" and another called "general attitude toward killing." After analyzing the data I found that this detailed analysis had been in vain because there was so little variability in the soldiers' statements. Nearly all of them explained that killing was routine and caused them no difficulties. The most frequent response to killing unarmed persons (men, women, and children) was "no feeling at all." When the killing involved unarmed children some soldiers expressed remorse. If the child was armed, a few soldiers said that they were "glad" they had killed it. A number of soldiers were glad that they killed women, particularly if the women had been armed. At the time of the kill, four Green Berets described an elated feeling, seven explained

'It was them or us," two stated that they felt "nothing at all," and one
aid he had felt "badly." Their reactions to the dead mutilated Americans
vere complete indifference in nine cases, nausea in two, two cases of increased hatred of the Vietcong, and one of sadness.

Personal Kills

CASE 210

had a 13-year-old girl shooting at me with a rifle. What am I suppose to
do, throw down my rifle because she is a girl and let her shoot me up? I shot
her. Then I picked up her body and threw it in the rice paddy so to contaminate
the rice. We put three other bodies in there too. The only thing I remember
about her was she was very pretty, but she was very deadly too.

CASE 212

got mad. This woman was firing at us. We didn't know it was a woman at
the time. I would have killed her anyway. But she was firing at us. I shot her
with a M16 rifle. The bullets went through her and killed the baby she was
carrying on her back. I felt bad about killing the baby. I didn't feel bad about
killing her. I don't believe the woman had any business in the war situation.
But that's the ground she chose.

CASE 215

was on reconnaissance and we came to a rubber tree plantation and decided
it was a good place to sit down and have lunch. So I took two men to scout
around the area. I walked I guess about fifty meters out in the rubber tree plantation and we spotted a guard just leaning against a tree. There must have been
a party or something because we were making all kinds of noise and he never
saw us. We just walked right up behind the tree and I just killed him with
my rifle butt. I used the back side of my rifle. I dumped my barrel and just
smashed him in the head with it. That was all. I didn't know I was going to
kill him, I think. It just happened.
    Once when I was moving across the trail, 'cause we never walk on trails,
you're just asking to be killed if you do, and my man gave me the signal to
come across, and apparently this fellow had been sitting in the bushes, going
to the bathroom [chuckle] or whatever the hell he was doing, and just stepped
out on the trail. He stepped out on the trail at the same moment and I guess
he was as surprised as I was, and I just reached my trigger quicker than he
reached his. And that one, he was just a few feet away. I was just faster. Just
plain habit. I was carrying a Swedish K, a nine millimeter submachine gun.
    The one time I was really close to one of them was with a woman. Well,
she was just a soldier in the company. She was dressed just like the rest of
them, carrying the same weapons as the rest of them, and we were to initiate
an ambush and being the advisor, I was supposed to start the ambush by firing
the first shot and she was just the closest person to me. But then she wasn't
really that close. Actually, she was about twenty meters away. You could see

that it was a woman. She didn't look like much of a woman. I mean, she ha
on the same uniform that the men had on, the same bandelero on her heac
even carried the same kind of weapon. In fact she was part of a point-elemen
so I figured she must have known something about combat if she was out o
a point. So I started the ambush by shooting her.

CASE 219

My job, our mission over there, was to kill VC. Well, close up I've probabl
killed, maybe fifteen or twenty where I was maybe from here to the door. Bu
other than that you can never say because you usually never see 'em the majorit
of the time unless you're in an ambush. During the daylight hours there's lot
of times you could see 'em but you couldn't actually tell if you shot that particu
lar man because when you have a whole platoon of people shooting and they're
shooting back at you, you're really not, really not looking at where you're shoot
ing. The most important thing is for you to get a large volume of fire, jus
a whole wall of bullets going his way.

We moved through this area and got hit hard and lost a lot of men. We
warned the civilians in the area that they were gonna get killed if they stayec
and they knew the Viet Cong were there and that the Americans were fighting
too, so I didn't feel bad about that. If they're stupid enough to stay there anc
get killed, well that's their business. . . . Yeah, there were women and childrer
in these villages as we moved through. Quite a few. They should have gotter
out too. We told them to, I mean our aircraft told 'em and sometimes, well,
you'd run across old men. They were crippled and all messed up. . . . On one
occasion I torched a house and there wasn't anybody in it. Then after I started
and the roof was on fire, I saw an old man crawl back in there. His leg was
all messed up. He looked like he had gangrene and he crawled back in there
and the house was on fire, and I don't know if he ever got back out or not.
I didn't have time to mess with him. So as we moved along that day we just
had to burn every village, blew up every bunker that we saw and completely
eliminated anything that could get behind us, 'cause we were constantly moving
forward and so we just had to burn it. That's the best policy, the best thing
to do. . . .

Yeah, I shot a lot of women and children. I mean, I didn't purposely go
around looking for women and children to shoot. On one occasion I was on
patrol and some of the local Viet Congs had detected us and we got fired at,
believe it or not, by crossbows, which is kinda discouraging because you don't
have any idea where the damn things are coming from. We had a mission of
staying there for a couple of days in a Viet Cong village. There were so many
Viet Congs around that we couldn't move for a whole day. Then we got reinforcements. Then we were given a sui, I call it a suicide mission, but it's really
a stupid mission. We had to attack the village the next morning. There were
only seven of us, seven Americans. There was probably a half a dozen houses,
so each of us picked a house and moved in as close as we could and since
they are straw houses they don't stop very many bullets. So on signal we all
just fired up those houses as much as we could and moved into 'em to check
out who we shot and there were several women and children in the house

hat I fired up, dead, and a couple wounded, but there were no Viet Congs. They had gotten out at night. We left 'em there, the wounded ones. Didn't have time to mess with 'em. Later on with one little girl we did evacuate. It was pretty risky bringing a helicopter in there. ... The other ones that were wounded in my hut they wouldn't have lasted very long anyway. They probably died shortly thereafter and we couldn't bring in a helicopter for 'em and we had no, no facilities or no means. There were just seven of us. In a Viet Cong area you're protecting yourself and you're not worrying about too many other people. But then there was this one real cute little girl who, uh, got hit two times and surprisingly enough it didn't mess her up too bad and I don't know, we just decided we were gonna try and get her out because we thought we could save her. And so we called in a helicopter and got her out and then continued up the road.

CASE 222

Oh yeah, I had personal kills on lots of occasions. We were working with small teams and could move pretty freely without being detected in an area, and one of our missions was to set up ambushes and just ambushing the enemy. I would say I got eight to ten that I'm positive. The closest was about fifteen feet.

We had this mission to check out an area. Of course, during these missions we had the secondary mission of setting up ambushes and just harassing the people and taking prisoners. We were going along this trail which wasn't on the map. I heard someone holler and it was one of our mercenaries. What it was was a bunch of VC coming up the trail behind us. Of course this Chinese did a stupid thing and pulled a pistol out and started shooting at them, which is one thing you don't do. Well, anyway, that kicked everything off. Well, actually, we were very fortunate that we pulled off the trail and made what we call a hasty ambush, and we got them good, a pretty good fire-fight there, and, uh, there were too many of them for us to handle so, I don't know, we killed five or six of them for sure. Then we stripped the bodies of their equipment. This is also one of our missions. We took rice samples and they were chemically analyzed so you could tell exactly what part of the country it came from.

Another time some choppers put us down on top of a hill at night. They must have heard us coming in. But they just layed there till the next morning until we got up. Evidently they had planned on hitting us when we were still in sleeping bags. Fortunately, one guy had to go to the latrine and when he did he just stumbled right over this one. That kicked everything off. The jungle was so heavy that you were just sneaking and crawling and peeking around trees and all this. There was this one guy over there. He fired several times and I knew he was there. He'd pop up and fire a few shots and then go back down and I just sat down and waited for him and when he stuck his head up I just fired. Well [chuckles] when he stuck his head up when I fired, he just stood up and went backwards and screamed.

Yeah, I saw some dead women, but not children. Saw them after bomb strikes on these small villages. Most of them were women soldiers carrying arms.

CASE 207

We were in this bad area and took a lot of kills and wounded. About an hour later they called in a Tiger Force. It's all volunteers. You can't get assigned to this unit. You have to volunteer to go to it. It's a suicide squad or whatever you want to call it. They go out and make contact without any support. It was such a bad area they couldn't operate. They got hit by a North Vietnamese battalion. And they called in for volunteers and I went and joined the Tiger Force. We went in with twenty-five men and took twenty-two casualties. I only volunteered that time to help out. I really didn't think too much of that unit because they were kind of crazy, most of them. They were the killers, you know. They were the kind that would kill just to kill. And I wasn't. I do it, I could do it right now to a VC. I couldn't go up to you [interviewer] in the street, you know, and think nothing of it.

CASE 226

Sure, definitely. I fired at women and children. Probably got some. I couldn't swear to it but I'd say yes. Yeah, say you get—I say firing. You've got people firing at you, you—naturally you shoot in a building and the bullets and you're going—you're going to kill innocent people. As a matter of fact, when you have your air attacks, you go in, you find . . . dead women and children. And at night you put out your—put out an ambush, and they come at night—they're dead. You have to do those things.

We're setting up just along the road and for a break, a rest, and always put a machine gun on, if possible cover your rear and one in the front, and one of the gunners looked up and noticed a Viet Cong, a woman, and a child come up front and got a little closer and he just started cutting them down, and killed them—the kid, the man, and wounded the woman real bad and he's just went ahead and done her in right there, had to kill her.

Anytime you've got a Viet Cong village or school or anything like this you always destroy. If you don't they'll come right back.

Yeah, I've called in artillery fire or air fire on a village. You're seeing all types of fire, all kinds of fire from a little village. You call in artillery, or aircraft, you move in there, you find dead people, but the people that's lying there, most of them is old women, old men, and uh, most of the young ones already left and I guess the old people, they think that you'll feel sorry for them, that they're too old to fight.

I never went up and just put my gun in a man's face and, uh, fired—killed. I've killed, I'd say five or six from a distance. Closest was about 100 yards. Shot them with automatic weapons. Start at the legs and round up. Yeah, they were pretty badly shot up.

CASE 213

We killed all six of 'em and we sort of patted each other on the back for a job well done. . . .

Well, it was the first time, I mean, it was just so cold-blooded that I didn't think about it at the time. Then I was sick afterwards. Just felt nauseated for a couple of hours. Then we ate lunch. . . .

We overran a village and killed everyone there, but that was normally—kind of a reprisal—you might say, for an attack . . . they could just gone in and aken all the young men of the village and just killed all of them and I'd be happy. I didn't feel the reprisal was quite needed, quite, as big and bad as they did it. . . .

No special feelings about dead children [very long pause]. Well, look, I've got no special feelings about killing somebody that has the capability of doing me harm . . . the women and children that were there weren't doing anything. They were just there. And that was enough reason for the montagnards to want to shoot them. I just couldn't see any reason in it . . . could have stopped it . . . just turned my back. . . .

I thought it was quite humane . . . let the blood squirt across the floor. . . .

But after I'd been in Vietnam for a while I lost respect for their lives. I had no respect for one of their lives whatsoever. It was—if he just died, well that was his problem. I had a job to do and if he died in the process, well, that was too bad. . . . You either gun-whored or you got dead.

Interrogations and Atrocities

CASE 207

I'm not going to mention names, but the platoon sergeant took a head and put it up in a tree. . . . And that was to show if you take any more heads, we're going to take them, you know. And the head in Vietnam is sacred. . . .

They brought in the guy, some sixteen year old. He was sitting there with a big grin on his face so I stuck a M16 in his face and pulled the trigger. It was empty, you know, and I knew it was empty, but I just did it to scare the hell out of him . . . Yeah, he was scared [chuckle]. His eyes lit up. I wasn't going to kill him because I knew he was an officer and officers give good information. I just did it for a little revenge.

CASE 210

Have you seen that picture? It's pretty famous. A VC hung upside down, tortured. If you ever get a hold of a magazine again, take a look at it. . . . That group right there, with the uniforms they wear, they're Vietnamese, not Special Forces. There's no Americans right there. The Americans—we got out of the way of that picture. That's where we had our name changed, but it's in the book. You can see it if you look. We were called Counter-Assassination Squad, that's what we were. . . . Well that picture in *Time*, uh, the Vietnamese tortured the P.O.W.'s. . . .

CASE 215

Oh, yes, I saw a few of them. I watched—they captured a 15-year-old girl. . . . soldier. . . . North Vietnamese. . . . uhm, real hard core type soldiers. . . . they captured her and tied her up and she was spittin' in people's faces and trying to kick them after she was tied up and captured. . . . I mean really indoc-trinated. We took a break and went to sleep and one of them woke me up.

... I woke up and he pointed over there and he had her staked out on the ground and all five of them had their fine time with her and they wanted to know if I wanted any before they killed her and I said, no thank you, uh just sit here, and then they killed her. ... Uh, he stabbed her in the both breasts with his bayonet until she died and then left her there. ... Yes, could have stopped it. ... I paid 'em, I led 'em. ... Boy, if I'd told them to kill one of the other men on the team, they'd have done it. They were totally loyal and when they started something like that, something they wanted to do just out of sheer hate, you have to take into consideration that if you stop them they're gonna resent it and you've got to live with these guys day after day. You've got to let your life depend on them and I just found it better at the time just to turn my back. . . .

I did some interrogation of my own. Don't know if you would call it an atrocity. I wouldn't. I thought it was quite humane according to the way they do things. We had a lieutenant that wouldn't talk. They had tried beating him with rubber hoses, they broke [chuckle] one of his legs, they tried everything. He'd'a' died first. Everytime they'd beat the guy up they'd bring him into my dispensary for me to fix him back up, wait a couple of days and beat the guy up again. I was getting kind of sick of it and I says, "Would you mind letting me interrogate him?" and he says, "Go ahead," and they had already tied him down to the bed so I just went into the office and I got out a ten cc syringe with an eighteen gauge needle and I walked up to him, put a tourniquet on his arm, the syringe was empty. I stuck it in a vein, took the syringe off the needle and just let the blood squirt across the floor and walked out of the room. I left him for about forty minutes and he did all the talking we wanted him to do, which I thought worked quite well. I don't consider that an atrocity. He lost a little over a pint of blood but it put the fear of God in him . . . No, I don't think I would have let him bleed to death [laughs a lot]. I would have had to clean up the mess. . . .

On one of my first missions I was with a NCO, one of the finest I've ever worked for. He got a direct commission to captain. . . . He interrogated three prisoners in front of me. He simply asked the first one a question and didn't even wait for an answer and stepped in front of the second one and blew the first one's brains out. ... That's one way of interrogating if you've got enough prisoners [chuckle].

CASE 217

The Vietnamese Special Forces techniques were beyond what we would do. . . . Well, for example, they had this one, I think a company commander. He knew where his units were. We interrogated him and we didn't get anything out of him so we gave him to them. And they were beating him up and everything, couldn't get anything out of him. So they went out and got a blasting cap and they tied it to his finger and blew it and blew the whole thing off . . . blew up the whole half of his hand. I came back and didn't ask him a single question. Just pulled out his dick and tied a new blasting cap to it and the guy started talking . . . After he talked they killed him. Shot him. ... He knew they would. . . . Just didn't want to be tortured. . . .

When we captured a VC and we'd turn them over like we're supposed
⊃, to higher headquarters, and we'd go out on operations a week later and
⌐e'd find the same people out in the field. They were released and these people
week later, they'd be out there shooting at us again. So how we going to
∍ll the people we work with to give them to us so we can turn them over
⊃ these people who will just turn them loose again? They just shoot them.
⌐hat way you don't have to worry about shooting them again or shooting at
⌐em.

'ASE 219

wasn't there at the time he had his penis cut off and stuck in his mouth
♦ut most of the time if you're dead, uh, being chopped up, I don't think it
♦others anybody too much. There's a purpose behind it. We chopped people
⌐p too. Uh, mainly because it's a big religious thing. . . . So they believe, the
⌐uddhists, if they cut off a person's arm or leg or something, this will condemn
⌐em to hell and so, uh, well, I'm not going to say that I ever did it because
⌐aughs] they're sending people to jail for that now. But I know quite a few
♦eople that have hacked off ears and arms and heads mainly for the main purpose
⊃ build up a tremendous amount of, uh, psychological warfare in the area. As
⌐ was we were known. . . . and when we were in the area the Viet Cong were
♦retty damn scared of us most of the time. . . .

Well, for instance, if a man is supposedly dead, you've already shot him
♦etween the eyes and you get up to his position, uh, what the hell is wrong
⌐ith cutting his ears off? I mean, he's already dead. I don't consider that an
⌐trocity. When you're dead, I mean, who in the hell could care? I mean, the
⌐uy who's dead doesn't care if somebody hacks him up. . . .

Yeah, I caught several prisoners. People in my squad and my platoon took
♦risoners and then I helped interrogate 'em. . . . Someone beats on the man's
⌐ead a little bit and tries to threaten and scare him as much as possible. Pain
⌐orks very good. Electricity works very good. . . . You have telephones, hand-
⌐ranked telephones, and you wire them up, women and all. . . .

I interrogated a few people and tried to scare 'em as much as possible.
⌐ever really enjoyed it. I had fun with 'em a couple of times. Oh, like one
⌐xample, uh, I painted a target on this man's chest and lined him up, oh excuse
⌐e, lined 'em up against the trees and had a big deal about it. My squad was
⌐l standing by and all pretended like we were having a firing squad. Had five
⌐uys line up, strictly military reg, formation, gave the man a cigarette and had
⌐y interpreter tell him it was his last, put a blindfold around him and wait
⌐ minute, in fact that one we didn't put a blindfold on. . . . The interpreter
⌐sked him some questions. He wouldn't say anything and so the interpreter
⌐odded to me and I called my men to attention and they brought their rifles
⌐p and cocked it and everything, you know. We didn't actually have to cock
⌐hem but it made more noise and it scared him more and aimed at him and
⌐nstead of calling fire I just started laughing [laughs]. You know, 'cause we knew
⌐ve weren't going to shoot him anyway because they got real professional interro-
⌐aters and there was a helicopter coming in to get him anyway so it was very
⌐ittle importance to us anyway. . . .

On another occasion I had fun. Well, I mean, it wasn't actually fun bu
I mean, you, uh well, it was kind of a joke, uh, I got a big kick out of it
This guy was tied up and he was in the usual Vietnamese squat, you know
where they are down on their feet and squat down and we tried to get thi
guy to talk and there was a large shovel there, well a big stick. It had a handle
on it, you know. And so, wham! I hit the ground right in front of his balls
about two, three inches from his balls and the guy was doing a backward shuffle
with his hands tied up and his feet tied up. I kept getting real close to him
you know, trying to scare him. He thought I was goin' to try and castrate him
I guess. We didn't hurt him at all, that once.

CASE 221

I saw one woman got shot by one of our men. She was the wife of a VC
lieutenant and we went into a village to capture her and try to get her husband
and took her and she had a little two-year-old baby and took her and the baby
out in the jungle and tried to get information out of her. And, uh, well, they
killed the kid trying to get her to talk, and, uh, she still wouldn't talk, so they
killed her too. I was the American on the operation. . . . Well, they threatened
to kill the baby and she was yelling and carrying on and so they took the
baby down to the bottom of the hill and turned her around to watch and they
killed the baby. Shot him. In the head. And the woman went into hysterics
and then first the interrogater shot both of her ear lobes off and then she still
wouldn't talk and they just centered it up between her eyes. . . . Yeah, I watched
the whole scene. . . . Yeah, first time I'd seen it with a woman. . . . No, it
didn't bother me a bit.

Tortured Americans

Seven soldiers report having seen the disfigured bodies of Americans
who had either been tortured to death or whose bodies had been cut up after
death.

CASE 207

Yeah, it was my first combat. We fell back and left three men behind. Then
we pushed 'em back and the three were dead. And they had cut off their heads.
And we had to ship these three men home. For two days we tried to find their
heads. And we never did, so we had to send these three guys home, well,
I knew one, without their heads. . . . A woman French reporter wrote an article
on how barbaric the Viet Cong were for taking, you know, men's heads.

CASE 212

The only time I really got upset was one time when a man was returned to
us without any skin on him and his teeth had been knocked out and his privates
had been cut off and sewed in his mouth. They sent him off with only one
tattoo on him and then charged us for the body so that the wife could receive
the death gratuity for the soldier.

CASE 215

No, not his head. We never got the head back. They sent us a piece of his body about once a week for a month. A hand one day, next week we'd get a piece of his arm. That was the only atrocity I saw done to an American. Oh, no, I take that back. I came across an infantry squad, that I don't know how it happened to them. Got no idea. They were all dead and they were cut up real bad after that, their throats were cut and both wrists were cut and blood all over the place and slashed elbows. Just mutilated with a knife. . . . Eight. Eight young soldiers.

CASE 219

I didn't actually see one. Uh, oh yeah. I did see, well, this wasn't an atrocity. He just had his hands tied behind him and was shot in the head. I wouldn't say that's an atrocity. He's a soldier. He gets killed. He was captured and they killed him later after about three days. He had a chain marks and rope marks around his neck. They'd taken him around from village to village on display and then they got tired of cartin' him around. . . . But there was a couple of people from my company that got burned alive but I never did see them . . . Eight of 'em had a fire built on their chest. I don't know if they were dead before they built the fire or not . . . Then one other guy I knew. I didn't see this. I wasn't there at the time he had his penis cut off and stuck in his mouth but most of the time if you're dead, uh, being chopped up, I don't think bothers anybody too much.

CASE 222

There was two Americans killed in that thing and we don't know if they were killed outright on the initial attack or if they were captured and then killed but, uh, when we found the bodies, this one particular young man, whom I knew fairly well, uh, I found his body in—they had cut him open—his complete front and booby-trapped his insides with a hand grenade . . . They cut him open, slipped the hand grenade inside him so when you touched the body the thing exploded. . . . The other American, who was not a fairly good friend of mine, I knew him for about three years, all we ever found of him was his leg. . . .

CASE 223

The only one I saw was an American major had his head cut off. . . . I was just there when they were bringing his body back. . . . It was cut off clean.

CASE 226

Well, I saw them with their, uh, they cut their penis off and stick it in their mouth and maybe cut their fingers off or just slice them up, maybe cut their ears off. Saw lots of Americans like that. . . .

Any time you come to a Viet Cong village or school or anything like this, you always destroy. If you don't, they'll come right back.

Impressions

CASE 226

Lasting impressions. The filth. The bad food. The water, no water. Recreation. The rainy monsoon. I don't mind the fighting or the duty . . . but couldn't relax . . . nothing to do at night.

CASE 227

. . . like I wiped out a couple of villages.

I'd seen guys wounded before . . . it didn't bother me . . . I just went up and searched the guy . . . [shot his head off]. There was flesh . . . around . . . parts of the head . . . it didn't bother me. . . .

It's the breaks of the game, I mean, that is what I feel, uh, you got a job to do and you go out and you do the job [killing women and children]. . . .

I enjoyed my tour.

CASE 207

I never felt that I killed a man as an individual, you know what I mean, but as the enemy.

I didn't see him take the head, but I really didn't like it. I don't believe in doing it. . . . And it got me kind of sick, I mean, I didn't throw up or anything, but, you know, I looked the other way. I didn't go up and stare at it and take pictures or anything like that, you know.

There was a big rumor back in the States about our taking heads. My mother wrote and asked me about it. And she thought I was still a clerk, you know. I never told her in the whole time I was there. I was in a combat unit until I got back to the States. . . . And she wanted to know what the Hatchet Brigade was. . . . It was in all the papers. There were seven men that bought hatchets through Sears and Roebuck, you know, to cut their way through the jungle . . . they used them to take heads . . . they called it the Hatchet Brigade. . . . It was in the papers and everything . . . that if you brought the colonel a head he'd give you a case of booze . . . he'd probably put you in jail for five years if you ever brought him a head. . . .

I could kill a VC right now.

Being a combat soldier was one of the most rewarding experiences of my life.

CASE 210

I got close enough to some to kiss 'em. . . . What was it like? I can't describe it. It's an accomplishment, more or less stalking a person, stalking something alive, just like going hunting for deer. You're stalking deer, you get in your position, you wait, you wait and finally the deer will come and you get him, and if you snag the deer, you feel—you feel good. It's the same way. If I had made one move I would have been shot. It was the same way. He would have been proud, if he heard a twig snap.

CASE 212

I don't want to bring anything back from Vietnam that is going to affect my family. I don't want to sit around my house and tell about things I might have seen or might have done that might upset my wife or children because they're impressionable and it's not only that they wouldn't maybe want to know what you did in the war, dad. You know this might cause problems in later life, in dreams or something like this.

You know, I like children. Over there I like children. I hate to see children get hurt, but . . . it's a war situation. Now if it was happening in the United States where my family is involved, naturally my attitude would be completely different, because this would be a self-preservation thing for my family. Over there it's only self-preservation for me. It's just the way it is. He's out there to kill me and I'm out to kill him because that's the way it has to be, uh, but that's not the way it has to be at home, so I can't see how I could draw a comparison between the two.

To be truthful about it, I really didn't think about it that much. Don't get me wrong, I don't think that people should kill each other but it just didn't seem like that . . . uh, I just figured this guy is trying to kill me so I just better kill him before he kills me. . . .

I'd rather fight a war in somebody else's country than in my own where my own wife and children are going to be subjected to the war situation. . . .

It didn't bother me too much when I saw American bodies. I didn't like the idea that Americans was being killed, but then again, I imagine the enemy doesn't like the idea of their soldiers being killed either. The only time I really got upset was when they returned a man to us without any skin . . . I was mad. . . . Don't know why anybody would want to commit something like that. It just doesn't make sense. I mean, it's a conflict, an act of war is one thing. Someone's going to die. But leave him his balls. You don't have to skin him. You don't have to take his privates off. . . .

I don't think war is any place for women and children, but if they choose that way, they should be expected to die, but they shouldn't bring their children with them . . . because they are going to get this child killed . . . would have been better if you had left it someplace else. It might be an orphan, but at least it's alive.

CASE 213

The first time you shoot someone it's all impulses, reactions. It didn't bother me . . . I wasn't sorry 'cause if we hadn't gotten them, uh, it could have been myself. . . . When I think back on it, all that flesh and blood and death, you'd think twice, I mean try and forget about it . . . I never had any problems eating after this, it just was something that didn't bother me . . . I had a sense of accomplishment, a part of the job, and that's all.

It hits on a sore spot when it's one of our troops, but it bothered me a little bit . . . when one guy got half his head shot off. I probably did say ugh to that when I saw it . . . seeing a man full of holes or his arm torn off isn't nearly as bad as seeing a man's head blown off.

For one thing I appreciate life more now and I feel a distinct honor in having been there, I mean I'm proud to wear the added awards and things of this nature.

CASE 217

Did you ever go deer hunting? You lead. It's just a lucky shot. Felt like having a party. Just a freak, lucky shot. . . .
   It was a lot of fun.
   . . . was never nauseous. No, from the heat, yes, not from what I saw. . . .
   Enjoyed Vietnam. Always something to do, twenty-four hours a day.

CASE 218

After I shot him, not really any particular feeling, I don't reckon. I didn't feel good. I didn't feel bad. I guess I didn't feel nothing . . . I don't reckon there was any feeling of satisfaction. . . .
   I didn't, I wasn't sick or nothing like that. I already seen people that was all messed up worse than that, so my, my sickness, I didn't, I didn't have any. I don't have it. . . .
   I saw a lot of dead ones [Americans] and a lot of live ones that weren't going to live. . . . I didn't feel nothing. I probably felt, maybe mixed feelings. I wasn't sick, maybe a little happy and unhappy—happy I wasn't one of the people that was messed up and unhappy that we had people messed up and sick.
   I didn't plan no kills or nothing like that. I have no notches or nothing. It's an impersonal thing. There's nothing in it. Nothing personal to it . . . you have no feeling for them people. I have none for them or anything. You don't have no hate for the man or anything like that. You're just doing what you're trained to do, what you're suppose to do.
   In what you call a kill-zone . . . the first man gives the signal . . . and everyone just shoots into them and nothing left there . . . they don't even get a chance to fire back or nothing. You just cut them to pieces there in less than ten seconds probably.

CASE 219

We chopped up people too, uh, mainly because it's a big religious thing. . . .
   It's like a little game [chuckles]. . . .
   I mean, a guy who's dead doesn't care if somebody hacks him up.

CASE 221

I just felt more relaxed [in Vietnam] and free of mind. There wasn't no pressure on me and I enjoyed relaxation even on operations. I enjoyed it. No money problems. No women problems. I just felt comfortable there. . . .
   They killed the kid trying to get her to talk . . . so they just killed her too . . . didn't bother me a bit.
   The women are just bloodthirsty. If you're a prisoner—they're harder than

a man can be. And if she's a VC I don't have no pity on her 'cause she would kill me just the same as a man can. . . .

I've seen a couple of ours shot in the back, but that didn't make me feel sick. One time, but it wasn't nothing to do with emotion. I had to go out and pick up a dead body . . . he was dead about three days and just the smell—if you ever smelled a dead person that's been dead for three or four days—that's one time that made me sick, from smelling him. . . .

Yeah, I want to go back. . . .

I don't care if they're woman, child, or man. It doesn't bother me a bit.

I do what I'm supposed to do. That is sometimes I question. Most times I don't question what I'm told to do. I wouldn't do anything else but stay in Special Forces.

CASE 222

Officially I was a radio operator. I was just another gun on the team, you might say.

Everytime we call in an air-strike on anything, whether it was a bunker or complex or what it was, we'd have to go in and pull a B.D.A., they call it, that was a bombed destruction analysis . . . just go in and analyze the destruction of bombs and count enemy bodies if there was any and all this.

CASE 224

Never felt sick at sight of blood or mutilated bodies, Americans or Vietnamese or women and children.

CASE 225

I actually felt badly about any one of them that got killed . . . and the reason is that I don't, I value human life pretty highly myself and for a man to die needlessly, that bothers me . . . yeah, they died needlessly, the ones I killed, I mean, of course, his views on life are a lot different than mine . . . he died needlessly fighting for communism and he believed in it so much . . . I can't see that attitude 'cause he's really only known communism and won't give anything else a chance. . . .

Well, uh, first of all I guess I was like anybody else. I didn't know whether I would be able to kill somebody or not . . . I used to look back and think, Christ, you're a soldier, soldiers kill and if you can't kill, you shouldn't be a soldier and that was the biggest conflict, whether or not I'd be able to. . . .

Well, it wasn't that hard, actually. You just went out and the situation arose, it was almost automatic. It was me or him. And that was that—that ended that. . . .

When I shot him [first kill] I think I felt a little elated because I hit him, which I don't know why. I just did. . . .

When they brought the body back [first kill] I just—I felt a little sorry for the guy, 'cause he—I don't know why. 'Cause I—they all look alike. He was just a Vietnamese peasant. When I looked at him I felt sorry, but I mean not enough to cry over it but I really felt something down deep there. You say, Jesus Christ, you know, the guy didn't do nothing, you—I killed. But that didn't last that long . . . I thought of it since quite a while. But I figured, what the hell. It's the chance he took, you know. It could have been me. . . .

The people, the people and the fear they have of the Americans . . . the farmers, the actual peasants—they were so damn afraid of the Americans, even though all we wanted to do was to help them. They were scared to death of the Americans . . . especially the little children. They never got over the fear. Never. Even though you'd sit there and talk to them. They wouldn't talk back, they wouldn't smile. Nothing. If they talked back, it was only through fear—fear that if they didn't, you'd kill them. That's the only reason.

CASE 226

It's by God my duty [to kill in battle].

Comments

Volunteering for combat duty in Vietnam was not a sudden decision for the Green Berets. Slowly and systematically the groundwork for this course of action was laid by their previous experience, only to be released by the appropriate situation. Describing how this potential was shaped was the task of the previous chapters. In this chapter, attention focuses on the conscious motivational framework and life circumstances surrounding their entrance into the Army and the Special Forces, and going to Vietnam.

One objective of this investigation was to study the origins of commitment. For me, commitment has two major components: the first alludes to a sentiment and the second to an action imperative of contractual character which tangibly unites the private sentiment with public behavior. In order to guarantee the selection of persons for whom the use of this word would be appropriate, I enlarged its meaning to include consequential risks to one's personal welfare. It was this intent which led me to discontinue a pilot study of soldiers who were volunteering for Vietnam for other reasons and instead to look for a group of men who would evidence a thorough sense of purpose and dedication to specific ideals. My assumption that I had found such persons in the Green Berets was at least partly fallacious. Just as sentiment need not lead to action, it is also true that action may not be based on the expected motives.

As I began talking to the Green Berets about their reasons for volunteering for the Army and combat duty in Vietnam, and the things they had seen and done during military duty, I discovered that my approach to this subject was different than theirs. I found myself asking what I thought were complex and psychologically penetrating questions to which they often gave brief and easy answers. In view of the risks they were taking, the controversy raging over the justification of American involvement in Vietnam, and particularly in light of the bad press American soldiers were receiving because of massacred civilian populations, I thought that these men would show signs of strain and use our talk as an opportunity to justify themselves.

I had also assumed that they would show reserve in connection with their combat experiences, particularly their own personal participation in interrogations, air strikes against civilian villages, mutilation of bodies, and the killing of women and children. However, the flavor of our conversations on these and many other subjects was very different from what I had expected; I had to learn that what seemed to be complex, obscure, or fascinating to me was often simple, obvious, or dull to them. Not only were many of my assumptions about these men false, but our entire modes of relating to ourselves and to the outside world were different. I also had to become accustomed to the fact that I was not talking to fervent and ideologically engaged persons but rather to socially and politically disinterested professional soldiers who were uninformed on social and political issues of the day and unconcerned with questions which were of the gravest concern to me. I had expected that when I asked a man what motivated him to leave his wife and children and risk his life fighting in a strange and distant land during a time of heated political debate, he would at least give me an emotionally convincing answer. Instead, I heard calm calculations, pragmatic considerations, ordinary statements which were as applicable to taking a cross-country trip, a few realistic references to the effects of war training, and several masochistic fantasies. In an almost indifferent tone, the soldiers explained that they had been sure that they were going to be killed in Vietnam. The only soldier who seemed to attach gravity to his own death had also counted on being killed in action. His approach to this was neurotically self-punitive in that he felt God would punish him for having committed adultery with the wives of two soldiers.

All this was a surprise to me at first. But after a few interviews, I began to understand that none of these men had joined the Special Forces or volunteered for Vietnam because of deep personal commitment to political, social, or religious ideals. It became clear that despite their pronounced distaste for communism their major reasons for going to Vietnam had little or nothing to do with the "defense of democracy." In the enumeration of their motives for going to Vietnam, only a few soldiers mentioned patriotism or stopping communism. When ideological reasons were mentioned at all they were usually tacked on almost apologetically at the end of the list. It was as if the men had suddenly realized the disparity between their real reasons and the reasons they were supposed to have.

Reasons for Joining Special Forces and Volunteering for Vietnam

Why did these men join the Army, volunteer for the Special Forces and thereby for probable combat duty in Vietnam? Their motives were largely private, professional, or financial. For example, they said that they initially joined the Army because they were unemployed and wanted to learn a profession, their friends had gone into the Army, their parents and friends felt it would be better for them to join, or they wanted to get away from their families; mostly they were seeking adventure and excitement. Between the ages of seventeen and nineteen these young men were confronted with dwindling prestige and the pressure to make something of themselves. The seven boys who went on to college were unhappy, bored, or doing poorly. Many of the others lost jobs and were unemployed. A few were vagabonding around the country. Their personal and professional lives had begun to stagnate and their professional prospects were meager. The social reinforcements of their high school years were gone. Many of them had nothing to do and were worried about getting into trouble. One had begun to associate with the Hell's Angels. Another had gotten a girl pregnant. Several felt that their girlfriends were pressuring them into marriage. Some were expecting to be drafted and others ran away from home. In one way or another, all of them ran away from their previous lives.

The men's reasons for joining the Special Forces were largely elaborations of the ones given above. They had been in the armed services for periods ranging from one to eight years before volunteering for the Special Forces. Several had returned to civilian life after their first tour of military duty and had again found themselves confronted with marital, occupational, and financial problems. They thought that the Special Forces would bestow prestige upon them, raise them to the status of elite troops, teach them special skills, and provide them with greater opportunities for travel, adventure, and excitement. Other reasons for joining included the desire to be "real men," "nothing but the best," or "jungle killers." They did not like to "take orders"; they wanted to put their military training to use, and they wanted to see combat. Many pointed out that service in the Special Forces meant greater freedom of movement than did service in a regular unit. Most of these men felt that volunteering for the Special Forces signaled their decision to become professional soldiers.

The parallels between their motives for joining the Special Forces and those underlying their sexual habits are striking. Such a strong desire to be a "real man," "to be nothing but the best," to seek excitement, to be in control, and to conquer must stem from a deep sense of uncertainty about oneself. I feel that just as these men felt the need to prove their potency again and again with women, they also required the external paraphernalia of the Green Berets to provide them with a feeling of importance. However, to concentrate solely on their apparent lack of self-confidence and their compulsive habit of bolstering their ego through external ensignia would be to oversimplify.

The decision to join the Special Forces and to volunteer for Vietnam had other psychodynamic features as well. For many men, these decisions were also continuations of habitual forms of behavior. Some had received explicit military training during childhood; all came from militarily structured families. The military training they received in the Army and in the Special Forces had a self-perpetuating feature. The soldiers practiced fighting techniques and strategies. These were the only occupational skills they knew and they wanted a chance to apply them, to test themselves, to find out if they were as good as they thought they were and were supposed to be.

The volunteers also had one or more pragmatic reason for going to Vietnam. Several were having marital problems and considered a combat tour a convenient escape. All were interested in the extra pay they would receive for being in Vietnam, and welcomed the opportunity of further financial gain through participation in special assignments. A few said they wanted to be able to tell war stories. A number of soldiers who had never been to Asia felt that a combat assignment in Vietnam would provide an opportunity to see that part of the world. Some emphasized the value of the Vietnamese war as a training ground for equipment, doctrine, and tactics.

Patriotism versus Professionalism

The American people did not receive proper psychological preparation for the war in Vietnam. Neither the political and military events which preceded and accompanied American involvement nor the interpretation politicians gave these events provided the foundation for a firm sense of national purpose. In fact, the very man who led the escalation of American involvement won his presidential campaign on an antiwar platform.

At the time the Green Berets I interviewed decided to go to Vietnam, the United States was preoccupied with its own domestic problems. Insofar as government and private organizations were successful in reactivating idealism in American youth, this idealism found its strongest expression in movements directed toward the alleviation of economic, social, educational, and political ills at home and abroad. During this period of social turmoil, when cities were burning, college campuses embroiled in revolution, the poor and the black marching for their rights, radical groups sprouting all over the country, unemployment and inflation increasing and beginning to threaten the security of the middle class, conditions were hardly ripe for an international adventure. Such a tactic might have succeeded in drawing attention away from domestic problems in a less sophisticated society, but in the United States many people did not see the merits of this course. Under such circumstances, it is not surprising that political, social, and moral idealism would not be deeply imbedded in the personalities of those men interviewed who voluntarily responded to the call to arms.

It was incumbent upon the United States government to try to give po-

litical and moral legitimacy to its activities in Indochina. It was also necessary, as in any war, that the image of the soldier be structured so that he
could see himself and be seen by others as an extension or embodiment of
the very ideals and cherished traditions which were supposedly at stake in
this conflict. The Special Forces soldiers and officers with whom I spoke
did not share this view. However strongly they might trumpet such ideas in
public or to outsiders, their private self-concept was composed of substantially different elements. The gulf between their politically inspired image and
their private self-concept is illustrated in their answers to several questions.

When I asked the Green Berets if they felt patriotic, all but one responded with an emphatic "Yes." However, when I asked them, "What
does patriotism mean to you?" they paused and looked puzzled. Their answers seem to indicate that at least some of the Green Berets believed they
were fighting in the name of principles which they could not explain or perhaps even understand. The answers of many soldiers reflect a manner of
thinking little advanced beyond sixth-grade school rituals. Quotations show
that some Green Berets saw themselves as guardians of their country. Yet
none was able to provide more than a superficial allusion to the distinguishing characteristics of this country whose welfare they were protecting. At the
same time, particular ideas begin to emerge from these quotations, suggestive
of the value system directing these men's behavior. Most fundamentally,
they saw themselves as professionals, as skilled technicians who were being
well paid to perform their tasks.

The Green Berets entered a contractual agreement with the government
of the United States. Aside from the need of some to try to justify this contract within the context of convenient patriotic notions, I do not feel that
their interest in the war in Vietnam extended very far beyond the benefits
they received from participating in it. Their contract enabled them to travel,
paid their bills, provided a pension, legalized their behavior and would have
cared for their families had they been killed. They had and have complete
medical benefits, regular vacations, interesting training programs, free education, and the opportunity—even obligation—to engage in a variety of such
outdoor sports as skydiving, scuba diving, mountain climbing, and skiing.
In return they have to complete their assignments and risk their lives. When
viewed from this perspective, the volunteers emerge as technicians who have
sold their skills at the best going price; if one were to bypass the issue of
what they actually do on the job, one could easily admire the dexterity with
which they landed a position with such a generous employer.

Probably the most important single reason for the inaccuracy of many
of my expectations about the self-concepts of these men was that I was exposed to the same propaganda efforts that they had been and I assumed that
men who would respond to such promotion would identify very strongly with
the image being propagated. It seemed axiomatic that American war volun-

teers would see themselves as especially courageous people who were acting out of a deep love for their country, its traditions and institutions, its promise of personal freedom and prosperity. I expected them to perceive themselves as the nation's best who were so selfless that they were willing to carry the banner of freedom to the farthest corners of the world and to defend it against aggression with their very lives. It was for this reason that it did not originally occur to me to ask them if they considered themselves professional soldiers. It never entered my mind to ask them if they would be willing to take up arms for another country or cause. These possibilities arose during the interviews. It was only after they explained their real motives for going to Vietnam and only after one soldier described himself as a "mercenary" that I realized that my own perceptions of these men had been more deeply affected by propaganda than their self-perceptions had been. It was at this point that I began to ask each soldier whether he viewed himself as a professional soldier and if he had considered working as a mercenary. Nearly all answered "Yes" to both questions. With few exceptions, the Green Berets made little attempt to disguise the fact that they saw themselves as hired guns, paid killers who were not particularly concerned with their employers or their victims. They expressed the kind of preferences about personally desirable working conditions that any employee might consider in choosing an employer.

Not only what the men said about themselves but also the ease and candor with which they said it came as a surprise. The days are past in which Western nations could successfully glorify wars and imbue them with religious and moral justification. Those who still think this way are, I suspect, in a minority. The majority learn to live with wars and to view them as necessary evils. We do not think about just how evil they can be and how one must think in order to participate in them without revulsion and without psychiatric breakdown (see the section on psychological disorders in Chapter 7 for a detailed clinical analysis). I posed this matter in a somewhat modified form to three Special Forces officers. I felt that they might be able to specify more clearly the personality characteristics of a man who is able to fight in the jungle one day and make an unproblematical transition to shopping in a modern supermarket the next. The officers' answers outline an idealized image of an achievement-oriented employee who is under consideration for a management position.

Colonel X: Let's say adaptability. In other words he's capable of adjusting to new and changing situations and stresses and he bears up well under pressure. He has ambition, seeks and welcomes additional and more important responsibility. Cooperation—works in harmony with others as a team. And dependability—consistently accomplishes the desired action with a minimum of supervision. The very nature of our business is that we're completely on our own with indigenous forces. We have no one to turn to. We do it ourselves. And we must be able to count on a man working with a minimum of supervision.

He's got to have enthusiasm, he's got to motivate others by his zeal. Got to have force, execute his actions vigorously. Ingenuity, the very basis of Special Forces operations—the ability to make something out of nothing. He's got to have initiative, in other words, the ability to take necessary and appropriate action on his own. Intelligence goes without saying. Judgment—thinks logically and makes practical decisions right down the line. Loyalty. Moral courage. Self-discipline.

Interviewer: What does **loyal** mean?

Colonel X: Uh, "with his faithful and willing support to superiors and subordinates." That's a book definition.

Interviewer: And what is moral courage?

Colonel X: Moral courage, then, we would say, intellectual honesty—a willingness to stand up and be counted.

Interviewer: And what does that mean?

Colonel X: It means that there reaches a point in everybody's life where you got to make a stand—it's either right, or it's wrong. I'm going to stand up for the right and I might get cut down for it. McArthur made his stand in Korea.

Interviewer: Could you give me some examples of moral courage from everyday field experience? In what ways would a man show moral courage according to this definition?

Colonel X: All right, we would be working with indigenous personnel. There'd be a guerilla leader here. Okay. The counterpart is the Special Forces 18th Commander and he doesn't have direct command over this man. He must by virtue of his personality and his ability inflict his will, if you will, on this commander. This guerilla leader, this indigenous man, is among his own people. Suddenly he decides to go out and blow this bridge over there and it's exactly this bridge which we know the conventional forces are going to come across a week later. So this commander's got to say, "Hold it, hold it, you can't do that!" If the guy still wants to destroy it, the 18th Commander stands up and is counted—"Hey, the bridge isn't going."

Interviewer: What else does the Special Forces soldier have?

Colonel X: Self-improvement. In other words, he takes actions to improve himself constantly. Stamina—performs successfully under constant physical and mental stress. Tact—says and does what is appropriate without giving unnecessary offense and understanding and appreciation of another's viewpoint. And when you mention personal traits, I pulled this right off an Officer's Efficiency Report, right down the line. That's where it comes from.

Interviewer: Do you know what that sounds like? It sounds like the Boy Scouts' Code.

Colonel X: You'd be surprised at how close we like to think the Army is to that. The men have to be, uh, an upright individual man and a good citizen. And that's what we're trying to train soldiers for, this exactly. . . . You must understand, of course, Doctor, that the ideas which I talk about are applicable to war or peace. A man can show enthusiasm in getting his paper work done or he can show enthusiasm and aggression in killing. The principles are exactly the same. Peace or war has nothing to do with all the things we have told you this morning. This guy can come back and adjust well, if that's what you want to call it, simply because he is emotionally mature. He hasn't got his head up his ass about any peace missions or anything like that.

Major Y: The hardest thing we put our boys through today, in comparison to Korea, is one day we send them into a village without a weapon. He's got bandaids in one hand and aspirins in the other and his pocket is full of lollipops. Two days later you bring him back to the same village on a search and destroy mission. The same man you gave bandaids to two days ago and you have to make a decision.

Interviewer: There are many patriots in the U. S. who couldn't make that decision. He may have the equipment to wave a flag but not to use a rifle.

Colonel X: You can't just say that.

Interviewer: You know very well that some people are built for flag-waving and others for carrying a rifle and perhaps some for both. But you can't expect the average American, ripped out of his environment in the U.S., to be able to function in that situation.

Major Y: I think you underestimate the average American.

Major Z: Every soldier goes through a period of training before he goes to combat. And during his time is when we try to teach him to become a soldier and be prepared to kill the enemy. The Special Forces soldier is different from an infantry soldier. He's really not there to go out and kill himself. He's there to train these other people, these Vietnamese. His mission is not so much to do the killing but teach the local people to do it. This may have a psychological effect on his thinking later on. He may say, ``I wasn't doing it, these people, the home-town folks, were doing it.''

Colonel X: We're not dealing with the hoi polloi here that comes in as private. These people have progressed much further. They're much older. They're old hands. They're old troopers. So you've got a man. He's a realist. He's not fooling anybody. He's lost his ideals, if you want to call them ideals, of youth and they're out of the way. He's over here today, tomorrow he's going shopping in the supermarket. Okay, it's a sad thing what's happening over there but it ain't going to break us, not the professional soldier. Not if he's trained correctly.

The colonel asked me to give him some psychological terms which he in turn might use to describe his soldiers. Being unsure of which terms to offer him I decided instead to give my initial impressions of the Green Berets and then see what he would correct, confirm, and complement. The following exchange took place:

Interviewer: The Special Forces soldier had been accustomed since early childhood to very hard, severe, and arbitrary discipline . . . in the form of whippings, intimidation, beatings. . . . There was little or no warmth in their families. . . . Punishments took violent forms. . . . There were weapons in the homes. . . . They've been accustomed to the use of weapons since early childhood. . . .

They hunted and used the weapons to kill. . . . They did not have strong ties to anything beyond the rest of the family. . . . The families were isolated units. . . . There were no positive expressive emotional ties within the family. . . . They began their sexual experience at a remarkably early age. . . . Average age for first intercourse would be about fifteen and a half. . . . Although they had intercourse frequently throughout adolescence they did not have emotional ties to these girls. . . . They don't report having had deep friendships with anyone. . . . They enjoy the service. . . . They have respect for law enforcement agencies and clearly know what can happen to them if they do something criminal. . . . They've killed many people, men, women and children in Vietnam and have no guilt feelings or nightmares.

Colonel X: You know, you have described Americanism at it's best. But somehow you have twisted it around to almost make it sound derogatory. We're so proud of having that kind of individual in Special Forces, it's unbelievable.

CHAPTER 6

Commitment to Peace

Beginnings of Commitment

CASE 101

Prior to my having gone to college I was never interested or involved. That was unfortunately symptomatic of the general tone of the community where I grew up, a general lack of concern in real social issues. And this being exposed to the picketing of the poor people . . . in this supposedly liberal educational institution and the administration won't even listen. They wouldn't even let their own cafeteria workers organize. That had an acute impact on me. I saw it with my own eyes. . . . It wasn't just a lesson in sociology. It was a lesson in real life.

CASE 104

In my sophomore year I met this family. I was eating dorm food and to go to suppers cooked by a good cook was absolutely fantastic. And the first time I went down I had a long discussion with them. And nothing like that had happened to me before. Stayed till one in the morning discussing my plans. And to understand that people can be good people. I mean, just something about them was good without being political. I was taught by experience to believe that the only good people were political people and the other people were shallow and lacking in something. And this was quite a shock. . . . They were interested enough in what I was doing to spend five hours discussing it . . . and I met a woman there and she taught me all that I know about decent treatment of people, interacting with people as individuals.

You know, and I could see it every day how a teacher can get you sick, literally physically sick for two weeks ahead of an exam depending on his attitude toward you. He has complete control over your total emotions if you're committed at all which I was all through school until this last year. It's absurd that somebody can have that much power over you without your knowing it. . . . And I always lied to myself looking forward to my courses. "Oh, wow! Great year! I can see all these fantastic courses". And that never lasted for more than a week or two. So that's why I dropped out of graduate school.

CASE 105

The main thing that characterized those years was the bitterness that I had and this anger. . . . About the world. About the inhumanity. . . . I just came to the city [New York City] and saw it. I saw how the people treat the black people. I saw the emphasis on getting good marks which seemed sort of exaggerated. I saw Christians who were preaching love and brotherhood and were bigots. I just saw the hypocrisy. . . . I don't know if it was all there before or not. . . . I just never saw it. Suddenly it just hit me and it knocked the hell out of me. . . . And I realized that the really unhappy people I was running into were just people like myself. People that were very sensitive and who could see all these things. You know, here are all these people at Columbia . . . a beautiful school and everybody is intelligent and most of the people are bigots. . . . And everybody is respecting all those people who are getting good marks and a lot of the people who are getting good marks can't respect anybody who doesn't look like them. And this was the whole college scene. . . . And I knew that a whole lot of people I had met who had never gone to college could offer me a whole lot more than these . . . college kids. . . .

This tremendous pride in America. I used to stand up when they played *The Star-Spangled Banner,* no matter where I was. I used to stand up, even if everybody else was sitting down or it was just on the radio. I had all this pride in this beautiful country and I just saw what all has happened. And if you have something taken away, it's a whole lot worse than if you hadn't had it.

CASE 120

All through this period I kind of really withdrew into myself. I had certain feelings about things that were going on, but I somehow felt detached. I felt myself like two persons. Like this person who's going through Columbia and becoming an engineer was somehow one person, and there was another person that I was, pushing into the background all the time. . . . I was watching myself go through Columbia successfully, but somehow that wasn't really essentially me out there. It was just that this was sort of the direction that offered the least resistance. . . . I was accepted by . . . [a prestigious graduate school] and I decided to go there because they are just about the best school on the East Coast for operations research. About that time I began to realize that I might have made a mistake in what I was doing and that possibly this direction was not the best direction for me. And not only maybe it wasn't the best, but I began to wonder if I could really continue to function. I also began to become aware that I had been a very passive person. There are certain things that I believed in but that I never gave any expression to or never let effect me in my activities to any great extent. . . . I was sympathetic with a lot of causes, but for some reason I didn't feel motivated to get myself personally involved. I don't really know why that was. I think it may have something to do with the fact that the person who was going to Columbia was somebody I had created. . . .

During that period, really beginning when I graduated from Columbia, I began to have serious doubts about the kind of life I had mapped out for myself and the kind of things that I was going to do. I saw the associations that I was forming and the things I was becoming involved in which I felt that I did not want to be involved in. Well, I'll give you an example. During my first semester at . . . [graduate school], I remember attending a lecture in game theory. I forget the fellow's name who gave it, but a very big name in the field, and he began to talk about placement of nuclear missiles to achieve a maximum kill. And this was just an indication of the kind of values that were prevalent there. There was no kind of, uh, reference to human values. He didn't even seem aware that he was talking about human lives when he talked about achieving maximum kill. And this is just an example of the kind of values that were there that I just couldn't function in that atmosphere. . . .

I was concerned with the role that I saw myself in. I didn't want to give my tacit approval to what was going on by maintaining this relationship with the university. And at the same time I was confused and didn't want to just break off entirely. In other words, I was still registered. At the end of the year I was asked to return, with the fellowship. But at that point I realized that I couldn't return, I couldn't function there anymore. I used to be able to psych myself up for work, get myself into the right state of mind . . . but now I couldn't do the work. I couldn't concentrate on it. I just couldn't do the work. I was concerned about the role that I found myself playing. I was becoming more aware of the fact that I have an obligation to myself and to others, to take some kind of stand in things that I believed. And I began to think about the question of the draft and about the war.

Commitment

CASE 100

One of the things Tom had said was that to apply for a conscientious objector status is like applying for a permit not to kill. . . . Killing should be the exception rather than the rule. . . . I began to think about it more and more and began to feel like all the other guys in the slums and who can't get 2-S deferments because they don't have the money and the education to go to school. And then the Resistance Movement began and on October 16 I finally made my decision and turned it [draft card] in personally at the national Selective Service headquarters in D.C.

CASE 101

I sent a letter to my clerk telling him to go fly a kite, that I just wouldn't cooperate any more, that you're not going to gain the acquiescence of people by killing them, and stop this political imperialism, you know. To what end? I've had it with you people. . . . No, I haven't sent them my draft card, I just told them I wouldn't have anything to do with it. . . . Both Bob and I reached this decision together within a day or so of each other, you know, cut our ties with [the Selective Service]. It was pretty much an individual thing. We weren't aware of what was going on in a lot of cities at the time. . . . I had been in the VISTA program and stationed on a Navaho Reservation, for about one and a half years. Began to realize things I had never conceived of before. I was beginning to become slightly cognizant of what the hell was going on, and became more and more interested in what was going on in Vietnam. And Vietnam has, at least to me, a very particular relevance to what had happened out there [with the American Indians] 100 years ago. And I saw many parallels between what happened out there in 1868 and in Vietnam now in 1968. . . . It was later, after I made my decision, that I really got into things and started working for Resistance.

CASE 107

I'm kind of undefined on what I feel. I can't see killing . . . I don't know what I'll do . . . I won't play games with files and forms. . . . If they induct me I don't know what I'll do. It may come down to not knowing until the time comes, you know, either stepping over the line or not stepping over it. . . . I'm so unconcerned about this whole draft thing. It's like a childish game. I don't see myself playing games.

If I go to jail, I'll go to jail. That's not something I'll have to do myself. That's something they'll have to do to me. Do you see what I mean? Like if they feel they have to do something or if they are going to do something, they'll just have to do it. I can't see fighting them. I could see me trying to make my beliefs known to other people. That might do some good. What should I do at the draft board? Tell them what they want to hear? Why do it? I'll tell them the way I feel and they'll probably not find it good enough. I'm not going to make any speeches . . . I'll cooperate with them. I'll give two years of service doing some good, anywhere in the world. I won't accept a destructive, negative assignment.

CASE 110

When my eighteenth birthday came around I just didn't have the strength to not register and it bothered me a lot. But I wasn't ready to do it, so I registered [with the draft board] and I decided that rather than seek a straight deferment which I thought was terribly cowardly I would take some risk in that I would try for a court case, a good test case for expanding C.O. and so I accumulated a lot of testimony from very reputable people, ministers and such, outside of the antiwar movement, saying I was a sincere conscientious objector with no religious background whatsoever. My fantasy was that I would blow open the C.O. provisions and thereby make my contribution and have taken my risk. I was going to prove that I was emotionally nonviolent, had never been violent, was very antiviolent, and prove it by testimony by reputable witnesses by the dozens. But instead they gave me a 1-Y for being loony and then a few months ago I finally decided I couldn't stay out of it any more, that it was really a growing movement, that it was important, and so I turned in my draft card and haven't heard from them since. I'm really surprised. It's almost six months now.

CASE 116

I refused induction a while ago. I turned in my draft card October 16, the first National Turning-In Day. . . . That was all over the country, you know, in forty or fifty cities, guys were turning in their draft cards. We had one in New York at the Federal Courthouse, Foley Square. This was after I came back from the South from civil rights work. I was thinking about things relating to the university and the antiwar movements and the radical movements and, uh, I pretty much set my mind that for the immediate future I was going to do radical activity and this tactic happened to include several years in jail as part of that immediate future. But, you know, I felt it was valuable enough politically that I should do it. . . . Where I was about 380 people turned in their draft cards. About 1,200 nationwide. Then they declared us delinquent and sent us 1-A reclassifications and eventually they ordered me for induction. They would rather fight an induction refusal which is clear and simple: "Did you or did you not wilfully refuse induction?" I went down to Fort Hamilton and they took me into a room, you know, they knew who I was, and they administered an oath and I refused to take it and within an hour I was out. My mother and sister were there and a lot of friends. I had written letters to all my relatives and former friends. None of them came, of course. But that was part of the tactic of influencing people immediately around you that "I'm going to jail. What are you doing?" . . . The most exciting time is turning in your draft card. Once you make that decision the rest of it is just a natural extension and I didn't get too excited about it. I got a very tremendous, uh, rush, sense of liberation when I turned in my draft card, but all the rest now is just sort of a matter of course and in a sense, that's just what we want to make it become, you know.

CASE 117

I'd like to hand in my draft card but I don't think it's the right thing to do. I don't know if I'm sure enough of myself to do it. As soon as I think I am, I would, I will. You know, it sets you apart from the middle class. I like—I like air-conditioners and flowers, but I don't like suburbia. I'm kind of, you know, I'm not down on wealth. If you hand back your draft card, you kind of cut yourself off from the mainstream of America right now. That might not be such a bad idea, but I have certain bourgeois feelings, you know, in me that to break away is, you know, not right or something. I don't want to work for the peace movement for the rest of my life, although that depends on the political situation. I want to study.

CASE 119

I was a Peace Corps volunteer for two years in Peru doing community development work in a squatters' settlement just outside of Lima. Then at the end of two years I came back to the States and worked in a training program during the summer at Yale and the following October went back to Guatemala, this time as a staff member. I worked in Guatemala for ten months and then in Venezuela for twenty months with the Peace Corps. Those five years overseas again heightened the social concerns on my part. There's nothing like seeing or living in or next to poverty and injustice to make you feel it acutely. But at the same time I became a little distant from concerns and problems in the United States. And so much had happened in five years. Five years is a generation gap as far as I'm concerned and this was brought out very vividly when I returned to the Stanford campus. I found a very, very interesting situation in that the students, I felt, had changed dramatically, were sharper, much more aware of what the world was all about, much more aware of their relationship to their environment. It was a good place to readjust to what was happening in the United States. I went away a liberal and still had the feeling I was a liberal and had people yell at me, just among friends. I just didn't catch the whole drift of the conversation. Somebody asked me if I thought I was liberal and I said yes, thinking that was pretty good as opposed to conservative and found out it was now bad. I came back in July and spent the summer there and was very much stimulated and jarred at the same time about things people were thinking and talking about. In addition to this I have a background, a whole orientation which I absorbed overseas, a way of thinking about the world, about people, that made a lot of what I saw in terms of political happenings, political events, governmental decisions, governmental programs—the spectrum or the parameters around decisions that were going on seemed so absurd and counterproductive, contrary to the very principles for which our country is supposed to stand. And so by October I felt strongly enough about it so that I felt I could and should send my draft card back to my local draft board, which I did, with a letter of explanation.

What I said is that we profess to believe in certain principles and I think in general the American people do believe them. But yet, in terms of day-to-day practice and certainly highlighted and presented quite vividly in the case of the war in Vietnam that we are acting contrary to our own principles. And then I contrasted what we were doing in Vietnam with what I had done as a Peace Corps volunteer and with what the Peace Corps is supposed to represent and then I said I found in them a hypocrisy which I couldn't reconcile in my own mind and as far as the war in Vietnam was concerned that I was returning my draft card and would not and could not serve in that war. . . . I decided that instead of doing it publicly I would do it alone.

CASE 120

I came to recognize that it would be better from a few points of view to do what I can do here first and then possibly, if I can't resolve the situation satisfactorily, to leave. So I'm making an application for C.O. status and will see what happens. If it doesn't work, maybe I'll go to Canada or England or Scandinavia.

CASE 126

I didn't do it because I didn't want to attract undue attention to myself. I'm not interested in going to jail. I suppose if there were some real mass turning in of draft cards, if it was really snowballing so that it would be impossible to stop it, then I'd be willing to do it. But I wouldn't go to jail for the peace movement.

Confrontations

CASE 100

A friend of mine slept out at the Federal Attorney General's Office on his eighteenth birthday demanding to be arrested for refusing to register. He was a noncooperator. He's the guy that said, "Applying for conscientious objector status is like applying for a permit not to kill. That should be the rule rather than the exception."

There is another guy, I didn't find out about it until I became a resister. He was a Green Beret. He quit the Green Berets and burned his draft card in Central Park about six months before the big draft card turning-in. He did it in uniform and got a lot of publicity and trouble.

That last demonstration. I mean, watching the hate and fear in both cops and demonstrators. Both the hate and fear were like right together and not separate emotions and the whole situation, realizing that the demonstrators had been programmed in a variety of ways and how the cops had been programmed in a variety of ways and watching the battle escalating and knowing step by step why it was happening and feeling, you know, my legs were trembling and watching a plain-clothesman smash a girl in the face and hit her head up against a lamp post for no apparent reason and things like that. And then seeing the demonstrators scream at the police and the police try and stop antidemonstration people from attacking the demonstration which is just ridiculous. The whole thing was just such a bad scene that I've become much more interested in more of the philosophy of nonviolence, reading and talking to people about what nonviolence means. It means more than just not hitting back.

CASE 104

Went down South for the summer to Mississippi to work in the civil rights movement. . . . There were lots of times I wanted to go home because we were being told, you know, people would say, "Damn, if I get a chance I'll shoot every single one of you." A lot of good black civil rights workers quit when they heard we were coming down and you just had to decide that it would be really bad publicity if whites started leaving and said they were being threatened and told to go home by blacks. That was the reason I decided to stay. Then we got to this nice little town where the masonite factories are located and ended up in the newly fire-bombed office of the movement. We were spotted the first night we got into town. This big truck full of rednecks came by just as we were getting out of our car. The sheriff and everybody else knew us immediately, as soon as we got there. We got along o.k. except for people driving by our house every night, constantly driving by, until one night they fire-bombed the place and shot, you know, God knows how many guns they were shooting into the place. There were holes all over the walls. They never did find out who did it. I had just gone to bed, I'd stayed up late and stepped on a wasp in the process of going to bed, so it was only two or three minutes after I turned out the lights. We were all sleeping on the floor from a knowledge of the way people shoot, when they shot into the house. Someone threw a gas bottle, a bleach bottle full of gasoline and it ran on the porch. The house was such that it probably just burned through the wall instantly. And the whole place was burning and these firecrackers started going off. I got up and started to get things out. I thought, what the hell, just shooting off firecrackers, trying to be funny. I had never heard a gun before, you know. So they pulled me down. The next morning, when we looked at the remains of the building, I noticed all these holes around where my head had been. And the bitter experience with the press in the North. We contacted all the press we knew about. The first thing they asked was, "Anybody killed or hurt?" We said, "No" and they said, "Well, we can't use it," and hung up on us.

Got beaten up that summer. We were picketing a store . . . because fifty percent of the customers were black, but no blacks worked there and they had a lottery and in fifty weeks there was never a black winner. The mayor was asked by the superintendent of the store to get us out of there. So he drew this line and said, "Anybody who walks over it will be arrested." So we all walked over it. I was the only white guy there. There were two white girls. The rest were black people from the community. . . . I was brought upstairs in the jail but they separated me out because I was white. It was a segregated jail. I wasn't going to cause any trouble and went along with this and was put in an open cell block with three other guys, all white. . . . One of them had just been arrested for being drunk, disorderly conduct at our picket line. He had also been taken out of his cell to watch us walking in and he saw me coming in with the black guys. The girls were put into separate cells. It was incredible the amount of noise they made in that place. Just unbelievable. I was talking to him about the noise and he turned around and told me to "Shut the fuck up and sit down." I realized I was in a very shady position there. And he brought in his friends to introduce them to me. One of them wasn't drunk, just high. There was a semi-drunk guy and a big, hawking mountain-man type, you know, 300 pounds, drizzle-whiskers, an old, beat-up hat, slightly longish hair and a big brown jacket. He was drunk and so far out he could hardly stand. The first guy immediately introduced me as "one of them freedom-riders" and then the semi-drunk guy started to rough me up. He got me up against the wall, but was drunk enough so that only one out of every two punches would land, you know. I stayed up as long as I could until I lost my wind. And then I went into this nonviolent curl and I was really stomped. The guy would run across and jump on me, pick me up and throw me against the wall. The mountain man was so drunk that he just stood in the corner and laughed and the other guy told him not to kill me, you know. "Do whatever you want, but don't kill him." I felt if I had tried anything at that time the mountain man would have got to me and that would have been it. . . . And then they decided they would try and get me in the back where they could really work me over. I lodged myself in the door and stayed there for a minute or so. If they had gotten me in the back, I would have had it. That would have been it. And the police came upstairs and I yelled bloody murder and they had to blackjack everybody to get them off me. One guy was taken to the hospital 'cause his skull was split, the police had to hit him so hard to get him off. That really shook me up. It was the first incidence of violence that I had undergone with no way to defend myself. . . . Afterwards, my attitude changed and I began to be a lot more withdrawn about the way I would participate in things. This was the first real beating I had ever gotten. The emotional shock was bad. Every time after that I would go out, it would take very definite active will. If I was going out alone I no longer walked through the white neighborhoods with the same abandon that I used to. I haven't been arrested since then.

CASE 105

I never thought of being a C.O. until I had to register for the draft. If you had asked me, I would have said, "What's a C.O.?" But when I had to register, I said, "What the hell is this thing?" And then I started to think about it [the draft]. If you had asked me then, if I would refuse to go into the Army I would probably have answered, "Something I'll have to think about, but there's a good chance." You know, I didn't hunt or fish and didn't even kill insects . . . if a spider had walked into my room, I would have picked it up and thrown it back out. You know, I always knew I didn't like to, uh, I always put myself in the other guy's place. As soon as I learned what a C.O. was, which was less than a year later, my thought was, "I'm going to have to find out about this because I might be a C.O." I'm not a pacifist, though. There's a difference, because I still play football [professional] and karate, which are both physically violent sports.

Then in college I started thinking about it a lot. I read a lot of things, but Bertrand Russell was the one who showed me something. I joined ROTC and then quit and told the Commander I was quitting because I decided that I was a C.O. . . . Then there was something that came about in my freshman year that really changed me. It really matured me. I read one of the great Greek tragedies. I remember there was this guy Ajax. He was a great big warrior. He was captured in the war by the enemy and he was going to lose his life unless he squealed on these other twenty guys and said where they were. Something like that. And Ajax realized that if he squealed on those twenty guys, that as soon as he did that, he had already died. And I thought about that for months. And I said that was beautiful. I would like to be like that, to be strong and to realize that if you don't do what you think is right, you're dead already. You know, physically alive doesn't mean a thing because you can't do what you have to do. So I thought about this and I hoped and was waiting for a chance to come along to prove this. And then . . . I got a parking ticket which I didn't deserve . . . I pleaded not guilty and when my trial came up I was found guilty. I told the judge there was no sign there and I knew I was right. And I got a three dollar fine. I don't know why I only got a three dollar fine. I think it was a woman judge and she like half believed me. But anyway, I said, "I can't pay that fine." And she said, "Why not? Don't you have any money?" I said, "Yeah, I have money, but I didn't do anything wrong." So I had to spend a day in jail. This was like the beginning.

CASE 112

This first demonstration I was at was in the fall of 1966, the first term of my junior year [of high school]. Before that I had spoken up about my dislike for the Vietnam war. I had a dislike that the communists would perhaps rule the country, but at the same time that the United States was again forcing its values and system down somebody else's throat and supporting dictators in the process.

Well, in 1963 or 1962 it was either the Bay of Pigs or the [Cuban] missile crisis, and I argued that it was an instance of intervention in another country's affairs. That was in seventh grade. But I felt a kind of happiness that we were beating the communists. You know, it was the kind of thing, it's not right that we're there, but I'm sort of glad that it's working out the way it is, that the communists are being gotten rid of. I would say, from about 1963 on my political awareness grew measureably. We talked about Vietnam more in class. I didn't know where Vietnam was at the time. Diem was overthrown and there was a lot of talk about the C.I.A. having a hand in it. . . . When a person studies American "gunboat diplomacy" in South America and is able to condemn it, and everybody condemned it in class, then why don't they condemn what we're doing today?

Well, then, in the fall of my junior year I took an American history course for college credit. We studied history in a manner I had never done before. I had always assumed history was known, and then you realize that no two historians agree on anything. I took an active part in the discussions and arguments in class and at the end of the year we were moving up towards foreign policy of the twentieth century and I guess I was the leading exponent of opposition to the Vietnam war, whereas the teacher was a supporter of it.

CASE 115

On the 21st of October we went to Washington and that's where I burned my draft card. Now that was the first real radical thing I had done. . . . I don't remember too much about it except that I was thoroughly disgusted and frightened by what I saw there. . . . Things were getting dangerous. People had been very badly beaten. People had begun to get very frightened where I was and began to leave. We were originally 1,000 and had dwindled to maybe 500 and I saw the absolute necessity to stay. Uh, I couldn't see people just leaving. The value of the demonstration would have been gone if we'd just got frightened and left. So I spoke to some of the people I was with. Some of the professors had decided to stay. Then people were still making speeches about let's leave, we're going to get killed. And then somebody got up and said, "We ought to stay." And it seemed to me he wasn't satisfying the crowd, and I got up and, uh, I told the people to stay. I told them, if anything happens to us here the people at home would come for us and support us. And then this fellow sat down and everybody decided to stay. There was a time when soldiers started walking up to us. We were surrounded, sort of huddled together. Everybody was expecting that they were going to get killed, and well, the soldiers never came. They stopped. But that feeling of holding each other and when you see the soldiers coming is just a very, very warm feeling. During the night eight or nine people shared one blanket. Girls and fellows and teachers and everybody just shared the blankets together. . . .

Then I went to Washington for the Poor People's Campaign. That introduced me to a new sort of people. And then we went to jail. I was in jail for ten days. When we first got arrested there were women, eighty years old, and mothers with their infants. . . . Well, it was the last day and everybody had to leave Resurrection City and we went to the Capitol to petition the Congressmen and other government officials. That wasn't allowed. You needed some sort of permit and so we got arrested. That was an act of civil disobedience, just asking the government for things that are due to us. It was really a frightening experience. . . . There were 1,500 soldiers there. Just walking in file like robots and they didn't look like men. They had masks on their faces and shotguns and bullet-proof vests. Quite frightening thing to see. When I left the city, they had shot tear gas at night, at about two a.m. indiscriminately around. . . . I understand there may have been one little infant that suffocated from the tear gas. It was like being bombed. I've never really been in a situation where I was getting bombed. Everybody sort of huddles together and doesn't know where to go or what to do. You don't know what is going to happen and it has a vague semblance to a Vietnamese city or village getting bombed. You can just imagine people running around after their arms and legs get blown off. When we got arrested there were blind people. A blind man was with me in jail for ten days. And these old women and young women with their infants. First they put us in a five by eight cell with eight, no, with six people. So we just had no place to sit or stand hardly and it was extremely hot. It was really rough and we didn't get fed in two days except for two Spam sandwiches. A very degrading thing. Then they moved us to another place with about seventy people where there was no place to sleep, uh, barely stand, very cold, and nothing to eat again. And then they shipped us to another place where we had beds at last and, uh, there we got food. Well, then they ordered us to work and we refused to work. But before we refused to work we refused to eat. So we went on a fast for four days and they took away our privileges. . . . Then the last night I had gotten involved in something and I got put in the hole. That's a cell with no bed, just a concrete floor with a toilet bowl. I remember it was about the width of my arms spread. I about reached the ceiling with my hands. They take all your clothes off and they just leave you your drawers on. One comical thing was that half my drawers were ripped so I had one cold buttock that night. The windows are open and they intentionally want to make you suffer . . . but now I can sort of empathize with people. So about the induction refusal. That was quite an experience. I wanted to stay at the Fort [Fort Hamilton Induction Center] as long as I could to speak to the inductees. Well, you get an induction physical. I refused to urinate for them. So they kept me downstairs. I told them that I was nervous and, uh, it was a traumatic experience for me and that's why I couldn't urinate. They accepted that and said, "Just wait a while." And they kept giving me water and I told them, "I'm sorry, I can't." During that time I was sitting downstairs and got into discussions with people taking physicals. Everybody knew who I was and that somebody was down there who was against the war. I travelled around to various offices and the whole Fort got to know me. I talked to a lot of people and I didn't find anybody who was for it [the war], and in two days that was about 300 people. . . . They accepted induction because they were frightened. They were very antiwar. It was very sad how they just accepted the induction without, without questioning. I found that the ones who volunteered didn't join the Army, you know, to go fighting. They wanted to get an education. That's why they joined. So let's see. They kept me overnight in the barracks with people who were awaiting transfer. Many of them had been to Vietnam. Some of them had been wounded and some had seen their buddies killed. You know, they just couldn't tolerate me, but they had no reasons for the war either, which was very sad. Here they went off to battle with no reasons. There was this one fellow. He had been in the service for seventeen years. He had all kinds of scars all over his body and he was going over to Vietnam in two or three weeks. They all drink. All drunkards. The "lifers" are, anyway, and the ones who aren't "lifers" just feel totally lost and have no idea or sense of what they're doing or what they should do. There was this other "lifer" who had been in for twenty-seven years and he was awaiting a medical discharge because he was an alcoholic. When he heard what I was talking about, he jumped off his bunk and, you know, got into a karate stance, and I thought for sure something was going to happen. And he ran up to me and jumped on my bunk. I thought he was going to kill me. And then he sort of relaxed and says, "I wanna talk to you." Well, we didn't talk too much because he was rather incoherent and couldn't stay on the conversation too long. His mind had really been affected. . . . This one young fellow from Germany who had just come back, he'd been to college for two years. I don't know how he was a soldier. He said that while he was stationed in Germany, when the riots were going on a couple of months ago, he said they got "lined up outside and there was 1,000 of us and 10,000 of them." He's talking about the students. "And I had a gun in my hand and I didn't want to kill anybody. Jesus, I didn't even want to join the Army. I had a metal plate in my skull and my leg is bad." And then he started crying and telling me this. There was another guy, just seventeen, who had enlisted and gone AWOL two or three times. Just a little itty-bitty kid. Then he had another friend . . . just little kids. So I got a general idea of what the Army's made of. Then the next day they took me down to the physical again and I told them I couldn't urinate and talked with the people there again. . . . They enjoyed the conversations. Occasionally, the Colonel would come down and ask what's happening. And they would tell him, I can't urinate. They can't force you to do anything and can't chase you off the Fort 'cause they have to fulfill their thing.

CASE 116

We went to Orangeburg, South Carolina, during the summer of 1965 and again in 1966 to help with voter registration. We knocked on doors, talking to people about voting and trying to get them to register, and bring them in carloads to the registration place and help them fill out the forms, so they wouldn't obviously get fucked over. At one point the registration process was slowing down, the registrars weren't showing up and stuff, and we had a sit-in with about fifty people, in which I got arrested. We spent the night in jail and the next day we got out. The trial was sometime later and was a sham thing. Our lawyer knew it. We were found guilty. We did very well in registering. Ironically the high school kids were tremendous. The college kids were really terrible. They went to this fraternity and football stuff. It was really impossible to crack those black colleges but the high school kids were very active and helped us out a lot. Just several months ago, the riots in Orangeburg were largely campus people, and these were the high school kids who helped us out several years ago.

CASE 122

Shortly after I burned my draft card we had a confrontation with Army recruiters on campus. And thirty of us got arrested. It was right after that that I dropped out of school. This was the first time any of us had been busted. The people at the school, the professors, came up with the bail for us. Thirty of us at 100 dollars each. They came up with 3,000 dollars in two hours and got us out. And we had long discussions about what to do and finally ended up hiring a lawyer. We all started by pleading not guilty. Most of the kids said they didn't have enough money to pay the lawyer. He wanted 1,000 dollars. I ended up getting a lot of money from my parents, 200 dollars, which was just supposed to be a loan. . . . Then it ended up that twenty-five of the thirty kids pleaded guilty. The arrest itself really radicalized the school. It got people thinking. Wherever you went on campus people were talking about it. You know, the war, whether or not it was o.k. to block the recruiters' table. A lot of people were saying they were against the war but [they didn't] think we should block the recruiters' table. Anyway, most of the kids said they didn't have enough money to pay the lawyer and pleaded guilty. Twenty-five of them pleaded guilty. They were fined fifty dollars and they paid it. All along they'd been saying, I don't have fifty dollars to pay the lawyer, but when it came to . . . [getting] out of jail, wham [claps his hands] they had their fifty dollars. And they paid it with no qualms. They changed their plea to "guilty" because if they stuck to their plea of not guilty they were going to have to come back sometime in the middle of the summer for their trial and it might have meant a longer sentence. So they copped out. It just sickened me. Well, five of us stuck to our plea of not guilty. The five of us were found guilty. It was July, just the end of June. I was in jail for the Fourth of July that year, this year too. They fined us fifty dollars too. And two of us refused to pay the fine. But it wasn't the damn guys who had been working so hard on campus. They all copped out. They all mumbled something about their jobs and school and that they couldn't go to jail for ten days. Well, I was working at the . . . Yacht Club and if I did ten days right then it meant that I was going to lose my job. . . . And I decided not to pay the fine, for many reasons. But first because I felt I was not guilty. And I figured I was facing jail for my draft activities, I'd better get a look at what it's like. So I did. . . .

This is something which has always bothered me. Here are supposedly committed people. No, sir. They get arrested and they cop out! They plead guilty. Anything to get out of it. Pay their fine. As soon as they find themselves where it might cost them a little bit of themselves, they start squirming. And I think that's sick. That's sick. I was back on campus for a little while this summer. I was just looking around. A lot of these kids dropped out of school and were involved in this peace group. Basically, they look grubby as hell. They're turning off everybody. And they aren't doing anything. They're goofing around town, not working, smoking pot—just alienating people. There wasn't anybody on campus who was really committed. It just made me a little bit sick. They talked commitment, but they didn't act commitment.

Later I found out about the Pentagon Walk for Peace, and I decided to join it. This was sponsored by the New England Committee for Non-Violent Action. I went down and joined them. And I was impressed by their commitment. These people were for real. They had a policy of paying no bail and no fine when they're arrested. They were all pacifists and nonviolent. And they really cared about people. This was another thing that really bothered me about the people on campus who said they were peaceniks. You could see the hostilities in them and hatreds. And yet they were supposedly trying to bring peace. And that bugged me. But these people on the Walk were beautiful people. I remember writing a letter saying that they leave love draped on the telephone wires as they walk past.

I was supposed to work for the Yacht Club driving a tender for a while, but I lost that job because I was in jail for ten days. Not only that, I was supposed to work for the New York Association for Brain-Damaged Children that year, but when I gave back my new draft card, 1-A, and this hit the publicity papers a lot, they asked me to rescind my contract because they said it would hurt them in getting funds. It hit the papers that I was going to work there for the summer with the brain-damaged children and that I was a draft resister. So I rescinded my contract. And then I worked here as a volunteer for cerebral palsy children making no money.

I went to this farm in Connecticut to learn more about nonviolence and then I was going from demonstration to demonstration. Two days after I got to the farm I got arrested in a civil rights march where we came to keep it nonviolent . . . and I got arrested by a policeman. The black protesters were marching to protest police brutality. They were going to march from the black part of town to the white part of town to the mayor's house. And when they tried to get out of the black part of town the police stopped them and started to push them back. The police came up to me and said, "Go back." And I said, "Why?" And they they'd say, "Go back." Then I'd say, "Why?" And then they put me in a paddy wagon. That was the first time I had totally noncooperated. I wouldn't walk. I wouldn't eat. They beat the living daylight out of me. The first time I had ever been beaten by the cops. Really hurt! They really hurt me. They never did arraign me. And they kept me for nine days in isolation. Then they finally let me go. They dropped charges. Six guys worked me over, kicking me, hitting me, and one of the things they used was a twister. It's a device that clamps on your arm and they clamp down and drag you by it. That was the first time it's been used on me. It's been used on me in Washington, D.C. Really hurts. And it really swelled up my arm too. And they bent my fingers back and they twisted my arm. . . . They were trying to get me to walk. I wasn't cooperating. They wanted me to walk upstairs to the jail and I wouldn't do it. And rather than just carry me up there they spent a half an hour beating me up. Six of them. They finally got me up there twisting my arm, dragging me by the twister. They could have just as easily carried me up there. They had an elevator. But they sometimes bashed me right in the mouth. They had another prisoner and he was handcuffed from behind his back. He was black.

And they banged me into him. Just kind of took me and shoved me into him.
And then they said, "Why did you bang into him?" And I said, "You pushed
me into him." And then they said, "Don't lie to me," and hauled off and
punched me across the mouth. I couldn't believe it, that that could happen.
This was another disillusionment. That was in Hartford. . . . You see, for me
it's been been a series of disillusionments. I started out believing that this country,
in this country entirely, in what it said it's good for, and then there's been
a series of disillusionments. Starting with the war and then this beating was
another one. That was the first time I had realized that the cops weren't your
friend. And they really hurt me. And then they finally let me go. They had
given me prison clothes which I wouldn't wear. I was in isolation anyway for
the whole nine days, just in my underwear. They just left me there to think.
One of the girls had been hurt. Her head had been cracked when they were
throwing her. She cracked her head on the paddy wagon. They didn't give her
medical attention and it hit the papers and everything. And she blacked out.
And finally they took her to the hospital. She had temporary blindness for a
while.

I helped plan a demonstration against the battleship U.S.S. New Jersey during the recommissioning ceremony down at Philadelphia on April 6. I got arrested for paddling a canoe in front of the U.S.S. New Jersey with a sign that
said, "Stop War." They charged me with a violation of the Espionage Law of
1917. But they dropped charges after a couple of days.

The farm where I was living in Voluntown, Connecticut, was attacked by
Minute Men. The police had gotten a tip from the FBI that the attack was going
to take place and staked out the place with police without telling us that the
attack was going to happen. The Minute Men got into the farm. They had submachine guns, World War I rifles, bayonets, and gasoline. Now it's hard to say
what they had in mind but it looks like their intention was to hurt someone.
The police came in. There was a shoot-out. One Minute Man got shot in the
face and is not going to be able to see again. One of the women at the farm
was shot accidentally by the police. Three other Minute Men were wounded.
As far as things can be ascertained, one Minute Man fired a shot. All the other
shots were fired by policemen. They only found one shell of any kind fired
by a Minute Man.

On the March on the Pentagon on October 21, 700 people got busted.
I was one of them. One of my primary aims for going to that was to keep
it nonviolent. And I also felt that this was an important thing to do. And it
was tremendous . . . with all those people and it was basically a nonviolent
thing. Thousands of people were sitting . . . [at] the Pentagon. I spent nineteen
days in jail down there, four of them in the hole without water. Then I stopped
drinking water and I was taken up to the hospital and force-fed. I was noncooperating again. I was sitting in the Pentagon parking lot. They lied, too. That's
another disillusionment. I was sitting there with my back to an MP. An MP
came along, grabbed me by the collar, dragged me under a flat-bed truck, and
arrested me for moving against . . . a police line. A marshall actually got on
the stand during my trial and testified that I had crawled backwards, on my
back, under this flat-bed truck through the police line. And I said I was dragged

by my collar. And they said we were guilty. Another disillusionment. These guys can't understand that they lied. Now it's rather commonplace. I've seen it happen quite often. Cops will get on the stands and lie! But yet they're supposed to be upholding the law. And the judges know they're lying. Everybody knows they're lying. That was a bad scene. Seven hundred kids got arrested. I was noncooperating. That time I wouldn't even give my name. They kept us in dormitories out in Virginia for a long while.

Dormitories?
Yeah. Akagwan, Virginia. That's a prison farm-type thing they have outside of Washington. And they put most of the people arrested in big dormitories. That was kind of nice [laughs]. At one point fifty of us got together. They didn't even have bars on the doors, but they had four guards sitting there in an office to keep us from coming out. We could go out into this courtyard. Then we'd have more bars to go through to get finally out to freedom. But fifty of us decided to get together and have a war trial. All together.

And I led it. And we walked—whoop!—right out the door. But these guards really got excited and bopped us, you know. And then we had a confrontation. I started thinking fast. Here we were all sitting. When once a cop would stop us we sat down in the doorway, all fifty of us. And the director of the prison just came along. And a few of the guys hadn't been allowed to make phone calls. . . . And so I said, "Well, you let these guys make phone calls. Let them go to the judge and we'll go back to the dormitories." I just thought of this on the spur of the moment [laughs]. My only purpose in leading this war path was, I wanted to go outside. And I think it's important. You just don't docilely submit to being in a cage. And I thought that it was good that we were kind of showing our feelings so in walking out this way. So I made these demands and some others too and they were met. And it was obvious that demands were going to be met. I said, "Do you want to walk back in?" And the guys said, "Yes." So we went back in. And there were no needs that I had. I was noncooperating. My general policy in prison is that I never ask for anything. . . . Other guys—especially regular prisoners as opposed to demonstrators—spend a lot of time yelling, "Give me cigarettes! Give me this! Give me that!" I never asked for anything. So I didn't want anything from them at all. . . . I didn't have any demands for myself, but these other guys. The director of the prison sent one of his goons in to get me, "Come out here and talk to the director!" And I looked out in this little office. And there the director was surrounded by four of his goons and I knew that they were going to drag. . . . "Tell the director to come in here." [laughs]. And he did. He came into the dormitory. And the director said something to the effect, "Well, what are your problems? And we don't want this kind of disturbance. Is there anything I can help you with?" And I said, "I have no problems, but some of these guys might." Everybody gathered around. So he spent a half hour there talking to these guys. Many of them had been arrested for the first time. And in the meanwhile I went up and fell asleep. I was tired. I spent the two weeks before the demonstration running around lecturing about nonviolence. And I had been up all night, the night of the demonstration. And I had been working to keep the demonstration nonviolent. So I fell asleep for the whole two days I was out there. But then they transferred me to the Washington, D.C. jail. And by this time most of the 700 people had been released. They either paid their ten-dollar fine or forfeited bail or walked into court. Eleven of us refused to walk into court. And they said, they wouldn't take us into court to be arraigned—I think it's illegal if I may say that—but they wouldn't take us into court, until we were ready to walk in there. Well, we said that we wouldn't walk in there. And we wouldn't wear prison uniforms. And we wouldn't submit to fingerprinting. And we wouldn't eat. We wouldn't walk, so they threw us in the hole. They took us to a Washington, D.C., jail and threw eleven of us in the hole, which is a stripped cell. It's got a commode with a little hole to go to the bathroom in. No toilet paper. And they stripped us naked and threw us in there. It was freezing. Concrete floor. There were three separate cells and four in two of them and three in the other. And they left us there! Overnight. And the next morning they came in and eight, I think it was eight, guards and they had the twisters again. And they took us out of the hole, one at a time. Dragged us down the hall. And I was naked and they took the skin off both hips. . . . And twisted the hell out of one arm with the twister while fingerprinting the other. They never did get clear fingerprints. They were hurting me too much. I couldn't even go limp. And they were hurting us again. Six guys in the face of that broke and they decided to walk and everything. Five of us decided to stick it out. And we responded to the hole by stopping to drink water. Three of us weren't drinking water. I'm never going to do that again. That hurts. But I went four days. I was going to stick it out and I did. . . . [They kept us in the hole] four days [pause]. Four days. Dark . . . stinking of urine. They finally brought in a mattress and a blanket. And we didn't know what was coming off. For each one of us. They brought in a mattress and a blanket. But it was still dark. . . . The press apparently had found out that we were in there and was making a stink. And they brought the press in. "See, they got a mattress and a blanket. It isn't true that. . . ." They bring the mattress in and a half hour later the prison director comes in, "See, they got a mattress and blanket". He denied that we were ever in there naked. As a matter of fact, for a while he was denying that he . . . had knowledge that we were in the hole. But he came in the night we were in there and supervised setting us in there.

Did you get to talk to the press? Did the press come in to your cell?
They just ran them by real fast and wouldn't let us talk to them. But . . . people were talking to the press when they got out.

Did the press print anything about that?
I think they did. There was a big, big thing, prison officials were lying. This is another thing I found too. Here you are, sitting in the hospital being force-fed and you read in the newspapers that somebody had brought in for you that we broke our fast voluntarily. And that you are now eating normally. And there you are with a tube down your nose.

How did they force-feed you?
They stuck a tube up my nose and down into my stomach . . . they jammed it up into my sinuses. The more I put my head down and then they put it in. And I took it out a couple of times, but then this nurse—I called her the

wicked witch—told me that if I took the tube out again, she was going to handcuff me to the bed and leave the tube. I finally ended up taking it out. I didn't mind the hospital that much anyway. And they ended up taking me back to a dormitory, because I had started eating again.

In the dormitory you're supposed to stand for count. They come in and yell "Count!" And everybody is supposed to stand up. And I wouldn't stand for count. . . . So they carried me into isolation—not the hole this time—but an isolation cell in a cell block. So I stopped eating again. And after two days the goon squad came along and said, "You're going to eat." And I said, "No." And they carried me up to the hospital and force-fed me again. So I had the tube in for a day or so and then I took it out and I started eating again. They took me back to the dormitory. For the last five days I was in the dormitory, but I wouldn't stand for count or abide by all their stupid rules. But they just ignored me. They made everybody else stand for count, but they let me do whatever I wanted to do. . . .

After nineteen days I was taken to court. We had our trial. . . . So after that I went back to the farm. And I started doing a couple of speaking engagements. Answering mail, working around the farm, and this kind of thing. Enjoyed being alive. Then I got busted again on December 4 for blocking an induction center in Manchester, New Hampshire. And I was only in jail seven days that time. Then I went back to the farm again. And kept on doing the same thing . . . couple of speaking engagements here and there, talking about nonviolence, answering letters, the same routine. Work on the farm.

Then I got busted again on April 6 for paddling a canoe in front of the U.S.S. New Jersey. That was in Philadelphia in April, '68. I refused induction on March 4 of this year. I got indicted on May 17 [1968] on one count, refusing induction. And I was supposed to show up in court on June 13 to be arraigned. Instead, I took sanctuary in the Washington Square Methodist Church. I was dragged out of church. And I wouldn't pay bail. Wouldn't cooperate with the court. And my first judge screamed at me, "You will stand up! Stand up!" Wouldn't stand up. Found me in contempt of court. Put me back to jail. They brought me back to court in a week, but I wouldn't walk in, because I was handcuffed. This was just this summer, beginning this summer. And he said I could sit in jail and rot until I was ready to walk . . . [into the] courtroom. But then they gave me a new judge. . . . That was a good scene. I was brought back to the courthouse again. Once again I wouldn't walk into the court because I was handcuffed. And I wasn't much inclined to cooperate. By this time I had been sitting in that dumb West Street jail for eighteen days fasting. I was taking milk and coffee which they'd bring in with meals. I wasn't eating anything. They came in and said, "Do you mind if you had a new judge?" And I said, "Not at all." They said, "Will you walk into court?" And I said, "No." The next thing, you know, the door of the south wing opens—and this is a neat story, I keep telling it to people. I had been reading *Pilgrim's Progress* by John Bunyan in jail, and the Bible. . . . I was in a spiritual mood. The fast and everything. It was the eighteenth day of my fast. All of a sudden the door in my cell in the courthouse flings open and this robed guy with this angelic smile walked in, you know. It blew my mind. Oh my God! Bunyan's

Pilgrim is coming into my jail cell. I didn't know what was coming off! I expected him to be holding a candle or something. And it turned out to be Judge——. And he said, "Mr.——, I hear you wouldn't walk into my courtroom, so I decided to come down and see you." And he brought the court recorder and the U.S. Marshall and the D.A. They all crowded into my cell and talked to me. And then he said, "Your behavior has been a little unusual." And I agreed that it had. He asked me if I could explain my behavior and I said, "Yes." Indeed, you know, he was anxious. While the other judge was trying to force, this guy was anxious. And he let me go on for about a half hour explaining my feelings. He asked some very intelligent questions. And when it was all over he said he was much concerned about the fact that I was going to defend myself. So they sent me over to King's County Hospital to get me a psychiatric examination to make sure that I was competent to defend myself. And I had to spend a week and a half on a mental ward, waiting to see a psychiatrist. I only saw him for fifteen minutes finally. We basically argued over why I was going to defend myself and he said, "You're sane." But that was terrible . . . that mental ward.

Did Judge——know that was going to happen?
Well, yeah. He sent me over there for psychiatric examination to make sure that I was competent enough to defend myself. . . . Since I was defending myself, he had to make sure that all my rights were protected and all his rights were protected. I don't think [he] knows what that ward is like. It's for criminally insane people. They send them there for observation. Not all of the guys are crazy. A lot of them were in there for observation, just like me. Boy, it was a rough place and they treated you . . . really less than human. The guards in the federal prison in the city here in the detention center treated me pretty well. They didn't give me a hard time. They treated me like a human being, even though I was locked in a cell by myself. But over at that mental ward it was terrible. I finally got out of there. And I came back into court, and I decided to break my fast in order to have enough strength to conduct trial. So I broke my fast after thirty days. Gave me a week of eating before the trial. And I did the trial myself. I defended myself in front of the court. I picked the jury and everything. I figured, if I had a jury they'd probably find me guilty anyway, because I obviously refused induction. I turned in two 1-A cards, burned one, and refused to take three physicals . . . as well as refuse induction. I had obviously, you know, resisted. . . .

The trial was a good scene. At the very outset Judge——told me that we were going to find out if I had refused induction. And not to talk about the war or anything else. Just to find out whether or not I had refused induction and whether or not that failure was willful. . . . And the first part of the trial, before the jury came in, they had to see whether I was properly classified. So they put the clerk of the draft board on the stand and it was obvious that I was properly classified. She mentioned all the draft cards, 1-A cards I had turned in, and the fact that I had burned my draft card was brought out and this kind of stuff . . . that I had refused to take three physicals, and I didn't have much defense. It was all true. And so Judge——decided that I was properly classified. They brought the jury in. We chose the jury and started the trial. And the prosecutor went first and presented his case. And the way he did it, he put this head clerk of the draft board on the stand. She was the only witness for the government. The indictment incidentally was the United States of America against [the subject]. Terrible . . . terrible. But he put his head clerk for the draft board on the stand. And she related all the times I had walked in and given 1-A cards back and all the physicals I refused. At one point, December 14, when I refused to take a physical, I sent them a box of Christmas cookies. And along was a note, saying "Hold me a Christmas cookie." They sent the Christmas cookies back and . . . [called] me [for] another physical. But this was all brought out in court, you know, which made it kind of a human thing. It was almost funny as they kept on going through, you know. "And then what happened?" "He came back into the draft board again and he returned the 1-A certificate again." "Again?" "Yes, yes." "And then what happened?" "Well, we saw him again about two months later when he was returning another 1-A certificate." "And then what happened?" "Well, we got a letter from him saying he burned a 1-A certificate over the altar of the Arlington Street Church." "And then what happened?" "We sent him a physical note when we first got word that he was in jail in Manchester. But then we got word that he wasn't in jail, but he wasn't going to take the physical, and he sent us some Christmas cookies." "But then what happened?" "We sent him another physical notice, but he refused it this time." It was rather laughable. . . . There were chuckles from . . . you see, a lot of my friends were there and my family was there. Nobody had seen me. I had been in jail for forty days and this was their first chance to see me. And I had been fasting most of the time. They had been worrying about me. And the courtroom was full. And Judge——never got excited. He never banged his gavel. And——too, the assistant D.A. He was pretty easy-going. They never got excited. Never yelled, "Clear the courtroom if you guys don't shut up!" Despite the fact that there was laughing, you know. As a matter of fact, I think Judge——even joined in laughing at times when all this was brought out.

One of the good things that happened, I had written a statement explaining why, every time I had turned in a 1-A card or had refused a physical. And [the judge] entered these letters into the record in order to show that I had intended to refuse induction. And he read parts of the letters where it said I definitely would not take a physical or that I would definitely not carry a draft card. And so when my turn came up for cross-examination, I said, well, since these letters had been entered into the record, I would like to read them in full. And they had no choice, but to let me do it. So I had about a half hour in which I stood there and read these six letters that I had written to the draft board, damning the war. And so I got in all my feelings about the war this way. And it was great. This was the prosecutor's case. And what I was trying to do was make a moral witness. I didn't give a damn about . . . some legal technicality. That worked out pretty well.

One of the things I wanted to do was show what kind of a human being was on trial. So I put four character witnesses on the stand. ——, who I had been working with on the New England Committee for Non-Violent Action. I really admire her. A friend of mine here in Huntington whom I've known for about eight years. He's just a good guy. The minister of the Unitarian Church here, whom I had gotten to know. And my Dad. I put him up. Incidentally, he had been sitting with me at the defense table. He had come up to give me a couple of words of advice. And Judge——said, "Do you want to sit at the table with him?" So my Dad was sitting at the defense table with me. I'm sure that the jury must have thought that Dad was acting as my advisor or something. Well, then I put him on the stand and said, "How long have you known Mr.——?" And Dad says, "Twenty-two years, eleven months and three weeks." He was a real ham. He just did a tremendous job up there as a character witness. And *The New York Times* said [my defending myself] . . . gave the trial a folksy, informal quality seldom seen in federal courtrooms. And I think it was Dad that gave it that idea, because he got up there on that stand and kind of slouched. Character witnesses are always allowed to talk about your truth, veracity, and integrity. . . . But in the case of my Dad, I said, I would like Dad to be able to talk about my school background and my job background. And the Judge said, "Fine." And my Dad did. I've had a number of jobs. I've been independent. But I worked. I ran a marina all by myself for one year. And at the same time I was working in a day camp. . . . I worked as a volunteer for cerebral palsy children. I was studying child psychology in school. And I wanted to bring all that out. And we did that. It worked out pretty well. I think that the jury and the prosecutor all would have to know what kind of human being was on trial by the time it was over. And then I put myself on the stand and said I had refused induction and [wanted] to explain why. And they stopped me. They kept on objecting.

Did you cross-examine yourself?
Well, I said, "Judge——, how are we going to do this?" And he said, "Well, just get up and narrate." So I did. . . . I argued along three basic lines. First . . . I didn't feel that refusing induction was a crime. Second, I would show that my intention was not to break their man-made law, but rather to uphold higher law. And call it what you want. Some people call it . . . God's law. It's very obvious that if we're going to live together in this world, we're going to have to learn not to kill each other. And I felt a duty to that higher law. I thought of it on the spur of the moment during the trial. They had to prove that it was willful failure on my part to refuse induction. And I said that in one case it was not willful failure. In one sense it certainly was. I knew I could get five years in jail for it and I certainly knew what I was doing. And in fact it was obvious during the course of the trial that I had almost forced this small confrontation. I would have been able to get some kind of deferment, so it didn't need to happen. But I had forced it. But in another sense, it wasn't a willful failure, because giving my feelings about humanity, which I tried to bring out on the stand with my character witnesses, and given the present political scene and the present state of affairs in the world, I had no choice but to refuse induction. And I could do nothing else. I had no other choice. No other avenue open to me. I had to refuse induction. So, in one sense it wasn't a willful failure. Certainly I'm not pleased with the thought of going to jail for perhaps as much as five years. And if I thought there was any other avenue open to me I would take it. But I see no other avenue. And I argued this in front of the court.
But I was found guilty by the jury. It took them about thirty minutes to

decide. It was really pretty open and shut. After they brought back their decision, Judge——said something to the effect that it was probably the right decision, that I had refused induction. But he said, "This . . . [may] be a man of the highest moral integrity and perhaps thirty years from now his feelings will be the law of the land, but right now we've got these laws to uphold."

The College Years

All but two of the war resisters had matriculated at college.* Nearly half of them won academic or combined athletic-academic scholarships. Most of them completed their four-year college programs and a few who entered graduate programs in engineering, chemistry, music, Latin American studies, and theology, received advanced degrees. The others voluntarily dropped out of college between their sophomore and senior years.

The resisters' academic progress in college was strongly affected by the increasing unrest in the United States as a whole and at their schools in particular. Along with their intensifying dissatisfaction with student life, most of them began to see their role as students as irrelevant and artificially isolated from the events of their times. They found most of their coursework to be a sterile and intellectually restricting burden. They also felt that most of the students and instructors operated in an academic straitjacket, demanded intellectual conformity and in doing so squelched creative impulses. Their attempts to adjust to academic life eventually failed when they discovered that this involved the suppression of deep needs which they were no longer prepared to deny.

There was a relatively close correspondence between the resisters' growing awareness of social and political questions and their first participation in social action and discussion groups. This in turn paralleled the decline of their grades. The actual decision to leave college, however, was precipitated by a variety of individual experiences. While only one student became deeply involved in campus politics, many others began to search for ways of expressing their concern about the domestic conditions and foreign policy of the United States. Many spent summer vacations on voter registration drives in the southern states, some became involved in government-sponsored social welfare programs and others moved directly into the antiwar movement. In each of these contexts the resisters made new friends and gained experiences

*Antioch College, Bradley University, Brooklyn College, Bucknell University, City College of New York, Colby College, Columbia College, Drew University, Eau Claire University Divinity School, Hobart College, Hunter College, Lafayette University Long Island University, New School for Social Research, State University of New York at Binghamton, State University of New York at Stonybrook, Queens College, St. Peters College, Stanford University, University of Chicago. Graduate schools: Columbia Graduate Faculties, John Hopkins University, University of Wisconsin, University of California/Berkeley, Union Theological Seminary. The two war resisters who did not matriculate in a college were among the five who had had serious conflicts with teachers and principals.

which highlighted their previous conflicts and unrest and helped them to define their role in society vis-à-vis immediate social issues more sharply. There were several resisters, however, whose decision to end their studies followed a long and completely private struggle with their conscience. They had remained detached from the student protest movements and had been only faintly aware of the political issues which were to play an important role in their lives. It was only after their private decision to demonstrate publicly against the war in Vietnam that they discovered other students who felt as they did.

When most of the resisters entered college they were still preoccupied with their private worlds. Insofar as they were aware of or interested in political and social issues, they tried to push these events away from their lives in order to avoid personal engagement. In many cases a single event shattered their previous image of the United States and left them deeply disillusioned. This disillusionment is only understandable in terms of their previous training. They had come from idealistic, patriotic families whose members had expressed a sometimes passionate reverence for the principles upon which the United States was founded. The resisters formed a deep attachment to these values and believed that American society was structured and functioned in accordance with them. Their college experience and the general unrest in the country opened their eyes to contemporary conditions and historical facts which were irreconcilable with their previous image and vision of American society. For some, this awakening began in the classroom, for others, in the streets or on their campuses. These insights resulted in an increasing estrangement from the competitive, materialistic and status oriented values and behavior of their fellow students.

During this period most of the war resisters attended colleges and universities with active chapters of Students for a Democratic Society and other New Left groups. Their reasons for not affiliating with radical student groups were many. Most fundamentally, their belief in the regenerative forces in American society had not been destroyed. Federal and local governmental agencies and nonviolent social action groups had succeeded in catching their imagination and had provided them with the opportunity of working toward social reforms within or alongside the institutional structure of the country. Even though they felt these programs were too small in scope, mismanaged, and ill-conceived, the alternative of revolutionary action was unacceptable because of its illusionary qualities and the violence and resulting injustice its programs implied. Those who had contact with radical student groups were appalled by their ideological dogmatism, intolerance towards "nonbelievers," coercive tactics, the personal habits of many members, and the fundamental hostility and anger these students radiated. As one resister put it, "They preached love of mankind but they didn't like people." Another said, "Basically, they look grubby. And they aren't doing anything. They're goofing around town, smoking pot, just alienating people. . . . They talk commitment, but they don't act commitment. ... There was another thing that was bothering me about some of the guys on campus who said they were peaceniks. You could see the hostilities and hatred in them. And yet they were supposedly trying to bring peace.''

Divergence

There was one major discernible difference between the movement subjects and other subjects. The other three subgroups still maintained strong educational, occupational, friendship, and aspirational links with conventional society, while nearly all of the movement members had completely extricated themselves from it and had formed a socially distinct marginal group. Despite the obvious implications of this difference for their life style, the elements of heterogeneity among the movement subjects themselves were so great that very few further differences emerged between them and the others. This observation is of some significance since there is a strong tendency to view the movement subjects as a uniform group.

Although most of the social activist, private, and convenience war resisters had only participated rarely and then in unusually large local demonstrations, nearly all were prepared to go to jail and a few to leave the United States rather than serve in the armed forces. Among the movement members, there were a few who did not feel that they would be willing to go to jail or to leave the United States, but most regularly attended large and small demonstrations, both locally and nationally, and helped organize some of them. Some of the movement members had not returned or burned their draft cards while some of the other war resisters had. Single, engaged, and married war resisters were equally distributed throughout all four subgroups; so were religious persuasions. These examples illustrate the caution which must be employed in making generalizations about the correlates of commitment. One can pursue private goals and thoughts as well within as outside an organizational framework. The heterogeneity of the war resisters also found direct expression in the kind and number of their ''commitment experiences.'' Some were content to work at a desk at the War Resisters League or to quietly enter an application for conscientious objector status. Others were occupied with giving lectures, organizing marches, preparing bulletins, or working in slum neighborhoods.

The examination of the resisters' expressed reasons for taking an antiwar stand revealed a greater degree of initial commonality than might have been expected, given the variability of their behavior. The two major reasons expressed were aversion to and rejection of violence and the obligation to take a public stand consistent with one's convictions. Nearly half felt that any kind of cooperation with the Selective Service System would imply legitimization of the United States' policy in Vietnam. A strong dislike for the

United States military was mentioned equally often. Religious considerations, a desire to help build the peace movement, personal expedience, and the rejection of deferments as discriminatory releases were mentioned infrequently as major motivations. There was a strong tendency for those war resisters who did not want to go to jail but did not want to leave the United States either to experience these extreme alternatives as genuine, situationally imposed threats, and to justify their application for C.O. status in terms of this dilemma.

My use of the interview method tended to promote an atmosphere in which the war resisters first spoke of motives and concerns which sounded well thought out. However, as the conversations progressed, most resisters began to mention additional motives, mostly of a temperamental character, which showed that plain and almost reflexive emotionality had figured decisively in their behavior. For example, one resister, after delivering a long and convincing analysis of American and world society, and asserting the importance of taking a moral position on every level to help cure the ills of the world, then explained that he most probably had refused to cooperate with the Selective Service System at first because he "hated red tape" and had "hated filling out college application forms" too, which he had "never gotten in on time." He had responded viscerally and with deep anger to the demand of his draft board to "return that form within ten days," exemplifying the individualistic manner in which most of the war resisters had been dealing with the choices open to them as opponents of the war in Vietnam. This, coupled with the complexity and functional irregularity of the administrative operation of the Selective Service System, the moody, disorganized, and sporadic activity of the antiwar movement, and the vast number of familial and other influences operating on their lives, explains the highly variable expressions of their antiwar sentiments. The variability is most clearly visible in the examples of "commitment experiences" contained in the quotations. There, the extremes in the temperamental qualities of the resisters are most apparent.

One of the major temperamental themes underlying many resisters' actions was, "Nobody is going to just tell me what to do." The manner in which this theme received personal interpretation is, in my opinion, one of the most interesting aspects of these reports. Unpredictability surrounded most of their "commitment experiences." Strong action was coupled with surprising passivity, novelty with banality, feelings of desperation with those of release. The actual course of the resisters' "commitment experiences" allows for few, if any, meaningful generalizations. It is necessary to deal with the psychology of each war resister individually as well as with his family, educational, occupational, and draft situation within the context of the antiwar movement during its varying phases in order to understand why he took a particular action.

For many people, participation in a march or demonstration is an act of only temporary significance and does not lead to further involvement. This was not true for the war resisters. More than half of them participated in demonstrations prior to their decision to resist the draft. Their experience at these demonstrations formed an important link in the series of events leading up to their decision to resist. For some, it was a rude and startling awakening. Others received a sometimes deceptive sense of belonging to a larger group of like-minded persons, and still others experienced demonstrations as confirmations of their already crystallized beliefs. Uniting all the resisters was a lesson of their childhood: to believe is to act.

CHAPTER 7

PERSONALITY CHARACTERISTICS: TEST DATA

This chapter is based on questionnaire results, some standard and in long use, others constructed for this study. Each section relies on the conception and construction of the individual questionnaire discussed. To aid the reader who may be unfamiliar with one or another of the instruments, short introductory explanations for each have been included. Statistics have been left when possible for technical appendices. An additional feature of this chapter is that it includes comparative data from the control group of thirty-five army draftees.

Two major trends emerged from the analysis of the questionnaire data. The profiles of the volunteers and draftees converged at many points, revealing a similarity which was far greater than that between either of these groups and the war resisters. On many individual questionnaire scales, the Green Berets and the draftees were very close to the ''normal'' standardization populations, whereas the scores of the resisters often departed substantially from the American norm. Since the meaning of questionnaire results is often found in the degree to which they approximate the general norms, the following general conclusion can be drawn: the most deviant men, relative to general American patterns, were the war resisters.

Psychological Needs

There exists a reciprocal relationship between a person's needs and his behavior. Unless a person is encumbered by psychological debility or environmental obstacles, he will try to behave in ways that satisfy his needs. Substantial differences in the major psychological needs of the Green Berets, draftees, and war resisters should appear in appropriate tests corresponding to the marked differences in their habitual modes of behavior.

To test this hypothesis the Edwards Personal Preference Schedule (EPPS), a questionnaire designed to measure the relative strengths of fifteen

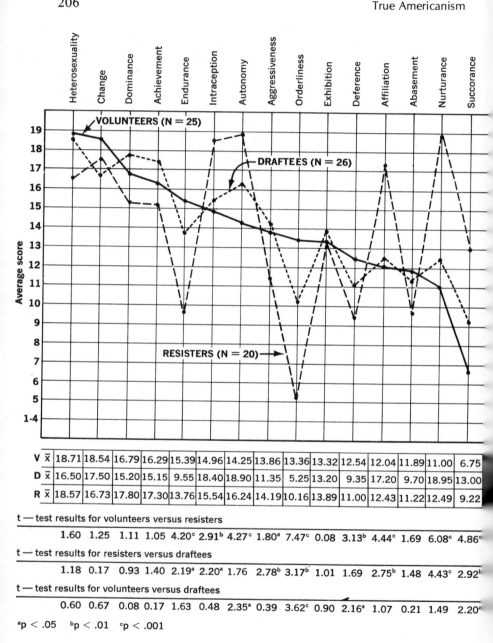

	Heterosexuality	Change	Dominance	Achievement	Endurance	Intraception	Autonomy	Aggressiveness	Orderliness	Exhibition	Deference	Affiliation	Abasement	Nurturance	Succorance
V x̄	18.71	18.54	16.79	16.29	15.39	14.96	14.25	13.86	13.36	13.32	12.54	12.04	11.89	11.00	6.75
D x̄	16.50	17.50	15.20	15.15	9.55	18.40	18.90	11.35	5.25	13.20	9.35	17.20	9.70	18.95	13.00
R x̄	18.57	16.73	17.80	17.30	13.76	15.54	16.24	14.19	10.16	13.89	11.00	12.43	11.22	12.49	9.22

t — test results for volunteers versus resisters

1.60	1.25	1.11	1.05	4.20[c]	2.91[b]	4.27[c]	1.80[a]	7.47[c]	0.08	3.13[b]	4.44[c]	1.69	6.08[c]	4.86[c]

t — test results for resisters versus draftees

| 1.18 | 0.17 | 0.93 | 1.40 | 2.19[a] | 2.20[a] | 1.76 | 2.78[b] | 3.17[b] | 1.01 | 1.69 | 2.75[b] | 1.48 | 4.43[c] | 2.92[b] |

t — test results for volunteers versus draftees

| 0.60 | 0.67 | 0.08 | 0.17 | 1.63 | 0.48 | 2.35[a] | 0.39 | 3.62[c] | 0.90 | 2.16[a] | 1.07 | 0.21 | 1.49 | 2.20[a] |

[a]p < .05   [b]p < .01   [c]p < .001

Figure 1. Group mean values on the Edwards Personal Preference Schedule arranged in hierarchical order according to the war volunteer results.

psychological needs, was administered to all three groups.* The questionnaire results can be evaluated in at least three different ways. The scores of each group on each of the fifteen need scales can be directly compared. The scores for each group can be placed in rank order from strongest to weakest need. The scores of each group on each need scale can be compared to the standardization populations surveyed by the author of this instrument. Each kind of evaluation gives the findings a new perspective.

In Figure 1 the average scores for each group of each of the fifteen needs are presented graphically. In eight out of fifteen scales, the draftees' mean values lie between those of the war volunteers and those of the war resisters. In the group comparisons the volunteers and draftees differed significantly (p > .05) on four scales (Deference, Orderliness, Autonomy and Succorance). The resisters and draftees differed significantly on seven scales (Affiliation, Intraception, Succorance, Nurturance, Endurance and Aggression). The resisters and volunteers differed significantly on nine scales (Endurance, Intraception, Autonomy, Aggression, Orderliness, Deference, Affiliation, Nurturance, and Succorance). These results show that the differences between the resisters and volunteers were most numerous and that differences between the resisters and draftees were more numerous than those between the draftees and volunteers, the latter groups having been most similar in their profiles.

When the content of the scales is examined, the meaning of these differences becomes evident. The war resisters' need to be independent in thought and judgement (Autonomy) was substantially stronger than that of the volunteers as was also that of the draftees. The Vietnam volunteers' need to defer to the judgment and leadership of others (Deference) was stronger than that of the resisters and the draftees. The war resisters' needs to be introspective and empathic (Intraception), to have many friendships (Affiliation), to help others (Nurturance), and to be helped by others (Succorance) were stronger than those of the war volunteers. The war volunteers' needs to be well organized and neat (Orderliness) were substantially stronger than those of both the war resisters and draftees. In comparison to the resisters but not to the draftees, the volunteers had stronger needs to complete a task they had begun (Endurance) and to be verbally aggressive (Aggression). The resisters' needs for close friendships, for introspection and to both give and receive help were stronger than those of the draftees while their needs to stick to a task and to be verbally aggressive were not as strong as those of the draftees. Finally, the draftees' need to receive help was stronger than that of the volunteers.

The construction of the Edwards Personal Preference Schedule to measure the relative strengths of many needs rather than the absolute strength of

---

*Five of the twenty-five resisters interviewed refused to complete the questionnaires. They objected to this form of inquiring because they found it "impersonal," "restrictive," "arbitrary," and "demeaning."

		Resisters	Draftees	Volunteers
High	1 2 3 4 5	Nurturance Autonomy Intraception Affiliation Change	Heterosexuality Achievement Dominance Change Autonomy	Heterosexuality Change Dominance Achievement Endurance
Middle	6 7 8 9 10	Heterosexuality Dominance Achievement Exhibition Succorance	Intraception Aggressiveness Exhibition Endurance Nurturance	Intraception Autonomy Aggressiveness Orderliness Exhibition
Low	11 12 13 14 15	Aggressiveness Abasement Endurance Deference Orderliness	Affiliation Abasement Deference Orderliness Succorance	Deference Affiliation Abasement Nurturance Succorance

Figure 2. The need structure of the war resisters, draftees, and volunteers in rank order from strongest to weakest showing inter-group similarities.

single ones reflects the realization that much of human behavior is understandable only through an analysis of patterning of many motives, their relative intensities and whether or not they conflict with or complement one another. This perspective was achieved by placing the needs of each group in rank order from strongest to weakest as shown in Figure 2.

A hierarchical analysis of these data offers a fuller understanding of the motivational structure of the research groups. Although the war resisters' need to receive help (Succorance) was substantially higher than that of the other two groups, it occupied the tenth position, low in their need hierarchy. The Heterosexuality, Dominance, and Achievement scale scores provide an even better example of the necessity for viewing these results in a hierarchical perspective. According to Figure 1, the war volunteers', draftees', and war resisters' needs in each of these areas appear to be equally strong. Yet in Figure 2 we see that they occupy positions 1 to 4 in the volunteer and draftee hierarchies and were among these groups' strongest needs. In the case of the resisters, they occupy positions 6 to 8 and were of secondary importance.

There are five major differences in the need hierarchies of these groups. The relatively strongest need among the war resisters was to help others (Nurturance). This need occupies the tenth position in the draftees' hierarchy and the next to last position in that of the volunteers. The need for many close friendships (Affiliation) occupies positions 4, 11, and 12 respectively in each group. The need to be free in thought and action (Autonomy) occu-

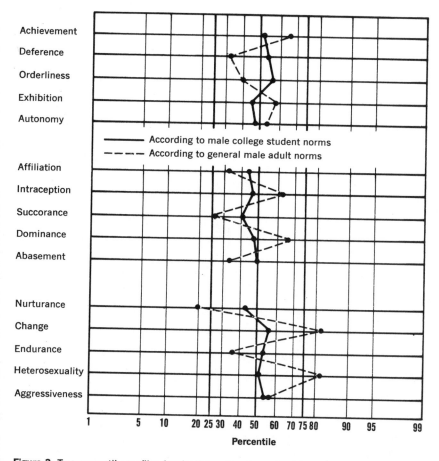

Figure 3. Two percentile profiles for the Green Berets on the Edwards Personal Preference Schedule using the "male college student" and "general male adult" norms (see Edwards, Personal Preference Schedule Manual, The Psychological Corporation, New York, 1959.)

pies positions 2, 5, and 7 respectively in each group. The resisters had their strongest needs in these areas, whereas for the draftees they occupy middle and for the Green Berets low positions. The draftees' and volunteers' relatively strongest need was for heterosexual contact whereas this need was of secondary strength for the war resisters.* Finally, the need to complete a task (Endurance) was among the volunteers' strongest, the draftees' secondary, and the resisters' weakest needs.**

*Since nearly all the Green Berets and draftees were cohabiting with wives or girlfriends at the time of the testing, this high score cannot be attributed to situational deprivation.

**It should be kept in mind that the content of the Endurance scale is weighted in the direction of prescribed rather than self-selected tasks, and completing these tasks uncritically simply because they have been started.

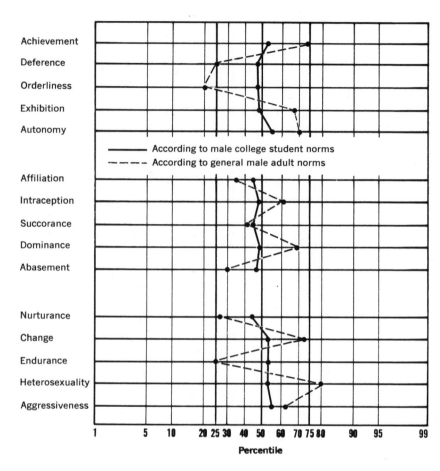

Figure 4. Two percentile profiles for the draftees on the Edwards Personal Preference Schedule using the "male college student" and "general male adult" norms.

Comparisons between the research groups and the general population on this instrument are problematical. Edwards' normative data are now fifteen years old. Also, separate norms were established for males and females and for "college student" and "general adult" groups. Should the research groups be compared with college students or with the general male adult population? If the resisters are compared with the college student norms and the volunteers with the general adult norms we have two distinct "normative" groups whose own comparability is not immediately apparent. I therefore decided to compare the scores of each of the three research groups separately with the normative data for both college students and adult males. The results are shown in Figures 3, 4, and 5. The solid lines represent the

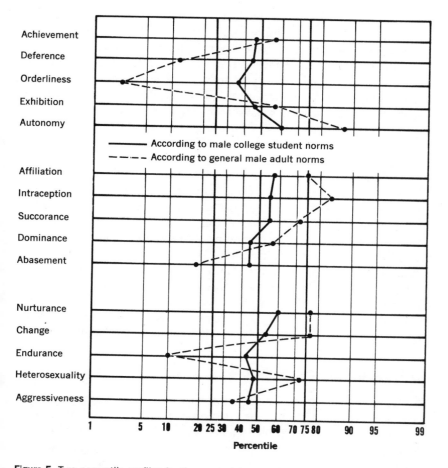

Figure 5. Two percentile profiles for the war resisters on the Edwards Personal Preference Schedule using the "male college student" and "general male adult" norms.

comparisons on the college student norms and the dashed lines the comparisons on the general adult norms.

Several general tendencies are immediately apparent. All three research groups are more similar to Edwards' college student than to his male adult sample. The profiles of the draftees and volunteers are nearly identical, differing primarily in elevation. Although the draftees are most similar to the mean of the college student norms,* the Green Berets are most similar to the male adult norms. The war resisters depart most from both the student and adult norms. A group mean was considered substantially different from

*This result is not surprising when we remember that the entire draftee sample were students in an introductory psychology course at the time of testing.

the norm when it equaled or was greater than the eightieth percentile or equaled or was lower than the twentieth percentile. (See Edwards Personal Preference Schedule Manual, 1959, Psychological Corporation, New York.) How similar are the Green Berets to the normative adult population? Their profile departs substantially from the norms at only three points: Nurturance, Change, and Heterosexuality. They were therefore on the average somewhat less nurturant and somewhat stronger in their need for change and for heterosexual activity than was the average male adult tested by Edwards. In the remaining twelve need areas no differences were found between the Green Berets and normative male adults.

The war resisters' profile departs substantially from the adult norms at nine points—Deference, Orderliness, Autonomy, Affiliation, Intraception, Abasement, Nurturance, Change, and Endurance—and is similar in six— Achievement, Exhibition, Succorance, Dominance, Heterosexuality, and Aggression. The similarities between war resisters and general adult male norms are as interesting as are the differences. These data suggest that the war resisters' atypical personality consists in part of relatively weak needs in the direction of subordination*—Deference, Orderliness, Abasement, Endurance—and relatively strong humanistic needs—Autonomy, Affiliation, Intraception, Nurturance. They also showed the war resisters to be no more aggressive or exhibitionistic than Edwards' adult male population.

Social and Political Attitudes

Both questionnaire and interview methods were used to assess various social and political attitudes. Five questionnaires were designed to measure Fascism, Dogmatism, Political-Economic Conservatism, Traditional Family Ideology, and Rigidity. Among psychologists, these questionnaire scales are thought of as measurements of attitude or general outlook dimensions. The interview questions, in contrast, dealt with opinions on specific issues, such as "Would you vote for a man for President of the United States if he were both qualified and Negro?"

The theory underlying the Fascism scale[1] is that people possess personality characteristics and, in some cases, a personality structure which can be viewed as anti-democratic. This theory does not presuppose that such people consciously and openly reject democratic institutions and processes. Rather, it suggests that a person's personality may make him susceptible to

*The term "subordination" refers not only to a structural position in an organizational hierarchy with superiors (parents, employers, officers, cardinals) giving orders and subordinates (children, employees, soldiers, chaplains) carrying them out. "Subordination" also refers to a state of mind and the manner in which one relates to one's social environment. In terms of the Edwards questionnaire scales, subordination can be viewed as the inclination to see oneself as inferior, the expectation that one's own feelings and thoughts do not count, the feeling that one must do things in socially prescribed ways, and the expectation that one is to blame when things go wrong.

autocratic ideals and methods, likely to initiate them when he has the power to do so, and willing to comply with them when they are exercised. Some of the personality characteristics this questionnaire attempts to measure are:

● Hierarchical thinking: i.e., evaluating people in terms of their power and prestige and their functional value rather than in regard to their individual personalities.

● Attraction/aversion relationship to authority figures: preferring autocratic leadership to democratic leadership and currying favor with authority figures in their presence, although having an underlying hatred of them which is not expressed for fear of punishment and loss of material advantages.

● A feeling of disgust toward weakness and powerlessness.

● The tendency to divide people into in-groups and out-groups, glorifying the in-groups and damning the out-groups.

● A general rejection of emotional matters, feelings, and sensitivities and attributing little or no value to them.

● Demanding a high degree of attitudinal and behavioral conformity from others.

● Ascribing unusual and higher powers to persons in positions of authority and placing one's fate in their hands.

● Regarding the state as more important than the individual and, for example, therefore regarding death in service of the state as a duty and an honor.

The Fascism scale was developed by refugees from Nazi Germany, and it is understandable that their conception of these phenomena would be strongly conditioned by the historical circumstances and cultural traditions in Germany to which they were exposed. Critics of the Fascism scale have pointed out that, among other things, the composite of autocratic elements can change, as can the ideological, political, and economic systems which give it expression. As Maslow pointed out in 1943, "A fascist cannot be identified by his geographical location, his nominal national citizenship, the language he speaks, his religion, his skin color, his economic class or social status. To make things worse, we cannot even trust what people say or do, for personal expediency as well as covert loyalties may cause the most astounding shifts in policy or in behavior."[2]

A principal criticism of the Fascism scale emerged later in response to research studies and historical realities. It was recognized that antidemocratic personalities occur in noncapitalistic and nonfascistic societies as well (as this study also shows, social science research is strongly influenced by historical conditions) and that the Fascism scale, because of its rightist ideological content, did not tap anti-democratic thinking among persons who subscribe to leftist ideologies. This led to the development of the Dogmatism scale.[3,4] This scale is not concerned with what a person believes but how a person believes and is neutral in political content. It assesses a person's ability to process new information critically, to distinguish between the source and the content of information, to hold contradictory beliefs without realizing it, and also measures readiness to expose one's attitudes and beliefs to scrutiny and to revise them when necessary. These capacities or qualities, which can perhaps be concisely described as possessing an open or closed mind, are independent of the kinds of beliefs one holds.[5]

The Political-Economic Conservatism scale measures just what its name implies.[6] It consists of a series of statements, some conservative and some liberal, on political and economic issues. The subject is asked to indicate his agreement or disagreement with each.

The Traditional Family-Ideology scale can be described as a democracy-autocracy scale for family life.[7] Since family background was one of the major research themes in this study and is still the central societal institution shaping fundamental social, political, moral, and behavioral patterns, I considered it crucial to find out how the subjects in the three research groups intended to conduct or were conducting their own family lives. The theory underlying this scale has three major premises. The first is that people are relatively consistent in their tendency to take a democratic or autocratic stand on matters of daily family life. Secondly, the individual's stand on "family ideology" is intimately related to his overall attitude toward social and political institutions. Thirdly, the democratic-autocratic dimension of family ideology reflects the same characteristics in personality. In short, this theory suggests that a person's approach to some aspects of organized social life, such as the family, is intimately bound up with his approach to others, such as church and government. The person who tends to be democratic in one would usually be expected to be democratic in the other.

The Rigidity scale is designed to measure flexibility, casualness, and self-centeredness in everyday behavior.[8] People who obtain high scores on this scale strictly separate work and play, organize their daily routines carefully and refuse to deviate from their schedules, insist on formality in social relations, value punctuality highly, think that they argue over matters of principle rather than over trivia, and assert that their judgments and perceptions are consistently correct.

The tendency for the members of each research group to think in the ways measured by the Fascism, Traditional Family Ideology, Political-Economic Conservatism, Rigidity, and Dogmatism scales are shown graphically in Figure 6. In analyzing and interpreting scores, careful attention must also be paid to the variability within each group. While the volunteers, draftees, and resisters can be easily differentiated in their average group scores, the individual scores of the volunteers and draftees overlap considerably on every scale. This means that it would be difficult, if not impossible in indi-

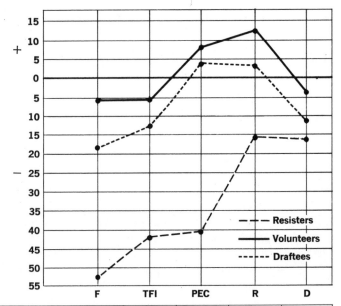

		F	TFI	PEC	R	D
Resisters	x̄	−53.04	−42.28	−40.50	−15.72	−16.10
	S.D.	12.68	12.14	12.37	17.62	18.66
Volunteers	x̄	−5.11	−5.4	8.85	12.6	−4.81
	S.D.	17.19	15.6	11.00	25.2	20.85
Draftees	x̄	−18.07	−12.32	4.31	3.68	−11.68
	S.D.	20.29	17.34	16.20	7.36	19.54

	Source	SS	df	MS	F
F	Between	29419.68	2	14709.84	43.06***
	Within	26302.38	77	341.59	
PEC	Between	36171.59	2	18085.79	86.36***
	Within	16125.11	77	209.42	

TFI	Median test	RxV	$\chi^2 = 28.81$,	df = 1,	p<.0001
R	Median test	RxV	$\chi^2 = 28.81$,	df = 1,	p<.0001
D	Median test	RxV	$\chi^2 = 1.79$,	df = 1,	n.s.

***p<.0005

Figure 6. Mean scores of the resisters, volunteers, and draftees on the Fascism, Traditional Family Ideology, Political-economic conservatism, Rigidity, and Dogmatism scales. (The score distributions were examined to see if they were normal. When normal, an analysis of variance was done. When not normal, a median test was done.)

vidual cases, to distinguish a volunteer from a draftee in the area of these basic attitude dispositions. At the same time it is also clear that the volunteers, as a group, described their thinking as more autocratic, both in regard to general society and family, more politically and economically conservative, more rigid in everyday life, and more dogmatic than the draftees did.* It is also clear that except on the Dogmatism scale, the resisters stand distinctly apart from the other two groups. Nearly all of them strongly disagreed with right-wing autocratic sentiments, autocracy in family life, political and economic conservatism, and rigidity in everyday life. Rejection was the most prominent aspect of the resisters' responses to the content of these questionnaires.

Despite the differences in their average scores, a statistical analysis of the variability within each group on the Dogmatism scale revealed two important findings. The individual scores of the volunteers, draftees, and resisters overlap so greatly that the differences in their group averages must be regarded as statistical or sample artifacts and therefore without interpretative importance. Moreover, the variability within each group is also so great that substantial intragroup differences in openness and closedness of mind are indicated. This means that within each group there were relatively open-minded, flexible, and ideologically nondogmatic persons, relatively closed-minded, inflexible, and ideologically dogmatic persons, as well as others at various points between these extremes.

One would like to know how the scores on these scales compare to those of other sections of the American population. Unfortunately, this question cannot be answered directly. There are many reasons for this. The authors of these questionnaires never bothered to standardize them. The number of versions of each scale is large, the number of questions in each version varies considerably, and many researchers have not been diligent in reporting the version and items they used. Therefore, judgments as to the relative intensity of the kinds of thinking measured by these scales can be safely made only in terms of the content and answer possibliities of the scales themselves.

Although the resisters achieved nearly maximum negation scores for fascistic thinking, autocracy in the family, and political and economic conservatism, the scores of the draftees and volunteers generally remained far removed from maximum possible approval. On the first two scales, the draftees and volunteers rejected a slightly greater number of autocratic statements than they accepted. The conclusions to be drawn from these observations are obvious. Just as we can observe that most Americans are unsympathetic toward uncamouflaged fascistic and autocratic ideologies, so are Green Berets and draftees. However, we can also observe that many Americans have

---

*The five black Green Berets had considerably lower scores on the Political-Economic Conservatism scale than did their white counterparts. In the interviews they expressed greater discontent and cynicism toward social and political institutions and policies in the United States.

a shallow understanding of what autocracy is. Many are fascinated by power, feel drawn toward militaristic and demagogic leadership, think in in-group and out-group terms, and are indifferent if not hostile toward the weak. This is also true for the draftees and volunteers in varying degrees. Large sections of the American population think conservatively on political and economic matters, but very few still expound eighteenth-century views. This too is true of the draftees and volunteers.

One final observation. It is often assumed that a common core of beliefs makes it possible for politicians to mobilize people to action. In my view, it is the use of propaganda and ideologies by politicians rather than the degree to which they are consciously accepted by a population which is responsible for this impression. The actual motives of the individuals participating in a political action may have little to do with the ideals being proclaimed. One does not have to be a believer to participate in war. The individual need not even feel threatened. The Green Berets have made this clear. It is also important to recognize that the thinking of the Green Berets on political, economic, and social issues and on the war in Vietnam is probably no different from that of large segments of the American population. Certainly, it is very similar if not identical to that of nonvoluntary infantry men who were serving in Vietnam in 1968, at the time I conducted my interviews in New York and Germany.

Quite consistently, the American combat soldier displays a profound skepticism of political and ideological appeals. . . . They dismiss patriotic slogans or exhortations to defend democracy with, "What a crock," "Be serious, man" or "Who's kidding who?" In particular, they have little belief that they are protecting an outpost of democracy in South Vietnam.

It should be repeated and heavily stressed that the reasons given for the war and the descriptions of Communism offered by the combat soldiers were always the result of extended discussion and questioning. When left to themselves, the soldiers rarely discussed the reasons for America's military intervention in Vietnam, the nature of Communist systems or other political issues.

The fact that the American soldier is not overtly ideological should not obscure the existence of those salient values which do contribute to his motivation in combat. Despite the soldier's ideological unconcern and his pronounced embarrassment in the face of patriotic rhetoric, he nevertheless displays an elemental American nationalism in the belief that the U.S. is the best country in the world. Even though he hates being in the war, the combat soldier typically believes—in a kind of joyous patriotism—he is fighting for his American homeland.[9]

I suspect that the basic difference between the Green Berets and the American infantrymen interviewed by Moskos is that the former fight professionally whereas the latter had had the "bad luck" to be sent to the front. I also assume that it was in large part good luck which separates the draftees in this study from Moskos' infantrymen.

Great and Evil Historical Figures

I presented each subject with a list of forty-seven deceased public figures* and asked them to write down the names of "those five persons whose deaths you personally think rid the world of dangerous and evil people" and "those five persons whose deaths you personally think represented the greatest loss to mankind." The subjects were free to write down the name of any other well-known public figure, but with few exceptions, the names chosen came from my list.

In order to properly understand each group's perceptual and value framework for historical figures, the explanations they gave for their choices must also be examined. However, several general conclusions can be drawn from the following listing of their choices. The disproportionate appearance of non-Americans among the volunteers' designations of evil persons corresponds to their stronger tendency to think in in-group/out-group terms and to perceive evil as being of foreign origin. Both the draftees and the volunteers rejected people such as Malcolm X and Che Guevara, whose attempts to upset the established order had not been legitimized in the mass media or through public acclaim, as had Martin Luther King's. The legitimacy of a person's popular image was of less importance to most of the resisters. Their predisposition was to celebrate personalities who worked against the current of their time, such as Gandhi, Malcolm X, Che Guevara, and Medgar Evers. (Of the resisters' eight positive choices, seven met violent deaths through assassination.)** The draftees and volunteers were also resentful of such an "un-American" figure as Lenin, whose "evil" rested in the fact that "he started communism in Russia." Although most of the volunteers were not sure who Patrice Lumumba was, many vaguely recalled that he was not well received in the American press, was "against United States interests," or "was a revolutionary," and rejected him.

It is interesting to observe that all three groups were largely in agreement that John F. Kennedy, Robert F. Kennedy, and Martin Luther King were great people, while Hitler, Stalin, and Mussolini were bad people. However, the reasons given by the resisters and volunteers for these choices varied in several essential aspects. Space limitations do not allow for the pre-

*Gandhi; Anne Frank; Leon Trotsky; Marilyn Monroe; Douglas MacArthur; F. D. Roosevelt; Cardinal Spellman; Martin Luther King; Albert Einstein; Medgar Evers; Sigmund Freud; Albert Luthuli; Che Guevara; Jayne Mansfield; Robert Kennedy; Henry Ford II; Malcolm X; Adolf Hitler; Tom Dooley; Paul Tillich; Nehru; Dag Hammerskjold; Clark Gable; Pope John; Stalin; Lumumba; Adlai Stevenson; Martin Buber; John F. Kennedy; Walt Disney; Lennie Bruce; J. R. Oppenheimer; Randolph Hearst; Herbert Hoover; Rosa Luxemburg; Churchill; Albert Schweitzer; Konrad Adenauer; Spencer Tracy; Berthold Brecht; Pope Pius XII; Lenin; Albert Camus; Rommel; Edith Piaf; Gary Cooper; Mussolini.

**These choices give further evidence of a tendency among many resisters to admire extreme self-sacrifice or martyrdom. The choices may also be interpreted as reflecting a secret yearning for violence. This interpretation is supported in part by the view of some resisters that violence may prove to be the only way of eliminating political oppression and economic exploitation.

	Resisters		Draftees		Volunteers	
	Great	**Evil**	**Great**	**Evil**	**Great**	**Evil**
Similar Views	J. F. Kennedy** R. F. Kennedy*** M. L. King*** Gandhi*** — — —	Hitler*** Stalin*** Mussolini*** —	J. F. Kennedy*** R. F. Kennedy*** M. L. King*** Gandhi** Einstein*** Churchill*** Schweitzer** Disney*	Hitler*** Stalin*** Mussolini*** Lenin***	J. F. Kennedy*** R. F. Kennedy*** M. L. King* — Einstein* Churchill* Schweitzer** Disney**	Hitler*** Stalin*** Mussolini*** Lenin***
Opposite Views	Malcolm X** Che*			Malcolm X*** Che***		Malcolm X*** Che***
Different Views	M. Evers* S. Freud	Cardinal Spellman** Lenny Bruce*	Pope John*		D. MacArthur** F. D. Roosevelt* M. Monroe[n.s.] J. Mansfield[n.s.] G. Cooper[n.s.] C. Gable[n.s.]	Lumumba[n.s.]

Figure 7. Historical figures most often named by the resisters, draftees, and volunteers as having been "great" or "evil". The asterisks indicate the significance level at which each name appeared in the lists of each group. Each of the forty-seven original names had a probability of 5/47 of being selected randomly.

* p .05 ∨
** p .01 ∨∨
*** p .001 ∨∨∨
n.s. — not significant

sentation of all the reasons given by the resisters and volunteers for their respective choices, so I have restricted this discussion to those explanations which best reveal the perceptual and value frameworks of these groups. John F. Kennedy possessed several qualities—youthfulness, charm, wit, inspirational power, and the promise of a rejuvenation of American life—which both the volunteers and the resisters found praiseworthy. However, while most of the resisters were disappointed with his leadership during the Bay of Pigs crisis and particularly with his escalation of American involvement in Vietnam, the volunteers explained that they viewed him as a kind of father figure since he had officially inaugurated the Special Forces.

Martin Luther King was considered a great man by both Green Berets and resisters. The resisters admired his principles, forcefulness, and dedication, and mourned his death. When the Green Berets were asked how they felt at the time of his assassination, most said they were glad he had been killed and considered his assassin a hero. A few remarked that they would have been glad to have killed King themselves. How does one explain that these very same people viewed Martin Luther King as a great man? In my opinion, the explanation of this apparent contradiction lies on several levels. First, the Green Berets respect accomplishments, deeds, and actions. King was a man of action, although to most of the Green Berets his skin was the wrong color and his actions in the wrong direction. They respected him, but were glad he was dead, because they did not like him. (Conversely, their only objection to men such as Che Guevara and Rommel, whom they admired, was that "they were fighting on the wrong side.") In addition, killing represented an accomplishment to some of them, a measure of professional skill. Satisfaction would be all the greater if the man killed were prominent and represented ideas alien to them. Hence, the fantasy or desire of some to have been King's assassin. Perhaps most important, the Green Berets were sensitive to public images. Whether they liked a man or not, they seemed inclined to say that he was great if he enjoyed general public acclaim.

Hitler, Stalin, and Mussolini were rated as evil by every resister, draftee, and Green Beret. The major differences emerged between the resisters and the military men in response to Hitler. They all called him a dictator, a murderer, and a maniac, using the words with the self-evident implication of badness. However, their emotional and intellectual understanding of what those words actually meant and the values they attached to them were different. The following quotations from Green Berets illustrate their remarkable perspective.

CASE 201 (black)

Uh, because, see, eventually, when he got rid of all the Jews and conquered the world, he may have thought of getting rid of the Negroes and stuff. I couldn't match into his description of the pure Aryan race, see, so it's just a matter of survival.

CASE 207

Well, he thought he was superior. Thought the Germans were the greatest men on earth, right? Didn't think too much of the Jews. Started wiping them out to start off with. And plus the concept of taking the world. I can see a war to take a few countries for, you know, population reasons and economic reasons, but not to rule the world.

CASE 212

Well, like Hannibal was a man that tried something that no other man had tried before. He beat a country, a power, that was considered unconquerable and did it with a minimum of men by attacking Rome from the North which had never happened before. . . . I think it was a pretty smart move myself. . . . It shows a lot of courage. . . . And Ghengis Khan conquered all the known world. I really don't know why I said Ghengis Khan because he was ruthless in everything he did but I think the feat he did was outstanding. . . . Hitler, I just don't like the way he operated.

CASE 214

Hitler built a great deal, of course, and he possibly saved Germany from Communism, which were good things. But he was also the figurehead of a machine, a very proud machine, and his death may have helped to dissipate that machine.
You said before that he also destroyed Europe.
Oh yeah, he destroyed Europe, you know. But that's not a very objective way to look at things. But he destroyed Europe, yes, and perhaps for that, possibly, he should die.

CASE 215

He [Hitler] was a madman. He was just a total madman and it was an asset to the world to have him gone.
In what way was he a madman?
A man that's less than six feet tall with black hair and brown eyes hollering that he wanted a super race of blond-haired people over six feet tall had to be mad because he didn't fit into the race to begin with. He wanted to annihilate the rest of the world and have this super race. And that's the talking of a madman. That's not a tactician, in my opinion.

CASE 217

Hitler was a thorn in the back but he had a lot of good assets too. . . . He could have accomplished conquering the world if he would have gone slow, used slower tactics about it. He'd either be a good loss or a bad loss. One of the two. For the world it's good he's dead.

Why?

Well, it's his atrocities in killing the Jews, his attitude towards children. If you're born blind or crippled, you're killed. For building a strong nation this is good in a way if you don't want to look at it mercifully. You don't need crippled children, crippled people. Granted, it's not their fault, but they're just a total handicap to themselves and the nation their entire life, the majority of them. There are individuals that show promise.

CASE 219

He was a sick individual really. In the military when he was a soldier he never got very high and wasn't a very good soldier. He was a strong politician and a person who got into power when it was easy to get into power. ... He didn't listen to his outstanding generals like Rommel and people like this that were militarists and knew what they were doing. He was just an ambitious greedy little dictator with sick ideas.

Well, what ideas were sick?

Oh, like burning all those Jews. I mean, I don't have too many emotions about the fact that he burned a lot of Jews. I think burning all those Jews was a pretty damn sick idea, really. Sure he was ambitious and dictators do eliminate a lot of their opponents usually, but that was pretty damn exaggerated. . . Now I can see enslaving them, oh, hell, using them in front of your soldiers and using them to blow up mines and anything like that. If that helps your soldiers to fight a world war, o.k. use them for something that's going to benefit you. But burning them didn't benefit him a bit. The amount of money he got from gold teeth and things like that damn sure didn't compensate for it. He could have used them as slave labor building roads, airports, working in munition factories and things like this.

So, in other words, it was just the idiocy of his impractability?

Right.

The Green Berets were not fundamentally concerned with such questions as whether to kill or not to kill, or even with the question of who could or should be killed. These matters are decided by others and the Green Berets' interest in them did not extend beyond practical and strategic considerations. For them, the only issue of fundamental importance was who may kill, and this question, too, is decided by others. In that a government had given their actions legal sanction they perceived themselves as legitimized extensions of governmental authority. For them, violent people were either declared enemies or did not act in the name of a particular Green Beret brand of law and order. They viewed demonstrators as violent simply because they demonstrated.

Moral Standards

Each subject was asked to indicate his relative approval or disapproval of gambling, drunkenness, smoking, lying, stealing, premarital intercourse for females, premarital intercourse for males, suicide, masturbation, and taking welfare payments. They indicated their attitude by checking one of the following alternatives: "always wrong," "usually wrong but sometimes excusable," "usually excusable but sometimes wrong," and "never wrong." The results from this questionnaire are consistent with earlier findings. Again there is a stronger similarity between the responses of the volunteers and draftees than between either of these groups and the resisters. When the ratings given by all the subjects to every question were examined collectively, the following pattern emerged. The volunteers used the condemning and disapproving alternatives most often, the draftees the disapproval and excusing alternatives, and the resisters the excusing and condoning alternatives.*

The volunteers condemned or disapproved of drunkenness, lying, stealing, premarital intercourse for women, suicide, and masturbation. They saw smoking and premarital intercourse for men as excusable or never wrong. Gambling was condemned by half and condoned by half. Taking welfare payments was disapproved of or found excusable.

The draftees gave the same responses as the Green Berets on gambling, drunkenness, smoking, and taking welfare payments. They were more tolerant of lying, stealing, and suicide, although disapproving of each. Premarital sexual intercourse for males and females was rated as "excusable but sometimes wrong." They found masturbation to be either excusable or never wrong.

Suicide is the only item which received "always wrong" evaluations from resisters. It was also the only issue on which their attitudes diverged sharply. The resisters' evaluations were equally distributed over the four alternatives. Masturbation and smoking were rated "never wrong." Premarital sexual intercourse for males and females and taking welfare payments were rated either as "never wrong" or "usually excusable but sometimes wrong." Gambling and drunkenness were rated as "excusable" and lying and stealing as usually wrong.

The volunteers' double standard on sexual matters as well as their condemnation of masturbation, noted earlier, are reconfirmed with these data. Although most of them admitted in the interviews that they drank heavily, lied, and stole, they uniformly condemned such practices. Again one must ask how they managed to reconcile an apparent contradiction. In my opinion, they experienced no contradiction at all. Just as they saw male sexual behavior as categorically different from female sexual behavior and judged both with different measuring rods, I am sure that they saw themselves as belonging to a special category in regard to drinking, lying, and stealing. For them, such habits were only qualifiedly bad—bad if someone else practiced them or if they themselves got caught practicing them, or if they did not practice them in the service of goals which have personal or professional legitimacy.

*The overall response pattern was analyzed with a 3 × 3 contingency table, yielding X^2 76.55, df = 4, p < .001.

Their attitudes toward killing were similar. Killing is something they do pro
fessionally with legal legitimacy but they "couldn't just go out onto the
street and shoot somebody." That would be murder.

Psychological Disorders

The war resister and the war volunteer are often objects of suspicion.
Their critics, but sometimes also their sympathizers, are prone to wonder
about such people's sanity. There are so many nice ways to spend one's
time, it is so easy to avoid danger, so why take risks? Moreover, the conformity and complacency of the general population engender distrust toward exceptions. One tends to think that there is something wrong with the person
who does things differently.

In choosing a method for a clinical appraisal, I placed particular emphasis on finding one which would be relatively free from personal bias. The
Minnesota Multiphasic Personality Inventory (MMPI), despite its many
flaws, seemed best suited to this job. Its purpose is to pick up pathology
and its language is that of psychopathology. Because of its unusually widespread use by clinical personnel and researchers during the past thirty years,
an enormous body of comparative literature exists on the scores of hundreds
of thousands of persons. Equally important, a computerized scoring and interpretation service for this instrument was inaugurated a few years ago.*
This service offered a reasonably objective diagnosis and personality description by analyzing each subject's scores according to the same criteria. The
full value of this diagnostic instrument is realized only when the configurational pattern of the scores is analysed. Since the number of patterns, pattern
elevations, and special scores to be considered is endless, only a computer
or a rare mind is capable of performing a configurational analysis properly.
The bulk of the MMPI evaluation presented here is based upon the computerized analyses of the following data: MMPI answer sheets and subjects'
age, educational status, and race.

Method

As with the EPPS, the MMPI data were analyzed in several ways. The
first analysis is based on group scores. The resulting group profiles are
compared with each other and with the normative population; the
interpretation is based in part on the computer analysis and in part on my
judgment.

A group profile is a statistical fiction. Depending upon the degree of
variability within a group, the profile of its averaged scores represents at best

*I would particularly like to thank Mr. Peter Blaser of Hoffmann-La Roche, Basel, for
his kind and indispensable help in securing the computerized interpretations. My thanks also to
Professor Raymond Fowler, the author of the computer program, for his explanations.

an approximation of the central trend within the group. Individual differences disappear. To compensate for this loss of information as well as erroneous impressions which may have arisen by treating the group profiles as though they were single individuals, each subject's answer sheet was submitted to a scoring company for an individual analysis. The content of the detailed personality descriptions was summarized as follows: each adjective and descriptive phrase and the frequency with which it appeared was registered. The resulting compilation allows for a quick assessment of each group's characteristics, its homogeneity, and its special features. Singly and collectively, the individual profile interpretations were far richer in content, yet consistent with the group profile interpretations.

Results of Group Profile Comparisons

In Figure 8, the average group profiles for the war resisters, draftees, and Green Berets are presented graphically. At first glance, several general findings are apparent. Except for the resisters' unusually high score on the masculinity-feminity interest scale, each group's profile is well within the so-called "normal range." On seven of ten clinical scales, the draftees' scores lie between those of the resisters and volunteers. On the whole, the volunteers' profile resembles more closely that of the "non-psychiatrically ill normative population." Conversely, the resisters' profile departs furthest from the norm on every scale. These observations stand independently of their meaning and independently of the interpretative material that follows.

Below, the computerized group profile interpretations are reprinted verbatim and are followed by explanation and commentary.

THE WAR RESISTERS

In responding to the test items it appears that these persons made an effort to answer truthfully without attempting to deny or exaggerate.

These persons may be experiencing periodic attacks of acute distress such as anxiety, tachycardia and intestinal cramps. Hysterical patterns are also a possibility. Although not severely depressed, some depression and fatigue are to be expected. The complaints are not likely to be severe and should respond to superficial treatment and reassurance.

They are sensitive and verbally fluent and may be somewhat feminine in their interest patterns.*

THE DRAFTEES

In responding to the test items it appears that these persons made an effort to answer truthfully without attempting to deny or exaggerate.

These persons appear to be passive but hostile individuals who maintain impulse controls with difficulty. Aggressive behavior is likely to be expressed

---

*In MMPI language, which is sometimes unfortunate, a feminine interest pattern refers to intellectual and cultural interests.

The Minnesota Multiphasic Personality Inventory

Starke R. Hathaway and J. Charnley McKinley

Scorer's Initials_____

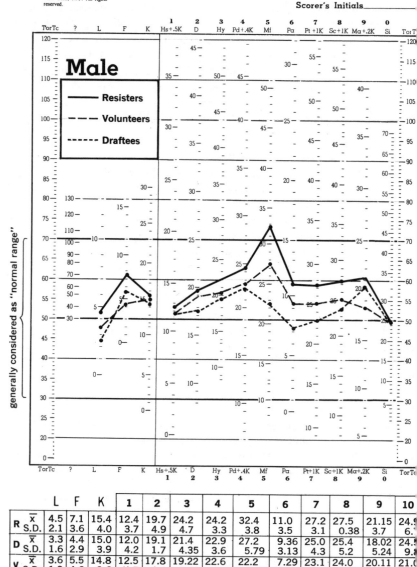

	L	F	K	1	2	3	4	5	6	7	8	9	10
R X̄	4.5	7.1	15.4	12.4	19.7	24.2	24.2	32.4	11.0	27.2	27.5	21.15	24.9
R S.D.	2.1	3.6	4.0	3.7	4.9	4.7	3.3	3.8	3.5	3.1	0.38	3.7	6.
D X̄	3.3	4.4	15.0	12.0	19.1	21.4	22.9	27.2	9.36	25.0	25.4	18.02	24.
D S.D.	1.6	2.9	3.9	4.2	1.7	4.35	3.6	5.79	3.13	4.3	5.2	5.24	9.
V X̄	3.6	5.5	14.8	12.5	17.8	19.22	22.6	22.2	7.29	23.1	24.0	20.11	21.0
V S.D.	1.9	4.6	3.6	4.7	4.4	3.79	4.6	3.11	2.95	5.2	6.8	4.2	6.

Figure 8. Configuration patterns for the war resisters, draftees, and Green Berets on th Minnesota Multiphasic Personality Inventory. Each group's mean and standard deviatio on each scale are listed beneath

indirectly and ineffectually with hostile intent denied. Sexual maladjustments, especially marital difficulties, are likely. Physical symptoms, if present, are unlikely to be acute or incapacitating.

THE WAR VOLUNTEERS

In responding to the test items it appears that these persons made an effort to answer truthfully without attempting to deny or exaggerate. These persons tend to be over-active, impulsive and irresponsible. They seek excitement and arousal and are characterized by a high energy level. They may expend great effort to accomplish their own desires but they find it difficult to stick to duties imposed by others. They may be sociable and outgoing but their poor judgment and lack of consideration tend to alienate others. Poor work habits and excessive drinking are likely.

Statistically significant differences between the research groups were found on six of the major clinical scales and on four "derived scales."[10] (See figure 8.) A number of general observations about the personality and emotional characteristics of the research groups can be drawn from their average profiles and the group comparisons.

The low elevation and nearly identical scores of all three groups on the control scales L, F, and K mean that the scores on the clinical scales can be interpreted without complications arising from response set, defensiveness, or tendency to exaggerate one's problems. This corresponds with two further findings. The scores of all three groups were normally distributed on both the Marlowe-Crowne and Edwards Social Desirability scales.* Further, there were no mean differences among the groups on these scales and there was a zero correlation between these response set measures and the MMPI clinical scales.

The groups' relatively low and statistically indistinguishable scores on Scale 2, Depression, indicate that they were not, as a whole, experiencing serious conflict, guilt, or depression. The slight elevation of the resisters' average score may be attributed to the feelings of futility and hopelessness some of them were experiencing, as well as poor morale in view of their forthcoming jail sentences. The absence of guilt and other depressing feelings in the volunteers' interviews is consistent with their score.

On Scale 3, Hysteria, the resisters' score is significantly higher than

---

*The Marlowe-Crowne Social Desirability Scale was designed to measure the tendency of people to reveal only those things about themselves which they feel are both good and culturally sanctioned (D. P. Crowne and D. Marlowe, *The Approval Motive* [New York: John Wiley & Sons, 1964]). The Edwards Social Desirability Scale is similar in intent to the Marlowe-Crowne but was designed especially to measure readiness to admit psychological symptoms and disorders according to their relative cultural undesirability (A. Edwards and L. B. Heathers, "The First Factor of the MMPI: Social Desirability or Ego Strength," *Journal of Consulting Psychology* XXVI 99-100; A. Edwards, *The Social Desirability Variable in Personality Assessment and Research* [New York: Dryden, 1957]).

that of the other groups. Scores at this moderate elevation indicate idealism, strong positive self-regard, and capacity for strong emotional response. The volunteers' relatively low score is significant for at least two reasons. It does not exclude idealism, positive self-regard, and emotional responsiveness in individual cases, but suggests that such persons would be exceptions within their groups. Further, it also reconfirms that the volunteers were not suffering emotionally from their Vietnam experiences. A very high score would have pointed to massive repression. Their low score indicates that they did not feel that they had anything to hide from themselves.

Although statistically significant differences between the groups did not appear on Scale 4, Psychopathic Deviate, the relatively higher score of the resisters suggests that they were more out of tune with societal norms. This is consistent with the fact that they were clearly moving against the dominant social and political current in the United States. The average scores of all groups on this scale are important for a further reason as well. They indicate that conventionally delinquent or criminal personality structures are not likely to be found among the individual case profiles.

The relatively large differences in the average scores on Scale 5, Masculinity-Femininity, point to several important differences between the groups. The high score of the war resisters is not unusual among college students. It reflects persons who are strongly internally oriented and who are reflective, introspective, and questioning. (This description corresponds closely to their dominant needs as measured by the EPPS.) The draftees' average score is typical of the average college student who, if only because of his studies, has some cultural and intellectual interests (all the draftees were enrolled in a college course). The mild elevation of the Green Berets' average score is an indication of the fact that these soldiers had all completed high school, that many had some college credits, and that some had literary interests.

High scores on Scale 6, Paranoia, reflect irrational fears. In the average to middle range, this scale serves as a positive sensitivity measure. The resisters' score suggests that they were more socially perceptive and attuned to what was going on in the world. The volunteers' score suggests insensitivity to the attitudes and feelings of others, which may be seen as inconsiderateness and self-centeredness. The draftees' average score lies between those of the resisters and of the volunteers and is not statistically distinguishable from either.

On Scale 6, Psychasthenia, the resisters appear to be mildly anxious, worried, and tense. This emotional state is probably situationally conditioned since the elevation does not suggest neuroticism. The volunteers, in contrast, appear cool and well adjusted. Nothing is likely to get under their skin. This corresponds to earlier findings. They had few or no ideological concerns which could cause tension, they did not worry about being killed in battle or about the fate of their families had they died, they did not become upset by what they saw and did in Vietnam, and they were generally satisfied with their style of life.

Scale 8, Schizophrenia, has a devastating label. In fact, high scores re-:ect the presence of such symptoms as delusions and hallucinations. At moderate elevations, scores on this scale suggest originality, imagination, and inventiveness, in short, an open and nonstereotyped mind. Scores which rise above this suggest intensifying degrees of loss of contact with reality ranging from day-dreaming to fantasy to delusional thinking. The resisters' score re-:ects an above-average degree of originality, imaginativeness, and inventiveness which, in some cases, may involve fantasy replacing real concerns. In contrast, the volunteers are highly variable on this scale. This variability. ranges from extremely low scores suggesting overly conscientious conformity through the average range and the imaginative range to bizarre thoughts and behavior.

On Scale 9, Hypomania, the resisters and volunteers appear to have an average energy level higher than that of the draftees. This reflects the ability to get enthusiastically involved in things, initiative, pep, and in some cases, impulsiveness.

Individual Profile Interpretations

Content analysis of the individual protocol interpretations provided by Hoffmann-La Roche permitted the isolation of a number of personality characteristics, emotional disturbances, and probable behavioral disorders, which, despite some overlapping, tended to be group specific, particularly in their combinations. Disturbances for which further examination and therapeutic care were advised occurred in several cases.

Symptom severity is not directly connected with the solicitation of professional care. This is true of persons with dental problems and applies even more to persons who feel personally troubled. This means that persons who do seek and receive professional psychological counseling are not necessarily those who need it the most. It also means that two people with roughly equal feelings of personal discomfort will react differently to the issue of professional care.[11]

On the basis of the earlier data it would be expected that a war resister would be more inclined than a Green Beret to consult a therapist. This expectation was confirmed by the fact that five resisters but no Green Berets reported having done so. These consultations by the resisters began prior to their sociopolitical engagement and their decision to resist the draft. At the time of the interviews, two were still in treatment. The MMPI interpretations help to explain this difference between the groups. Insofar as distressing emotional problems were found among volunteers, they appeared along with the observations that they would be denied, that they would be expressed as vague physical symptoms for which no organic basic could be found, that these persons would reject a psychological explanation of their problems, that they had little or no insight into their problems, and that their treatment prognosis was poor. Moreover, the presence of the descriptions "poor insight into personality and problems" in three-quarters of the volunteers' protocols and "complains often of physical symptoms for which no organic basis can be found" in more than one-third shows that these were pervasive characteristics of the entire group rather than restricted to the few who admitted distressing emotional problems. The statement "overconcern with bodily functions and health" appeared in four-fifths of the volunteers' profiles. Although this concern is undoubtedly related to the physical hazards of their work and the broken bones, wounds, and illnesses of many, it also reflects, particularly in connection with the absence of introspective elements, the predisposition of this group to take an apsychological, organic attitude toward their personal problems.

The opposite pattern was pronounced among the resisters. Somatic or bodily complaints, usually involving headaches and gastrointestinal problems, appeared in seven protocols, five of them from movement members. This may be connected to the extraordinarily irregular eating habits and poor diet which were common among the movement members. Whatever their cause, these complaints did not occur in connection with denial, repression, or poor insight, although each of these descriptions appeared at least in one resister's protocol. The protocols of many resisters pointed to the presence of distressing problems which were being experienced more directly in the form of worry, discouragement, anxiety, and tension, usually unaccompanied by physical complaints.

THE GREEN BERETS

The most frequently appearing personality disturbances in the Green Berets' protocols centered around impulse control and social relations. The terminology used in describing these problems varies from protocol to protocol and points to different severity levels. Three typical descriptions follow.

This person tends to be overactive and impulsive. He seeks excitement and arousal and is characterized by a high energy level. He may expend great effort to accomplish his own desires, but he finds it difficult to stick to duties imposed by others. He may be sociable and outgoing, but his poor judgment and lack of consideration tend to alienate others. Poor work adjustment and excessive drinking are likely. Among adolescents, college students, and various low socioeconomic groups this pattern occurs fairly frequently and may have less serious implications. However, acting out and impulsiveness may be anticipated.

He has some difficulty in dealing with hostile feelings. To the extent that he controls the direct expression of these feelings, he may be a bitter, resentful, and perhaps somewhat irresponsible person. Where control factors are not present, however, the hostility may be expressed in direct antisocial behavior. In any event, he is likely to have problems in establishing close personal relationships.

This person exhibits contradictions in his behavior and in his view of himself. The contradiction may appear behaviorly as an alternation of phases. For a period, he may act with little control or forethought, violating social restrictions and trampling on the feelings and wishes of others. Following such a period of acting out, however, he may show guilt, remorse, and deep regret over his actions, and for a while he may seem overly controlled and contrite. These activity swings may be associated with excessive drinking and various socially unacceptable behaviors. While his conscience pangs may be severe, even out of proportion to the actual behavior deviations, his controls do not appear to be effective in preventing further outbreaks.

Such paragraphs appeared in seventeen of twenty-five volunteer protocols. They point to a high energy level which is variously labeled as "energetic," "overactive," "impulsive," "restless," and "seeks excitement and arousal." The second predominant feature of the pattern refers to disturbances in interpersonal and broader social behavior. Here the descriptions are "violates social restrictions," "difficulties in interpersonal relations," "direct anti-social behavior without controls," "poor close interpersonal relations," "tramples on the feelings and wishes of others," and "keeps people at a distance." In most cases several of these descriptions occurred in each of the seventeen protocols as well as in three others in which high energy characteristics were absent. As often as not, this pattern emerged in persons who were either described as "sociable, friendly, and cheerful" (eleven times) or "bitter, resentful, and irresponsible" (ten times). Twelve of the fifteen descriptions "self-centered" and "immature" and the five descriptions "excessive drinking likely" also occurred among those seventeen volunteers with the pattern described above.

The remaining five volunteer protocols contained few of the elements presented above. I have given the first three protocols the titles "dominant aggressive," "good-natured stable," and "cheerful-venturesome" in accordance with the major features of their content.

This person takes an active, assertive role in dealing with groups. He is likely to be seen by others as sociable, enthusiastic, and outgoing, although these same characteristics may cause others to regard him as blustery, impulsive, or immature. Similarly, his competitiveness, persuasiveness, and aggressiveness may cause others to see him as an opportunistic and manipulative person.

This person is characterized by a denial of anxiety or worry. He expresses self-confidence, affability, and self-acceptance.

He appears to be a balanced, independent person who is able to mobilize his resources effectively. He emphasizes achievement as a means of gaining status and recognition.

He appears to be a steady, adaptable, controlled individual who desires power and recognition but lacks aggressiveness and assertiveness. He is likely to be seen by others as a compliant and cautious person who is, however, obliging and good-natured.

He appears to be a cheerful, optimistic person who is free and spontaneous in thought and action. He is an active, energetic person who is generally seen by others as good-natured and pleasant.

He appears to be an independent, venturesome person who prefers action to contemplation. He lacks insight and may have difficulty emphathizing with others or understanding their reactions to him. He is likely to be seen by others as a contented but perhaps somewhat uninteresting person.

For easier identification, I gave the following protocol the title "defensive, confused, aggressive and contrite." The defensiveness described in the first two paragraphs appeared in seven other protocols as well.

The test results on this person reflect an extreme defensiveness about revealing himself psychologically. Because of his unwillingness to tolerate any suggestion of personal inadequacy, the test results are of doubtful validity. The pattern may be the result of conscious deception, extreme rigidity and naiveté or generalized negativism and refusal to cooperate. His tendency to present a distorted image of himself is likely to generalize to the treatment situation and may be expected to interfere with the development of a therapeutic relationship.

He seems to be attempting to minimize or deny faults in himself. He is hesitant to admit to psychological problems, perhaps because he perceives them as weaknesses. In some normally functioning individuals this apparent defensiveness may represent self-assurance and good self-concept. In an individual with current difficulties, however, it is more likely to represent resistance and reluctance to enter treatment.

This person exhibits contradictions in his behavior and in his view of himself. The contradiction may appear behaviorly as an alternation of phases. For a period, he may act with little control or forethought, violating social restrictions and trampling on the feelings and wishes of others. Following such a period of acting out, however, he may show guilt, remorse and deep regret over his actions, and for a while he may seem overly controlled and contrite. These activity swings may be associated with excessive drinking and various socially unacceptable behaviors. While his conscience pangs may be severe, even out of proportion to the actual behavior deviations, his controls do not appear to be effective in preventing further outbreaks.

He tends to be somewhat overproductive in thinking and action. He may be restless, overtalkative and, in the face of frustration, irritable, aggressive, and impulsive. The normal expression of this trait is enthusiastic, energetic, and persistent goal-directed activity.

There are some unusual qualities in this person's thinking which may represent an original or inventive orientation or perhaps some schizoid tendencies. Further information would be required to make this determination.

The last volunteer protocol received the identifying title "disoriented, perplexed, hyperactive, and idealistic." Careful attention must be paid to the third paragraph in this description since is appears in sixteen percent of the volunteer, fifty-seven percent of the description since is appears in sixteen percent of the volunteer, fifty-seven percent of the draftee, and all of the resister protocols.

This person spends a great deal of time in personal fantasy and daydreams which may approach or reach the level of delusional thinking. He keeps people at a distance and avoids close interpersonal relations. Projection and repression are his major defense mechanisms. The general picture is of a disoriented, perplexed but restless and hyperactive person who tends to disorganize under stress. Psychiatric patients with the test pattern are frequently schizophrenics who require hospitalization or intensive outpatient care. Psychotherapy is rarely the treatment of choice, and the prognosis is poor.

He has some difficulty in dealing with hostile feelings. To the extent that he controls the direct expression of these feelings, he may be a bitter, resentful, and perhaps somewhat irresponsible person. Where control factors are not present, however, the hostility may be expressed in direct antisocial behavior. In any event, he is likely to have problems in establishing close personal relationships and he may be undependable in treatment.

He appears to be an idealistic, inner-directed person who may be seen as quite socially perceptive and sensitive to interpersonal interactions. His interest patterns are quite different from those of the average male. In a person with a broad educational and cultural background this is to be expected and may reflect such characteristics as self-awareness, concern with social issues and an ability to communicate ideas clearly and effectively. In some men, however, the same interest pattern may reflect a rejection of masculinity accompanied by a relatively passive, effeminate, noncompetitive personality.

The third paragraph outlines two alternative interpretations. If the person involved has a broad educational and cultural background, unusual interests are to be expected which may be seen to reflect self-awareness, concern with social issues, and an ability to communicate ideas clearly. For a person without a broad educational and cultural background, however, the same interest pattern may reflect rejection of masculinity accompanied by a relatively passive, effeminate, noncompetitive personality.

Which alternative matches the personalities of the four Green Berets whose protocols contain this descriptive paragraph? The previous data suggest the latter alternative. However, in order to avoid a premature and inaccurate appraisal, the life histories of these subjects were reviewed. It turned out that they shared a number of characteristics which were highly atypical for their group. They had unusually cold, abusive, and punitive mothers who also dominated the family life and issued the severest corporal punishment. Their fathers were either passive, dominated by their wives or absent, mechanical, peripheral figures in daily family life. Three of the four had never been struck by their fathers. Two were the only ones whose earliest memories possessed sexual content. One distinctly recalled taking his mother's breast and sucking on it, and had been plagued "through the years" by the thought that this might only have been a fantasy and that he had never really been breast-fed. The other's earliest memory was of "some old Catholic ladies trying to catch me to see if I was circumcised." Two of these four volunteers were also the only ones who remembered incidents from their childhood in which they were objects of humiliation. One explained that the children at school always laughed at him because he had to wear flannel pants (his mother was both severely punitive and overprotective). The other had been afraid of snakes and worms as a child. This brought humiliation from his friends who taunted him and from his father, who as "a military man all the way" found such fears "unmanly."

In high school these volunteers were serious students with academic and cultural interests. Two of them were the only Green Berets who belonged to their high school drama clubs, and they performed in several high school productions. Two were the only volunteers who received college scholarships. Two were the only Green Berets who had considered entering the ministry and another was one of the two volunteers who converted to Catholicism. In comparison to all the Green Berets, these four were the only ones who had ever read serious literature and who also read for pleasure. One of them was the only Green Beret who had written independently and creatively.

Several of the findings which are characteristic of the sexual development and practices of the entire group of Green Berets are especially pronounced in these four cases. Their average age at first intercourse is one year lower (14.2 versus 15.1) and their estimated number of different sexual partners (prostitutes, pick-ups, girlfriends) ranks among the highest in the Green Beret sample. Self-defeating and self-punitive behavior is also clearly visible in their sexual histories. Two of them had been married twice and one of these two divorced twice. The other two, both black, were single when interviewed and gravitated toward white women. They had all had long, frustrating, and chaotic affairs with women who were either frigid or became pregnant by other men (the first marriages of the two soldiers were to frigid women). These soldiers also described qualitative differences in their emotional response to fights. When they fought they were usually scared and upset and they were especially vicious and vengeful. Finally, one, who had become a medic, requested that his MOS (Military Operations Speciality) be changed in Vietnam because he could "no longer stand the sight of blood."

In my opinion, both alternatives outlined in the MMPI protocols are necessary for a proper characterization of these soldiers. During the interviews they impressed me with their verbal articulateness, introspective and egoistic self-consciousness, and curiosity about themselves. They also appeared more interested in my comments and questions than most of the other Green Berets, and were the most culturally sophisticated in their group. These characteristics correspond to the first interpretative alternative. The other alternative, "rejection of masculinity, passive, effeminate, and noncompetitive," requires modification. Outwardly, these soldiers, as the others, made neither passive nor effeminate impressions and there is little, if anything, about their work which can be described in such terms. However, in contrast to the majority of Green Berets, they seemed more conscious of their sexual and masculine insecurity. The other soldiers with equally hectic sexual histories gave the impression of fornicating out of spite, because it was a challenge to break taboos and because sex was fun. These soldiers seemed to be consciously aware of their search for approval. They therefore tended to be more concerned with a woman's emotional reactions to them and expressed deeper bitterness when they were disappointed. This is related to their attraction to women who would frustrate them, who represented difficult conquests, as well as their fear of renewed failure which drove them to avoid emotional involvement. The origin of this pattern may lie in their family background. Whereas the other soldiers were exposed to dominant, hard, cold, demanding, and punitive fathers with whom they could later identify, it was the mothers of these soldiers who wore the pants in their families. This undoubtedly resulted in identity conflict and insecurity aggravated by their academic and intellectual interests, childhood fears, sexual memories, and early experiences with social ostracism.

One must also ask whether the atypical characteristics of these four Green Berets support the possibility that they were less competitive than the others. The conflict between fear of failure and the desire for achievement and prestige which initially drove all the Green Berets into the security of military service and later into the prestige of the Special Forces was most conspicuous in their life histories. In one case the inconsistency between the soldier's goals during high school and his behavior upon graduation was so striking that I asked him the following question:

The surprising thing about you is that you had everything going for you in high school—good grades, extracurricular activities, lots of prestige, a rich, steady girlfriend whose father was willing to help you through college. You looked like the well-rounded, all-American high school student destined to take a degree in journalism, architecture, or medicine. Instead, you drop everything and go and get trained to be a mercenary. How do you explain that?

He could not explain it. But he acutely remembered his indecision and conflict at the time. The same was true of the others. Their fear of failure was strongly connected to academic performance. They knew that college would be far more demanding than high school and thought that they would be less successful. More generally, it is not accidental that so many Green Berets held private, professional aspirations which were far beyond their present possibilities. It should also be remembered that noncompetitiveness can be a situationally determined response as well as a persistent personality trait. The volunteers tried to avoid competition when failure was likely or superior achievement appeared unattainable.

THE WAR RESISTERS

As was pointed out, the protocols of all twenty resisters who took the test contained the paragraph discussed with regard to four Green Berets. It was also the only paragraph which appeared in all resister protocols. We established in earlier chapters that the war resisters did have many and also atypical interests, were persons with broad educational and cultural backgrounds, did not identify with a stereotyped masculine role, and were also idealistic, introspective, sensitive to interpersonal relations, concerned with social issues, and highly verbal, although they were anything but clear in their communication of ideas.

Were they also passive, effeminate, and noncompetitive? At the time of our talks, they were no longer competitive in academic or career ambitions. A few seemed effeminate. These were the same who had shown the greatest amount of sexual anxiety and inhibition. Passivity is problematic. One cannot very well label people who risk physical abuse and jail sentences as passive. On the other hand, they were all advocates of passive resistance. There were several war resisters whose total resistance style impressed me as especially passive. They, as the four volunteers previously described, were experiencing an acute conflict. On the one hand they felt morally obligated to oppose the war in Vietnam and to suffer the consequences. On the other hand several feared the consequences so greatly that they sought relief in half-way solutions.

The remaining content of the resisters' MMPI protocols describes emotional and social characteristics and disturbances. In comparison to the volunteers, two clusters of social behavior characteristics rather than one emerged. The resisters' protocols average about twice as long as those of the volunteers and provide a correspondingly more detailed portrayal of emotional qualities. Given the higher average elevation of the resisters on all ten clinical scales, this was expected. It is undoubtedly connected to the fact that the resisters had a far more active emotional life. Emotional characteristics, however, are not systematically related to either pattern of social behavior in the MMPI protocols.

I gave the label passivity to the first cluster. It contains eight descriptions, which are listed in the table (Figure 9) along with the frequency of their appearance in individual protocols. They range from reserve and shyness to the possibility of caution and inhibition and the probability of a his-

Case No.	100	101	103	112	115	116	120	121	122
1. Reserved				x	x		x		
2. Hesitant in New Situations				x	x		x		
3. Keeps People at a Distance	x							x	
4. Avoids Close Interpersonal Relations	x							x	
5. Difficulty in Establishing Close Interpersonal Relations				x	x		x	x	
6. Difficulty with Hostile Feelings				x	x		x	x	
7. History of Disrupted Social Relations						x			x
8. Unlikely to Act Out Socially				x			x		

Figure 9. "Passive" social behavior characteristics and disturbances among the war resisters

tory of disrupted social relations. Difficulty with the control of hostile feelings and the unlikelihood of acting them out are also in this cluster. The nine protocols containing these statements are noteworthy for two further reasons. First, neither high energy nor active social behavior characteristics appear in them. Secondly, the war resisters who expressed or indicated hostility toward their families in the interviews or came from broken homes are so identified, with one exception, in their protocols with the statements "may have frequent home maladjustments" or "seems to be repressing, with considerable effort, hostile feelings towards persons close to him, especially his family." None of these five persons is portrayed as socially active or highly energetic. Four were among the nine resisters described as socially passive and the dominant characteristics of the fifth are low energy combined with a number of anxiety and depression symptoms.

The second social behavior pattern contains active or extroverted descriptions as shown in the table (Figure 10). In all four cases, these descriptions are combined with high energy characteristics, and only in one case with anxiety and tension. Although this pattern has a strong resemblance to the dominant pattern among the volunteers, it can be distinguished from the former in several respects. The volunteers' protocols are generally more extreme in that they contain such statements as "violates social restrictions" and "tramples on the wishes and feelings of others." Overconcern with bodily functions and frequent complaints of physical ailments for which no organic basis could be found are integral parts of most volunteer protocols. Among the resisters, physical symptoms are seen as likely under stress in nine cases, but this is unconnected to any of the patterns described so far. Finally, although bitterness and resentment are associated with the active pat-

Case No.	107	111	113	118
1. Alienates Others through Poor Judgment and Lack of Consideration	x	x	x	x
2. Acting Out Possible	x	x	x.	x
3. Hostile	x	x	x	
4. Excessive Drinking Probable*		x	x	
5. Suspicious		x	x	

Figure 10. "Active" social behavior characteristics and disturbances among the war resisters

*In the two cases where excessive drinking was viewed as probable, it had occurred. It is interesting that both fathers were also heavy drinkers, but socially passive. The sons' heavy drinking began in high school, intensified during the confusion after they quit college, and terminated after they began their antiwar activities.

tern among the volunteers, and occurred twice as often in their protocols, they arise only in the protocols of the four socially passive resisters from broken families.

The remaining seven resister protocols contain neither the active nor passive social behavior clusters and otherwise have little in common with one another. With the exceptions noted below, their content is a mixture of elements already described (without clustering) and those to be presented.

Introspection and emotional responsiveness as well as the situational stress of their oppositional position was reflected in a variety of emotional symptoms. Irritability, aggressiveness, and impulsiveness were among the most prevalent and are indicated in nine protocols. Other states such as worry, depression, self-dissatisfaction, discouragement, and fatigue as well as tension, anxiety, disorientation, perplexity, restlessness, fears, rumination, and compulsivity each appear between two and six times and in fourteen of the twenty protocols. Although these symptoms occur somewhat more often among movement than among nonmovement resisters, and also somewhat more often among resisters with passive rather than active social behavior descriptions, their appearance with or without these patterns indicates that the war resisters, as a group, were distressed. Of the twenty resister protocols, there are only three which contain no indications of social disturbances or emotional distress.

THE DRAFTEES

In twenty-three of thirty-five draftee protocols there were statements representing variations of the central characteristics of the group—passivity combined with hostility, indirectly expressed and then denied. These characteristics are reminiscent of the reactions of people caught in a highly charged avoidance-avoidance conflict.[12] They do not like the situation they are in, but the ways of getting out are equally or more unappealing. Some adjust passively, others become argumentative and embittered, still others appear openly hostile and may strike out intentionally or perform poorly. The major annoyance is rarely attacked directly because severe consequences are feared. Therefore, when acting out occurs, it is most likely to be directed at secondary objects.

Distress symptoms occurred more often in draftee than in resister or Green Beret protocols. Again, in twenty-three, clinically relevant degrees of tension, worry, depression, anxiety, sexual problems, restlessness, and reduced self-esteem were found. In fourteen more protocols, problems in interpersonal relations, including antisocial behavior, poor hostility control, and uneasiness, were indicated. Finally, in contrast to the Green Beret protocols, acting out among the draftees was characterized as self-punitive; fantasy and daydreaming were coupled with escapism, and in four cases suicidal preoccupation was seen as likely.

Conclusions

In their individual clinical profiles, the draftees appeared more distressed than either the resisters or the volunteers.* This result would not have been predictable from the averaged group profiles since the resisters' averaged profile elevation was consistently and on many scales significantly higher than those of the other two groups. The group scores generated the expectation that the resisters' individual profiles would show the most frequent and more severe signs of emotional turmoil.

How is this discrepancy to be explained? It seems to me that an adequate explanation must consider and integrate several factors: the manner in which members of each group were generally disposed to handle emotional difficulties; the individual's attitude to his life situation in terms of the degree to which he felt instrumental in creating it; the role of situational stresses and the degree to which they may have contributed to personal discomfort; and the boundaries and limitations of each situation for the satisfaction of basic emotional needs as well as for acting out sexual and aggressive impulses.

There can be little doubt that the vast majority of both volunteers and

---

*It is the resisters' remarkably small standard deviation (0.38) on Scale 8, Schizophrenia, and the unusually large deviations of the draftees (5.2) and volunteers (6.8), rather than their respective mean values, that contain the clinically most relevant data. At the low extremes, these scores indicate persons with little emotional activity who are also incapable of emotional responsiveness. At the higher and highest levels (approximately thirty percent of the draftees and volunteers scored higher than eighty-four percent of the standardization population and approximately sixteen percent higher than ninety-eight percent of the standardization population) the scores point to heavy blocking of emotionality as well as to deep-seated and intense conflict, fear, and anxiety. The latter pattern will also coincide with bizarre thoughts, delusional thinking, inappropriate affect, self-destructive tendencies, interpersonal insensitivity, and massive guilt.

resisters felt committed to their respective lifestyles and saw themselves as instrumental in achieving them. For both of these groups, considerable effort, sacrifice, planning, and decision had gone into their careers as pro- and antiwar activists. Both groups showed firm identification with their roles and gained a sense of purposefulness from their activities. Therefore they were also prepared to accept the dangers and deprivations as unavoidable dependencies of their personally chosen positions. This could not be said of the draftees. It was rather a sense of purposelessness, of wasted time and senseless effort which characterized the private and organisational climate in which they lived.

The fundamental importance of a sense of purpose for general psychological balance as well as for the readiness and ability to endure various kinds of stress must be emphasized.* However, we must also examine the continuities in personal behavior within the context of situational restraints in order to gauge both the individual's needs for personal expression and the degree to which a situation will allow for it. It was action, decisiveness, and dedication to ideals or careers which placed the resisters and volunteers in situations which enabled them to take continuing and personally satisfying action. It was passivity, born of conflict, which motivated the draftees to let the government make the first move; this placed them in a situation they despised and in which individualistic and instrumental action was impossible. This is perhaps why the interpretation of their group MMPI profile was of passive but hostile persons who express their anger indirectly and then deny it. One further indication of the depth of their conflicts which will be discussed at length in the concluding chapter is that while none of them approved the war in Vietnam or wanted to be personally involved in it, the majority felt they would welcome the opportunity to kill an enemy soldier.

---

*"In our study of the late effects of concentration camp incarceration we found several prominent personality and situational correlates among persons who survived this ordeal in relatively good or in relatively poor health. Those persecutees who were able to relate and understand their persecution and their suffering in terms of a well-defined ideology (Jehovah's Witnesses, Communists, some socialists, priests, and Orthodox Jews) withstood the concentration camp experience best. They had also organized themselves hierarchally within the concentration camps, had been personally disciplined, cooperative and helpful to members of the in-group. The vast majority of the persecutees, however, were never able to grasp the reason for their suffering. They experienced their ordeal as senseless, found little or no purpose in the experience, and felt they had not derived any benefits from it. In the concentration camps they tended to be socially isolated, uncooperative and they were also mistreated more often and more severely by the camp guards. They also tended to receive the more debilitating kinds of work assignments and therefore, in terms of objectively definable stresses, suffered more.

"Within the latter majority group of nonideologists, it was possible to isolate a small subgroup which also survived the camps in relatively good health. These persons had reacted to the incipient persecution actively by trying to flee. Once caught and interned, they were also opportunistically active in the camps. They disobeyed orders, stole, lied, bribed the guards and also managed to obtain relatively better working conditions." (See P. Matussek, et al., *Die Konzentrationslagerhaft und Ihre Folgen* [Berlin: Springer Verlag, 1971]. Translation mine.)

Contrary to general expectations and consistent with an implicit and unspoken misunderstanding in both professional and lay circles on the problems of Vietnam-era veterans, it has been support troops in "peace" zones rather than combat troops in "war" zones who have been most conspicuous clinically.[13] This paradox is most relevant here but its full elucidation goes beyond the possibilities of this research. It does seem useful, however, to briefly mention and discuss several possible reasons for this.

The morale of American combat troops in Vietnam appears to have been higher than that of their support troops. Group norms in combat units as well as operational dangers and demands may well have worked against preoccupation with personal problems. It seems plausible to assume that combat troops would have found a psychiatrist's office less accessible than support or peacetime troops. Obviously combat troops had many more sanctioned opportunities to ventilate their anger and rage. It is also likely that there were important differences in medical and psychiatric policy as well as in the attitudes of medical specialists and their assistants toward psychological problems, depending upon the military situation. As Daniels (1970) and others have pointed out, war-zone psychiatrists established higher tolerance levels for personal distress than did their counterparts in other zones.[14] This attitude undoubtedly is passed on to the troops and may influence their self-perception as well as their readiness to seek psychiatric help.

If we assume that the individual soldier internalizes his peer group and the psychiatrist's norms, or at least measures himself against such standards and then applies them in his test-taking behavior, we may obtain an additional clue in our attempt to understand the discrepancies in symptom type, frequency, and intensity between volunteers and draftees. Such an assumption indicates that the groups are really more similar clinically than the data indicate and that the volunteers tended to suppress and also to disclose and the draftees to more directly experience and air their personal difficulties when given the chance. In my personal contact with both groups I found that the volunteers had few gripes and felt they had nothing to gripe about. The draftees spent a good portion of their time complaining.

The fact remains, however, that the volunteers were exposed to a great many more hardships in the military than were the draftees. These differences cannot be easily brushed away with sophisticated arguments about response sets. On the one hand they strongly suggest that there are people who remain relatively immune to battlefield stress and who do not respond later with the variety of symptoms (guilt, rage, uncontrolled violence, feelings of deception, suicide, nightmares, flashbacks) now being generally found among Vietnam veterans. On the other hand, this observation does not preclude the possibility that noncombat troops express "milder" problems in greater numbers while suffering more because they are constrained from acting out their more serious ones.

Notes

1. Of the thirty-two Fascism scale items used in this study, sixteen were reversals suggested by R. Christie, J. Havel, and B. J. Seidenberg, in *Journal of Abnormal and Social Psychology*, LVI (1958), 243-249. Others were originals taken from Forms 40 and 45, in T. Adorno et al., *The Authoritarian Personality*, New York: Harper and Brothers, 1950, p. 255. The Adorno originals 22, 31, 33, 38, and 44 were omitted either because satisfactory reversals could not be formulated, because the item was antiquated, or because according to Christie upon analysis the item failed to discriminate between highs and lows.

2. A. H. Maslow, "The Authoritarian Character Structure," *Bulletin of the Journal of Social Psychology*, Society for Psychological Study of Social Issues, 1943.

3. M. Rokeach, "The Nature and Meaning of Dogmatism," *Psychological Review*, LXI (1954), 194-204.

4. The items used in this study were taken from K. Roghmann, *Dogmatismus und Autoritarismus* (Meisenheim: Verlag Anton Hain, 1966).

5. This was nicely demonstrated in a study by E. N. Baker, "Authoritarianism of the Political Right, Center and Left" (Unpublished doctoral dissertation, Columbia University, 1958).

6. The version used in this study contained twenty-five items and was taken from Form 60, page 163, in Adorno et al. The wording of a few items was changed to bring them up to date.

7. The items for this scale were taken without alteration from D. Levinson and P. E. Hoffman, "Traditional Family Ideology and Its Relation to Personality," *Journal of Personality*, XXIII (1955), 251-273.

8. The items for this version were taken from J. C. Brengelmann, "Extreme Response Set, Drive Level and Abnormality in Questionnaire Rigidity," *Journal of Mental Science*, CVI (1960), 171-186.

9. C. C. Moskos, Jr., *The American Enlisted Man* (New York: Russell Sage Foundation, 1970), 148-151.

10. W. G. Dahlstrom and G. S. Welsh, *An MMPI Handbook* (Minneapolis: University of Minnesota Press, 1962). See pages 443 to 468 for scale names and item composition.

11. A. Hollingshead and F. Redlich, *Social Class and Mental Illness* (New York: John Wiley & Sons, 1958); L. Srole, T. Langner, S. Michael, and M. Opler, *Mental Health in the Metropolis: The Mid-Manhattan Study* (New York: McGraw-Hill, 1962); B. and B. S. Dohrenwend, "The Problem of Validity in Field Studies of Psychological Disorder," *Journal of Abnormal Psychology*, LXX (1965), 52-69.

12. K. Lewin, *A Dynamic Theory of Personality* (New York: McGraw-Hill, 1935).

13. This observation is based on personal communications from several military psychiatrists who were involved in related research or who had extensive practical experience in Vietnam. It is also based on my personal observations during a six-year

association with U.S. military personnel and installations in Europe and on my continuing research in this area. (See P. G. Bourne, "Military Psychiatry and the Vietnam Experience," *American Journal of Psychiatry*, CXXVII, no. 4, 123-130 and "The Vietnam Veteran: Psychosocial Casualties," *Psychiatry in Medicine*, III, 23-27; R. J. Lifton, "The Scars of Vietnam," *Commonweal*, Feb. 20, 1970, 554-556 and "Experiments in Advocacy Research," *The Academy* (Newsletter of the American Academy of Psychoanalysis), XVI, I (1972), 8-13; D. Mantell and M. Pilisuk (eds.), "Soldiers In and After Vietnam," *Journal of Social Issues*, in preparation; C. Shatan, "The Subversion of the Super-Ego: Uses of Identification With the Aggressor in Basic Combat Training," paper presented at Annual Conference of Psychoanalytic Psychiatrists, New York City, 1972, "Soldiers in Mourning: The Post-Vietnam Syndrome, "*The Berkshire Eagle*, June 23, 1972, and "Post-Vietnam Syndrome," *The New York Times*, May 6, 1972; G. F. Solomon, "Casualties of the Vietnam Conflict with Particular Reference to the Problem of Heroin Addiction," *Modern Medicine*, Sept. 20, 1971, 199-215 and "Three Psychiatric Casualties from Vietnam," *Archives of General Psychiatry*, XXV (1971), 522-524.)

14. A. K. Daniels, "Normal Mental Illness and Understandable Excuses: The Philosophy of Combat Psychiatry," *American Behavioral Scientist*, XIV, no. 2 (1970), 167-184.

CHAPTER 8

CONCLUSION

Normal, Average Families

Few social institutions are permitted greater freedom in the use of violence than the family. Adults display far more aggression and cruelty toward each other in the guarded sanctuary of their homes than in any other social context except war. The frequency with which the arbitrary use of aggression, autocracy, and violence occurs between married adults is exceeded only by the frequency of their use by parents against their children. We find that parents usually have a ready justification for such practices; they consider these practices to be legitimate outgrowths of their parental obligation, and continue to use them both reflexively and vengefully even after their purposive failure is evident. Most children, to the degree that they are exposed, learn to accept this treatment passively.[1] One might argue that the turbulence and violence of family life rarely ends in the serious physical injury or death of its members, but that is beside the point. These are fundamental social learning experiences which shape the human beings' capacity for violent expression in later life.

If we are to come to grips with the causal factors underlying mass and individual violence, this realization must become firmly anchored in our thinking, in our social, political, and educational analyses as well as in action programs. The war in Vietnam is but one example of politically inspired and—as this study has illustrated—individually waged violence. The potential for that violence has been wittingly and unwittingly prepared in the American family. Parents instill attitudes, values, prejudices, fears, and a variety of behavioral patterns and predispositions (response hierarchies) in their children. Were these psychological and behavioral preconditions absent, nations would not possess the human material to wage wars. Just as politicians are children who have grown up, so too are soldiers. The first bring to public office and the second to the battlefield the lessons of childhood.

Violence does not emerge in a vacuum. It is not a mysterious, unpredictable, uncontrollable inborn drive. It is planted by example and continually reinforced or extinguished by experience. If reinforced it becomes an ever-present potential in the emotional make-up and behavioral repertoire of its practitioners.

In addition to the family, other social institutions—mass media, peer groups, and the schools—have direct access to the child during his or her formative years. However, as Peck and Havighurst discovered in their extensive investigations of the development of character structures in adolescents, "the much-debated effect of movies, comic books and similar media, as far as could be told, did little to change the kind of character structure or specific values any given child had learned from family experiences."[2] As for the peer group, it "appears to be less an originator than a reinforcer of moral values and behavioral patterns developed in the family."[3] The same holds for schools. Peck and Havighurst report that schools "seem less to shape character than to crystallize and throw into sharper contrast the punishments for undesirable behavior and the rewards for proper behavior. Even more extremely, the schools tend to discriminate widely, and rather persistently, between those individual children who show inadequate character and those who show good character. . . . It was surprising to find how high character maturity correlated with school grades. . . . It is amply evident that school teachers reward rational-altruistic, irrational-conscientious, and effective conforming behavior and literally mark down children of expedient and amoral character. It appears, in summary, that the basic qualities of personality structure and interpersonal attitude are predominantly created by the child's experiences with his parents."[4]

Parents and society are aware of parental responsibility as legal and moral imperatives and as behavior-shaping power. Social scientists can hardly question the premise of parent-child causality, but can merely try to document the direction and contingencies of influence. This awareness and understanding, however, succumbs to other interests under particular circumstances. Rarely will any degree of persuasion or evidence move parents to accept accountability for the "evil" they or others perceive in their children. This undertaking must fail because adults so often disown moral and legal accountability for their own behavior and show no greater readiness to accept blame for the behavior of another.[5,6]

Independent investigations have repeatedly shown strong and consistent correlations between family atmosphere characteristics (the kinds, combinations, and intensity of parental discipline practices), moral development, and the occurrence of hostility, aggression, and violence in children.[7] Previous literature has been concerned with aggressive and violent behavior in family and school settings and in peer groups, with special emphasis on the violence of gangs and juvenile delinquents. I interpret the data reported in this book to show that the same factors which lead to aggression in the above-mentioned settings promote militaristic attitudes and behavior. A strong correlation exists between the degree to which children have been exposed to arbitrary authority, physical abuse, and intimidation and their later readiness to submit to these practices and make use of them.

Imitation is one of the fundamental ways in which social behavior is acquired. Children imitate their parents and carry the behavior they learn at home into new contexts which often have no apparent external resemblance to their homes. The child "properly reared" in the authoritarian tradition learns enough at home to enable him to adjust to military and other societal institutions, nearly all of which contain structures similar to the one he grew up in. He learns to conform at home, to accept and bow to arbitrary and demeaning authority, to discipline himself by squelching the direct expression of resentment, to be beaten and intimidated, and to justify these conditions as well. The children who do not learn this, or who are raised differently, are likely to get into trouble in authoritarian settings.

However, society is threatened less by social deviants than by the cruel and violent traditions, institutions, policies, and attitudes which we have inherited, with which we consciously and reflexively identify, and which we continue to refine. Masked and open violence, habitual and systematic training for violence, are integral parts of our civilization. So are the values, prejudices, fears, and ideologies which help to perpetuate them from generation to generation. The collective violence of groups and nations is the combined and multiplied violence of their individual members. In the absence of war or other socially sanctioned outlets, people may be hard-pressed from time to time to keep the expression of their aggressive and violent impulses within the bounds of legality. This is one of the reasons that the home environment, with its familiarity and safety, proves to be such a popular arena for the ventilation of these urges.

A Tradition and Morality of Violence

What can this research contribute to the understanding and control of violence? There are consistent patterns in the developmental histories of young Americans who volunteered for combat duty in Vietnam and those who refused to participate in that war. The patterns first emerged during early childhood in the homes where the subjects received their core socializing experiences. We were able to relate their subsequent behavior as well as the dominant cognitive, affective, and perceptual aspects of their social, religious, sexual, intellectual, and moral development to early social learning in the family. By reconstructing the early learning situation we gained a plausible explanatory framework for their prowar and antiwar decisions.

Traditional Authority and Teamwork

Every Green Beret had one strict parent and most had two strict parents. (See "Characteristics of Parent-Child Relationships as Reported by Volunteers and Resisters," in Appendix.) Mechanical formality and parental dominance existed in nearly all cases between one parent and son and often between both parents and the son. In twenty-one of twenty-five families neither parent showed respect for the son's rights or individuality. Eleven Green Berets were granted some freedom of movement by one parent, usually the mother, but none experienced this from both. Although the majority did not feel they had been rejected by their parents or that their parents were generally hostile toward them, most experienced continuous irritability on the part of one or both parents. It is significant that eighty percent of the volunteers never experienced emotional closeness with either parent, and only forty-eight percent reported receiving parental affection. This affection came from both parents in only twelve percent of the cases. Approximately equal numbers remembered both parents showing or both parents not showing patience and helpfulness. It is also of interest that nearly half the Green Berets perceived their mothers' attention as overprotective.

The Green Berets' perceptions as to which of their parents played a more dominant role in their upbringing seem to have been based on the sheer intensity and severity of parental behavior. When the father dominated the mother, he also dominated the children. However, the same pattern of dominance and influence based on discipline and fear was also present in those families in which the mother was the central authority figure. In these families the pattern was simply reversed. The mother dominated the father and the parent-child relationship, issued most of the discipline, was stricter, delivered the severer corporal punishment, and was feared more. The father remained a background figure or assumed the milder stance which characterized a few of the mothers in the father-dominated families. In neither mother- nor father-dominated Green Beret families were there differences of opinion or practice between the parents with regard to child-rearing practices. Parents were strict disciplinarians, threatened their children with corporal punishment, delivered corporal punishment, demanded unswerving obedience from their children, and maintained control over them primarily through fear.

One weakness of this child-rearing pattern is its inflexibility. Parental treatment of the child is guided by deeply ingrained attitudes, ideals, and habits which remain largely unreflected upon and undiscussed. The parents themselves are not in close emotional contact with each other and therefore have virtually no leverage for bringing about a positive change in each other's behavior toward the child; an undesirable aspect of the other's behavior is likely simply to be tolerated.

Prohibition of "inconsiderateness" is one example of the lopsided character of the parent-child relationships in these families. The Green Berets' parents showed little concern for the inner lives of their children in their actual behavior or in their proclaimed standards. Importance was attached to the child's behavior, which was required to conform strictly to parental wishes. Yet these same parents required their sons to pay careful attention to parental feelings. This demand was formalized in the values of considerateness and respect. Its application was broad, so that the child's asking for something the parent did not want to give, speaking to the parent while he was preoccupied, making noise, or in any other way interfering with adults was treated as inconsiderate and disrespectful. It was, of course, the parents who decided when this label would be applied.

All parental values and demands carry implications for moral concepts, judgments, and perceptions. Children are inclined to view the acts their parents prohibit as morally wrong and to feel guilty if they do them. The Green Berets' parents prohibited cheating, lying, and stealing. They also prohibited disobedience in general, back-talk, and the display of emotion. By prohibiting and punishing these behaviors as moral transgressions, they completed the circle of control over their sons. The fathers and mothers could simply be autocratic and did not always need to employ physical violence or its threat to gain their sons' compliance. Since the value system they imparted declared desires that ran counter to their own as morally wrong, they were able to count on their children's own self-censure as an effective means of discipline.

The Green Berets were raised to be emotionally tough. Their parents gave them behavioral and moral standards which they accepted uncritically, and still held at the time of the interviews and tests. Their lives are based on the principles of propriety, respectability, pride, hard work, obedience, respect for authority, and professionalism. Their childhood and adolescent years revealed a remarkable continuity of social experience with their peer groups, teachers, coaches, ministers, and scout leaders, all of whom seem to have made demands and extolled virtues closely resembling those of the men's families. The Special Forces soldiers were exposed to like-minded people from their earliest childhood and there is no evidence that they ever sought out persons who thought or acted differently. They tended to live their lives on a day-to-day basis with little thought for the past or future. They had firm beliefs about who they were and what they stood for. Their ability to recall few people other than their parents who had influenced them, or experiences which had left an impression on them, was equivalent to saying that they could not remember any changes in their lives, that they had always been the same.

Unlike ideologically committed authoritarians,[8] the Green Berets were relatively unengaged politically, and were unemotional about the use of their professional skills. However, they were somewhat threatened by the beliefs and actions of persons who repudiated Green Beret values or professional status, or who escaped prosecution for actions resembling something the Green Berets themselves might have contemplated doing. An example of the latter is their stated readiness to change their uniform to fight for another cause if the pay and working conditions were good. Military virtue is independent of political belief. Many Green Berets would have been glad to assassinate American Army deserters who had fled to Sweden. They were more tolerant of war resisters and conscientious objectors, whom they would only send to jail or force to go to Vietnam. Objections to Hitler and his policy of wanton extermination of "undesirable" populations illustrates that some of the Green Berets valued human life pragmatically, while others found it entirely meaningless.

In the military, these men were not pervasively meek and submissive, or strongly interested in gaining a position of power within a social hierarchy. The latter would involve continuous subordination to superiors, restrict mobility, and require bureaucratic work, all of which they detested. Their interest in social hierarchies seemed to have less to do with administrative power than with the prestige, freedom of movement, and freedom from conventional responsibilities and censure that some hierarchies, like the military, can grant.

The Green Berets were too elitist in their thinking, narrow in their interests, and hungry for adventure to derive satisfaction from membership in a broad social movement or conventional organization. They preferred the intimacy of the small group, which for them was their team. In the Special Forces the team is a group of from five to ten soldiers; each member is trained in a particular Military Occupation Specialty (MOS)—such as medic, intelligence, demolitions, radio operator, light and heavy weapons, or combat engineer—to a high level of proficiency and then cross-trained in the specialties of the other team members.

Although the soldier remains embedded within a stringent military hierarchy composed of officers (most Green Berets never go beyond the rank of a noncommissioned officer) and derives considerable prestige as well as additional material benefits from membership in this military unit, his primary allegiance is to his team, to the small group of men with whom he trains daily and upon whom his life will depend in combat. These men become his peers. They bestow approval, give support, and can impose severe sanctions. While the team demands devotion and even heroic self-sacrifice, it resents and suppresses individual glory seeking. An aggressive individual may lead a basketball team to victory, but he is likely to get a combat team liquidated. Devotion to the team does not rest on devotion to social and political principles or to a higher ideology. What matters is the efficiency of the team. The team serves others only to the degree necessary to maintain its legitimization.

Perhaps the basic significance of the Green Berets' continuous involvement with teams—from high school athletics to the Special Forces—is their belief that they cannot succeed as individuals. The Special Forces team, like their high school athletic teams, provides support, approval, and constant reinforcement. Not being contemplative or introspective, the team members do not know how to be alone and do not value solitude. Not having known privacy as children, feeling that their fate was tied to that of their parents, having escaped parental domination either through attainment of physical equality with them or by fleeing, they have no internal anchor and therefore seek it in the group. Easily bored, they require constant activity and adventure. Despite the temporary benefits these players derive from their team and their loyalty to it, they regard themselves and each other as dispensable. Their relations with each other are to be seen in this light. As one soldier put it, "I'm just a cog in the wheel. Nobody knows whether I live or die."

A New Morality

Whether he lives or dies is of considerable importance to a war resister. He shows no readiness to risk his life for material benefits, for peer approval, out of fear of censure, or for ideological convictions. This attitude derives from intellectual conviction and a basic respect for life in general, including his own. Most people are afraid of death, but people are not equally attached to life, nor do they show equal readiness to preserve their lives.

As a group, the war resisters broke more strongly and irreversibly with ingrained concepts of conventional American morality than did any other group of noncriminal young Americans who have not opted out of society altogether. They did not pursue any obvious material benefit and in their activities they destroyed little property. For the most part they acted alone rather than in unison. They allowed themselves to be assaulted physically and psychologically and did not strike back. Instead of accepting the socially and legally sanctioned last resort of conscientious objector status, many became convicts. None is in a position to say that his sacrifice had any perceptible influence on the course of the war he wanted to end.

Even sympathetic observers may be suspicious of such people. Underlying surface agreement with their stand and their principles is a gnawing feeling of uneasiness, bound up with the realization that most of us are not ready to make a similar sacrifice for our convictions. Privately, and sometimes in the press, a cynical, defensive attitude prevailed toward the war resisters. It went something like this: "You people want to be martyrs. It doesn't pay. It doesn't change anything. It's bad for your career. It's unhealthy. It's fanatic. That means that you're sick. You must have had a troubled childhood. Go see a psychiatrist."

Did the war resisters have troubled childhoods? Objectively, they had far less to complain about than did the Green Berets, and yet most of them were more openly critical of their parents. None experienced parental rejection. Only one was exposed to a parent perceived as generally hostile. Only three felt that one of their parents had been largely indifferent toward them, and only one saw a lack of respect for his rights and individuality in both parents. The majority felt that both parents had been helpful, patient, and affectionate, and had allowed them increasing freedom of movement and independence. One complained of parental overprotectiveness and a few of parental strictness, formal coldness, irritability, or excessive dominance. The majority recalled close emotional bonds with one or both parents.

It is a long leap from childhood influences in the home to the character structure of young adults. Many influences, particularly those of the peer group, of the school, and of other persons of reference, are present in the intervening years. We found that the war resisters searched out groups and persons in their surroundings and even organized groups which took critical, constructive, activist stands toward contemporary American society.

The war resisters' ability to point to a continuous stream of friends, classmates, teachers, ministers, girlfriends, neighborhood adults, and chance acquaintances who influenced them contrasts sharply with the paucity of persons outside the extended family named by the Green Berets. The resisters never seemed ready to sacrifice their private values for group membership. They do not seem to have gained an extended sense of identification from any group to which they temporarily belonged. Instead they stood on the fringe, experimenting, looking in, picking and choosing persons and elements, gaining a personal challenge and experience, and then moving on. The Green Berets were also on the fringe, yet they stayed with one conventional group or another, unable to relate to it personally or intellectually, unable to say what they might have derived from group membership, yet only leaving the group upon formal, biologically, and chronologically determined graduation.

The war resisters were basically searching for their own approval. Being relatively autonomous in their decision-making, they were likely to choose the rules they wished to live by and to revise them according to the demands of their consciences and a particular situation. Being reflective and intellectual, they are involved with questions of morality. Being introspective they question their own motives and the moral adequacy of their acts. When they feel that they have not fulfilled a moral precept or have violated their own principles, they will be troubled by intense guilt. And since they are likely to have broken with virtually all sources of traditional moral authority, they are not able to accept packaged solutions for their own moral dilemmas.

Like the Green Berets, the war resisters are very much products of American cultural traditions. They see themselves as individualists first and foremost and do not want to account to others for their actions. They resent authority figures and structures, are disdainful and suspicious of ideologies and mass movements, are nonconformists of a passionate variety, and value their freedom of movement above almost everything else. The similarities between them, however, end here. Whereas the resisters identified with Martin Buber and Henry David Thoreau, the volunteers exalted John Wayne, Che Guevara, and Rommel. The resisters defied traditional authority openly, the volunteers only when it wasn't looking. The volunteers liked the good life and were willing to risk their personal welfare only if the pay were right. The resisters tended toward asceticism and moral values rather than material luxuries were their priorities.

While many secondary values could be listed to characterize the resisters' moral code, nonviolence, the starting point of their Selective Service System confrontation, was the primary value. It would be stretching the facts to assert that all the war resisters interviewed had a natural, self-evident relation to nonviolence stemming from the practices and moral teachings of their parents. Yet many could not recall a single incident of their parents threatening or striking each other or their children. The range of motives, the level of emotional, social, and moral maturity, the specific values and their sources vary among the war resisters. These differences are suggested in the typology of the resisters explained in the Introduction. Had the original sample been larger, it might have been possible to provide an empirical foundation reaching back through developmental experiences for each of the four types of resister. Lacking a broader pool of data, it is only possible to review the divergent trends in the data and to point out their continuities where these seem pertinent.

Nearly all the war resisters' parents used rational, consistent discipline, and were far more likely to punish their children with disapproval, explanations, appeals, and withdrawal of privileges and affection than with threats or force. These discipline measures have been identified elsewhere as producing "autonomous-altruistic"[9] and "rational-altruistic"[10] character structures, moral judgment based on "individual principles and conscience"[11] and "independent, non-violent"[12] persons.

In ten war resister families the parents, usually the fathers, made some use of violence against their sons in the form of a spanking or slap. In about half these cases a single such incident occurred in late childhood or early adolescence. In these families, the mere occurrence of violence indicated mild to severe disharmony in the home. The five resisters from broken homes were spanked. In some of the others there was considerable tension between the parents over financial difficulties arising from the father's alcoholism, neglect of his profession in favor of peace activities, or illness. These difficulties are also related to other nonrational disciplinary practices, including appeals to God, responding to the child's behavior as if it were a personal affront, openly crying and showing distress, withdrawing all affection from the child for an extended period, and demanding complete obedience.

Those war resisters who came from broken or relatively disharmonious homes and were exposed to repeated irrationality and even one incident of parental violence were more sympathetic than their fellows to the practices of violent revolutionary groups in Asia, Africa, and Latin America. They were also more readily able to envision circumstances which would justify the use of violence by dissident groups reacting to discrimination within the United States. Disharmony in the home was also related to a more troubled sexual development, a more fearful and yet more hostile attitude toward law enforcement agencies, and greater wavering and uncertainty in oppositional attitudes and behavior. The final solution to the Selective Service dilemma, however, involving the extremes of active confrontation and avoidance techniques was not related to family discord and violence.

A different cluster of home life circumstances seemed to surround a more reasoned and cautious approach to antiwar activities and the Selective Service. These subjects, mostly in the social activist and private convenience groups, tended to come from clearly matriarchal homes. Their fathers were described as quiet, rational, distant figures who took little part in family life. After the day's work they preferred to read the newspaper, watch television, or engage in a solitary hobby. They tended to avoid confrontations with their energetic, emotional wives by staying out of the way.

As a result of the divorce of his parents when he was seven, one war resister, who later became the most creatively dedicated of those interviewed, experienced both the above patterns. He described his father as a quiet, peaceful, ultimately rational man who spent virtually no time with his family, though he was often at home. Instead he spent his spare time with engrossing hobbies and with handicapped or troubled young people. This father never lost his temper and told his son, "Never raise your voice. Speak quietly and patiently until you get your point across." The mother was portrayed as a dynamic, temperamental, jealous woman who dominated family life. After divorcing her husband she married a wealthy lawyer and gained custody of her son. The stepfather later went bankrupt through his alcoholism and neglect of his practice. The mother also became alcoholic and submitted to the views and practices of her husband. He was a strict disciplinarian who, particularly when drunk, beat his stepson mercilessly. It was here that the resister found his first use for the nonviolent tactics he later used with the police. No matter how severely his stepfather beat him he never cried or tried to run. He took it until the man "wore himself out."

The early neglect of the child, the mother's jealousy and vengeance toward her husband, the stepfather's beatings, and the father's moral code and behavior all left their mark. In late adolescence he fell in love with a girl whose love for him filled a deep gap in his life. When she decided to break the relationship he lost control of himself and "beat her up." Recognizing at that time the depth of his need for warmth and love, and his vulnerability to hurt, combined with his horror of his capacity for violent behavior, he considered remaining celibate. He had, however, learned how to judge and to deal with his own violence and the violence of others at home. Had he known only his stepfather he might have become a Green Beret. This case is exceptional in containing the dominant patterns of both the war resister and the Green Beret family life styles.

*   *   *   *   *

The test data show that the personality profiles of the Green Berets and inductees are similar to those of the cross section of the American population. The profiles of the resisters depart more sharply from these norms. Green Berets, then, are more like the majority of Americans. The Green Berets followed traditional authority, went to war, and experienced what they liked best—adventure, excitement, and the performance of professional military skills. The war resisters represent a minority trend in American life, a very old and honored position of putting an individual conception of honor above all other concerns. They rejected traditional authority, asserted a morality that they considered superior to prevailing morality, and refused to go to war.

People like the Green Berets may be necessary in potential soldiers if the United States is to survive as a world power. For the United States to survive as an idea, we will need people like the war resisters. We can hope to nurture such men.

Notes

1. See D. Gil, *Violence Against Children: Physical Child Abuse in the United States* (Cambridge, Mass.: Harvard University Press, 1970), for an excellent study of the cultural patterns and individual experience of child abuse in the United States.

2. R.F. Peck and R.J. Havighurst, *The Psychology of Character Development* (New York: Wiley, 1960).

3. *Ibid.*

4. *Ibid.*

5. D. Mantell and R. Panzarella, "Obedience and Social Responsibility," unpublished.

6. D. Mantell and M. Perlmutter, "Responsibility: A Semantic Profile," unpublished.

7. See W. Becker, "Consequences of Different Kinds of Parental Discipline," *Child Development Research,* M.L. and L.W. Hoffman, eds. (New York:

Russell Sage, 1964) II; and L. Kohlberg, "Development of Moral Character and Moral Ideology," *Child Development Research,* I, for excellent reviews of the literature.

8. D. Wright, *The Psychology of Moral Behavior* (Baltimore: Penguin, 1971).

9. *Ibid.*

10. Peck and Havighurst, *op. cit.*

11. Kohlberg, *op. cit.*

12. Becker, *op. cit.*

BIBLIOGRAPHY

Adorno, T. *et al. The Authoritarian Personality.* New York: Harper, 1950.

Bandura, A. and Walters, R. *Adolescent Aggression: A Study of the Influence of Child Rearing Practices and Family Relationships,* New York: Ronald Press, 1959.

Barker, E. N. "Authoritarianism of the Political Right, Center and Left." Unpublished dissertation. Columbia University, 1958.

Becker, W., "Consequences of Different Kinds of Parental Discipline," in M.L. and L.W. Hoffmann, eds., *Child Development Research,* Vol. II. New York: Russell Sage, 1964.

Brengelmann, J. C. "Extreme Response Set, Drive Level and Abnormality in Questionnaire Rigidity," *Journal of Mental Science,* CVI (1960), 171-186.

Bourne, P. G. "Military Psychiatry and the Vietnam Experience," *American Journal of Psychiatry,* CXXVII (1970), 123-130.

———. "The Vietnam Veteran:Psychosocial Casualties," *Psychiatry in Medicine,* III (1972), 23-27.

Christie, R., Havel, J., and Seidenberg, B. "Is the F Scale Irreversible?" *Journal of Abnormal and Social Psychology,* LVI (1958), 143-159.

Crowne, D. P. and Marlowe, D. *The Approval Motive.* New York: Wiley, 1964.

Dahlstrom, W. G. and Welsh, G. S. *An MMPI Handbook.* Minneapolis: University of Minnesota, 1962.

Daniels, A. K. "Normal Mental Illness and Understandable Excuses: The Philosophy of Combat Psychiatry," *American Behavioral Scientist,* XIV (1970), 167-184.

Dohrenwend, B. and Dohrenwend, B. S. "The Problem of Validity in Field Studies of Psychological Disorder," *Journal of Abnormal Psychology,* LXX (1965), 52-60.

Edwards, A. *Edwards Personal Preference Schedule.* New York: The Psychological Corporation, 1959.

———. *The Social Desirability Variable in Personality Assessment and Research.* New York: Dryden, 1957.

Edwards, A. and Heathers, L. B. "The First Factor of the MMPI: Social Desirability or Ego Strength," *Journal of Consulting Psychology,* XXVI (1962), 99-100.

Gil, D. *Violence Against Children: Physical Child Abuse in the United States.* Cambridge, Mass.: Harvard, 1970.

Hollingshead, A. and Redlich, F. *Social Class and Mental Illness.* New York: Wiley, 1958.

Kohlberg, L. "Development of Moral Character and Moral Ideology," in M. L. and L. W. Hoffmann, eds., *Child Development Research,* Vol. I. New York: Russell Sage, 1964.

Lane, R. E. "Fathers and Sons: Foundations of Political Beliefs," *American Sociological Review,* XXIV (1963), 502-511.

Levinson, D., and Hoffmann, P. E. "Traditional Family Ideology and Its Relation to Personality," *Journal of Personality,* XXIII (1955), 251-273.

Lewin, K. *A Dynamic Theory of Personality.* New York: McGraw-Hill, 1935.

Lidz, T. "The Family and the Developmental Setting," in E. J. Anthony and C. Koupernik, eds., *The Child in His Family.* New York: Wiley, 1970.

Lifton, R. J., "The Scars of Vietnam," *Commonweal,* Feb. 20, 1970, 554-556.

————. "Experiments in Advocacy Research," *Newsletter of the American Academy of Psychoanalysis,* XVI (1972), 8-13.

Mantell, D. "The Potential for Violence in Germany," *Journal of Social Issues,* XXVI (1971), 101-112.

————. "Warnung vor dem Durchschnitsbürger." Basel: *National-Zeitung,* Jan. 13, 1973, 1.

Mantell, D. and Panzarella, R. "Obedience and Responsibility." Unpublished manuscript, 1973.

Mantell, D. and Perlmutter, M. "Responsibility: A Semantic Profile." Unpublished manuscript, 1973.

Mantell, D. and Pilisuk, M., eds., "Soldiers In and After Vietnam." In preparation for *Journal of Social Issues.*

Maslow, A. H. "The Authoritarian Character Structure," *Journal of Social Psychology,* Society for the Psychological Study of Social Issues Bulletin, XVIII (1943), 401-411.

Matussek, P. et al. *Die Konzentrationslagerhaft und ihre Folgen.* Berlin: Springer-Verlag, 1971.

Milgram, S. "Behavioral Study of Obedience," *Journal of Abnormal and Social Psychology,* LXVII (1963), 371-378.

————. (1964) "Issues in the Study of Obedience: A Reply to Baumrind," *American Psychologist,* XIX (1964), 848-852.

Moskos, Charles C. Jr. *The American Enlisted Man.* New York: Russell Sage, 1970.

Peck, R. F. and Havighurst, R. J. *The Psychology of Character Development.* New York: Wiley, 1960.

Roghmann, K. *Dogmatismus und Autoritarismus*. Meisenheim: Verlag Anton Hain, 1966.

Rokeach, M. "The Nature and Meaning of Dogmatism," *Psychological Review*, LXI (1954), 194-204.

Rosenthal, R. and Rosnow, R. *Artifact in Behavioral Research*. New York: Academic Press, 1969.

Shatan, C. "Soldiers in Mourning: The Post-Vietnam Syndrome," *The Berkshire Eagle*, June 13, 1972.

———. "Post-Vietnam Syndrome," *The New York Times*, May 6, 1972.

———. "The Subversion of the Superego: Uses of Identification With the Aggressor in Basic Combat Training." Paper read at Annual Conference of Psychoanalytic Psychologists, New York, 1972.

Smith, R. B. "Disaffectation, Delegitimation and Consequences: Aggregate Trends for World War II, Korea and Vietnam." Paper read at the conference on "The End of the Mass Army," Amsterdam, March 29-31, 1973.

Solomon, G. F. "Casualties of the Vietnam Conflict With Particular Reference to the Problem of Heroin Addiction," *Modern Medicine*, Sept. 20, 1971, 199-215.

———. "Three Psychiatric Casualties from Vietnam," *Archives of General Psychiatry*, XXV (1971), 522-524.

Srole, L., Langner, T., Michael, S., and Opler, M. *Mental Health in the Metropolis: The Mid-Manhattan Study*. New York: McGraw-Hill, 1962.

Thorne, F. "A Factorial Study of Sexuality in Adult Males," *Journal of Clinical Psychology*, XII (1966), 378-386.

———. "Scales for Rating Sexual Experience." *Ibid.*, 404-407.

———. "The Sex Inventory." *Ibid.*, 367-374.

Thorne, F. and Haupt, T. "The Objective Measurement of the Sex Attitudes and Behavior in Adult Males," *Journal of Clinical Psychology*, XII (1966), 395-403.

Wright, D. *The Psychology of Moral Behavior*. Baltimore: Penguin, 1971.

APPENDIX

Parents' Educational Background

	Volunteers				Resisters			
	Fathers		Mothers		Fathers		Mothers	
	N	%	N		N	%	N	%
Elementary school or less	7	28	6	24	1	4	0	0
High school not completed	4	16	4	16	3	12	2	8
High school diploma	4	16	4	16	5	20	10	40
College not completed	4	16	5	20	4	16	2	8
Nursing school	0	0	0	0	0	0	2	8
College diploma	1	4	1	4	5	20	3	12
Graduate degree	1	4	0	0	6	24	6	24
Unknown	4	16	4	16	1	4	0	0

Parents' Occupations

	Volunteers				Resisters			
	Fathers		Mothers		Fathers		Mothers	
	N	%	N	%	N	%	N	%
Self-employed businessmen	1	4	0	0	3	12	0	0
Professional	1	4	2	8	8	32	7	28
Management or executive	3	12	0	0	4	16	0	0
Clerical and sales	1	4	5	20	3	12	9	36
Police	1	4	0	0	0	0	0	0
Skilled manual	9	36	0	0	4	16	0	0
Unskilled manual	8	32	4	16	2	8	0	0
Housewife			14	56			9	36
Unknown	1	4	0	0	1	4	0	0

External Cohesion of Families

	Volunteers		Resisters	
	N	%	N	%
Family intact, living together	18	72	21	84
Death or divorce, remarriage of parent(s)	3	12	2	8
Death or divorce, long period of outside help	1	4	2	8
Family irreparably broken, child given to outside agent	3	12	0	0

Raters' Judgments of Parental Harmony/Disharmony

	Volunteers		Resisters	
	N	%	N	%
Very harmonious	3	12	5	20
Generally harmonious	7	28	8	32
50/50	3	12	4	16
Generally disharmonious	4	16	4	16
Very disharmonious	6	24	4	16
No answer	2	8	0	0

Raters' Judgments of Families' Psychological Stability

	Volunteers		Resisters	
	N	%	N	%
Highly Stable	8	32	15	60
Stable	8	32	5	20
Shaky but intact	4	16	2	8
Shaky and Crumbling	1	4	1	4
Completely unstable	4	16	2	8

Raters' Judgment of Dominance/Submission Relationship Between Parents

	Volunteers		Resisters	
	N	%	N	%
Father dominant	15	60	4	16
Mother dominant	5	20	5	20
Equal	1	4	12	48
Separate ways	3	12	3	12
Does not apply (orphan or only one parent)	1	4	1	4

Explicit Child-rearing Values Held Most and Least Frequently by Parents

	Volunteers				Resisters			
	Fathers		Mothers		Fathers		Mothers	
	N	%	N	%	N	%	N	%
Respect for property	24	96	24	96	12	48	14	56
Respectability	23	92	25	100	12	48	17	68
Work and diligence	22	88	21	84	22	88	22	88
Orderliness and cleanliness	21	84	21	84	8	32	10	40
Discipline	21	84	23	92	3	12	8	32
Conformity within the community	21	84	24	96	10	40	12	48
Obedience and submission to authority	20	80	22	88	2	8	7	28
Physical strength	20	80	5	20	2	8	0	0
Good manners	19	76	22	88	16	64	21	84
Independence	19	76	10	40	21	84	17	68
Thrift	16	64	17	68	14	56	15	60
Individual achievement	16	64	10	40	22	88	21	84
Respect for adults	16	64	21	84	0	0	0	0
Emotional toughness	15	60	0	0	1	4	0	0
Material wants and pleasures	14	56	12	48	5	20	4	16
Mutual help within family	12	48	14	56	8	32	18	72
Love of animals and nature	9	36	5	20	6	24	8	32
Intellectual achievement	6	24	9	36	20	80	23	92
Rationality and reasoning	6	24	3	12	20	80	17	68
Individual privacy	5	20	4	16	19	76	15	60
Kindliness	5	20	11	44	17	68	24	96
Love of life	5	20	12	48	21	84	22	88
Community responsibility (sociopolitical engagement)	4	16	2	8	14	56	15	60
Philanthropy	3	12	8	32	8	32	17	68
Social justice	1	4	1	4	17	68	19	76
Love of art, music, literature	1	4	4	16	11	44	17	68
Humanitarianism	0	0	3	12	17	68	24	96

Age at Time of First Complete Sexual Intercourse

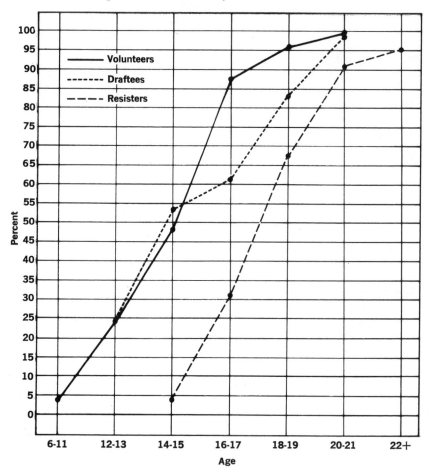

Characteristics of Parent-Child Relationship as Reported by Volunteers and Resisters

	Father only		Both parents		Mother only		Neither parent	
	Volunteer	Resister	Volunteer	Resister	Volunteer	Resister	Volunteer	Resister
Strictness	2	1	18	3	5	5	0	16
Mechanical-formal-cold	7	1	12	1	3	3	3	20
Parental dominance	8	3	9	0	5	2	3	20
Freedom of movement (permissiveness)	2	1	0	13	9	4	14	6
Respect for child's rights and individuality	1	4	1	15	2	5	21	1
Hostility	4	1	1	0	1	0	19	24
Rejection	4	0	2	0	1	0	17	25
Indifference	5	3	6	0	1	0	12	22
Irritability	3	5	8	0	5	6	9	14
Overprotectiveness	0	0	1	1	11	1	13	23
Helpfulness	0	4	9	15	7	7	9	2
Patience	2	6	8	14	5	4	10	1
Affection	0	2	3	14	9	4	13	4
Emotional closeness	2	3	0	5	3	9	20	8

Criteria for Definition of Peer Sub-Groups

	Members of peace movement (N = 15)		Social activists (N = 3)		Private (N = 5)		Personal comfort (N = 3)	
	N	%	N	%	N	%	N	%
Burned or returned draft card	10	67	1	33	0	0	0	0
Wrote draft board and refused cooperation	5	33	1	33	0	0	0	0
Refused induction at induction center	10	67	0	0	0	0	0	0
Awaiting trial in federal court	6	40	0	0	0	0	0	0
Awaiting sentencing or already served sentence	2	13	0	0	0	0	0	0
Appealed case in federal court	5	33	0	0	0	0	0	0
Classified for immediate induction (1-A)	10	67	1	33	0	0	0	0
First contact with subject made at War Resisters League where he worked	13	87	0	0	1	20	0	0
Prefers jail sentence to administrative cooperation with Selective Service System	13	87	1	33	0	0	0	0
Previous jail sentences due to participation in antiwar demonstrations	11	73	1	33	0	0	0	0
Gave considerable time to antiwar movement	15	100	0	0	0	0	0	0
Best friends directly involved in antiwar movement	12	80	0	0	0	0	0	0
Intends to devote himself to antiwar movement	11	73	0	0	0	0	0	0
Past activity in: VISTA, Peace Corps, civil rights organizations, Urban League, Volunteers in Asia, ghetto work etc.	0	0	3	100	0	0	0	0
Personal dedication to nonviolence without organizational affiliation	0	0	3	100	5	100	0	0
Applied for conscientious objector status	1	7	1	33	3	60	1	33
Personal comfort: does not want to serve in army	0	0	0	0	0	0	3	100

High School Questionnaire*

		R	V	D
1.	Thinking back to your High School days, were there any teachers who you liked very much?			
	(a) all	0	1	1
	(b) many	3	6	9
	(c) a few	13	16	18
	(d) one or two	3	5	5
	(e) none	1	0	4
2.	During this same time were there any teachers you strongly disliked?			
	(a) all	0	0	0
	(b) many	3	1	2
	(c) a few	9	8	19
	(d) one or two	8	12	10
	(e) none	0	4	6
3.	Would you say that you enjoyed school or that you disliked school?			
	(a) enjoyed it very much	4	8	7
	(b) enjoyed it more than disliked it	7	5	12
	(c) enjoyed it sometimes, disliked it sometimes	4	11	12
	(d) disliked it more than enjoyed it	1	1	4
	(e) disliked it very much	4	0	0
4.	Were you a liked student or a disliked student by most of your teachers?			
	(a) very well liked by all teachers	4	9	5
	(b) liked by some	9	7	17
	(c) liked by some and disliked by others	7	9	13
	(d) disliked	0	0	0
	(e) very disliked	0	0	0
5.	Were you more liked or disliked with most of the other students?			
	(a) very well liked	5	6	8
	(b) liked	6	15	13
	(c) averagely liked or disliked	9	4	14
	(d) disliked	0	0	0
	(e) very disliked	0	0	0

*In this questionnaire and the one that follows, R = resister, V = volunteer, and D = draftee.

6. Were you well-known in the school or not
   well-known?

	R	V	D
(a) very well-known	4	9	7
(b) well-known	7	9	12
(c) average	5	6	14
(d) not well-known	3	1	1
(e) hardly known at all	1	0	1

7. Can you remember teachers having given you an
   unfair grade? Did this occur

(a) always?	1	0	0
(b) often?	0	0	0
(c) sometimes?	8	1	6
(d) rarely?	10	20	21
(e) never?	1	4	8

8. Can you remember teachers having been angry
   with you? Did this happen

(a) all the time?	0	1	0
(b) often?	0	1	0
(c) sometimes?	11	12	14
(d) rarely?	9	11	21
(e) never?	1	0	0

9. Can you remember teachers having treated you
   unfairly? Did this happen

(a) all the time?	0	0	0
(b) often?	0	0	0
(c) sometimes?	9	1	5
(d) rarely?	10	15	25
(e) never?	1	9	5

10. Can you remember getting mad at teachers? Did
    this happen

(a) all the time?	0	0	0
(b) often?	2	1	2
(c) sometimes?	9	11	17
(d) rarely?	8	12	14
(e) never?	1	1	2

11. When you disliked a teacher, did you try to get
    back at the teacher

(a) always?	0	0	0
(b) often?	0	1	0
(c) sometimes?	4	1	7
(d) rarely?	8	6	10
(e) never?	8	17	18

12. Did you ever have the feeling that a teacher didn't   R   V   D
praise you for a good job?

	R	V	D
(a) always praised me	0	0	1
(b) often gave me praise	11	4	6
(c) sometimes gave me praise	8	17	23
(d) rarely gave me praise	1	4	5
(e) never gave me praise	0	0	0

13. Do you think you could have done better work in High School if you had tried harder?

	R	V	D
(a) extremely better	3	5	10
(b) much better	6	12	16
(c) somewhat better	8	7	6
(d) a little better	2	1	3
(e) no better	1	0	0

14. Do you feel badly about not having done better work in High School?

	R	V	D
(a) miserable	0	1	1
(b) very badly	0	6	5
(c) somewhat badly	2	6	13
(d) a little bit badly	3	6	11
(e) not at all badly	15	6	5

15. When you were in High School, did you get into fights

	R	V	D
(a) all the time	0	0	0
(b) often?	0	2	1
(c) sometimes?	0	10	8
(d) seldom?	10	11	17
(e) never?	10	2	9

16. Do you have the feeling that when you got into a fight you were

	R	V	D
(a) always ready to fight?	0	1	0
(b) sometimes ready to fight and sometimes not?	1	6	5
(c) usually wanted to avoid a fight but were ready to fight?	5	10	14
(d) wanted to avoid fights and had to fight against your will?	2	6	11
(e) wanted to avoid fights at all costs and only fought when forced to?	7	2	5

17. When you got into a jam in High School and needed help, did you have

	R	V	D
(a) many friends who would help you out?	2	7	8

			R	V	D
(b)	several friends who would help you out?		8	10	16
(c)	a couple of friends who would help you out?		8	7	10
(d)	one friend who would help you out?		1	0	0
(e)	usually no friends who would help you out?		1	1	1

18. In High School, did you have

		R	V	D
(a)	many close friends?	1	7	11
(b)	several close friends?	7	11	10
(c)	a couple of close friends?	9	6	12
(d)	one close friend?	0	0	1
(e)	no really close friends?	3	1	1

19. When it came to doing favors for each other

		R	V	D
(a)	did you always do more favors for your friends?	0	2	0
(b)	did you sometimes do more favors for your friends?	6	4	8
(c)	it was about 50:50?	13	19	26
(d)	did your friends sometimes do more favors for you?	1	0	1
(e)	did your friends always do more favors for you?	0	0	0

20. Did you have the feeling that your friends failed you in some way?

		R	V	D
(a)	all the time	0	0	0
(b)	often	0	0	0
(c)	sometimes	6	5	10
(d)	rarely	10	16	22
(e)	never	4	4	3

21. Did you have the feeling that

		R	V	D
(a)	you liked most of your friends much more than they liked you?	0	1	1
(b)	you liked some friends more than they liked you?	4	5	1
(c)	you and your friends liked each other equally well?	14	19	18
(d)	some of your friends liked you more than you liked them?	2	0	5
(e)	most of your friends liked you more than you liked them?	0	0	0

22. Do you feel that the distinction between good friends and aquaintances is

		R	V	D
(a)	very important and necessary?	3	5	12
(b)	justified and at times necessary?	7	9	8
(c)	worth having in mind?	9	10	10
(d)	not particularly necessary?	1	1	5
(e)	not necessary at all?	0	0	0

23. Thinking back to your High School days, do you remember ever swearing at a teacher for any reason *out loud?*

	R	V	D
(a) many times (more than 10 times)	0	0	1
(b) several times (8–10 times)	0	0	1
(c) a few times (3–7 times)	1	1	4
(d) once or twice	4	5	6
(e) never	15	19	23

24. Do you remember swearing at a teacher to yourself, under your breath?

	R	V	D
(a) many times (more than 10 times)	3	5	8
(b) several times (8–10 times)	1	5	2
(c) a few times (3–7 times)	7	6	11
(d) once or twice	4	8	12
(e) never	5	1	2

25. Do you remember arguing with teachers?

	R	V	D
(a) many times (more than 10 times)	5	1	6
(b) several times (8–10 times)	3	1	6
(c) a few times (3 to 7 times)	5	5	6
(d) once or twice	3	11	14
(e) never	4	7	3

26. Do you remember having been very angry about something in school but *not* doing anything about it? Did this happen

	R	V	D
(a) many times?	3	1	2
(b) several times?	2	0	6
(c) a few times?	8	6	15
(d) once or twice?	5	12	7
(e) never?	2	7	5

27. When you got angry at a teacher, did you usually

	R	V	D
(a) tell the teacher openly and directly why you were angry?	7	4	12
(b) refuse to carry out teacher's order?	2	1	1
(c) carry out teacher's orders but purposely do a bad job?	1	1	3
(d) try and bury your anger so none would know?	4	12	13
(e) try to avoid contact with the teacher?	6	7	6

28. How did you feel afterwards, after letting the teacher know you were angry about him or her?

	R	V	D
(a) felt very uncomfortable about it and tried to make it up in some way	2	6	3
(b) felt it wasn't smart and wished I hadn't shown anger	3	12	11
(c) felt it probably wasn't good but he (she) deserved it	3	3	10
(d) felt the teacher deserved it	9	3	5
(e) felt that the teacher deserved a lot more than I gave out	2	1	3

	R	V	D

29. Do you recall any occasions when you asked teachers for advice in some matter?

	R	V	D
(a) never asked teachers for advice on any matter	2	1	2
(b) rarely asked teachers for advice and then only about schoolwork	5	4	8
(c) asked teachers for advice on schoolwork occasionally	6	5	8
(d) often asked teachers for advice, on schoolwork and other things	5	12	13
(e) asked teachers for advice on all matters, often, whenever I thought they could help	2	3	4

30. When you were in High School, did you feel that

	R	V	D
(a) praise and recognition from your teachers was very important?	7	5	6
(b) praise and recognition was helpful but good grades were most important?	4	16	22
(c) praise and recognition were unimportant and that good grades were only important for getting into college?	4	3	1
(d) praise, recognition and good grades didn't matter?	3	0	3
(e) never thought about the importance of grades, praise or recognition?	2	1	3

31. Do you feel that your teachers

	R	V	D
(a) were very interested in their students and always ready to help?	1	13	5
(b) were generally interested in their students but not always?	9	9	20
(c) were evenly divided between those who were interested in their students and those who were not?	6	3	4
(d) were by and large bad, there were only a few who were sincerely interested in their students?	4	0	6
(e) were all bad and never showed any sincere interest in their students?	0	0	0

32. During your school years, did you

	R	V	D
(a) have many arguments with your schoolmates?	0	0	0
(b) have frequent arguments with your schoolmates?	1	0	5
(c) have occasional arguments with your schoolmates?	10	13	17
(d) seldom argue with your schoolmates?	8	12	12
(e) never argue with your schoolmates?	1	0	1

33. Among your schoolmates, were there

	R	V	D
(a) very many you didn't like?	0	0	0
(b) quite a few you didn't like?	0	0	3
(c) several you didn't like?	12	6	14
(d) just a couple you didn't like?	8	18	17
(e) none who you didn't like?	0	1	1

34. Among your schoolmates, were there

		R	V	D
(a)	very many who you hated?	0	0	0
(b)	quite a few who you hated?	0	0	1
(c)	several who you hated?	1	1	0
(d)	just a couple who you hated?	7	7	17
(e)	none who you hated?	12	17	17

35. Among your schoolmates, were there

		R	V	D
(a)	very many who you liked?	5	12	11
(b)	quite a few who you liked?	8	10	15
(c)	several who you liked?	6	4	7
(d)	a couple who you liked?	1	0	2
(e)	none who you liked?	0	0	0

36. When you particularly disliked a kid in school, did you

		R	V	D
(a)	refuse to have anything to do with him and ignore him?	15	14	21
(b)	snub him so that he knew that you disliked him?	0	2	5
(c)	let him know you didn't like him by telling him so?	2	7	7
(d)	tell him to keep out of your way?	1	2	2
(e)	challenge him to a fight and settle the scores?	0	0	0

37. Was the approval and recognition of your classmates of you

		R	V	D
(a)	absolutely unimportant, didn't care what they thought of you?	1	5	4
(b)	a little bit important?	5	4	11
(c)	important enough so that you tried to please them on some things?	6	9	6
(d)	generally important so that you usually tried to do things they liked?	8	4	14
(e)	very important to you and made you want to do almost every thing in a way they would like?	0	3	0

38. When you think back of the kids you went to school with, were there

		R	V	D
(a)	many who you liked *very* much?	1	6	1
(b)	several who you like *very* much?	8	9	20
(c)	a few who you liked *very* much?	6	7	8
(d)	one or two who you liked *very* much?	5	3	6
(e)	none who you liked *very* much?	0	0	0

39. During your high school years, would you characterize your sexual experience as

		R	V	D
(a)	social gatherings (parties, etc.)?	4	1	1

	R	V	D
(b) some mild petting and kissing?	4	1	2
(c) occasional kissing and petting but no intercourse?	7	9	12
(d) frequent petting, intercourse on one or more occasions?	5	12	17
(e) frequent intercourse?	0	2	3

40. How many times did you have intercourse between your 12th and 14th year?

	R	V	D
(a) never	19	19	25
(b) once	0	0	5
(c) twice	1	1	1
(d) three times	0	1	2
(e) more than 3 times	0	4	2

41. How many times did you have intercourse between your 14th and 16th year?

	R	V	D
(a) never	14	9	19
(b) once	2	3	2
(c) twice	3	2	4
(d) three times	1	0	2
(e) more than 3 times	0	1	8

42. How many times did you have intercourse between your 16th and 18th year?

	R	V	D
(a) not at all	14	2	13
(b) once	0	1	1
(c) twice	1	1	1
(d) three times	0	1	0
(e) more than 3 times	5	20	20

43. How many times have you had intercourse between your 18th and 20th year?

	R	V	D
(a) not at all	3	0	4
(b) once	2	0	3
(c) twice	0	0	0
(d) three times	3	1	1
(e) more than 3 times	12	24	27

44. How old were you when you started to masturbate?

	R	V	D
(a) 8 to 11	2	8	3
(b) 12 to 15	14	7	21
(c) 16 to 19	2	5	7
(d) 20 to 23	0	0	1
(e) have never masturbated	2	5	3

45. How old were you when you had your first wet dream?

	R	V	D
(a) 8 to 11	0	3	4

	R	V	D
(b) 12 to 15	18	14	17
(c) 16 to 19	1	4	12
(d) 20 to 23	0	2	1
(e) never had a wet dream	1	2	1

Military Life Questionnaire

1. How resentful do you think soldiers in combat
   outfits feel about troops who have rear-area jobs?

	V	D
(a) very resentful	3	4
(b) fairly resentful	11	8
(c) not so resentful	3	10
(d) hardly resentful at all	6	11
(e) not resentful at all	2	2

2. In the Army, some jobs are naturally harder and
   more unpleasant than others and the Army has to
   put men where it thinks they are needed.
   Considering everything, do you think the Army is
   doing its best to see that as far as possible, no man
   gets more than his fair share of hard or unpleasant
   jobs?

	V	D
(a) not doing anything	0	1
(b) doing a little bit	3	16
(c) doing a fair job	14	14
(d) doing a good job	8	3
(e) doing an excellent job	0	1

3. How well do you think "Headquarters"
   understands the problems of the soldiers?

	V	D
(a) headquarters doesn't understand the soldiers at all	0	4
(b) headquarters has some understanding for the soldiers	5	16
(c) headquarters understands the soldiers well in some respects	14	10
(d) headquarters understands the soldiers fairly well in all areas	5	4
(e) headquarters understands the soldiers very well in all areas	1	1

4. How many men in your company would you say
   are good all-around soldiers?

	V	D
(a) almost none	0	5
(b) a few	0	17
(c) about half	1	5
(d) most	22	5
(e) all	2	3

5. Does it ever bother you that there are some soldiers
   who never get sent into combat?

		V	D
(a)	it bothers me all the time	0	0
(b)	it bothers me frequently	5	0
(c)	it bothers me occasionally	8	1
(d)	it hardly ever bothers me	3	11
(e)	it never bothers me at all	9	23

6. On the whole do you feel that the Army is giving
   you a chance to show what you can do?

(a)	no chance at all	0	7
(b)	a poor chance	0	10
(c)	an average chance	7	9
(d)	a fairly good chance	7	3
(e)	a very good chance	11	6

7. In general, how do you feel about being in the
   Army?

(a)	it's a complete waste of time	0	9
(b)	I could be doing better things	2	16
(c)	it's all right	5	4
(d)	I like it	13	3
(e)	Army life is great	5	2

8. In general, how do you feel about the amount of
   time you have to sleep?

(a)	never have enough time	0	0
(b)	usually don't have enough time	0	3
(c)	sometimes enough, sometimes not enough time	3	14
(d)	usually have enough time	18	16
(e)	always have enough time	4	4

9. In general, do you feel that the Army has changed
   you?

(a)	very much for the worse	0	2
(b)	somewhat for the worse	0	7
(c)	hasn't changed me at all	4	5
(d)	somewhat for the better	13	16
(e)	very much for the better	8	5

10. In what ways has the Army changed you for the
    worse? (If the Army has not changed you for the
    worse, leave this blank. You may also check more
    than one alternative.)

(a)	made me more nervous, tense, short-tempered	1	0
(b)	made me more bitter, harder, more hard-nosed	3	2

	V	D
(c) made me more dependent—have trouble making decisions	0	0
(d) made me wilder, more carefree	2	2
(e) made me dumber, less well-informed	0	1

11. In what ways has the Army changed you for the better? (If the Army has not changed you for the better, you may leave this question blank. You may also check more than one alternative.)

	V	D
(a) has made me become better informed and smarter	1	0
(b) has made me more independent and responsible	4	5
(c) has made me more confident and sociable	0	2
(d) has made me think deeper and understand people better	6	3
(e) has made me more self-controlled and disciplined	3	3

12. How many of your present officers are the kind who try and look out for the welfare of the enlisted man?

	V	D
(a) none	0	4
(b) a few	5	17
(c) about half	4	5
(d) most	16	6
(e) all	0	3

13. How many of your present officers are people who you would like to mix with socially?

	V	D
(a) none	0	8
(b) a few	10	17
(c) about half	5	1
(d) most	10	7
(e) all	0	2

14. How many men in your outfit are the kind who look out for the other guys' welfare?

	V	D
(a) none	0	0
(b) a few	8	15
(c) about half	8	13
(d) most	16	6
(e) all	0	1

15. How many men in your outfit are the kind who you would like to mix with socially?

	V	D
(a) none	0	1
(b) a few	4	16
(c) about half	5	9
(d) most	16	8
(e) all	0	1

16. How would you describe your feelings about being
    separated from your mother and father when you
    were first shipped overseas?

		V	D
(a)	was really glad to get away from them	2	1
(b)	thought it was good that I could get away from them for a while	6	16
(c)	never thought about it	17	15
(d)	thought the separation would be too long and we would be too far apart	0	0
(e)	felt badly about the long separation ahead	0	3

17. How do you feel now about your separation from
    your mother and father?

(a)	very glad to be able to lead my own life	6	4
(b)	think the separation is good	8	12
(c)	never think about it	10	12
(d)	think the separation is too long	1	3
(e)	feel badly about such a long separation	0	3

18. Since you have been separated from your parents,
    do you worry about them?

(a)	never	4	2
(b)	seldom	8	12
(c)	sometimes	10	18
(d)	frequently	3	4
(e)	all the time	0	0

19. How much do you think your parents worry about
    you?

(a)	never	2	0
(b)	seldom	3	4
(c)	sometimes	6	17
(d)	frequently	10	11
(e)	all the time	4	2

20. How often do you write home to your family?

(a)	never or almost never	7	4
(b)	once every few months	10	4
(c)	once a month	2	12
(d)	once every two weeks or so	6	9
(e)	once a week or more often	0	6

21. How often do you receive mail from your parents?

(a)	never or almost never	4	2
(b)	once every few months	8	3
(c)	once a month	5	7

	V	D
(d) once every two weeks or so	4	16
(e) once a week or more often	4	7

22. If and when you get into a combat, how well do you think you will stand up?

(a) don't know	2	11
(b) not well at all	0	0
(c) not very well	0	3
(d) fairly well	9	15
(e) very well	14	6

23. How would you describe your physical condition now?

(a) bad condition	0	1
(b) not so good	0	5
(c) average	4	12
(d) fairly good	9	9
(e) very good	12	8

24. Do you feel that you are now trained and ready for combat or do you need more training?

(a) badly trained and not ready	0	5
(b) undertrained and not ready	0	11
(c) need some more training, but ready	5	8
(d) fairly well trained and ready	5	5
(e) well trained and ready	15	5

25. Which of the following statements best describes your own feeling about getting into combat in Vietnam?

(a) I'm definitely against the war	0	6
(b) I don't see the point of getting involved over there	0	11
(c) I don't care whether I go or not	1	5
(d) when my turn comes I want to go	21	12
(e) I want very much to get over there	3	1

26. If you were sent into actual fighting after finishing one year of training, how do you think you would do?

(a) I don't think I would do very well	0	1
(b) I think I would have trouble at first and then be all right	3	5
(c) I haven't any idea of how I would do	2	6
(d) I think I would do fairly well	9	16
(e) I think I would do very well	11	7

27. Do you ever worry about getting injured in combat?

(a) never worry	7	6

	V	D
(b) worried once or twice	4	13
(c) worry once in a while	10	14
(d) worry fairly often	3	1
(e) worry a great deal of time	1	1

28. How do you think you would feel about killing a Vietcong?

(a) I would really like to kill a Vietcong soldier	3	1
(b) I would feel it is part of my job without liking or disliking it	18	5
(c) I would feel it is part of my job, but I wouldn't like it	4	19
(d) I would probably be able to do it, but would feel very badly	0	10
(e) I don't feel I would kill a Vietcong soldier	0	0

29. How do you think you would feel about killing Vietcong women soldiers?

(a) I would like to kill Vietcong, men or women	1	0
(b) I would feel it is part of my job, without liking or disliking it	19	5
(c) I would feel it is part of my job, but I wouldn't like it	4	14
(d) I would probably be able to do it, but would feel very badly	1	15
(e) I don't feel that I could kill a woman	0	1

30. Supposing you were in an infantry squad operating in an area where the Vietcong were causing heavy casualities to the American Forces and a village nearby was giving the Vietcong active support. What do you think should be done?

(a) the village and its inhabitants should be put out of action permanently	2	2
(b) several members of the village, preferably the leaders, should be executed as a warning and punishment	1	·0
(c) the village should be burned and the inhabitants moved to another area	14	16
(d) the village should be given a stern warning not to support the Vietcong and receive sanctions	1	6
(e) There isn't much that can be done about this except to try to win the village over to our side	7	11

31. What do you think lies behind the war in Vietnam?

(a) an attempt by the Communists to take over the world	10	2
(b) an attempt by the North Vietnamese Communists to take over South Vietnam	5	14

	V	D

    (c) it is basically a Civil War between the Communists and Non-Communists in South Vietnam   2   9

    (d) it is just another arena for the struggle between East and West, between the Communist and the Capitalist systems   6   10

    (e) the most basic cause is the United States trying to protect its own interests   2   0

32. If you were to volunteer for Vietnam or have already done so, which of the following would best describe your reason for doing so?

	V	D
(a) advance one's military career	3	1
(b) earn extra money	3	14
(c) get some different and new military experience	7	4
(d) serve our country	11	9
(e) chance to see another part of the world	1	6

33. Which kind of assignment would you prefer in Vietnam?

	V	D
(a) front line combat	12	1
(b) intermediate combat	1	1
(c) support	0	12
(d) makes no difference	9	5
(e) intelligence	3	16

34. Which kind of assignment do you feel is most important in pursuing the war?

	V	D
(a) front line	6	1
(b) support	0	0
(c) pacification	0	4
(d) medical	1	2
(e) all of equal importance	18	28

35. How do you feel about a soldier who goes AWOL from the front after having seen combat for only one or two weeks?

    (a) I think that a soldier who goes AWOL from the front line should be considered a deserter and shot   4   2

    (b) I think that a soldier that goes AWOL from the front line should be considered a deserter, should be court-martialled, dishonorably discharged and imprisoned for at least two years   6   5

    (c) I don't have any use for deserters who let their buddies down   4   4

    (d) he shouldn't have let the other fellows down, but he probably couldn't help it. Should give him a non-combat assignment   1   16

	V	D

(e)   this man is probably disturbed and should receive medical
      care   10   8

36. How many officers in your present outfit are the
    kind who are willing to go through anything they
    ask their men to go through?

(a)   all of them   2   1
(b)   most of them   18   10
(c)   about half of them   1   8
(d)   only a few of them   4   9
(e)   almost none of them   0   7

37. How do you feel about a soldier who tries to get
    out of combat by going on sick call when he really
    isn't sick?

(a)   he's just as bad as a deserter and should be shot   1   0
(b)   he is the same as a deserter and should be court-martialled
      and imprisoned   3   5
(c)   the man is a coward and should be dishonorably discharged   3   4
(d)   the man is obviously unfit for combat and should be given
      a non-combat assignment   7   16
(e)   this man should receive a medical and psychiatric
      examination   11   10

38. What do you feel should be done to a military
    doctor who refuses to train medics for Vietnam?

(a)   since this is war-time he should be shot for
      disobeying a command   1   0
(b)   he should be court-martialled and imprisoned   9   7
(c)   he should be court-martialled and dishonorably discharged   10   5
(d)   he should be sent to Vietnam as a combat medic   2   4
(e)   he should be given another assignment which he is willing
      to carry out   3   19

39. What would you like to see happen to the Vietcong
    after the war?

(a)   they should be wiped out   2   0
(b)   they should be made to suffer plenty   0   1
(c)   they should be forced to leave the country   10   10
(d)   they should be allowed to remain within the country   6   6
(e)   they should have the same rights as all other Vietnamese
      including a voice in the government   7   18

40. How does seeing Vietcong prisoners make you feel
    about the Vietcong?

(a)   makes me want to kill them all the more   1   0

	V	D
(b) makes me feel they have to be stopped	16	11
(c) makes me feel they deserve to lose	0	2
(d) makes me feel they are just like us	8	21
(e) makes me feel that we have no right to fight against them	0	1

41. When you read about or see pictures of Vietcong atrocities against American soldiers, do you feel

	V	D
(a) that the Vietcong must be killed to the last man?	0	1
(b) that there is no longer any reason to show Vietcong any mercy?	8	3
(c) that we should have no qualms about how to treat Vietcong prisoners?	6	2
(d) that we have to win the war as quickly as possible?	10	17
(e) that this war is senseless?	1	12

42. When you see pictures of Americans who have been tortured by the Vietcong, does this

	V	D
(a) make you sick in the stomach?	1	3
(b) make you sad to realize that these young men died this way?	10	19
(c) not affect you at all—it's part of the war?	0	1
(d) make you wonder how it must have been for them?	1	6
(e) make you want to pay the Cong back?	13	3

43. If you were in a battle zone in Vietnam and a 14- to 15-year-old Vietcong tried to shoot you, how would you feel about shooting him?

	V	D
(a) I would want to shoot him.	15	5
(b) I would feel it is part of my job to shoot him.	10	9
(c) I would feel it is part of my job, but would feel badly.	0	8
(d) I would only shoot him if it is unavoidable and would feel very badly about it.	0	13
(e) I couldn't shoot a 14- to 15-year-old boy.	0	0

44. If you were given a group of men and told to take charge of them yourself on a mission under enemy fire, how well do you think you would do?

	V	D
(a) excellently	9	4
(b) well	9	14
(c) average	6	14
(d) not so well	1	2
(e) badly	0	1

45. Supposing after a tough battle with many American casualties one of the men in your company took a captured Vietcong who had just killed one of his

buddies and shot him between the eyes. How
would you feel about this?

		V	D
(a)	I would congratulate him for having the courage to do it.	0	0
(b)	I would feel he did the right thing.	1	1
(c)	I would understand how he felt and not criticize him.	13	9
(d)	I would think he should have controlled himself and not done it.	9	19
(e)	I would have to consider him a cold-blooded murderer.	2	6

46. It is well known that many villages in Vietnam
actively support the Vietcong. Usually, the men of
the village fight during the day and return to the
village at night to eat and sleep. Supposing, as has
happened many times, the people of the village,
consisting of old men, women, and children, are
warned not to support the Vietcong many times but
nevertheless continue to do so. One night your
company is attacked by the Vietcong from this
village and suffer heavy casualties. The next day a
patrol catches several old men and women laying
mines, which in the past had badly damaged
American convoys and resulted in American
casualties.

A. What do you think should be done to the village?

(a)	The village and all its inhabitants should be destroyed.	2	0
(b)	The village should be destroyed and all adults, particularly those laying the mines, should be shot.	4	2
(c)	The village should be destroyed and all persons remaining in the village should be imprisoned.	9	10
(d)	The village should be evacuated, the inhabitants dispersed to many different camps for the duration of the war.	10	15
(e)	One can't destroy the village or evacuate the inhabitants. All that can be done is to try and pacify them and meanwhile keep close guard.	2	8

B. If you were given a direct order to join a squad
which had been ordered to destroy the village and
its inhabitants, how would you feel?

(a)	I would gladly join the squad.	2	0
(b)	I would feel that it was part of my job and that the village deserved it.	10	4

	V	D

(c) I would feel it was necessary, but wouldn't like it.   8 10

(d) I would ask to be relieved of the assignment, but if ordered to do it, would carry out the order.   4 18

(e) I would refuse to carry out the order even if it meant a court-martial.   1 3

C. If the squad was to consist only of volunters, would you volunter?

yes   18 5

no   7 30

47. Which of the following best describes the way you feel about getting into an actual battle zone?

(a) I want to get in as soon as possible   1 0

(b) I am ready to go at any time   22 14

(c) I'd like to go before the war is over, but I am not ready yet   3 21

(d) I hope I don't have to go   1 0

(e) I won't go   17 9

48. Which 3 of the following, in order of importance, do you think will be the most unpleasant aspect to be in Vietnam?

(a) threat of my life   2 1

(b) bad climate   5 25

(c) bad food   0 0

(d) separation from my family

(e) separation from my friends

(f) the insects and filth

(g) sight and sound of dying men

(h) loss of freedom of movement

(i) not having any girls or sex for 1 year

(j) lack of privacy

(k) fatigue

(l) long periods of boredom

(m) threat of disease and injury

(n) not counting as an individual

49. Which do you think would bother you most in combat (check only one)?

(a) seeing a dead friend   12 20

(b) seeing an enemy atrocity on an American soldier   8 7

(c) seeing a dead child   5 8

50. Have you ever seen a dead person?   V   D

    yes   24   30

    no   1   5

51. If you have seen a dead person, please write down
who this person or persons is/are (friend, family
member, accident, victim, etc.). (Note: See chapter
on adolescence for further discussion of this item.)
Who or what was this person?
How did this person die?
Under what circumstances did you see this dead
person?
How old were you?

52. Would you say that you think about what it is like
in Vietnam?

    (a) all the time   0   1

    (b) a lot   6   1

    (c) some   12   16

    (d) a little   6   17

    (e) not at all   1   0

53. Would you say that you discuss the war in
Vietnam?

    (a) a great deal   3   2

    (b) a lot   5   7

    (c) some   12   13

    (d) a little   5   11

    (e) not at all   0   2

54. Have any friends, family members, or Army
buddies of yours been killed in action in Vietnam?

    A. yes   24   19

        no   1   16

    B. If yes, how many?

    C. Please list these people who you have known and
who were killed in action in Vietnam stating the
nature of your relationship to them (family, friend
from civilian life, Army buddies), how old they
were and how you found out they were killed.

        Relationship (friend, family, Army buddy)
        Age at death
        Rank
        How did you find out?

55. Do you know anybody who volunteered for duty in
    Vietnam?
    A. yes   24   34
        no   1   1
    B. If yes, about how many?
    C. As in 54, please list these people, explaining your
        relationship to them, their rank, and approximately
        when they volunteered as best you can remember

        Relationship (friend, family, Army buddy)
        Age
        Rank
        Date volunteered